The World Beat Series

WILLIAM H. BEEZLEY, University of Arizona
DAVID E. LOREY, The Hewlett Foundation
Series Editors

The World Beat Series consists of books designed for use in under-graduate courses in the social sciences. The general focus is social issues and social change, with many selections highlighting the stories of individuals and communities. All volumes include readings drawn from around the world, presenting a global offering of perspectives and information. Each book provides a mix of previously published articles, unpublished pieces (some of them commissioned specifically for the volume), and primary documents on a particular topic. An introduction by the volume editor places the general topic and the individual selections in their broader contexts. Texts in this series are an easy way for professors to "globalize" their courses in one stroke. World Beat books easily replace outdated course readers and old supplementary texts for undergraduate classes at both the introductory and advanced levels.

Volumes Published

David E. Lorey and William H. Beezley, editors. *Genocide, Collective Violence, and Popular Memory: The Politics of Remembrance in the Twentieth Century* (2002). Cloth ISBN 0-8420-2981-8
Paper ISBN 0-8420-2982-6

Wendy F. Kasinec and Michael A. Polushin, editors. *Expanding Empires: Cultural Interaction and Exchange in World Societies from Ancient to Early Modern Times* (2002). Cloth ISBN 0-8420-2730-0
Paper ISBN 0-8420-2731-9

David E. Lorey, editor. *Global Environmental Challenges of the Twenty-first Century: Resources, Consumption, and Sustainable Solutions* (2003). Cloth ISBN 0-8420-5048-5   Paper ISBN 0-8420-5049-3

Brian Loveman, editor. *Strategy for Empire: U.S. Regional Security Policy in the Post-Cold War Era* (2004). Cloth ISBN 0-8420-5176-7
Paper ISBN 0-8420-5177-5

Paul Ganster and David E. Lorey, editors. *Borders and Border Politics in a Globalizing World* (2004). Cloth ISBN 0-8420-5103-1
Paper ISBN 0-8420-5104-X

Borders and Border Politics
in a Globalizing World

Borders and Border Politics in a Globalizing World

THE
WORLD
BEAT
SERIES

Edited by
Paul Ganster and
David E. Lorey

No. 5

SR Books
Lanham • Boulder • New York • Toronto • Oxford

Published by SR Books
A imprint of Rowman & Littlefield Publishers, Inc.
A wholly owned subsidiary of The Rowman & Littlefield Publishing Group, Inc.
4501 Forbes Boulevard, Suite 200
Lanham, MD 20706

PO Box 317, Oxford OX2 9RU, UK

British Library Cataloguing in Publication Information Available

Library of Congress Cataloging-in-Publication Data

Borders and border politics in a globalizing world / edited by Paul Ganster
    and David E. Lorey.
        p. cm. — (The world beat series ; no. 5)
    Includes bibliographical references.
    ISBN 0-8420-5104-X (pbk. : alk. paper) — ISBN 0-8420-5103-1
(cloth : alk. paper)
        1. Boundaries—Case studies. 2. Ethnicity—Case studies.
    3. Nationalism—Case studies. I. Ganster, Paul. II. Lorey, David E.
    III. Series.
    JC323.B667 2005
    320.1'2—dc22

                                                            2003023428

Printed in the United States of America

♾ ™The paper used in this publication meets the minimum requirements of
the American National Standard for permanence of paper for printed library
materials, Z39.48, 1984.

Acknowledgments

Many individuals have contributed to this volume. At the Institute for Regional Studies of the Californias at San Diego State University, research assistants Alison McNee, Nathan Gallagher, and Martina Sánchez all helped with obtaining permissions to use the essays, developing the glossary of terms, and evaluating the suitability of the essays for undergraduates. Bertha Hernández, Associate Editor at IRSC, assisted with copy editing tasks. Harry Johnson, staff cartographer at the Department of Geography at San Diego State University, created all the maps used in this book.

About the Editors

Paul Ganster is Professor of History, Director of the Institute for Regional Studies of the Californias, and Associate Director of the Office of International Programs at San Diego State University. He is the author of more than fifty articles, book chapters, and edited works on policy questions of the U.S.-Mexican border region, border environmental issues, Latin American social history, and comparative border studies. He has been a Fulbright Lecturer in Costa Rica and served as a consultant on programmatic development for the United States Information Agency at universities in Mexico, Bolivia, Costa Rica, and Ecuador. Ganster also has been a visiting professor at the School of Economics of the Universidad Autónoma de Baja California in Tijuana. He received his B.A. from Yale University in Latin American studies and his Ph.D. from the University of California, Los Angeles, in Latin American history.

David E. Lorey received his B.A. in history from Wesleyan University and his M.A. and Ph.D. in Latin American social and economic history from the University of California, Los Angeles. From 1989 to 1997 he directed the program on Mexico and was Visiting Professor of History at UCLA. From 1997 to 2003, Lorey directed the U.S.-Latin American Relations Program at the Hewlett Foundation. His publications include *The U.S.-Mexican Border Region in the Twentieth Century* (1999) and *Global Environmental Challenges of the Twenty-first Century: Resources, Consumption, and Sustainable Solutions* (2003).

Contents

Introduction, **xi**

Glossary, **xxiii**

Borders as Barriers

1   JOHN J. WILKES, Hadrian's Wall,   **1**

2   CHENG DALIN, The Great Wall of China,   **11**

3   FREDERICK BAKER, The Berlin Wall,   **21**

Borders, Migrants, and Refugees

4   DAVID FITZGERALD, Sahuayo, Mexico, and Its U.S. Colonies,   **51**

5   DAVID A. MCDONALD, LOVEMORE ZINYAMA, JOHN GAY, FION DE VLETTER, AND ROBERT MATTES, Migration from Lesotho, Mozambique, and Zimbabwe to South Africa,   **73**

Borders and Partitioned Groups

6   J. D. HARGREAVES, West African Boundary Making,   **97**

7   CATHERINE ELTON, The Jívaro People between Peru and Ecuador,   **107**

8   ANSSI PAASI, Boundaries as Social Practice and Discourse: The Finnish-Russian Border,   **117**

Borders, Perceptions, and Culture

9   PIRJO JUKARAINEN, The Attitudes of Youth toward the Other Side: The Finnish-Swedish and Finnish-Russian Borders,   **137**

10   ROGER GIBBINS, Meaning and Significance of the Canadian-American Border,   **151**

11   MICHAEL IGNATIEFF, Northern Ireland,   **169**

12   THOMAS L. FRIEDMAN, The Fault Line between Israelis and Palestinians,   **177**

Borders and the Environment

13 Norris Clement, Paul Ganster, and Alan Sweedler, Environment, Development, and Security in Border Regions: Perspectives from Europe and North America, **199**

14 Brian Erskine, Disaster on the Danube, **237**

15 Pascal O. Girot, Border Regions and Transborder Conservation in Central America, **247**

Borders, Goods, and Services

16 Kirk S. Bowman, The U.S.-Mexican Border as Locator of Innovation and Vice, **269**

17 Dallen J. Timothy and Richard W. Butler, Cross-Border Shopping: Canada and the United States, **285**

Maritime and Space Borders

18 Daniel J. Dzurek, Maritime Agreements and Oil Exploration in the Gulf of Thailand, **301**

19 Malcolm Anderson, New Borders: The Sea and Outer Space, **317**

Suggested Readings, **337**

Index, **341**

Introduction

Contemporary borders present an intriguing paradox. Globalization is proceeding everywhere at an astounding pace, merging economies and cultures through world trade, regional economic integration, the mass media, the Internet, and increasingly mobile populations. But, at the same time, political borders separating peoples remain pervasive and problematic. Rather than being purposefully erased by humans or dissolving of their own accord as boundaries between economies and cultures fade, borders between nations and ethnicities appear to be as strong as ever—and are perhaps growing more so. This paradox of borders in our globalizing world is found even at single sites such as at the U.S.-Mexican or the mainland Chinese-Hong Kong borders, for example. There, people are at the same time both more closely united and more carefully divided through increased physical and legal barriers to restrict crossing by people from both sides of the boundary. Is there a tension between globalization and the continued pervasiveness of borders that will result in their fading over time? Or will border regions, with their social and political complexities and stresses, be a defining feature of our more globalized world?

The editors of this volume have become convinced that in the twenty-first century, humankind will face mounting challenges at both international borders and at subnational boundaries where ethnicities and cultures meet in conflict. These challenges—from resolving political and social conflict to managing migrant flows to dealing with transboundary environmental issues such as toxic-waste disposal and the overuse and pollution of fresh water—will demand responses from regional, national, and multilateral authorities. The most problematic of these issues will be those that have the potential to lead to deadly conflict within regions, deadly conflict between nation states or ethnic groups, social and public health stresses, and irreversible decline of natural ecosystems.

We can begin to prepare for these challenges by seeking to better understand the complexities of border regions—how they work and do not work, how they facilitate cooperation, and how they create tensions. Borders and border regions remain remarkably poorly understood. In this volume, we present leading-edge work on the histories of borders, their social development, their politics, and the daily life that characterizes them. Our authors place their various treatments of these issues within the global context, stressing how borders are affected by, and how they affect, global processes. The selections are intended to provide a window onto current understanding of human interactions at and along national and interethnic boundaries—interactions that we think will characterize borders and border politics through at least the first half of the present century. A second purpose of the book is to raise awareness about the importance of borders, border conflict, and border politics to our common future. As the authors of the following chapters demonstrate, some of the coming challenges that will face humans along the borders they have created can already be identified and others can be reasonably predicted from current knowledge. Many, however, are sure to be unexpected. These are the challenges for which we most need to prepare.

This book addresses the following seven specific issues: borders as barriers; borders, migrants, and refugees; borders and partitioned groups; borders, perceptions, and culture; borders and the environment; borders, goods, and services; and maritime and space borders. It should be noted that the division of these issues into separate groups is an arbitrary one, for each issue is integrally bound up with the others. To give just one example, the continued warming of global climate is expected to have, by midcentury, the effect of reducing rainfall in important transboundary watersheds. It is estimated that surface flows in the Colorado and Rio Grande river basins in the United States and in Mexico could be reduced by between 10 and 40 percent by midcentury, which would have far-reaching impacts on large populations straddling the international boundary in the arid southwest of the United States and in the far north of Mexico. A reduction in rainfall of this magnitude would force significant changes in human water-use patterns. It would also result in significant conflict among the U.S. states of the Colorado River basin and between Mexico and the United States.

In selecting these essays, we have not attempted to be comprehensive. Rather, we have chosen what we think is some of the most suggestive literature on borders and border politics. We have sought to represent border regions from throughout the world, believing that a comparative approach to the evolution of these regions over time will yield the most suggestive and meaningful insights for the reader. Yet, we have also been greatly influenced by the extent and quality of the published works on world borders. For example, the literature for the U.S.-Mexican boundary is much more extensive than for any other border region, and relatively little work on borders exists for Asia or South America. We have avoided articles that focus primarily on the legal and diplomatic creation of borders.[1] For all seven divisions of the book, we have selected articles that give a sense of the complexity of the issues; none of the selections offers or implies easy solutions. We have also concentrated on essays that treat border regions as historically coherent areas, that adopt a region-centered focus (emphasizing cross-boundary social, economic, environmental, and political issues), that address the relationship between social and political issues, and that consider social and political change in border regions from the inside—that is, from the perspective of people who live along borders. For the most part, the selections in this volume focus on two types of boundaries: national boundaries that resulted in the eighteenth and nineteenth centuries from the processes of state building and colonization; and boundaries between and among ethnic and religious groups.

Part of the challenge of studying and understanding borders and border regions stems from the difficulty of defining their scope, both geographically and temporally. Where and what, for example, is the U.S.-Mexican or Soviet/Russian-Finnish border region? In contrast to most regions, border regions are defined by boundaries that run *through* them. How far does a border region extend outward from the political boundary that defines it? Does a border region that functioned one way in the past function the same way at present? And how do borders—in their various social and political manifestations—evolve?

The U.S.-Mexican border provides a good example of the difficulties in clearly defining border regions. The political boundary is nothing more than a line that is marked and maintained by both governments. In some places it is denominated by a tall wall, in some places by a barbed-wire fence. In other places it is an imaginary line drawn in the middle of the Rio Grande or between physical boundary markers set in the deserts and mountains. The regional economy was always delineated by U.S. and Mexican twin cities, which formed spheres that integrated binational economic activity. However, with the implementation of the North American Free Trade Agreement (NAFTA) beginning in 1994, economic integration has spread far beyond the border zone. Cultural features such as language, food types, architecture, and music were once confined to the region adjacent to the international boundary, especially twin cities such as San Diego-Tijuana, El Paso-Ciudad Juárez, or Brownsville-Matamoros, and to a few places away from the border such as Los Angeles. Now, huge areas of the U.S. Southwest and northern Mexico share many of these border features. Environmental agreements between Mexico and the United States define the border zone as sixty miles on either side of the boundary. So when we speak of the U.S.-Mexican border region, we must realize that the features we are considering define its extent. The same is true, in varying degrees, for many other border regions around the world.

Even if borders occasionally appear to follow the natural features of a landscape, they are still human constructs. Boundaries determined by geography are no more "natural" than walls or lines in the sand. Rivers, for example, although frequently used to demarcate boundaries between people, represent only the approximate middle of the vast watersheds that drain into them. It would be difficult to argue that the Taiwan Strait forms a natural boundary between the Nationalist Chinese on Taiwan and the Communist

Chinese on the mainland. Rather, boundaries between peoples are human inventions and thus reflect human visions of the social and political world.

Humans have created borders to separate one group of people from another for a variety of reasons, apparently for thousands of years. But the people who actually end up living at and along borders tend to ignore them when that serves their interests and to take advantage of them when that is more convenient. The most obvious example is transboundary trading, where merchants and consumers both become extremely savvy about short-term and short-distance variations in prices created by a border.[2] Greatly complicating matters is the fact that international and other boundaries are frequently set, administered, and maintained by outsiders in places distant from the borders.

Borders and border regions come in many varieties. Scholar Oscar Martínez has identified four ideal types.[3] First are alienated borderlands, in which transboundary exchange is either nonexistent or very modest, principally due to animosity between peoples on each side. The second ideal type is what Martínez terms "coexistent borderlands"; here, relations between peoples on either side are characterized by regular contact and by generally friendly associations between two polities. Third, Martínez describes an interdependent borderlands; in this type, peoples on both sides of the border are involved in a symbiotic relationship characterized by significant flows of goods, services, and individuals back and forth. Martínez's fourth ideal type is an integrated borderlands, where practically all barriers to trade and human movement have been eliminated. One of the great advantages of Martínez's typology is that it can be applied to both international and various other sorts of borders, including those between ethnicities and religious groups. The typology works well, for instance, in comparing and contrasting the very different kinds of borders between the French and English (across a so-called natural water boundary), between the English and the Scots or Welsh, and between English-speaking Protestants and Catholics in Northern Ireland.

Borders are hardly ever static for long. They have distinct histories, emerging and becoming more rigid over time and then eventually disappearing. They existed before nation-states and can, apparently, exist just fine when nation-states are suppressed. The European Union is an excellent example of this last point: a unified Western Europe now struggles not over internal boundaries, but rather with the incorporation of new members—Eastern European countries beyond the borders of the present Union. Although borders are established for distinct purposes, their creation and development frequently have unexpected and unintended consequences.

The U.S.-Mexican border region is a good example of how the historical process of border development can unfold and how, in a relatively short period of time, major transformations take place. At the middle of the nineteenth century, the U.S.-Mexican border region was a vaguely defined territory in which sparse populations, separated by an international boundary, came into uncertain contact. The border presented little inconvenience to residents of the states and territories that abutted the demarcating line, for although the border was defined, local populations crossed back and forth in most areas with little inconvenience. A century and one-half later, the 2,000-mile international boundary defines a region in which "two civilizations face each other and overlap."[4] The U.S.-Mexican border region is now characterized by a binational economy of astounding complexity, having transformed itself from a cattle-ranching and mining area that attracted American and European capitalists in the late nineteenth century to an area of a lucrative vice- and pleasure-based tourist industry to a region that attracted after World War II an extraordinary amount of international capital to its manufacturing and services sector. During a century and one-half of rapid and dramatic change in both the United States and Mexico, the border came to unite as well as divide the two countries and their historical experiences.

By generalizing—and there are many exceptions—we can identify a three-part process that allows us to establish a chronology shared by many borders. First, a frontier period, or a time of multiple interpenetrating frontiers, lasts from first contact between peoples to the point where contact becomes mixing. Second, a borderlands era develops, during which peoples intermix and interact without any attention to or attention from national powers. Third, there is a period during which a distinct border region is formed with clearly demarcated boundaries and definable social and political responses to the boundary. In addition to these three periods of development, we might add a fourth of dissolution. In the long run, most borders are erased or dissolved. Although we tend to think of borders as being immutably fixed in time, in fact the most common ultimate outcome for an individual border is its eventual dissolution.[5]

In both geographical and historical terms, the definition of border regions must remain flexible. Economic, social, political, and cultural borders fall in different places; there are subregions that only relate loosely to international or interethnic boundaries. U.S.-Mexican border phenomena are now experienced as far from the international boundary as Chicago and New York, as far as the states of Washington, Oregon, and Colorado in the United States, and as far as Sinaloa, Durango, Jalisco, and the Yucatán peninsula in Mexico, where assembly-plant production has pulled people into the border world.[6] To deal with this complexity, Michiel Baud and Willem Van Schendel have identified three essential regional units of analysis for border study. One is the border heartland, which abuts the border and is dominated by its existence and where social networks are shared directly by the border (for example, the Basel region where Germany meets Switzerland and France, and the borderlands between Singapore and Malaysia). A second category is that of intermediate borderlands, a region that feels the influence of the border but in intensities ranging from moderate to weak. Finally, there are the outer borderlands, which only under specific circumstances feel the effects of an international or interethnic border.[7] The long-term trend seems to be for border regions that continue to expand in social, cultural, and psychological ways. The social networks that are created and the cultural patterns that are established constantly shift the boundaries of the border world outward.

Borders are characterized everywhere by their amazing social complexity; it is this complexity that gives rise to the difficulty and explosiveness of border politics. Oscar Martínez has developed a schema for understanding the complex social landscape of the U.S.-Mexican border world in his *Border People*, which is also useful for other borders, both national and subnational. Martínez includes in his typology the following groups: transient migrants (people residing only briefly in the border region); newcomers (people newly arrived in the border region); nationalists (long-term residents of the border who do not partake of the culture of the other side of the international boundary); uniculturalists (people who live wholly in the culture of one side or the other); binational consumers (persons whose main experience of the other side is commercial); settler migrants; commuters who move back and forth across the border on a regular—usually daily—basis to their work; biculturalists (persons, generally bilingual, who have roots and live adult lives on both sides); binationalists (people, frequently business people and professionals, who live and do business on both sides and operate at a very high level of transboundary social integration); and people who reside permanently, perhaps after retirement, on the other side of the border. In addition, Martínez notes, each border has special cases: in that of the U.S.-Mexican border, winter resident communities and U.S. communities in which persons of Mexican origin dominate politics and business and persons of European extraction sometimes feel marginal or marginalized.

A key aspect of the border social complexity is the development, in the twentieth century, of twin-city urban areas as a defining characteristic of modern borders. Twin-city pairs shared some growth characteristics and differed in others. They often grew up together as commercial hubs straddling the lines of communication across borders, as tourist nexuses, or as sites for industrial or assembly production. Twin-city pairs developed complex interrelationships and interdependencies. At the U.S.-Mexican border, for example, daily movement between twin cities grew to the point that by 1990, northbound traffic—most of it commuters, tourists, and shoppers—exceeded 274 million, a number greater than the population of the United States and three times that of Mexico.[8]

The border politics to which these realities give rise, and which are a principal focus of this book, are as complex as the social milieu. Baud and Van Schendel provide the useful typology of border politics. The quiet borderland is one in which nations, regional elites, and local populations are kneaded into a coherent power structure with relatively low tension. Territorial control by either state does not lead to major confrontations in the borderlands. The variance of the quiet borderlands is best described by examples. The Dutch-Belgian borderland since 1830 can be termed harmonious, while the boundary between North and South Korea since 1953 is an enforced version. An unruly borderland exists when power structures are less coherent and when neither the state nor the regional elites has a commanding position over local border populations. Local people resist the new social and territorial boundaries and the rules that come with them. The authority of the regional elites is sometimes weakened because it serves as an agent of the national state rather than as a protector of local rights and concerns. Northern Ireland is a classic case of an unruly borderland where, in the late 1960s, a Protestant elite backed up by the British state lost its ability to control a local population. Finally, we can speak of rebellious borderlands, where regional elites side with local populations against a national state that seeks to impose its authority on the border. Rebellions can be regionalist, separatist, or irredentist in their objectives. An example of a rebellious borderland is the golden triangle straddling the borders of China, Laos, Thailand, and Burma, where various guerrilla groups have been fighting state armies and each other for decades in attempts to set up separate states. Complicating this typology is the fact that different sides can fall into different categories: for example, one side can be quiet while the other is rebellious (for example, the Yugoslav [Kosovo]/Albanian borderland in the 1980s).[9]

The first set of selections in this book, Borders as Barriers, addresses walls—the most obvious way that humans, across long periods of time, have separated themselves from one another. The first chapter explores Hadrian's Wall, constructed in the early centuries A.D. by the Romans across one of the narrowest points of Great Britain. The wall, some seventy-four miles (119 kilometers) in length, was built to control the marauding tribes to the north, thereby providing stability for the Roman province of Britannia to the south. The Great Wall of China, another defensive structure designed to protect the Chinese empire from its warring neighbors to the north, is the subject of the second chapter. Constructed over a period of nearly 2,000 years, the Great Wall extended more than 3,728 miles (6,000 kilometers). Chapter 3 focuses on an equally famous wall of modern times: the Berlin Wall, built beginning in 1961 to separate the Soviet-controlled zone of Berlin from those controlled by the United States and its allies. The Wall symbolized the division of Europe into two spheres during the Cold War (1945–1989), and its destruction symbolized the end of the Cold War. The Berlin Wall, in contrast to the Great Wall of China and Hadrian's Wall, was built more to keep people in the Soviet sector of Berlin rather than to keep others out.

The second section of the book focuses on how migrants and refugees are affected by borders. While the chapters consider both legal and illegal migrants, the distinction between the two is not particularly important from a global perspective. While attention tends to center on illegal migration, legal flows are generally much more important. At the U.S.-Mexican border, for example, only 1 percent of people crossing the border on a regular basis do so illegally.[10] Yet this percentage frequently constitutes the only border story deemed worth reporting in the mass media of both Mexico and the United States. Compared to the dozens or hundreds who may cross illegally every day, approximately 40,000 people daily cross legally from Tijuana to San Diego to work. Every year the border sees 250 million legal crossings each way, mostly Mexican shoppers who spend an estimated $25 billion in the United States and pay $2 billion in sales taxes without receiving any government benefits.

This second section includes selections from the U.S.-Mexican border region and from southern Africa. The central point is that migration across borders is occurring in many parts of the world. Driven by political unrest, famines and drought, and economic disparities, improved communications and transportation and globalization of the economy have all contributed to increasing flows of people from poor to less poor areas. Nations with expanding populations and little economic opportunity see tens of thousands of their citizens cross borders in search of a better life in more developed countries. Every highly developed country is faced with significant flows of legal and undocumented immigrants. None has developed adequate policies for coping with this mass of humanity that impacts on both the sending and receiving nations but is most clearly evidenced in border areas.

The third set of selections focuses on borders and partitioned peoples. While migrants and refugees cross international boundaries in search of safety and economic opportunity, there are many cultures and ethnic groups that have been divided by the establishment of international political boundaries. Most often, these demarcations were the result of European powers dividing up the colonial world. This section, for example, includes readings on cases of partitioned peoples from West Africa, the Peru-Ecuador border, and the Russian-Finnish border.

The fourth set addresses culture and perceptions with case studies from the Finnish-Swedish and Russian-Finnish borders, the Canadian-U.S. border, Northern Ireland, and the Israeli-Palestinian "fault line." Historically, many border regions were far from the center of the nation, adjacent to the enemy. Institutions were often weak in these border regions and their peoples were economically and politically marginalized. These factors led to the development of negative stereotypes that often remain long after the reality has changed. The U.S.-Mexican border has long been seen negatively by both the United States and Mexico. The 1920s saw it depicted as a haven for gambling, prostitution, and vice, an image that has continued while other layers have been added. Next, the view of the border as the center of worker exploitation in assembly industries (*maquiladoras*), of serious environmental problems, and of uncontrolled urban growth has broadened. Finally, the flow of illicit drugs across the border to consumers in the United States has encouraged the perception of the region as one characterized by drug wars and corruption. These stereotypes have been widely disseminated by Mexican cinema as well as by Hollywood.

Perceptions of how border cultures view themselves and how they view their neighbors on the other side of the international boundary are a central theme of this same section. Canada has some 75 percent of its population located near the border with the United States, and living next to a huge economic, social, and military power has conditioned how Canadians see themselves and their neighbors to the south. Mixed in with perceptions in Canada and in the essays about Finland's border regions and Northern Ireland is the issue of nationalism. In the case of Northern Ireland, the aspirations of the two principal segments of the population are tied to religion and affiliation with Ulster or Great Britain. Finally, the reading on Israeli-Palestinian issues also explores topics of culture, territory, borders, and nationality.

The fifth section of this book addresses transboundary environmental issues. Political boundaries often pass through important natural resources such as rivers and lakes, and pollution does not respect boundaries established by nations. As a result, neighboring countries frequently fall into conflict about natural resource and environmental issues. Indeed, water is a key issue in the transborder context. The social and political importance of water will become ever more apparent in the twenty-first century as its relative scarcity increases. Many observers believe that freshwater will be the source of violence among communities and nation-states in the not-too-distant future. One of the selections considers a massive hydroelectric project on the Danube River, which has raised concerns not only within the main project partners of Hungary and Czechoslovakia (now Slovakia) but also with other nations of the Danube basin. Management of other natural resources in border areas is also quite complicated, as the essay on transborder conservation initiatives in Central America illustrates.

The sixth section examines transboundary exchanges of goods and services with examples from different regions of the world. Borders between neighboring countries with different economic systems, legal regimes, taxes and tariffs, and cultures are places where residents and others acquire goods from the opposite side of the boundary—goods and services not available locally or available only at a high price. At most borders, this trade is very evident. Sometimes consumers are found on both sides of the border, sometimes the purchases are by one side only. The U.S.-Mexican border is a good example of this sort of complex activity. U.S. tourists flock to Mexican border cities to purchase arts and crafts, sex industry services, pharmaceuticals at bargain prices, dental and health care at prices considerably lower than in the United States, and access to alternate health therapies not available at home. Mexicans cross into the U.S. border towns to purchase foods, manufactured goods, clothing, and many other items not available south of the border for the same price, quality, and selection. Mexicans also seek high-tech health care in U.S. border towns. For the U.S.-Mexican border, this exchange is no longer a minor issue about smuggling and petty trading but rather a huge economy unto itself. As people crossing from Tijuana to San Diego spend perhaps one billion dollars annually in the retail and service sectors, trade officials from the two cities travel the world together to invite productive facilities to their international, twin-city site.

The final group of selections in this volume addresses maritime and space borders. In the modern globalizing world, new technology has enabled nations and companies to exploit resources and find economic benefits in regions formerly ignored and thought useless. The mining of undersea resources and the ability to use outer space for commercial and strategic purposes have increasingly focused concern on maritime and space borders. The establishment of borders in these areas is the subject of complicated discussions among many nations and will be an ongoing important theme in the future.

As noted earlier, it is hoped that this volume will raise awareness as well as inform readers. It is an inescapable fact that our global village is characterized by walls that one cannot climb and by streets that one had better not cross. How these boundaries affect future development in sites around the world is not preordained, however. Our authors have shown a great variety of practices in the development and evolution of border regions and political borders. The challenges that humans will face along the boundaries that unite and divide them in the twenty-first century are tremendous, and the solutions of which we are capable are not obvious or easy. Readers of this book in their teens, twenties, and thirties are likely to be directly affected by the continued prominence of borders in a globalized world. The editors hope that this collection of information and analysis on borders and border politics in the context of ongoing globalization will shed light both on international and subnational boundaries and on the unfolding process of globalization.

A Note to the Reader

This volume has been designed for use by university students as well as by the general reader. A number of elements have been incorporated into the book to improve access to the content of the articles. First, the Introduction provides an overview of the collection and places the essays within the context of comparative studies of border regions and globalization. Second, the Glossary offers short definitions of terms that might be unfamiliar to the reader. Third, each chapter has a locator map, permitting easy identification of the geographical location of the border region discussed; a few of the essays also have more detailed maps as well as photographs. Fourth, a head note opens each chapter, to discuss its major themes and offer brief biographical information about its author(s). And finally, a list of Suggested Readings is provided for those who might wish to learn more about border regions throughout the world.

Notes

1. On these aspects of borders and border politics, see J. R. V. Prescott, *Political Frontiers and Boundaries* (London: Allen and Unwin, 1987); Malcolm Anderson, *Frontiers: Territory and State Formation in the Modern World* (London: Polity Press, 1996); and René Barendse, *Borderlands: A Theoretical Survey* (Rotterdam: Centre of Border Studies, 1994).

2. Michiel Baud and Willem Van Schendel, "Toward a Comparative History of Borderlands," *Journal of World History* 8, no. 2 (Fall 1997): 211–42. Much of the discussion that follows here draws heavily on this important article. See also Norris Clement, "International Transboundary Collaboration: A Policy-Oriented Conceptual Framework," in Paul Ganster, ed., *Cooperation, Environment, and Sustainability in Border Regions* (San Diego: San Diego State University Press, 2001), 17–31.

3. Oscar J. Martínez, *Border People: Life and Society in the U.S.-Mexico Borderlands* (Tucson: University of Arizona Press, 1994), 5–10.

4. Stanley R. Ross, ed., *Views across the Border: The United States and Mexico* (Albuquerque: University of New Mexico Press, 1978), xii.

5. See Ellwyn R. Stoddard, "Frontiers, Borders, and Border Segmentation: Toward a Conceptual Clarification," *Journal of Borderlands Studies* 6, no. 1 (Spring 1990): 1–22. See also the five stages of growth identified by Baud and Van Schendel, "Toward a Comparative History of Borderlands," 223–25.

6. The fastest growth of Mexico-origin population in the 1990s was experienced in the nonborder states of Oregon (55 percent growth between 1990 and 1996), Nevada (77 percent), Nebraska (70 percent), Iowa (52 percent), Arkansas (104 percent), Tennessee (58 percent), Georgia (70 percent), North Carolina (73 percent), and Vermont (55 percent). See Edwin Garcia and Ben Stocking, "Latinos on the Move to a New Promised Land," in *San Jose Mercury News*, August 16, 1998.

7. Baud and Van Schendel, "Toward a Comparative History of Borderlands," 221–22.

8. U.S. International Trade Commission, *The Impact of Increased United States-Mexico Trade on Southwest Border Development* (Washington, DC: Government Printing Office, 1986); Paul Ganster, "Percepciones de la migración mexicana en el condado de San Diego," *Revista Mexicana de Sociología* 53 (1991): 259–90; "Impact of the Peso's Devaluation on Retail Sales in San Diego County," *San Diego Economic Bulletin* 33 (March 1985).

9. Baud and Van Schendel, "Toward a Comparative History of Borderlands," 227–29.

10. In 1996 only 1.1 percent of the U.S. population was made up of illegal Mexican migrants; only 15 percent of the Mexican-origin population of the United States is in the country illegally. See Frank D. Bean et al., "The Quantification of Migration between Mexico and the United States," *Binational Study of Migration between Mexico and the United States* (Washington, DC; Mexico City: U.S. Commission on Immigration, Mexican Ministry of Foreign Affairs, 1998), 61.

Glossary

a fortiori: with more convincing force

Agenda 21: global plan of action for sustainable development adopted at the Rio Earth Summit in 1992

alae: Roman cavalry regiments

Alliance for Sustainable Development: an agreement signed by Central American presidents in 1994 to promote sustainable development in the region

antagonism: actively expressed opposition, hostility, or antipathy

antipode: direct or diametrical opposite

antithetical: of, relating to, or marked by opposition

apartheid: policy of racial segregation in South Africa from the late 1940s through the early 1990s by the white minority that sanctioned political and economic discrimination against the nonwhite majority

aquifer: underground formation of gravel or porous rock that contains water

asbestos: mineral that separates into long fibers suitable for uses where incombustibility is required

ASOCODE: Asociación de Organizaciones Campesinas Centroamericanas para la Cooperación y el Desarrollo (Association of Central American Rural Organizations for Cooperation and Development); this organization counts as members 80 percent of all organized small farmers in Central America, or four million heads of household

asymmetrical: out of balance, unequal, as in asymmetrical military or economic power

aufheben: raising, lifting; preserving, keeping

autarky: policy of national self-sufficiency and nonreliance on imports or economic aid

balaclava: warm woolen hood covering the head and neck and worn by soldiers and others

battlement: wall that consists of alternate solid parts (merlons) and open spaces (crenels) for defense

bayou: slow-moving stream that meanders through lowlands and enters a larger body of water

bonanza: source of great wealth or prosperity

book: place where bets on sporting events are taken and placed

bracero: Mexican laborer admitted to the United States under immigration treaties for seasonal contract labor in agriculture or industry; the program lasted from the end of World War II to 1964

Brezhnev-era hubris: general feeling of overconfidence, especially in regard to not taking the environment into account, as expressed by Communist states around the time when Leonid Brezhnev was in charge of the Soviet Union

by-products: something produced in the making of something else

CACM: Central American Common Market; a trade organization started in 1960 by Guatemala, El Salvador, Nicaragua, and Honduras, which later added Costa Rica

campesino: small farmer or farm worker in Latin America

cantina: Mexican pub or bar

cardenismo: support for the policies and beliefs of former Mexican president Lázaro Cárdenas, who was in power from 1934–1940

cerveza: beer

cholo: half-breed

CIS: Commonwealth of Independent States; an economic union created in 1991 that now includes twelve former Soviet republics

coffers: financial resources; funds

cohesive: sticking together

core-periphery: core countries' economies are characterized by advanced development and wealth; the periphery includes developing countries with economies based on low value-added activities such as raw material extraction or labor-intensive industries

de facto: in fact, in reality

delta: low triangular area where a river divides before entering a larger body of water

desarrollo: development

dikes: embankments of earth and rock built to hold back floodwaters

DM: deutsche mark; monetary currency used in West Germany from 1948–1990 and in Germany from 1990–2001; now replaced by the euro

dredging: deepening river channels or harbors by machine to rid them of obstructions and accumulated sediment

EEZ: exclusive economic zone; maritime territory extending 200 nautical miles beyond the coast. A country has sovereign rights to all natural resources and other economic resources within its EEZ, but other countries have rights of navigation and overflight

egregious: noticeable, bad, or offensive

EMU: European Monetary Union; the European countries that have adopted the euro as their common currency and share a common monetary policy as set by the European Central Bank

enclaves: enclosed territory that is culturally or economically distinct from the territory surrounding it

EPZ: export processing zone

EU: European Union; an economic and political confederation of European nations that are responsible for a common foreign and security policy and for cooperation on justice and home affairs

EU Interreg Programme: EU community initiative designed to support cross-border cooperation, social cohesion, and economic development between the regions of the European Union

EU Tacis programme: European initiative for the New Independent States (states that became independent with the collapse of the Soviet Union) and Mongolia, which fosters the development of economic and political links between the EU and these partner countries

FEDEPRICAP: Federación de Entidades Privadas de Centroamérica y Panamá (Federation of Private Businesses of Central America and Panama); an alliance of business and nonprofit groups in Central America that seeks to assist the economic and social development of the region

federalist: member or supporter of a decentralized form of government

fief: something over which one has rights or exercises control, such as in the case of a dominion overseen by a duke

FMLN: Frente Farabundo Martí para la Liberación Nacional (Farabundo Martí National Liberation Front); a political party in El Salvador

fratricide: the murder or killing of one's brother or sister

frontera: border

fronterizos: people from the northern border region of Mexico

FSLN: Frente Sandinista de Liberación Nacional (Sandinista National Liberation Front); a leftist Nicaraguan political organization that, after a prolonged period of civil war, held power from 1979–1990

garrison: permanent military post

gastarbeiter: foreign worker

GDP: gross domestic product; the total value of all goods and services produced within a country in a given year

GDR: German Democratic Republic; a Communist country encompassing the easternmost part of modern-day Germany from 1949–1990; also called East Germany

globalization: worldwide dispersion of culture, ideas, economic processes, and political power brought by advances in transportation and communications and economic integration through trade

GNP: gross national product; an economic indicator of the total value of goods and services produced within a country in a given year along with net foreign trade

GNRBS: Gabcikovo-Nagymaros River Barrage System of the Danube River basin

gringo: a foreigner in Latin America, especially an American or English person with fair features

hedonism: doctrine holding that behavior is motivated by desire for pleasure and avoidance of pain

herald: announce

hydroelectric: production of electricity by waterpower

hydropower: generating electricity by conversion of the energy of running water

ICJ: International Court of Justice; world court set up in 1945 to settle legal disputes between countries

iconographies: sketches, descriptions

IICA: Interamerican Institute for Cooperation in Agriculture; an organization established in Central America in 1942 to promote agriculture and rural development

IMF: International Monetary Fund; an organization of 184 member countries established to promote international monetary cooperation, exchange stability, and orderly exchange arrangements

IRA: Irish Republican Army; a paramilitary organization in Northern Ireland seeking to end British rule there

Iron Curtain: term coined by British prime minister Winston Churchill in 1946 that referred to the dividing line between the Free World and the Communist World during the Cold War era

isthmus: narrow strip connecting two larger masses of land

JDA: joint development area; an overlapping economic zone in the Gulf of Thailand established to resolve the competing claims of Thailand and Malaysia to hydrocarbon resources there. The Malaysia-Thailand Joint Authority governs this area

kaffiyeh: cloth headdress fastened by a band and usually worn by Arab men

kashrut: Jewish dietary laws

kibbutz: collective farm or settlement in modern Israel

Koran: book of sacred writings accepted by Muslims as the basis for their religion

kosher: fit or proper according to Jewish law

ladinos: in Central America, Spanish-speaking or acculturated Indians; mestizos (of mixed Spanish and Indian ancestry)

latifundio: large landed estate found in many regions of Latin America

lignite: mineral coal retaining the texture of the wood from which it was formed

macroeconomics: study of the overall aspects and workings of a national economy

maquiladora: manufacturing plant in a developing country that imports foreign materials and parts for assembly by low-cost local labor and exports the finished product to markets in developed countries. Thousands of these assembly plants are found in Mexico's northern border region

masato: traditional drink of the Amazon region made from fermented yucca (manioc)

matzo: brittle, flat unleavened bread, eaten especially during the Jewish Passover celebration

megawatt: unit of electric power equaling one million watts

menorah: holy candelabrum holding seven candles, used in Jewish rites

MERCOSUR: Mercado Común del Sur; a customs union encompassing Brazil, Argentina, Uruguay, and Paraguay

mezzotint: method of engraving a copper or steel plate, first utilized in the eighteenth century, from which etchings are made

milecastles: small forts spaced one mile apart along Hadrian's Wall

minaret: tall tower attached to a mosque from which a muezzin calls Muslims to prayer

minifundios: land subdivided into small subsistence plots characteristic of many areas of Latin America

Mormon: member of the Mormon Church, also called the Church of Jesus Christ of Latter-day Saints

mosque: Muslim house of worship

muezzin: crier who calls the Muslim faithful to prayer five times per day

NATO: North Atlantic Treaty Organization; a military alliance encompassing the United States, Canada, and Western European nations and originally designed to stop an invasion from the Soviet Union

neo-colonization: term used when a dominant power exercises control over a weaker political entity, not through direct political means but through economic control

norteño: person from the north of Mexico

OAS: Organization of American States; an organization of the countries of the Western Hemisphere that seeks to promote democracy and human rights in the region

OECD: Organization for Economic Cooperation and Development; this organization includes thirty members, all of which have market economies and are democratic, and most of which have developed economies

OPEC: Organization of Petroleum Exporting Countries; an oil cartel that includes eleven countries and accounts for 40 percent of the world's annual oil output and 75 percent of proven oil reserves. OPEC works to influence and stabilize the price of oil on the world market

Orangeism: attachment to the principles and practices of the Society of Orangemen, a secret organization founded in 1795 in Northern Ireland to maintain the political and religious ascendancy of Protestantism in the region

PAN: Partido Acción Nacional (National Action Party); a center-right party in Mexico that won the first opposition governorship in 1988 and the presidency in 2000 with the electoral victory of Vicente Fox

panista: supporter of the PAN political party of Mexico

parapet: wall, rampart, or elevation of earth or stone to protect soldiers

peccadilloes: slight offenses

peripheries: areas on the edges (borders) of a nation that have less political power and wealth; nations of the Third World with less power and wealth

platos típicos: traditional foods

PLO: Palestine Liberation Organization; a coalition of various groups founded in 1964 with the intent of establishing an independent Palestinian state

praxis: habitual or established practice; custom

PRD: Partido de la Revolución Democrática (Party of the Democratic Revolution); one of Mexico's major political parties

PRI: Partido Revolucionario Institucional (Institutional Revolutionary Party); the Mexican political party that maintained power from its date of establishment in 1929 until 2000

priísta: supporter of Mexico's PRI

protectorate: direct control of regions of Africa by the European powers

quisling: traitor, or collaborator with the enemy

rabbi: person trained in Hebrew law for the leadership of a Jewish congregation

regionalization: process by which activity is concentrated in regions (either within a nation or straddling nations), either by political dictate or by *de facto* market or social forces

remittances: payments sent by Mexicans working in the United States back to their families in Mexico. These payments are one of the largest sources of foreign currency for Mexico

Sabbath: seventh day of the week; Saturday, the day of rest and worship for Jews

SADC: Southern African Development Community

SAMP: Southern African Migration Project; an international partnership network linking organizations in Canada and six southern African states committed to collaborative research, training, public education, and policy development on migration issues

schadenfreude: enjoyment derived from the mishaps of others

sentry: soldier standing guard

shekels: silver coins of the ancient Hebrews

Shin Bet: Israeli counterintelligence and internal security service

SICA: Central American Integration System; an ongoing process of economic integration among Central American countries that will ultimately include free trade among members and a customs union

SIECA: Central American Secretariat for Economic Integration; the coordinating body for the Central American Integration System

simulacra: images or representations

sluices: artificial channels for conducting water, with a valve or gate to regulate the flow

synagogue: place of meeting for worship and religious instruction for those of the Jewish faith

tahini: thick paste made from ground sesame seeds that is part of the daily diet in many areas of the Middle East

teetotaler: one who practices or advocates total abstinence from alcoholic drinks

theocratic: of, or pertaining to, being administered by a religious authority

trawler: fishing boat that drags a conical net along the sea bottom

turret: small tower on top of a larger tower

UN: United Nations

UN/OEA: joint effort between the United Nations and the Organization of American States (in Spanish, Organización de Estados Americanos)

UNESCO: United Nations Educational, Scientific, and Cultural Organization; it supports the collaboration of nations around the world in areas of education, science, culture, and communications

unpalatable: not pleasant or agreeable

vis-à-vis: face to face, compared to, in relation to

Volstead Act: the 1919 act of Congress, authorized by the 18th Amendment, which prohibited the manufacture, transportation, and sale of beverages containing more than 0.5 percent alcohol

xenophobic: fear and hatred of any or anything that is strange or foreign

yarmulke: skullcap worn by religious Jews

yuppies: young professionals under age 40 who prospered during the 1980s

zeitgeist: the spirit of the time; the perspective of a given generation

1

Hadrian's Wall

John J. Wilkes

This article discusses the construction of a fortified wall across the northern frontier of the Roman Empire in what is now Great Britain. Emperor Hadrian, who visited the region in A.D. 122, ordered the building of the wall, beginning in the second century. The purpose of the structure was not to hold back an invading army; rather, its function was to control an imposed political boundary and to check smuggling and other illicit activities—much like many modern borders. The wall had fortified gates, watchtowers, a deep ditch on either side, and occasional Roman legion garrisons. Civilian settlements developed around the garrisons and checkpoints, a common feature of borders. Hadrian's Wall served its purpose for some four centuries.

John J. Wilkes is Yates Professor of Greek and Roman Archaeology, Emeritus, at the Institute of Archaeology, University College, London. His research interests include history and archaeology of the Graeco-Roman world in general with specializations in Britain and Southeast Europe, Roman inscriptions and topography, and settlements and site archaeology.

Hadrian's Wall in Great Britain crosses one of the island's narrowest points, between the estuary of the river Tyne on the east and Solway Firth on the west, a distance of about eighty Roman, or seventy-four English, miles. It is one of the largest surviving monuments from the four centuries when most of Britain, along with the bulk of Europe, the Middle East, and North Africa, was part of the Roman Empire. For a long time the identity of the emperor who ordered its construction was a subject of controversy among historians;

From John J. Wilkes, "Checkpoint Hadrian," *Natural History* 4, no. 89 (April 1989): 64–72. Reprinted with permission from *Natural History*. Copyright 1989 by the American Museum of Natural History.

it was therefore known as just the Roman Wall or the Picts Wall, after the Picts, whose attacks harried the Romans toward the end of their rule. The matter was only settled during the first quarter of this century, when excavations confirmed that the builder was Hadrian, who visited Britain during his rule (A.D. 117-38).

Britain was first invaded by Julius Caesar in 55 B.C. By then the Romans, who had already begun to acquire provinces under their republic, had good grounds for believing that the gods had assigned them the task of ruling the inhabited world. Carthage had been leveled a century earlier, and there was no other rival for power to be seen. The Parthians, who inhabited roughly what is now Iran, were a source of occasional disturbances but presented no real problem, and contacts with the Indians beyond them suggested a respectfulness that might soon turn into subservience. Everywhere else there were just barbarian tribes, whose leaders, if properly handled, would provide stable regimes to insure peace and security along the borders of the Roman world.

After Caesar's invasion of the island and victory over the British ruler Cassivellaunus, Britain seemed in line for annexation as a province, along with the rest of Caesar's new conquests in central and northern France (Gaul). But the takeover of Britain was dropped from the Roman agenda early in the reign of Caesar's successor, his great-nephew and adopted son Caesar Octavianus, who ruled from 27 B.C. to A.D. 14 as Rome's first emperor, Augustus. Along with a major reorganization of the Roman provinces, Augustus apparently reached a satisfactory diplomatic settlement with the kings of Britain that avoided the expense and bother of military conquest. As the contemporary Greek geographer Strabo explained, the Britons posed no threat, while occupation of their territory would never repay the costs of administration and a garrison. Besides, the taxes imposed on cross-channel trade—at external rates—provided a much better income.

When it came in A.D. 43, the Roman conquest of what is now southern England, and its transformation into the province of Britannia, served the purpose of surrounding the new emperor, Claudius, with the sorely needed aura of a military victory. But the large and expensive army of four legions and their auxiliaries (totaling about 40,000 men) became bogged down in inconclusive guerrilla warfare in Wales, northern England, and Scotland, until later emperors ordered victories and new conquests. Not until A.D. 83, when the governor of Britain, Julius Agricola, defeated the Caledonii in the Scottish Highlands, did the conquest of all of Great Britain seem to have finally been achieved.

Meanwhile, whole Roman armies were wiped out in what is now Romania by the rising power of the Dacians. These catastrophes, calling for reinforcements on the Danube front, led to the withdrawal of one legion from Britain, which later proved to be an act of overconfidence. Worse still, the military enterprises of Trajan, who ruled from A.D. 98 to 117, left his successor, Hadrian, with an empire reeling from the effects of war. Despite glorious victories in some quarters, including the eventual conquest of Dacia (achieved in A.D. 106, on the second attempt), the picture elsewhere was very different, as constant troop movements left some areas exposed to rebellion from within or sudden attack from without. The Parthian expedition at the end of Trajan's reign was ultimately a disaster.

Hadrian's Wall follows the contours of the landscape across England, 1996. *Photograph by Paul Ganster*

On becoming emperor, Hadrian drastically changed the organization of the army and of the frontier provinces where it was stationed. This signified a shift in Roman attitudes toward the peoples along the empire's borders. Conquest without limit gave way to a consolidation of conquest, the policy Augustus had sought to establish more than a century before. As a fourth-century historical biography states:

> When he assumed power, Hadrian immediately reverted to an earlier policy, and devoted his efforts to maintaining peace throughout the world. For at one and the same time the peoples subjugated by Trajan had risen in revolt, the Moors went on the offensive, the Sarmatians started a war and the Britons could not be held under Roman control.

Hadrian's intention was to achieve, through alliances and the subsidizing of chosen barbarian rulers, peace along the borders, where the army could maintain the status quo through regular peacetime training and maneuvers. "And so," the biography states, "having recognized the army in truly royal fashion, Hadrian set out for Britain. There he set many things right and he was the first to construct a wall, eighty miles long, that separated the Romans from the barbarians."

The emperor journeyed from the Rhineland to Britain in A.D. 122, mindful that the Romans there had suffered significant casualties in previous years. In fact, scholars long believed that the Ninth Legion, based at the fortress of York, had been destroyed. More likely, it was transferred from Britain only to perish either in a Jewish rebellion during Hadrian's reign or later in a war against Parthia. Whatever the fate of the Ninth, its place was taken by the Sixth Legion Victrix, which may have accompanied the emperor from the Rhineland. The other two legions in Britain were the Second Augusta, based at Caerleon, and the Twentieth Valeria Victrix, at Chester.

Having surveyed the unstable situation in Britain, Hadrian issued orders to build the wall that now bears his name. The planned length was seventy-six Roman miles, but the eastern end was extended to eighty. The wall followed the line of the Tyne Valley across northern England, a few miles in advance of an existing line of Roman forts. Where possible, the central sector of the wall was perched along the crest of a chain of north-facing volcanic crags now known as the Whin Sill. Today this area contains some of the best-preserved parts of the wall. Little remains in the east, where it followed the north side of the Tyne Valley for about twenty-five miles, or in the west, where it followed the Irthing Valley to Carlisle (Luguvalium) and the marshy shores of Solway Firth.

The wall itself, consisting of a rubble core faced with sandstone blocks, was eight to ten feet thick and probably fifteen feet high. Perhaps because of a shortage of limestone, which is used for lime mortar, the westernmost thirty-one miles was temporarily built of turf, but was entirely replaced by stone by the end of Hadrian's reign. In Hadrian's original scheme, only two types of structures were to be attached directly to the wall. The larger of these, known today as a milecastle, was a fortified portal at every Roman mile. Each had inner and outer gates and, to the side, a soldiers' barrack and a cooking oven within an enclosed area about sixty feet square. The second was an observation tower (now usually called a turret), twenty feet square, which was built into the wall and had stairs from ground level. Two such turrets were evenly spaced between each pair of milecastles.

The turrets were used for surveillance and, by means of a signaling system, for communication along the line of the wall; demonstrating their importance, they were built from the outset in stone throughout the system, whereas the milecastles were also constructed of turf in the turf wall sector.

The surveillance system also extended beyond the western terminus of the wall, probably as far down the coast as Saint Bees Head some forty miles away. A timber palisade may have formed a continuous barrier along some stretches of the coast in place of a stone or turf wall.

The wall's design included two additional features: parallel to the wall, some twenty feet north, was a V-shaped ditch about thirty feet wide and ten feet deep. A flat-bottomed ditch, twenty feet wide and ten feet deep, flanked by mounds of the dug-out earth thirty feet to either side, ran south of the wall, rarely more than two hundred yards away and often much closer. This ditch diverged from its parallel alignment in order to encompass some of the forts and milecastles and to skirt the crags of the Whin Sill.

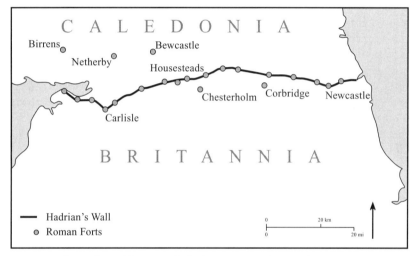

For a long time this second ditch, known today as the Vallum, was the most puzzling element of the wall system to archeologists, and not all that long ago, some believed that it was the original frontier established by Hadrian. Based in part upon a confused late Roman tradition, they considered the stone wall itself to have been the work of a later emperor, Septimius Severus, who fought the Britons for four years until his death at York in A.D. 211. The Reverend John Hodgson, however, in his *History of Northumberland* (1839), used the evidence of inscriptions to prove that the Vallum was not the original frontier, and excavation by Frank G. Simpson in the first quarter of this century showed that the entire complex—ditch, wall, milecastles, turrets, Vallum, and almost all of the associated regimental forts—was completed between A.D. 122 and 126, following Hadrian's visit to the province. The Vallum is now presumed to have been the boundary of the military zone, marking the area off limits to civilians and protecting army supplies from pilferage.

Although the imagination of some artists has left us with vivid images of Hadrian's Wall as the scene of conflict between the Romans and the Britons of the unconquered north, the wall was never intended to function as a battlement in the event of full-scale military conflict. It was instead an imposed line of political demarcation, equipped to prevent illicit passage beyond the checkpoints. Among its principal targets were smugglers attempting to evade the taxes imposed on trade in either direction. In principle it was like the less-permanent fortified boundaries established elsewhere in the empire wherever an artificial barrier was required, such as the boundary line that extended from Mainz on the Rhine to Regensburg on the Danube. Comparison can even be made to the wall that has divided the city of Berlin for a generation. Had such things been available, Hadrian's Wall would certainly have been laced with mines, electric fences, and barbed wire.

According to Hadrian's original scheme, the military manpower to operate this frontier system was to have come from auxiliaries stationed not far to the south. Three bases were also established at Birrens, Netherby, and Bewcastle, north of the wall in the west. For reasons as yet unknown, soon after Hadrian's visit the plan was changed, placing fifteen or sixteen army forts, varying in area from roughly three to nine acres, along the south side of the wall and down the western coast. This produced a total garrison of about 12,000 troops, mostly in infantry regiments, although some of these had mounted companies. The governor of Britain at the time of the wall's construction was Aulus Platorius Nepos, an ex-consul with considerable experience of command elsewhere in the empire. He later fell from Hadrian's favor, perhaps in part because the wall diverged somewhat from the emperor's original order.

As things turned out, Hadrian's Wall, even in its modified version, proved unsuitable in the view of Hadrian's rather dull and inactive successor, Antoninus Pius (ruled A.D. 138–61). Although we do not know why, within a few years of Hadrian's death the Roman frontier in Britain was moved 100 miles farther north and set across the narrows of central Scotland between the estuaries of the Forth and the Clyde. Perhaps the Romans decided that too much good territory had been left out of the province. Topography aside, there was no major ethnic, cultural, or historical division that dictated the placement of the northern frontier. If anything, a more natural boundary fell between the more settled eastern lowlands and the less tame west.

The return to the north was directed by the governor Quintus Lollius Urbicus, who apparently saw to the construction of the new fixed frontier line, completed in A.D. 142. Many of the bases first occupied under Agricola half a century before were reinstated, as large numbers of army units moved north. The victory of the new emperor was proclaimed, and coins portrayed the image of a dejected and defeated Britannia.

The Antonine Wall, as the new frontier is known, was, at thirty-seven miles, only half the length of its predecessor. It started a few miles east of

Edinburgh and followed the south edge of the lowland corridor formed by the Forth and the Kelvin, meeting the north bank of the river Clyde a few miles downstream from Glasgow. It was a turf barrier, perhaps twelve feet high, set on a stone foundation fourteen feet wide and fronted by a ditch forty feet wide and about thirteen feet deep. It had gates, similar to the milecastles of Hadrian's Wall, and army forts, which were attached to the wall from the outset. There were about nineteen such forts, generally smaller than those of Hadrian's Wall and more closely spaced, at about two-mile intervals. North of the wall, a line of forts was maintained through the Stirling Gap and along the valley of the Earn as far as the river Tay.

Despite differences in the design, the purpose of the new line was similar to that of Hadrian's Wall—to maintain comprehensive and effective control over all movements into and out of the Roman province. The new frontier line was built by men from the same three legions that had constructed Hadrian's Wall. When completed, the new frontier bore many symbols of Roman victory in the form of elaborately carved stones (now called distance slabs) that recorded which of the three legions had been responsible for that sector and their emblems, as well as scenes of sacrifice and military victory.

Little more than twenty years after its completion, the Antonine Wall was given up and Hadrian's Wall once again became the limit of the Roman province. Why this happened remains a mystery. The historical sources begin to fail us, and the task of the archeologists becomes much more difficult, as the same military bases are occupied, abandoned, and then reoccupied within a few decades. A major attack on the frontier is recorded for the year A.D. 180, when the northern peoples broke through Hadrian's Wall, killed a general, and caused much damage. Other stories suggest that in this period the Roman army in Britain was disaffected, perhaps feeling neglected after its earlier days of glory. Eventually, the emperor Severus (ruled A.D. 193–211) and his successors made Hadrian's Wall the lasting frontier of the province by thoroughly reorganizing the garrison and totally reconstructing the wall and the forts, both those along the wall and others to the north and south.

Most of the century following the death of Severus was a time of peace along Hadrian's Wall and in the civil settlements that arose near the forts. Life in these places was probably similar to that in and near a great military base of modern times. Everything was dominated by the presence of the army units stationed there, usually about 10,000 full-time professional soldiers, each serving a standard engagement of twenty-five years.

These forces were not the famed legions, the heavily armed infantry divisions of 5,000 men, but the auxiliaries, consisting of smaller infantry cohorts, 500 to 1,000 strong, and cavalry regiments known as *alae*. At one time there had been a clear distinction between the legions, recruited from among Roman citizens in Italy and Italian colonies, and the auxiliaries, enlisted from the ethnic groups on the fringes of the empire. The auxiliaries, originally dispatched to serve outside their homelands, included cohorts of Gauls, Germans, Spaniards, Illyrians, Thracians, and even Britons.

By the time of the emperor Severus, however, these distinctions were fast disappearing. Most soldiers who served in the auxiliary cohorts that manned Hadrian's Wall appear to have been Roman citizens, a privilege granted the sons of the non-Romans who served. Moreover, even though the units continued to carry the names of the ethnic groups from which they had originally been recruited, the majority of serving soldiers came from Britain or Gaul, often from the very civil settlements that prospered outside the forts along the wall. The emperor Caracalla, Severus's son, made citizens of every free-born man and woman in the empire by edict in A.D. 212 or 213.

The forts and associated civil settlements became miniature garrison towns containing, in addition to the dependents of serving soldiers, every service that an army demands—shops, brothels, and taverns, no doubt thronged with traders, bogus preachers, miracle workers, and quack doctors with patent medicines. Two settlements grew to acquire the character of full-sized towns. Corstopitum (modern Corbridge) lay on the river Tyne where the main Roman road from the south crossed the river. A military works and stores depot manned by legionaries from elsewhere in the province, it was also remarkable for the many religious sculptures and offerings made to the gods by civilians. Luguvalium (modern Carlisle), on the river Eden, was instead the urban center of the Carvetii, identified in late Roman period sources as the native people who inhabited the Lake District of northwest England.

Among the forts that have been excavated is Housesteads, where archeologist Eric Birley found evidence of a murder: the remains of a man who had been knifed to death lay hidden beneath the stone floor of a house in the settlement. (Naturally this was reported to the district coroner, but since nineteen centuries had passed, inquiries were not pursued.) At the time of the murder, the dispensing of justice would have been the responsibility of the garrison commander, an educated man from a wealthy family and probably from elsewhere in the empire.

Until recently, most of what we knew of the people who lived near Hadrian's Wall had been based on tombstones and similar monuments bearing Latin epitaphs, recorded and collected over the past three or four hundred years and now on view in museums at Newcastle, Corbridge, and Carlisle. In 1974, however, Robin Birley began excavations at Vindolanda, a fort incorporated into the Hadrian's Wall system but not actually attached to it. Here, in the form of Latin letters and other documents written in ink on thin sheets of birchwood, he found a truly sensational record of life from just before the wall was built. Hundreds of these precious but fragile documents, which were preserved by wet conditions, have come to light. Since the documents date to the period from A.D. 95 to 105, some of the people who wrote them may still have been there when Hadrian came and ordered the building of the wall.

Some documents are lists of stores and provisions issued at regular intervals to the soldiers, including barley, goat's meat, young pig, ham, and venison, along with good quality beer and wine. One is a parade state—a list of what everybody was doing on a particular day—for one of two units known from other sources to have been stationed at Vindolanda during this period: the Eighth Cohort of Batavians, originating from an area that now lies in Holland; and the First Cohort of Tungrians, from eastern Belgium. From it we learn that of a total of 750 men, only 270 were in fact on station; the rest were on leave, patrol, or some sort of detachment. And no less than a tenth of the unit is listed as sick. A hint of garrison life in northern Britain is reflected in a letter from home to a serving soldier: "I have sent you pairs of socks from Sattua, two pairs of sandals, and two pairs of underpants. Greet . . . Tetricus and all your messmates with whom I hope you live in the greatest good fortune."

At a more elevated social level we have an invitation from one lady to another: "Claudia Severa to her Lepidina, greetings. For the third day before the Ides of September, the day of the celebration of my birthday, I give you a warm invitation in order to make sure that you come to us, to make the day more enjoyable for me by your arrival, if you come. Give my greetings to your Cerialis. My Aelius and my little son send their greetings." Then, to this invitation, presumably written by a clerk, there is added in another hand: "I shall expect you, sister. Farewell, sister, my dearest soul, as I hope to prosper, and hail." Finally the address is added in a third hand: "To Sulpicia Lepidina, wife of Flavius Cerialis, from Severa." From other documents, Flavius Cerialis is known as one of the garrison commanders at Vindolanda, and we can identify Severa's husband as Aelius Brocchus, known as a cavalry commander on the Danube frontier but at this time presumably commanding a regiment somewhere in northern Britain. What makes this pleasant social exchange even more interesting is that the message in the second hand, rather more clumsy and less elegant than the first, is a personal note from Claudia Severa herself and is the earliest known original document in Latin written by a woman.

On a very different note, another document is evidently an official report on the fighting qualities of native Britons: "The Britons are not protected by [armor]. There are very many cavalry. The cavalry do not use swords nor do the Britons [the word used is the disparaging *Brittunculi*, or 'little Brits'] hold fixed positions when they throw javelins." Whether these remarks were about the opposing forces or allied enlistees is unclear. The many other finds from Vindolanda—including shoes, clothing, textiles, and every variety of timber and metal implement—are also of great interest, but nothing compares with these written accounts, more of which certainly remain to be found.

There is ample evidence that Hadrian's Wall remained an effective northern boundary of Roman territory in Britain as late as the second half of the fourth century A.D. But it cannot have survived the collapse of the Roman Empire in the west during the early years of the fifth century. For a time the forts and other structures of Hadrian's Wall may have been used as dwellings by the native populations, possibly including descendants of the wall's garrisons. The English historian and theologian Bede refers to remains of Roman Carlisle still being visible in the seventh century. But most of the forts and civil settlements must soon have been stripped of their building stone for new towns and villages that grew up in response to local needs, not to sustain the military system of an imperial frontier.

2

The Great Wall of China

Cheng Dalin

The Great Wall of China extends across the north of the country for more than 6,000 kilometers (3,728 miles). Comprised of high walls with low parapets on the top and guard and garrison towers at intervals, it was constructed over a 2,000-year period. The Great Wall was the major defense system of ancient China and served largely to protect the country from incursions from nomadic groups from the north. Rather than forming an impenetrable barrier, it permitted controlled movement of goods and people. Construction of the wall, the stationing of troops, and ongoing maintenance led to building of access roads and establishment of towns. These activities brought economic development and better integration of the Far North with the rest of China. The similarities in form and function of the Great Wall of China with Hadrian's Wall are striking.

Cheng Dalin is a photographer and writer who lives and works in China. He spent over five years and traveled more than 30,000 kilometers (18,640 miles) in his quest to visit all sections of the wall and document it with photographs and text.

Throughout the ages the Great Wall has been regarded as symbolic of China. To a space-traveling astronaut looking back at the earth, the Great Wall is the most conspicuous object among the visible man-made structures.

Walls high and low criss-cross the vast expanse of China, but the wall lying across the north is the greatest in magnitude. From the pass of Jiayuguan

From Cheng Dalin, "Symbol of the Past, Inspiration for the Future," in *The Great Wall of China* (Hong Kong: South China Morning Post Ltd. and New China News Ltd., 1984), 9–17. Reprinted by permission of Cheng Dalin.

in Gansu province in the west, it snakes eastwards to the Yalu River, a distance of more than 6,000 kilometers—or 12,000 *li* in the Chinese unit of length. The Chinese call it "the Great Wall of 10,000 *Li*." Like a colossal dragon, the wall crawls over high mountains, boundless grasslands and vast expanses of desert, and terminates on the banks of the Yalu. Time-honored, stupendous in dimensions and superb in architectural engineering, the Great Wall of China has been acclaimed as a wonder of the world comparable to the pyramids of Egypt, the Taj Mahal of India and the legendary Hanging Gardens of Babylon.

The First Line of Defense

The Great Wall was the greatest defense system in ancient China. It was beginning to take shape in the form of connected systems of walled towns and beacon towers as long ago as the Spring and Autumn and Warring States periods (475–221 B.C.), when rival dukes had to protect their own fiefs from encroaching neighbors.

The wall varies in size from one place to another, as it was built according to the configurations of the local terrain. Some sections are as much as 7.8 meters high, 6.7 meters thick at the base, and five meters wide at the top to allow five horses or ten warriors to march abreast. They are surmounted on the inner edge by one-meter high brick parapets, and on the outer side by battlements with two openings in each merlon—the upper one a peephole and the lower an embrasure.

There are buttressed platforms and guard and garrison towers on the wall. Sentries kept watch from the protruding buttressed platforms, which have battlements on their outer edge and small brick rooms where wall patrols could shelter. The guard towers are two-story elevated structures with brick cells on the lower floor to house 50–60 troops. The upper floors have peepholes and embrasures, and in some cases are installed with equipment for building beacon fires. Garrison towers, very much resembling modern forts, were built at strategically important points that were not easily accessible to attackers. Garrison troops were summoned from them to fight in emergencies. Much larger than guard towers, they are usually two-storied. The top floor was used as a lockout post and a firing platform and the lower floor for storing bows and arrows, arms and gunpowder. Ladders were used to climb up and down.

All along the Great Wall there are beacon towers, mostly perched on high hilltops or at turning points on plains. They were used to relay alarm signals. Whenever the presence of the enemy was detected, columns of signal smoke were produced during daylight and bonfires lit at night. Wolf dung was regarded as the fuel that produced the tallest and straightest columns of heavy

The Great Wall near Beijing, 1996. *Photograph by Paul Ganster*

smoke visible from afar. In classical Chinese literature widespread fighting was often described as "a rash of wolf-dung bonfires all over the land."

Under a rule in force during the reign of Ming Emperor Chenghua, the presence of an enemy force of 100 men was signaled with one lighted beacon and one round of cannon fire; 500 strong required two fires and two cannon shots; three fires and three cannon shots meant an enemy force of 1,000; and five fires and cannons indicated 5,000 men—a primitive but novel system of audiovisual communication. The sight of an enemy would touch off a swift chain of bonfires across the length of the wall from one command to the next. It was said that in half a day an alarm message could be relayed across a distance of 500 kilometers.

The Work of Many Dynasties

The construction of the Great Wall actually engaged a succession of dynasties. Starting as far back as 500 to 400 B.C. during the period of the Warring States, the work went on for more than 2,000 years and involved more than twenty dynasties, including the reigns of vassal states.

The period of the wall's beginning was a splendid juncture in Chinese history, when China was moving from a slave society to a feudal one, emancipating its productive forces. Already there were towns large enough to hold hundreds of thousands of people, and a canal linking the Yangtze and Huaihe valleys.

In its early years the Zhou dynasty (1100–256 B.C.), with the aim of tightening its control over the slaves, had divided its domain into fiefs and parceled them out to more than 800 dukes. Because of the subsequent uneven economic development of these vassal states, however, some grew stronger than others and a process of encroachment and annexation followed. By about 500 B.C. several big states, Qin, Qi, Chu, Wei, Yan, Zhao and Han, survived alongside a small number of tiny dying ones. Annexionist wars raged among these bigger states, reaching increasingly formidable proportions. Hundreds of thousands of men would be mobilized in a single campaign, and infantry became increasingly important. Hitherto chariots had been the principal instrument of war between the vassal states in the central plains. But they were abominably awkward, especially in difficult terrain, and the northern vassal states suffered a series of embarrassing debacles in wars against national minorities whose infantries showed far greater mobility. Heeding this lesson, the state of Jin used infantry to devastating effect in its war with Qi. In their actions against slave uprisings, the dukes of the central plains also learned to use infantry as a supplementary force. Consequently troops were able to move much faster, and mobile war and outflanking tactics were increasingly adopted. The trend sent military strategists back to their drawing boards to develop new defensive measures.

The state of Chu in the south was the first to build fortresses and a defense line where natural barriers were used to good advantage and sound military strategy was evident. Their fortresses were known as "square-walled cities." Then followed the state of Qi, which took 200 years between the 5th and 3rd centuries B.C. to construct a defense line consisting of beacon towers, castles and tall ramparts, starting in the suburbs of Jinan, the present-day provincial capital of Shandong, and running eastwards along the northern foot of Taishan Mountain, through the natural divide between Lushan and Yimeng mountains and down to the seashore off the city of Qingdao. Five hundred kilometers long, this defense line was China's first long wall. Qi was followed by Wei, Qin, Zhao and Yan, which built their own long walls. Zhongshan, a tiny state of a minority people surrounded by vassal states, also built a wall of its own.

These long walls were mostly used as boundary barriers against the acquisitive greed of other vassal states. The three northern states, Qin, Zhao and Yan, while contending among themselves for control over the central plains, also had to fend off minorities in the north, and built walls on their northern borders as well.

In 221 B.C. the state of Qin succeeded in unifying China, and a centralized feudal state of many nationalities was established. The supreme ruler was Qin Shi Huang, the First Emperor.

With his supremacy over China established, Qin Shi Huang was faced with the problem of protecting what he had won, particularly from a powerful rival from the north—the Xiongnu (Hun) nationality. The Xiongnu were pastoral nomads with a long history who had been quickly developing from a primitive society into a slave society while the vassal states in the central plains were busily fighting each other. They had become united in a great tribal union, and their first chieftain, Touman, had his headquarters in what is known today as Touman City, north of Langshan Mountain in Nei Monggol (Inner Mongolia).

The Xiongnu, who earned their living mainly in animal husbandry, were in the habit of increasing their resources and population by making predatory raids on their neighbors and taking captives as their slaves. The developed and populous central plains states had become their principal prey. Now they posed a threat to the Qin dynasty, in that they were damaging its developing economy and destroying citizens' lives and property. Counter-measures were necessary, and a great wall to fend off the Xiongnu became imperative.

In 215 B.C., four years after the unification of China, the Qin court sent General Meng Tian in command of 300,000 troops against the Xiongnu. He succeeded in driving them 350 kilometers off to the northern bank of the Yellow River and out of their political center, Touman.

No sooner had Meng Tian and Fu Su, the Prince of Qin, set up their garrison at Suide than they began building the Great Wall. Over a period of nine years a million soldiers and civilian laborers were recruited to work on the project. Earlier walls built by the vassal states of Qin, Zhao and Yan were repaired and connected up, and many new sections were built. Starting from Lintao county in eastern Gansu province, the new wall ran eastwards to the farthest part of Liaoning province, a distance of 5,000 kilometers, and a new chapter was opened up in the history of the long walls of China.

Three later dynasties—Han, Jin and Ming—were also great builders of long walls each exceeding 5,000 kilometers (10,000 *li*). The Han wall was a two-fold project, complete with many connected square-walled towns, outposts, ramparts and beacon towers. Emperor Wu (140–87 B.C.), in carrying out the work, rebuilt the great Qin wall and extended it to the west with new sections. A chain of outposts and barriers built at far-flung positions crept out for 20,000 *li* to Yanze in today's Luobupo region of Xinjiang, where relics of some of them are still discernible today.

The Ming dynasty attached an even greater importance to building the wall. Its aim was to prevent a comeback of the remnant forces of the preceding Yuan dynasty, and to forestall the rising Nuzhen nationality in northeast China. The first emperor of the dynasty, Zhu Yuanzhang, at the very outset of his reign (1368) assigned his son Zhu Di and General Xu Da to repair the existing Great Wall and its defile forts at Juyongguan, Shanhaiguan and in the eastern part of Liaoning province. From the Yalu River to Jiayuguan, several thousand new garrison towers, defile defense works and beacon towers were constructed along the 12,000-*li* Great Wall. The project took 200 long years to complete.

The Qing dynasty began with the pursuance of a modified policy towards the national minorities to the north, and for some time there was peaceful coexistence with them. Emperor Kang Xi even composed a poem in which he denigrated Qin Shi Huang for having built too great a wall, depleting the nation's resources but still failing to save his realm from collapse.

But the good relationship with the minorities began to wane before long, and national antagonisms resurfaced. In the eighth year of his reign (1669), the chieftain of the Mongolian tribe of Dzungar, Galdan, established himself as the Khan in an open challenge to the Qing regime. This development compelled erstwhile Great Wall critic Kang Xi himself to order the reinforcement of the fortifications and the manufacture of arms and ammunition. Moreover, in the 17th year of his reign (1678) he made an inspection of the defense situation at his frontiers. A dozen years later he had personally to lead an armed expedition, though to little avail. The next year the Great Wall was garrisoned almost in its entirety.

Many Nationalities Involved

China has always had a great variety of peoples, some of them immigrants, others indigenous. Many of these were nomadic tribal groups who were subject to frequent rises and falls in their fortunes. Very often when one nationality grew powerful another would be lurking behind its back, ready to take its place.

During the past 2,000 years there have risen and fallen, or perished, on the vast Chinese territory the Xiongnu, Donghu, Wuhuan, Liaoling, Yueshi, Wusun, Xianbei (Sienpi), Rouran, Tujue, Qidan (Khitan), Nuzhen (Nuchen), Mongol and Man (Manchu), living at times in peace and friendship, at others in enmity and war. Many of them adopted the traditional Chinese method of defense—the long wall. The wall built by the Jin dynasty of the Nuzhen (1115–1234) in the north was an extraordinary barrier more than 5,000 kilometers long. Later, the Yuan dynasty of the Xiongnu (1280–1368) repaired the existing Great Wall for its own use. Over the past twenty centuries, long walls were built not only when the Han people were at loggerheads with national minorities, but also when one of the latter was at war with another. The Northern Wei dynasty (386–577) built a long wall to fend off the Rouran to the north. The Northern Qi dynasty (550–577) had a similar barrier erected to defend itself from the Rukou, Tujue, Kumoxi and Qidan. The Jin dynasty put up its own long wall to fend off the Liao dynasty of the Qidan. The Great Wall was actually the joint creation of many nationalities of China.

The long walls built by the various minority groups were located according to their distribution, the mutual balance of strength between them and the invulnerability of the terrain. Those living outside a long wall at one time could be inside it at another. Hence the Great Wall was neither the boundary between the Han people and the northern minorities, nor a barrier separating civilization from barbarism or agricultural from pastoral societies. It would be even more preposterous to regard the Great Wall as the national boundary of China in the north. The Great Wall was simply the major military defense system of ancient China, and it was never considered as anything else.

The Great Wall is a shining example of two conventional Chinese ideas: that defenses should be built where the terrain makes access difficult, and that locally available materials should be used to the fullest possible extent in any construction project. In fact the entire wall is built on terrain where natural barriers provided by high mountains and deserts are fully exploited to make the structure easy to defend and difficult to capture. The fortifications on the wall differ according to the configurations of the local terrain, but are ingeniously integrated into a complex whole. Thanks to the maximum use of local materials, the cost was kept as low as possible.

It has been estimated that the earth and stone used in the body of the wall could build a wall around the equator, one meter wide and five meters high, more than ten times over.

The number of annexes is simply incalculable. Historical data handed down from the Ming dynasty show that Commander Qin Hong alone built as many as 14,000 fortresses of different sizes in his garrison region, which encompassed the provinces of Shaanxi, Gansu and Ningxia, during the period 1501–1505. The walls of these fortresses, averaging two kilometers each in circumference, could alone be straightened out to circle the equator. In 1555, Ming imperial Minister of Defense Yang Bo constructed 2,800 beacon towers, using enough earth and stones to make a 2,100-kilometer wall one meter wide and one meter high.

As construction of the Great Wall continued for more than two millennia and involved thousands upon thousands of commanding generals and officers, its fortifications all have their own distinctive features.

Many of the earliest ramparts and walls dating back to 2,000 years ago in central and northwestern China were built with sand and reeds, with hammered earth or with rubble. Some of them still exist today. This is in itself extraordinary, and says much about the superb architectural skills of ancient China.

The Great Wall of the Ming dynasty is considered the best example of Chinese long walls, as it epitomizes the military strategy of the ancient Chinese as well as their wonder-working aptitude in the organization of labor in construction projects and in architectural engineering.

An Investment in Human Lives

The Great Wall as a project entailed an enormous investment of human and material resources. In one mobilization in 215 B.C. alone, Emperor Qin Shi Huang recruited 300,000 soldiers and 500,000 civilian laborers. In A.D. 550 the Northern Qi dynasty sent as many as 1.8 million drafted laborers to build a 450-kilometer-long section of wall from Datong in Shaanxi province to Juyongguan in Beijing.

The laborers who were torn away from their homes to become Great Wall builders were condemned to unbearably hard toil and were frequently worked to death. Historical documents show that of the one million laborers pressed into construction service in A.D. 607 by Emperor Yang of the Sui dynasty, who was building a 500-kilometer section of the wall in north Shaanxi and Nei Monggol, only half survived to return to their homes. The rest died on the job, an average of one death for every meter of wall. Hence there was a saying in ancient times that the Great Wall was "ten thousand *li* of human bones and earthwork."

The various dynasties engaged in the project went to great lengths to amass the financial and human resources required. Emperor Wu of the Han dynasty (140–87 B.C.) managed to overcome the state's financial difficulties caused by his war on the Xiongnu and his Great Wall project through a host of measures, including new taxes to extort wealth from merchants and other sectors of the population.

One historical record of the Ming dynasty shows that state revenue in 1550 could hardly meet one-third of the defense costs along the Great Wall, and that new taxes had to be introduced, giving rise to serious social unrest.

Benefits from the Wall

The Great Walls would of course have no strategic value in any modern war, but they proved quite impregnable against warriors wielding swords, spears, pikes or bows and arrows. Even fast-moving and highly mobile cavalry were unable to surmount it. The Great Wall allowed the dynasties to develop the nation in peace, and in this respect contributed much to China's economic growth through the ages.

The Great Wall for its greater part is sited in areas that were thinly inhabited and poorly developed economically and culturally. To ensure its security, and to provide supplies for its garrison forces, settlements were established along the wall by one dynasty after another. For example, in 221 B.C. the Qin dynasty organized the resettlement of 30,000 families in Nei Monggol in the vicinity of the first Great Wall. The later Han dynasty in 119 B.C. settled 720,000 people along its wall in Gansu, Ningxia and north Shaanxi.

Meanwhile the garrison troops of the wall were ordered to reclaim wasteland and plant crops. To supply their needs, access roads and canals were constructed. While building the Great Wall, the Qin dynasty paved an avenue more than 700 kilometers long from Xianyang in Shaanxi province to Baotou in Nei Monggol. The Ming dynasty extended the Grand Canal up to Tong county on the outskirts of Beijing so that supplies from Henan, Shandong and even the Yangtze and Huaihe valleys could be transported up to the Great Wall. All these undertakings were militarily significant, but they also played an important role in promoting economic and cultural development in many remote areas.

In the Han dynasty (140–87 B.C.), when Emperor Wu commanded a counter-expedition against the Xiongnu, he built a road leading to the west which linked inland China and Xinjiang and greatly helped to increase the country's trade and cultural exchanges with the southern, central and western parts of Asia and even the coastal states of the Mediterranean. To make sure that the road remained open and secure, an extension of the Great Wall flanked by beacon towers was built. This was later to become known as the "Silk Road."

Thus the metallurgical techniques, farming methods and water conservancy know-how of inland China, along with bolts of silk fabrics, were introduced into Xinjiang to enrich the lives of the people there, stimulating their economic and cultural development as a result. On the other hand horses, camels, woolen goods and farm and orchard products ranging from clover to grapes flowed into China from Central Asia together with its religions, cultures, dances, acrobatic arts and music, to be subsequently merged into traditional Chinese culture and become part of it. The cultural intercourse begun then exerted such a wide and far-reaching influence that it was felt all over China. The Magao Grottoes at Dunhuang and the grotto of Maiji Mountain are examples of such influence.

For the people on either side of it, the wall was never a barrier impeding their cultural and economic interchange. There was no such thing as a "closed-door" policy. Instead, through the reigns of all the dynasties, official and civilian fairs were held along the wall, interrupted only in wartime. Salt, tea, cotton and silk fabrics and tools from inside the wall were exchanged for cattle, sheep, horses and woolens from the other side, and business was brisk.

Being itself China's largest single cultural relic, the Great Wall is at the same time a huge cultural treasure house. Builders, garrison soldiers and artisans left behind many precious objects, including inscribed tablets, arms, household articles and writings.

A beacon tower from the Han dynasty which was excavated by archaeologists 100 kilometers west of Dunhuang in 1979 led to the discovery of 1,200 written bamboo slips and a great variety of household articles ranging from toys to writing brushes and rice paper. The finds are extremely valuable to the study of the defense institutions of the Great Wall and the everyday life of its garrisons during the Western Han dynasty, and also to research into the relations of the regime with the countries of Central and South Asia.

Since the founding of the People's Republic, the government has attached great importance to preserving the Great Wall, the ancient world's most stupendous architectural work. The sections of the wall at Mount Badaling, Shanhaiguan and Jiayuguan have been listed as priority cultural sites for preservation. Specialized institutions endowed with huge funds for repair and maintenance have been set up to take care of them as tourist centers and objects of research.

Standing in bold relief against the vast expanse of northern China, the Great Wall is an eternal monument to a nation's glorious history. It is a symbol of the early civilization of China, and an embodiment of the wisdom, talent and determination of its people. Many who have been to the Great Wall have said that without the knowledge of the wall one can never truly understand China and her long civilization.

3

The Berlin Wall

Frederick Baker

The Berlin Wall was erected in 1961 through the heart of the city of Berlin by the government of East Germany to prevent its citizens from fleeing to the west. It came to be the most vivid symbol of the Cold War, the period of tension between the Soviet Union and its allies and the United States and its allies in Western Europe from 1946 to the late 1980s. With the decline of the Soviet Union and the growing rapprochement between the East and the West, the East German government permitted free passage through the wall in November 1989. Shortly thereafter, citizens spontaneously began destroying the wall and selling pieces as souvenirs. Eventually, after the reunification of Germany, the government began to preserve sections of the wall, along with the graffiti art created on them, for posterity.

Frederick Baker (B.A. Hons., M.Phil. Cambridge University) is a bilingual Austrian-British writer and filmmaker. Born in Salsburg, he was brought up in London. He studied archaeology and anthropology at Cambridge, Tübingen, and Sheffield universities. He has just published The Reichstag Graffiti, *with Lord Norman Foster (Berlin, 2002).*

Though it was only built in 1961, the Berlin Wall is today an archaeological monument. Four years after its opening on 9 November 1989, less is left of the Berlin Wall than of Hadrian's Wall. To trace its former course through Germany's capital would now test the skills of many a field archaeologist. For archaeology, the study of material objects in a historical perspective, contemporary material objects, especially those of complex meaning and history

From Frederick Baker, "The Berlin Wall: Production, Preservation and Consumption of a 20th-Century Monument," *Antiquity* 67, no. 257 (1993): 709–33. Figures omitted. Reprinted by permission of Frederick Baker.

21

like the Berlin Wall, are as valuable as the older border fortifications of China or of Northumberland.

The Wall is important for several reasons. No single object better encapsulates the 20th-century European experience than the Berlin Wall. It was the central monument of the Cold War, 1945–89 in Europe, a conflict that had its roots in the European wars of 1914–18 and 1939–45. As the notorious part of the "Iron Curtain," the petrified front-line of the Soviet empire from the Baltic to the Black Sea, it was also an emblem of the division of the late 20th-century world into two political spheres. The Wall's building was the symbol of the Cold War, its destruction a symbol of its end.

The Berlin Wall exemplifies features common to many monuments which carry special weights of symbol or meaning; the memory that has been preserved suffers from partiality, not just in how little physically remains, but also in its representation to the public today.

This article approaches the Berlin Wall in two stages: first it sets out the nature and development of the Wall up to its fall in 1989; then it examines the way in which parts of the Wall were preserved to be consumed by the tourist industry, and the distorted view of the Wall it offers.

The Berlin Walls

There was no such thing as "the" Berlin Wall; there were several Berlin walls.

This is true at many levels, in time and in space. The "border security system for the national frontier west," as it was officially known, went through several phases ("generations") of construction. And "The Wall" was a set of in-depth border fortifications that consisted of *two* parallel walls: an interior and an exterior one enclosed a "death strip" and watch towers. But even these walls were not walls: the internal wall was often constituted of old boarded-up buildings, as at the Bernauer Straße, or by the banks of canals or rivers. Only 37 km of the wall ran through areas of housing; 17 km ran through industrial areas, 30 km through woods, 24 km along waterways, and 55 km along rail embankments, fields and marshland (Rühle & Holzweißig 1988: 145). So in some places the Wall was made of wire fences, not concrete, or was a line through a lake or a bridge, like the infamous Glienicker bridge, where spies were swapped between East and West.

The Wall's complexity goes beyond bricks and mortar, for its meaning was very different according to whether you lived on its East side or on its West side. This difference is best illustrated by the two German words that translate as the English word "wall," *Mauer* and *Wand*. While *Mauer* means wall in the sense of a barrier, *Wand* means wall in the sense of the "face" of a wall. According to Martin Walser, the novelist who predicted the fall of the Wall, "The English can never fully understand what '*die Mauer*' meant for us Germans, because your word wall doesn't differentiate between *Wand* and

Mauer" (1991, pers. comm.). When the Wall was built and all contact was broken off, the Wall was very much a *Mauer* for Westerners and Easterners alike. By the 1980s, when crossing from West into East had became easier for Westerners, the Wall was less *Mauer*, more *Wand*. For East Germans the Wall remained firmly a *Mauer*.

There had been a large city wall around Berlin, long before the Wall of 1961–89. The Brandenburg Gate's position, adjacent to the 1961 Wall, is no coincidence; it is the only survivor of the old Customs wall which was demolished in 1867 (Ribbe & Schmaedeke 1988: 107). That Prussian kings had built a Customs wall which in places was followed by the exact course of the most recent Wall was often used to normalize the division of Berlin by another wall.

The Cold War and the Construction of the Wall

The Wall was constructed in 1961, in the stalemate phase of the Cold War in Europe, before the focus of tensions turned to Cuba, Indo-China and Africa. The Soviets, having liberated Berlin during the Second World War, felt a moral right to its total occupation. Only with reluctance did they allow the Americans, British, and later the French, to take up an agreed four-powers supervision of Berlin on 1 July 1945.

The frontier within the divided Germany that separated the Soviet zone (after 1949 the German Democratic Republic: East Germany) from the combined American/British/French zones (after 1949 the German Federal Republic: West Germany) ran about 200 km west of Berlin (Wagner 1990). Berlin, as the old German capital, was divided between the Allies; the Soviet zone, East Berlin, was soon integrated into East Germany; the American, British and French zones, united as West Berlin, remained a Western island inside East Germany, closely linked to the West German Federal Republic and joined to it by air and surface access corridors through East Germany. The division line within Berlin, later the line of the Wall, followed the old boundaries of the historical local government boundaries, chopping across the old centre, through the middle of the Potsdamer Platz, the city's greatest square, and within a few yards of the Reichstag, united Germany's parliament building. The trains on some north-south underground railway lines went under East Berlin from the West, running non-stop through shut-down "ghost stations" before reaching Western territory again.

The foundations of the Wall were laid in late 1945 when the USA changed its policy from attempted co-operation with the Soviet Union to "containment," according to the new policy's progenitor George F. Kennan: "if the West was not willing to 'go the full hog' [*sic*] to block the USSR, the only alternative was to split Germany, partition Europe into two spheres and decide the 'line beyond which we cannot afford to permit the Russians to exercise unchallenged power' " (McCauley 1983: 52). With two spheres of influence established, Berlin was the Western island of influence inside the Eastern zone that could become "the West's weakest spot" (McCauley 1983: 77). In 1948 Stalin blockaded surface access to West Berlin; the Western Allies kept Berlin provisioned by a massive air-lift. The episode hardened anti-Communist sentiment in West Berlin and proved to West Berliners that their half of the city was viable on its own.

The Wall was constructed in 1961 as a climax of the "Berlin Crisis." Its international dimension started with Khrushchev's 1958 ultimatum to the Western Allies that they abrogate their right of residence under the four-powers status of Berlin (Rühle & Holzweißig 1981: 11), one of the several episodes of Soviet-American brinkmanship that culminated in the Cuba crisis of 1962.

In 1958 refugees told Western security services that the East German Communist Party had been preparing plans since 1951 for "a hermetic and fixed border with West Berlin" (Rühle & Holzweißig 1982: 18).

A combination of economic difficulties in East Germany, the collectivization of agriculture, a hard-line phase of party policy, and Khrushchev's threat to Berlin led to a dramatic increase in the number of emigrants from East Germany, which reached 30,000 a month in July 1961 (Weber 1985: 321). In March 1961 the Warsaw Pact vetoed the plan of the East German leader, Walter Ulbricht, for a barbed-wire fence across the border to stem the flood.

In July U.S. President Kennedy laid down the fundamentals of Western policy on Berlin: the presence of the Western powers, the right of free access to Berlin, and political self-determination for the population of West Berlin (but not East Berlin) (Asmuss 1987: 103).

On 3 August 1961 a desperate East German leadership gave a Warsaw Pact meeting in Moscow three alternatives: closing the air routes to Berlin; building a wall; or shutting the ring around greater Berlin (Weber 1982: 326). Ulbricht favoured the most radical course, "a final blockade of Berlin." As that prescription was too drastic for the Soviets, Ulbricht was authorised only to cut off the traffic between the Eastern and Western sectors of the city (Craig 1982: 52–3). The documents show that it was very much Erich Honecker's Wall. Later to lead the GDR, he was then the secretary of the national defence council and with three others planned the operation in secret. The archives reveal that the Central Committee of the Communist Party was only officially informed two days after the Wall was built (Möbius & Trotnow 1991).

The construction of the Wall allowed Ulbricht to stem the crippling flow of c. 2.7 million people who had left East Germany since 1949 (Weber 1982: 325), and to show the West a strong front, without infringing on Kennedy's fundamentals, which could have triggered a world war. In a message to the West German ambassador in Moscow, Khrushchev said, "I wouldn't want to conceal from you that it was I who in the last instance gave the order for it.

. . . I know that the Wall is an ugly thing. It will also disappear. However only when the reasons for its construction have gone" (in Rühle & Holzweißig 1988: 18–19).

From the beginning the Wall had a second function. Beyond stopping mass emigration, it was given great symbolic significance from both sides. In the propaganda of the German Democratic Republic (GDR), the Wall was a contribution to world peace, "a foundation stone for the success of our policy of relaxation and peaceful co-operation" (Honecker, 1973, quoted in Mehls & Mehls 1979: 43). In Party rhetoric, the Wall was an "anti-fascist protection wall" (Honecker 1980: 205) not to keep Easterners in, but to keep the Western influence out. It was anti-fascist, because Honecker saw West Germany's capitalist economy and the formation of an army within NATO (which included some ex-Wehrmacht military men) as putting the Federal Republic on a par with Nazi Germany. On the first anniversary of its construction, the Party paper said, "Now that a year has passed, we can establish that the protection wall that we built against the aggressors has proved itself to be tenable and has secured the peace" (*Neues Deutschland* 1962, in Rühle & Holzweißig 1988: 156). Just as rhetorically, American President Kennedy said on his famous visit in 1963, "The Wall is the most repulsive and strongest demonstration of the failure of the Communist system" (in Möbius & Trotnow 1990: 14). For West as well as East, the Wall was a useful visual short-hand. It showed each side who they were, by creating a clear enemy, a clear image of what they were not. As Edelmann (1985) has pointed out, for most people politics today is nothing more than a sequence of pictures from the TV, newspapers and magazines; the Wall provided the perfect image to sum up the Cold War world, the picture bite to go with the sound bite. This was the basis of the power of the Wall, and the aura that each fragment carries.

The First Wall, 13 August 1961 to 1964

The construction of the Berlin Wall started at 2:15 A.M. on 13 August 1961, when members of the East German security forces started to break up the pavements at the Friedrich-Ebert Straße with pneumatic drills. At the Potsdamer Platz concrete posts were put up along with rolls of barbed wire. By the afternoon the border was complete, West Berlin was surrounded. Simultaneously, a few hundred kilometres to the west, a double row of barbed wire fences was being put up from the Baltic to Bohemia, along East Germany's border with West Germany (Gerig 1986). Then, "When no effective Western retaliation materialised they replaced the temporary barrier with a cement wall" (Craig 1982: 53). This barrier of earth, breeze blocks, concrete, Spanish riders and barbed wire formed the first phase of the Wall. Round the outskirts of the city, multi-layered barbed wire fences formed the Wall (Hildebrandt 1988a: 9). This "ring around Berlin" consisted of "12 km of wall, 137 km of barbed wire fortifications (made up of 8,000–10,000 km of barbed wire) and 450,000-500,000 square metres of no-man's-land." Before the Wall was built, 10,000 West Berliners had allotments or holiday homes in East Berlin, 53,000 East Berliners had jobs in the West, and 1,100 school-children commuted from the East to the West. The Wall cut across eight overground (S-Bahn) and four underground (U-Bahn) railway lines, and 193 roads. Before, there were 81 crossing points into the Soviet sector; after, there were only 7 (Rühle & Holzweißig 1988: 145–7).

This initial phase saw the forced evacuation of buildings on the border, infamously the moving of almost 2,000 people from their flats on the Bernauer Straße (Möbius & Trotnow 1990). Many people jumped into the Western sector from high windows. Four died (Petschull 1990; Rühle & Holzweißig 1988: 146).

Mander (1962: 10) described this first-generation Wall:

> It does not look very impressive, even in photographs. Close up, it is even
> less so. When I first saw it I was impressed by its flimsiness. It was the sort
> of wall that asked to be pushed over—a tank or a bulldozer could flatten it.

The point was not lost on the Americans who planned to dynamite the Wall on New Year's Eve 1961, a project vetoed by the British. Some Berliners took things into their own hands; in the first two years 23 violent attacks were recorded on the Wall. On 2 December 1962, a big bomb did rip a hole in the Wall, but for the politicians the Wall was already part of the status quo. West Berlin's mayor Willy Brandt criticized the bomb, saying: "Explosives are not just no argument, explosives damage Berlin" [*Berliner Zeitung* 1992a]. From then on, words were the only dynamite to be flung against the Wall. However flimsy, the first Wall did its job for Honecker: the number of emigrants dropped from 14,821 in September to 2,420 in December 1961 (Rühle & Holzweißig 1988: 154).

East Germany then felt secure enough to allow the first contact between East and West Berliners. The first visits by relatives took place between 19 December 1963 and 5 January 1964 (Möbius & Trotnow 1990: 56).

The Second Wall, 1964–1976: "The Modern Border"

Exact phasing of the Wall's construction is difficult, because the Wall was organized in local sections, each with different commanders, terrain and re-sources; detailed investigations reveal local idiosyncrasies in construction, in the timing of changes and the way modernizations were carried out (Trotnow pers. comm.)—the same local differences one can see in other great walls of history. What makes this second Wall stand out is its pre-calculated nature.

Gone were the improvised materials of the first Wall. This second Wall was made of standard, pre-fabricated parts and for the first time had the typical smooth pipe along the top, replacing the barbed wire (Hildebrandt 1988a: 12). Peter Schneider describes it (1983: 52–3):

Cold War Berlin
East and West Sectors

The ring around West Berlin is 102.5 miles long. Of this, 65.8 miles consist of concrete slabs topped with a pipe; another 34 miles is constructed of stamped-metal fencing. 260 watch-towers stand along the border, manned day and night by twice that many border guards. The towers are linked by a tarred military road, which runs along the border strip. To the right and left of the road, a carefully raked stretch of sand conceals trip wires: flares go off if anything touches them. Should this happen, jeeps stand ready for border troops, and dogs are stationed at 267 dog runs along the way. Access to the strip from the east is further prevented by an inner wall at the foot of which are spikes which can literally nail a jumper to the ground, spiking him on 5-inch prongs. Long stretches of the inner wall still consist of the facades of houses situated along the border, but their doors and windows have been bricked up. Underground in the sewers, the border is secured by electrified fences, which grant free passage only to the excretions from both parts of the city.

The Third and Final Wall, 1976 to 9 November 1989

With the boast was that this was "the best security system in the world" (Hildebrandt 1988a: 73), the third Wall was started in 1976, intended as the final version. It was final, not as Honecker had hoped in the sense of permanent, but in the other sense of last. The huge L-profile prefabricated blocks of this third Wall are what we see in all the TV pictures being toppled to the great cheers of the crowd; it is these portions of the last Wall which have gone down in the public imagination as the Berlin Wall.

On 28 October 1969, West German Chancellor Willy Brandt said he was prepared to deal on equal terms with the GDR, in a Germany that was "two states, but . . . one nation" (Diemer 1990: 83). Against the background of Brandt's *Ostpolitik*, a new "Four-powers agreement over Berlin" in 1971 stabilized West Berlin's position and eased the number of visits possible to East Berlin (Diemer 1990: 88). By 1973 the GDR, accepted into UNESCO, had established diplomatic relations with Great Britain and France. It could think of the third-generation Wall as the final Wall, firm in its belief. "The Berlin Wall will also be standing in 50 and also in 100 years. . . . The Wall protects us from robbers," said Erich Honecker in early 1989—just seven months before he and his Wall were destroyed (*Berliner Zeitung*, 20 January 1989).

The Western, outer barrier of this "final" Wall had a height of 3.6 m; it was built of pre-cast slabs set side by side. The sections were of a steel-reinforced concrete of high density (Möbius & Trotnow 1990: figure 71), which included large amounts of asbestos, reaching levels of up to 75% (Malzahn 1989). This form and the smooth flat surface it offered was to have a big impact on the graffiti art of the Wall's Western face. According to Lapp (1987: 139), 111.6 km of the border around Berlin were by then walled; there was 124.9 km of electric fence, a 124-km road along the death strip for patrol cars and bikes, 258 dog runs, 298 watch towers and 52 bunkers. Although it had more wall, the politically more sensitive Berlin border was not the most brutal. In Berlin there were no tripwire-activated gun systems as there were on the inner German border to the west until 1985, when under pressure from the West these were dismantled (Lapp 1987: 140).

This new Wall was more efficient as a barrier. Its visual strength and force bore a symbolism as well—to heighten the crime of fleeing the republic. Samson (1992: 32) says of Offa's Dyke, a frontier defence that was immense in the technology of its own era: "if Offa's Dyke appears to have involved an unnecessary amount of effort in erection, so the 'illegal' crossing of it would have been seen as more serious." The symbolic discouragement should not be exaggerated in comparison with the physical: the order to shoot, in operation on the border since the 1950s, became a part of the official constitution in May 1982. Latest figures put the fatalities since the building of the Wall in Berlin at 122, on the Inner German border 144, and in the Baltic at 81. Twenty-five East German border guards were shot by Western agents, by escapees and by colleagues while attempting to flee (Hildebrandt 1993).

The Fall of the Wall

A factor in creating the limbo after the Wall opened was a Western inertia, the shock from an event which a whole generation had been convinced was impossible. Among the very few to predict the fall of the Wall was novelist Martin Walser (1989: 100), who said on 3 October 1988: "The majority of the opinion makers, left and right, work at making the division rational. . . . One would like to think that . . . the Germans would vote in both their states for a way to unity." In 1989, architects at Darmstadt University analysing Berlin's urban structure concluded that social, cultural and economic barriers in both halves of the city "influence the development of both half cities much more than the Wall" (Drosdeck et al. 1989: 34).

By the late 1980s the standing Wall had already been run through by the new media, which no medieval city wall had to cope with: "The broadcast frequencies reach well over it. Policies of political relaxation have created the possibility to travel across—albeit that these are unequally divided. . . . The Wall is undermined by a natural gas pipeline from the Soviet Union and an optic cable leading to the Federal Republic" (Eckhardt 1987: 39).

The late 1980s were also witness to a bizarre manifestation of a slow thaw in the Cold War. East German border guards helped West Berlin ecological radicals to flee across the Wall when the Western police cleared the Linné triangle (Smith 1991). Once over the Wall, they were given a cup of coffee and taken back to the West when the demo had died down.

The *Zeitgeist* of this suppressed longing to overcome the division is captured brilliantly in Wim Wenders & Peter Handke's (1989) film *Wings of Desire*; its heroes are two angels with wings to fly and invisible to the human eye, who can traverse the Wall at will and even stroll along the death strip. It is an amazing premonition of today when the former no-man's-land is the largest cycle path and promenade in the city.

Power relations in the GDR were crucial, since the control of the Wall became a symbol for a larger debate; as Samson (1992: 32) says, "Without the authority and power to make them function, walls cannot act as barriers, far less as serious fences; they are neutral without the social relations necessary to make them work." He continues (1992: 36): "The symbolic function of town walls is reflected by Gregory of Tours' belief that their collapse was an unmistakable sign that the king would die." As the king of East Berlin's city Wall, Erich Honecker fell; so did his handiwork a few days later. History had now overtaken him; the decade demanded not the hero of the Wall's construction but a "real hero of deconstruction," "a hero of a new kind, representing not victory, conquest and triumph, but renunciation, reduction and dismantling" (Enzenberger 1989: 136). As in the construction of the Wall local factors in East Germany combined with international factors in the Soviet Union. Crucial to the fall of the Wall locally was Honecker's successor Egon Krenz; however the real architect of demolition was Khrushchev's successor in the Kremlin, Mikhail Gorbachev. As early as 1987 Gorbachev recalls feeling "the archaic nature of the 'Iron Curtain'" (1988: 194). When he came to the celebrations of the 40th birthday of East Germany, a few weeks before the Wall fell, Gorbachev made it publicly clear he saw no future for a GDR which did not recognize the changing times. Krenz soon suffered the archetypal fate of the historical demolition man: "in doing his job he ended up undermining his own position. The dynamics he set in motion hurled him aside, and he was buried by his own successes" (Enzenberger 1989: 138).

The Wall started to fall not in Berlin but in Hungary, where on 11 September 1989 the government chose to let 6,500 East German tourists cross the Iron Curtain to Austria (Aanderud & Knopp 1991). The pressure of the New Forum movement and the numbers fleeing via Prague, Warsaw and Budapest built up. On 6 November, Klaus Hartung could already title an editorial commentary "The fall of the Wall" (1989). Three days later, on the evening of 9 November, the East German government spokesman Günter Schabowski announced that citizens of the GDR could "cross the border" (Geisler 1992: 262). With this event the East German revolution had changed gear; the ordered stride of the autumn's demos now became a rush (Warnecken 1992: 21). As word spread, crowds pushing forward to the border crossings were to their astonishment let through to the West.

With hindsight, we see this was the end of the Wall (Darnton 1991: 51):

> On 9 November it still cut the heart of Berlin, a jagged wound in the centre of a great city, the great division of the cold war. But on the 10th it was a dance floor, a picture gallery, a blackboard, a cinema screen, a video cassette, a museum and as the cleaning lady in my office said, "just a pile of stones." Like the storming of the Bastille the breaching of the Wall changed the world.

One must remember that the Wall only *opened* on 9 November. No one knew whether it would close again or whether it would crumble, as it did not just at the Potsdamer Platz, but also along its whole length. The whole city was in a state of limbo. All East German institutions, the border forces included, were paralysed by a crisis of authority. A state of anarchy activated and empowered individuals to take the political and physical future of the Wall upon themselves, a champagne bottle in one hand, a chisel in the other. The next day, 10 November, the West Berlin paper *Volksblatt* carried two headlines next to each other: "The Wall has fallen," and "Bonn calls for the demolition of the Wall." Darnton (1991: 51) comments: "Both were correct. The Wall was there and no longer existed."

According to Gottfried Korff (1990: 156), "it was a situation in which the past was negated, erased, cast aside, but the future hadn't begun yet." It is in light of this tension that the attempts at preserving, as well as consuming, the Berlin Wall must be understood.

Consuming the Wall

The fall of the Wall gripped the world (Smith 1990: 75–6):

> As the news from Berlin rippled outward, dousing everyone in instant history, tourists began pouring in, from the rest of Germany, and from Europe and America and Japan, just to see, pick up a souvenir, take pictures, live briefly in a moment of significance. 1989 was a boom year for Berlin tourism, and in the first week after the opening, British Airways carried 30% more passengers to Berlin than at the same time a year before. By the Wall there was a good deal of strutting by those who felt their system vindicated.

For the tourist industry the Wall was the defining feature of Berlin. The Wall had become the eighth wonder of the world in the West. TV showed the world within seconds the Berliners' instant reaction—to take physical possession of it, first climbing on it, and then hacking at it. Characteristic of 1980s tourism is the consumption of goods, a means to prove attendance at the history that one is consuming: "One day, maybe, stores and museums will become the same . . . with everything for display, inspection and sale" (Bayley 1989: 7). That day came with 9 November 1989. Within hours, pieces of the Wall were on sale in West Berlin's premier shopping street.

Why did people buy a bit of the Wall? The skillful marketing of the heritage industry cannot be responsible, since this souvenir trade was not directed by professional merchandising. In a world where history is kept in the hands of professionals and its physical artifacts are locked away in museums, the collapse of political authority over the Wall left a vacuum which allowed everyone access to fragments of a historical object imbued with historical significance. The Wall belonged to anyone with time on their hands.

At the Wall, more was at work. Television played a crucial role in the events of autumn 1989 (Garton Ash 1990: 23), its clearest images the joy and the destruction of the physical substance of the Wall with pick-axes or crowbars. The personal pleasure of meeting was mixed with the *Schadenfreude* of climbing onto the forbidden Wall and smashing it. These images went into the homes of the world. When tourists later made it to Berlin, the joy had gone, but the *Schadenfreude*, the central passion of our reaction, remained;

you could yourself attack the Wall or just take a piece of it. You could buy a piece, or pay 5 DM [deutsche marks] to hire a hammer and chisel for 20 minutes and get your own pieces. If as Michel Butor said (in Hildebrandt 1988a: 64), "you have to touch the Wall to believe it is reality," then you have to strike the Wall to believe its destruction. Even Ronald Reagan had a go at Wall-pecking when he visited Berlin on 12 September 1990 (Aanderud & Knopp 1991: 24). A crowd of "Wall-peckers" made a profession of chipping pieces off the Berlin Wall and selling them to tourists (Baker 1992a). It was the marginals of German society (students, pensioners, and Polish, Italian or Turkish *Gastarbeiter*) who most frequently tried to make some quick money from this symbol of German history.

Mass consumption demands mass production. When the supply of Wall fragments carrying genuine graffiti stopped, the demand did not. One evening in February 1990 I met a man in no-man's-land. He was smashing pieces out of the east side of the Wall, carefully following the line of a chaotic band of colour he had sprayed on to the grey surface. At his feet lay a bag full of spray paint cans of every colour. I asked him what he was doing. He answered: "I'm producing Wall fragments for my stall by the Reichstag. I'm getting a pneumatic drill next week. That will give me a year's supply." But why did he have to spray the grey east face of the Wall first? "Because fragments with graffiti sell better, and otherwise people wouldn't believe that the fragments were real. Anyway the Wall-peckers have chiselled off all the graffiti on the West side." Mr. De Carolis, an Italian labourer in Berlin for 15 years, was forging history, with genuine materials. The small flakes of Wall that the tourists bought at his stall by the Reichstag were genuine pieces of Berlin Wall, but these originally grey pieces of a *Mauer* which 189 people died trying to cross, had been converted into the harmless *Wand*, West Berlin's colourful scribble-pad and wonder of the post-modern world. The impact of tourism was again to distort: "The local and 'exotic' are torn out of place and time to be repackaged for the world bazaar" (Robins 1991: 31). The Berlin Wall was consumed by our little purchases at the souvenir stalls in a post-modern era when we are "condemned to seek history by way of our own pop images and *simulacra* of that history, which itself remains forever out of reach" (Jameson 1984: 71), and seems best explained by Daniel Miller (1987), who has described how the desire to personalize, to appropriate and finally to re-contextualize objects is a prime motivation for consuming them.

Graffiti Art: Just One of the Wall's Four Faces

At the heart of this paradox is the opposition that Walser summarized between *Wand* and *Mauer*. And the story shows that the florescence against the absence of graffiti is the direct visual corollary.

The image the final Wall presented to the East was of an absolute, insurmountable barrier, painted with military order in pale grey-green-coloured panels. The image to the West that is remembered of the same physical barrier is a surface wildly coloured with graffiti. The graffiti became a crucial hallmark of the Wall in the popular imagination, and now provides the dominant European memory of what the Wall was like.

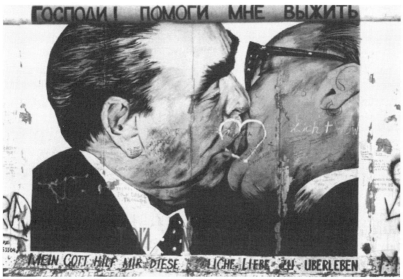

Graffiti on the Berlin Wall shows Soviet leader Leonid Brezhnev kissing East German leader Erich Honecker, 1995. *Photograph by Paul Ganster*

The graffiti of the Wall have their own structure and their own history. Most of the graffiti starts with the second of the Wall's three generations when "at the end of the 60s the students' movement discovered the Wall as the perfect medium for visual protest" (Kuzdas 1990: 10). "In the early years this was paintbrush work, often done at night. There were some arrests by the East German border guards for defacing People's property" (Smith 1990: 20–1). The rough slatted surface of the early Wall was not conducive to proper painting; when Frank Liefeoghe wanted to paint the Wall on the Wilhelm Straße he had to attach plywood boards to make the Wall a usable surface (Hildebrandt 1988a: 22).

As the GDR tried finally to turn its back on the West, it created the final form of the Wall with a beautifully polished, pristine surface that just begged to be defiled. The panel of the final Wall provided such perfect frames that "each single panel of the Wall ironically obeys the law of the classical column, with a 'base,' 'pillar' and 'capital' " (Kuzdas 1990: 10). The Wall provided a frame as well as a surface. Artists even used to sign their works on the round concrete tube that ran along the top and made an upper "frame" for the picture.

According to Hildebrandt (1988a: 48), Lew Nussberg of the 1962 Moscow non-conformist "Movement Group" who emigrated with his followers in 1976 was the first internationally known artist to express a wish to paint on the Berlin Wall. There followed Boucher & Noir's "Statues of Liberty" and Keith Haring's 100 m-long chain of human figures (Kuzdas 1990: 12); Haring, it will be remembered, was a New York graffiti artist whose street style became fashionable fine art.

"Overcoming the Wall by painting the Wall" was the crucial ambition of much of the art on the Wall, summarized in the title of an exhibition organized by Dr. Rainer Hildebrandt's (1988a) private Checkpoint Charlie Museum in 1984. The 3,000-mark prize went to East German dissident Mattias Hohl-Stein.

By the mid-1980s, with the arrival of the spray can, the Wall's paintwork had become a permanently changing exhibition proclaiming the slogans of every struggle in Europe. Some of its graffiti was passionate and witty. The bulk wasn't. Much was in English, the work of non-Berliners.

In late 1986 a group of expelled East German dissidents from Weimar painted a broad white line at eye level along the whole length of the by-then colourful Wall between Mariannen Platz and the Potsdamer Platz: "The Wall must be seen again for what it is. It is not a tourist attraction." Their white line symbolically wiped out Wall art. They opposed the Wall being considered the "eighth wonder of the world" (Kuzdas 1990: 55). Their act shows how, even before the Wall fell, there was a struggle and a difference in the perception of the Wall and its graffiti between Easterners for whom it was a wall, a barrier and the Westerners for whom it was a canvas, a wonder of the world.

The word *graffiti* was first used by classical archaeologists to distinguish between officially sanctioned inscriptions and unofficial texts (Stahl 1989: 12). Even after the fall of the Wall this official/unofficial [distinction] defined the graffiti. Lieutenant Colonel Karsch, who served with the border regiment for 25 years from the age of 18 recalls (Fischer & Von der Schulenburg 1990: 27):

> Well, all of a sudden our artists from East Berlin began to paint the Wall at this point, without asking the border guards for permission. So we had to give the guards a pot of paint and a brush and order them to paint over it. If they had asked for permission, then they would have got it, straight away, no problem. But as it was we had no choice but to order the guards to paint over it. I'm sure you understand.

The reaction is understandable. It was soldiers who built, manned, maintained and therefore *defined* the Wall. Till now they had been the sole Eastern Wall artists, the only ones able to paint it. Even when it was breached, they tried to control who could paint on it and what they painted. It was a military structure, the product of the orderly military mind.

Censorship had not been confined to the East. The Wall was built a metre or two to the east of the exact frontier line, so even its Western, painted face was on the territory of East Berlin. Smith (1990: 108) notes:

> For years and years they fought against graffiti; the Western police discouraged it, there was so much uncertainty what the other side might do, could do. In some points such as the Potsdamer Platz, which were very sensitive points, they tried to keep it white, continually whitewashing. When Jimmy Carter came to West Berlin the West whited out anti-American slogans there. But eventually they gave up in the mid eighties.

In early 1990 a long section of Eastern Wall near the Oberbaumbrücke was given over panel by panel to an international collection of artists. Dubbed the "East Side Gallery," the signed and copyrighted panels were to be removed and sent round the world as a travelling exhibition to art museums, transferring the Western tradition of high art on the Wall to the East. The East Side Gallery remains in place along the Mühlen Straße, saved from removal by its local popularity.

The last chapter in the artistic history of the Wall was reached by the sale of complete concrete segments with fine pieces of Western Wall art. In January 1990 the East German government, estimating the value of the total Wall at DM800,000,000 (about £3.7 million), set to marketing segments to museums, companies and rich individuals (Grant 1992: 150). Some of the best pieces went to art galleries like the Museum of Modern Art in New York (Aanderud & Knopp 1992: 124). Others of what was now a sculpture were sold at auction in Monte Carlo to the Vatican (Escaut-Marquet 1990), and to the Expo in Seville (*Berliner Zeitung* 1992b; Grant 1992; Gow 1991). After German reunification on 3 October 1990, the Defence Ministry in Bonn, as the Wall's new owner, staked its claim on the money raised from the art sales to help pay for the Wall's removal. "Artistic" sections of the Wall are now spread between 18 countries, from Fatima to Japan (Koch in Hildebrandt 1993: 47). The other parts are in "graveyards" awaiting recycling into 0.54 mm granules for road-building at DM23 (£9.20) per ton. Metal fence posts go to gardeners, farmers and steelworks (Wedow 1992).

The dialectical nature of art's relationship with the military structure which was the Berlin Wall had reached its conclusion; the art had the effect on the Wall of *Aufheben* in the Hegelian sense of the word. *Aufheben* has two meanings: raising or lifting as well as preserving or keeping (Gonzsalez-Marcen & Risch 1990: 102). Art had been a symptom of relaxing East-West tensions. It so captured the public and political imagination as a metaphor for a pluralistic open democratic society, that it became a force in finally lifting and removing the Wall. But art had also the power to preserve the Wall; the art painted on the west face of the Wall as an attempt to overcome the Wall came to save some pieces from destruction.

The Berlin Wall and the Bastille

So while everyone from labourers to the Defence Minister are busy consuming the Wall, a comparison with the treatment of the Bastille after its revolutionary fall in 1789 reminds us of the Wall's symbolic function; which gives fragments a special national aura, and affects both their consumption and preservation.

Commentators have reached back to the French Revolution of 1789 as an analogy for the events of 1989 (Biermann 1991: 9; Darnton 1991: 51). Chippindale (1990a) noted a specific analogy. The collapse of the Berlin Wall was the great symbolic event in the revolutions of the late 1980s in Eastern Bloc Europe, just as the storming of the Bastille was the great symbolic event in the French revolution of 1789. There are telling similarities in what happened to each: the rage of the people that was let loose on the monument, its rapid demolition and the turning of fragments into souvenirs, touchstones of the revolution's reality and meaning.

On the evening of 14 July 1789 Pierre-François Palloy started the job of demolishing the Bastille. He had helped storm the old fortress earlier that day. Within a year only foundations and a pile of rubble remained. Palloy, more than a demolition contractor, was a self-professed "Apostle of liberty" (Lüsebrink & Reichardt 1990: 136). Presenting a piece of the Bastille to the *département* of Calvados, he wrote: "It was not enough for me to have been there and contributing to the destruction of the walls of this; I also have the urge to immortalize the memory of its horror" (Lüsebrink & Reichardt 1990: 137).

In October and November 1790 Palloy sent miniatures of the Bastille, carved from the dismantled blocks of that "Temple of Despair" to each of the 83 French *départements* at his own cost, accompanied by "Apostles of freedom" to give public readings of Palloy's tracts. The new *départements* were new land divisions sweeping away the old "intendencies," each new entity launched with a physical part of the Revolution.

Palloy did not see the Bastille stones purely as "reliquaries" of a new patriotic cult, but also as "emblems" or a "dead pledge of Liberty," which irreparably unite the regenerated body of the nation and give it new energy (Lüsebrink & Reichardt 1990: 139–40). Dubbed "destroyer of the Bastille" by the press in March 1792, Palloy produced medals for the 900 members of the French parliament, made from the iron bars and chains of the Bastille (1990: 141). Bastille stones were even used as settings in patriotic jewellery of liberty.

Ken Smith (1990: 189) reports of Wall fragments: "Some mount their chips as badges, brooches, earrings, sculpture, assemblages of wire and glazed surfaces. Others are set in PVC resin. Others are authenticated by various sorts of certificates." Stall-holders equip themselves with rubber stamps, which they print on fragments as "proof" of authenticity. Again the paint is important as a talisman; at the stalls round the Reichstag in 1990, every one of the many hundred fragments of Wall on sale was painted; the pattern of paint on a big, expensive chunk showed it had been painted *after* it had been broken off.

On the first anniversary of the storming, Palloy threw a "revolutionary party. Here there will be dancing, there will always be dancing." The dance-floor was erected on stones from the Bastille. Palloy's workers gave tours of the Bastille cellars, which they had rebuilt and fitted out as a horror and torture chamber. At Palloy's house a *papier-maché* copy of the Bastille was stormed to the cheers of the crowd, who freed a heavily chained white-haired "prisoner," and then all processed in triumph through the streets (Lüsebrink & Reichardt 1990: 143).

Berlin's equivalent to Palloy may be Hagen Koch, the Stasi officer who left his commission in 1985 and who collects representative elements of the Wall for the Checkpoint Charlie Museum (Dobberke 1993). But typically his case is more complex; it was he who drew the line across the road at Checkpoint Charlie where the Wall-builders had started on the night of 13 August 1961. The destroyer-cum-recorder-cum-preserver had himself been the builder. Interviewed in 1990, he made clear the political purpose behind his collection of Wall sections for the museum (Thames 1990) was ". . . to confront people walking past with the former defence systems of the border, and to remind the people of this topic because it cannot be that many countries will receive parts of the wall via me . . . and in Berlin there is nothing left for future generations."

Palloy understood the need to make abstract ideas—tyranny, freedom, liberty—physically tangible and accessible for the general public; like the Bastille, the Berlin Wall is a "'collective symbol" (Drews et al. 1985), an easily identifiable, emotionally charged, physical embodiment of the political system which made it—both symbol of tyranny and symbol of liberation from tyranny.

In Catholic France in 1789, the politics followed religious metaphors. A tract of 1792 declares (Lüsebrink & Reichardt 1990: 138–9): "France is a new world, and in order to maintain this achievement, it is necessary to sow out the fragments of our old enslavement, just as when Leviticus in the Book of Moses distributed the limbs of his wife in all directions of the wind, to wreak revenge." In secular Berlin in 1989, metaphors were mixed; the Wall fragments went with travel souvenirs, rock concerts, art or "history."

In Berlin the rock concert became one of the experiences through which people collectively expressed themselves in those first heady weeks, in which there were more Berliners than tourists. They danced three times on the Wall: at the opening of the Wall on 9 November, at the opening of the Brandenburg Gate on 21 December, and at New Year on 31 December 1989. In the Berlin "Wall dance," there was neither music nor dance steps, people shouted and gesticulated like they do at rock concerts (Darnton 1990: 79). But there was also carnival, fireworks, bottles opened. "The dancers wore jeans and anoraks. Many of them were young, almost all of them under 30 . . . most of them born after 1961, the year of the Wall's construction" (Darnton 1991: 82). At these rock concerts, the folk dances of our age, the merchandising led on the commodification of Wall memorabilia, particularly T-shirts; one said thank you to Gorbachev as "GORBATchev Man" smashing through the Wall in the figure of Batman.

Large concerts were staged on the West side of the Wall near the Reichstag. One can be seen (Darnton 1991: 83) as

> the key event, which gave the East Berlin demonstrations lots of impulses. It took place on 19 June at a Michael Jackson concert. While Jackson filled the air with sound near the Reichstag on the Western side of the Wall, a group of young people gathered on the Eastern side to listen. The police tried to drive them away, but the crowd defended itself . . . Rock on one side of the Wall, riots on the other. At the big Wall dance at New Year 1990 they came together.

Rock came back the following summer, 1990, as a medium for consuming the Wall and echoing Palloy's re-enactment of the storming of the Bastille. A huge wall of polystyrene blocks was smashed down as the climax to Pink Floyd's performance of their concept album and film *The Wall* (*Spiegel* 1990).

A final collective medium for the appreciation of the Wall was the modern chronological concept of history. As Hermann Bausinger has noted, the collective concept of history in the 18th century had a very close horizon of two to three generations; the days when Grand-Dad was a child were as distant as the Romans. In 1989, "However imprecise the historical comprehension of the people, consciousness of history and the historical is no longer foreign for them, and the 'limited horizon' . . . has finally fallen for ordinary people" (Bausinger 1986: 134). Souvenirs quickly appeared in which fragments of graffiti-ed Wall were mounted in a case of clear plastic, along with the Wall's chronology 1961–89: instant scientifically fixed and chronologically fixed history ready for the museum. And the idea of a historical record, remains for which one was responsible to future generations, led to attempts to preserve Wall sections in situ in a pristine condition.

Some graffiti pleaded, "Don't disturb History." "*Prière de ne pas toucher au mur pour ne pas toucher à histoire*, MERCI." "This part—only this part(!!) is for you! but please take care for the other pieces of these" (Kegel pers. comm.—original emphasis). That these messages at the Potsdamer Platz should be in English and French as well as German, shows the Wall as a world monument, not just a Berliner's or even a German's concern. The considerable tension between local and international perceptions of the Wall has many manifestations.

Preserving the Wall

Wall nostalgia combined with 1980s heritage awareness of conservation (Assion 1986: 353; Lübbe 1990: 41; Bausinger 1986: 98) in a complex conservation debate, which ran both in parallel with and in reaction to the consumption of the Wall.

"It is typical for us Germans that at the end of an historical era we want to rip everything down and forget it ever happened. It occurred with the Nazi sites, now it's happening with the Berlin Wall," said Dr. Alfred Kernd'l, Berlin's chief archaeologist (pers. comm.). He continued, "It is indicative that I as an archaeologist have responsibility for 20th-century sites, which were first demolished and then had to be re-excavated, like the former Gestapo-SS HQ on the Niederkirchner Straße" (pers. comm.). The Active Museum of Berlin, who initiated that excavation (Baker 1988a; 1990a; 1990b) warned, "The destruction of the Berlin Wall is taking place with unparalleled ferocity. There is a danger that no section of the Wall is going to be preserved as an historical document." "Save the Wall!" said Sabine Weissler, cultural spokesperson of Berlin's Green Party. "The Wall did not just divide Berlin, it also made it an island. The Wall is the key to understanding the past 30 years of the city. Where parts of the Wall remain they should be kept" (Weissler 1990).

In 1990 Chippindale (Thames 1990b) warned, "The Berlin Wall is the central symbol of the Cold War. It is the most significant monument of the 20th century, and there is a danger that like the Bastille which is the central monument of the 18th century, the Wall will all be sold off to tourists, leaving nothing for future generations."

According to Sabine Weissler, "The Wall must remain where it is part of the historic context" (pers. comm.). Her colleague Eberhard Elfert has proposed a history trail, like the "freedom trails" in Boston (Massachusetts), along the strip of no-man's-land from the Oberbaumbrücke in Kreuzberg to the Bernauer Straße so as "to show the layeredness of history" (in Scheub 1992). But which bit of history, relevant to whom? Three major sections remain standing under conservation orders: at the Niederkirchner Straße, Bernauer Straße and the Invaliden Friedhof. Controversy centres on the first two locations.

Niederkirchner Straße

Halfway between Checkpoint Charlie and the Potsdamer Platz, the Wall runs for 200 m alongside what was in its time the most feared address in Berlin, the former Gestapo and SS HQ of Himmler and Heydrich. On the other side of the road, in former East Berlin, is the Luftwaffe ministry (1938), from where Goering planned the Blitz. Completing the historical landscape is the Kaiser's 19th-century Prussian Parliament building.

"We have to keep the Wall here, because the Wall is a result of Hitler's War and the Nazi terror which was planned and administered from this site," argues Silvia Lange of the Active Museum (pers. comm.). "It is crucial to preserve this physical relationship, so as to confront visitors with the interrelationships of German History."

Dr. Kernd'l (pers. comm.) disagrees: "If you leave the Wall standing here, then everyone will come and say: 'Oh, look, there is the Wall next to the Gestapo headquarters, they were just as bad as each other, the Gestapo and the Stasi were just the same," and they were not. The danger is that leaving the Wall standing here will relativize and therefore dilute the crimes of the Nazis.

"People already compare the Nazis and the Stasi," counters Silvia Lange, "and keeping the Wall here will provoke debate. It all depends on how the site is presented."

Kernd'l replies (Thames 1990), "With the Wall there you can't understand the Gestapo-SS site. We've still got remains of the old pavement there, and we ought to concentrate on presenting the Nazi period here properly and deal with the Wall properly elsewhere, the Bernauer Straße for instance."

In the latest architectural competition for presenting the site (1993), the winning design has left the Wall exactly where it is. Dr. Kernd'l seems to have lost.

Bernauer Straße

The Bernauer Straße is the other centre of present controversy. For Berliners this is the most notorious and tragic part of the Wall (Hildebrandt 1988b). In August 1990 a sign appeared on the Wall at the Bernauer Straße addressed to the "Wall-peckers":

> Dear Wall-peckers, please don't peck at this part of the Wall. The area of border between the Acker and Garten Straße is, with the support of the East and West German governments, to become a memorial to the Berlin Wall. Join in conserving an authentic and worthy memorial to the victims of the Wall.

The notice was signed by Pastor Manfred Fischer, a young Protestant minister, whose old church—isolated in no-man's-land by the Bernauer Straße—had been dynamited by East German border troops five years before.

Pastor Fischer's neighbours are 200 old people in the Lazarus Nursing Home (Möbius & Trotnow 1990: 31). Interviewed in 1990 (Thames 1990), its matron Sister Christa Heckel took a different view:

> The Wall on the Bernauer Straße has to go as fast and as completely as possible. I speak not only for myself, but for 200 old people, who live in the nursing home overlooking the proposed museum. They experienced the terror of this Wall being built, had to live with it for 29 years and are now suffering psychologically from still seeing it outside their window long after the border has opened. When this place was a hospital, this was where they brought all the injured escapees. Part of the Wall should be kept, but not opposite 200 old people. Tourists can go, these old people can't. The Wall should also go, so we can have direct access to the graves of our Diakonissen order, which we were previously unable to visit, because they were in no-man's-land.

Among Pastor Fischer's powerful allies are Hagen Koch and the German Chancellor Helmut Kohl's new Museum for German History (Baker & Korff 1992a; 1992b). Koch remembers the fall as a dream from which he was afraid to wake up from and find out it wasn't true. The Berlin Wall was not just a wall, but a whole military system with an interior wall, watch towers, water patrols and minefields. In order to show this, he thinks (pers. comm.), we need an authentic Wall Museum.

"What they want is a chamber of horrors. You can't get authenticity. The Wall is an ambiguous object and it would be more appropriate to get artists to interpret it," says Sabine Weissler (pers. comm. 1990).

For Dieter Havichek, the local Mayor, the plans for the museum on the Bernauer Straße run counter to the stated popular sentiment in the boroughs of Mitte and Wedding:

> There is no space for Walls in Berlin any more. The legacy of the Wall's victims demands that divisions be irrevocably removed. The Bernauer Straße must become a normal street where people live and go shopping again. The division must be overcome. Moreover, the Wall is causing the old people in the Lazarus Nursing Home psychological stress; that too, has got to be understood.

Pastor Fischer believes Havichek has less altruistic reasons for opposing the Wall museum. "It is all part of the preparations for an Olympic bid. The two stadia would be near here and they want to build a ring road and link the two. The Bernauer Straße is a key link in such a plan" (pers. comm. 1990).

Challenged, Havichek defends himself. "It would be perverse if a Wall museum held up plans for a new ring road. I am not against a Wall memorial, but not here. There should be one central memorial perhaps on the Niederkirchner Straße" (pers. comm. 1992).

In the end the view of the Deutsches Historisches Museum has been followed; in 1992 it launched an architectural competition to design a memorial and museum to go with the section of Wall (Trotnow pers. comm.).

Although the preservers moved to save the Wall here, and it was fenced off, they were already too late. The watch tower had been cut down, the concrete segments of the outer Wall had been hammered through to the reinforcing bars, and much of the inner Wall had been torn down. "Preserving" the Wall at the Bernauer Straße will be more a work of reconstruction than of preserving what is presently there. Now the discovery of World War II graves under the site is delaying these plans.

Invaliden Friedhof

North of the former crossing-point Invaliden Straße, a stretch of the Wall still runs between the Berlin-Spandauer-Schiffahrtskanal and the Invaliden cemetery, where many of the former Prussian military leadership are buried; the most famous is Scharnhorst, who is buried under an imposing monumental grave [sic] designed by the famous Berlin architect Karl-Friedrich Schinkel. In contrast, Gestapo boss Reinhard Heydrich's grave is today unmarked. The Nazis buried him there after his Prague 1942 assassination, aware of its links with Prussia's military tradition: the same links which prompted conservationists to argue that the Wall should be left here, precisely because the graveyard so visibly showed the Wall's historical roots in German militarism. Apart from murmurs that Heydrich's grave should be marked, this site has been uncontroversial.

Checkpoint Charlie

At the private Checkpoint Charlie Museum the collection, "Topography of the German-German border," consists of individual segments of Wall and representative examples of bunkers and border-posts, mixed in with sculptures inspired by the Cold War. Each artifact is displayed like a work of art with a blue-and-white plaque of the Haag [Hague] Convention for the protection of world cultural heritage, prominently displayed to replace the artist's signature as a guarantee of authenticity. The problem with Koch's collection is that his exhibits are not warnings, but just larger versions of the rubber-stamped Wall fragments sold to the tourists on the street outside. By reducing the Wall to the museum equivalent of the sound bite it may be more easily consumable for passers-by, but it is also more forgettable. A lapse of memory definitely seems to have occurred with the developers of the planned American Business Centre at Checkpoint Charlie. Their plans threaten to destroy the very 24 m of Wall at which U.S. Sergeant Pool threw a line to an escapee and dragged him to the West (Kugler 1991).

Kapelle Ufer

The stump of a watch tower stands next to five relocated segments of Wall with the word "ART" painted on them. Highly visible from the train, this has been the site of frequent freelance artworks such as the recycling artist's "Mutoid Waste" arch made from three abandoned armoured personnel carriers (APCs).

Oberer Freiarchenbrücke

A command tower has been saved from demolition at the former crossing point Puschkin Allee next to the lock where the Landwehr canal enters the river Spree. Ironically, amongst the group who saved it are young East Germans who themselves fled across another part of the Iron Curtain in Hungary in the spring of 1989. Now called Museum der Verbotenen Kunst (Museum of Forbidden Art), it has a very libertarian anti-censorship agenda. It has exhibited censored Stasi files and the border guards' own Wall photos (Nürnberger 1992).

Schiffbauerdamm

The stretch of the inner Wall . . . is still extant. Today it has a double function. The eastern face encloses the car park of a Toyota repair workshop. The western face is now a "Memorial for the Victims of Violence and War." Clearly visible from the crosses of the Wall dead next to the Reichstag on the other river bank, a stark black-and-white mural chronicles the Wall's victims. Starting at 1961, each of the Wall's 29 years gets one segment with that year's death toll painted on it (Cleven 1993). The death strip has been planted with a so-called "Parliament of trees" and three relocated Wall segments form a sign for a "Europe memorial," which consists of earth banks arranged to form the words "EUROPA ERDE WIEDER" (Europe Earth Again), so that they are clearly visible to passengers in the passing trains.

Pankow

A very long stretch of western outside Wall has been preserved as a factory wall parallel to the railway line between Wilhelmsruh and the Nordgraben.

Potsdamer Platz

A guard tower along with some little graffitied segments of back Wall are still standing between the Leipziger and Stresemann Straße in the coalyard next to the offices of the archaeological section of the former East Berlin Academy of Sciences.

Nostalgia for the Wall?

Tourists, fed on the TV images of November 1989. could scarcely imagine an opinion poll amongst Berliners asking "Do you want the Wall back?" in which 1 in 4 West Berliners, and 1 in 5 East Berliners said they were nostalgic about the Wall. But that is exactly what the Gewis poll (1990: 26) found in May 1990. One in four said they had thought back to the period before the fall of the Wall with nostalgia. Westerners were more nostalgic for the time of the Wall than Easterners (27% to 17%). When they put the same question in October 1990, the number of nostalgic West Berliners had grown to one in three. Particularly prone were West Berliners under 30 years old, 39% of whom "had shed a tear for the passing of the Wall" (Gewis 1990: 26).

In 1961 the Wall was experienced as a noose around the Western part of the city, which threatened to kill it, but in 1989 one saw the Wall in West Berlin as a source of support. The Bonn government made billions of marks available to the city thanks to this monument.

The special status of Berlin also freed men from having to do military service. For those who lived opposite the Wall, it provided silence and seclusion (Smith 1990), a seclusion much missed once the Wall opened. The Wall, protecting the East from crime, AIDS, pornography, drugs, etc., also protected West Berliners from military service and recession. Western subventions to this "front-line" city protected culture and the arts from the cold winds of recession when they blew throughout Europe. This may be a reason why the degree of Wall nostalgia is particularly strong amongst young West Berliners (Gewis 1990); it is an argument for preserving the large and *in situ* section of the Wall which will be needed to explain to future generations how East and West Germans are, paradoxically, "two totally different generations of the same age" (Kutter in Pokatsky 1990).

Conclusion

In the end the archaeologist stands before the question, What is the Berlin Wall?

As is true of the Roman walls, the Berlin Wall which is now available for preservation is the last phase and is ruined, atypical of the monument's original purpose and life-span. For example: the Berlin Wall has the image of the Iron Curtain, but no!—the Iron Curtain ran mostly through countryside, as a fence not a wall, and far to the west of Berlin. The Wall was typical of Berlin, but no!—much of the city border was fenced instead and ran through fields. The Wall was massive and flat surfaced, but no!—only in its last phase. The Wall was unprecedented, but no!—a wall had existed on the very same border 100 years before. The Wall was the biggest graffiti art gallery in the world, but no!—the graffiti only really came with the last phase of the Wall and only on one of the Wall's four faces. The Wall was an impenetrable barrier, but no!—it wasn't impenetrable to Westerners.

Security system. Sculpture. Art canvas. Historical monument. The Berlin Wall, in its construction, consumption and preservation, has been all of these things. For the Cold War warriors and the TV audience, it stood for the binary world of opposing systems; a Wall flake or one Wall segment is enough to be "The Wall" as long as it has only two sides. For the relatives of Easterners who died crossing the Wall the military aspect is important; [for] the Museum on the Bernauer Straße the security system is the Wall. The Wall had effect and visual force from its going on for ever. Preserving a section of Wall even 50 or 100 metres long misses the point if you can see it ending; it ought to look endless. Fragments as large as a single cast segment or as small as a painted crumb give a visitor a fundamentally different experience and interpretation of what the Wall was (Chippindale 1990a).

The role of art and graffiti shows the paradoxical, mutually dependent relationship between the consuming and the preserving of monuments. The Wall was painted in order to overcome it. It is those painted sections which are preserved. At the East Side Gallery a grey Eastern *Mauer* has been turned into a coloured Western *Wand*. The key question is: If a public which sees politics as a succession of images is shown the Eastern *Mauer* visually transformed (reduced) into the Western *Wand*, then what becomes of the memory of those who died at the Wall and of the perspective of Easterners who were locked behind the Wall?

If the Wall shows that monuments are diverse in their forms and meanings, then the only way to do justice to their preservation is to demand and to tolerate an equally diverse spectrum of preservation.

Since the first piece of Wall was hacked out under the fire of water cannon on 9 November 1989, the historical memory of the Berlin Wall has been atomized into a million fragments. The relationship between consumption and preservation is more a dialectical than a simple opposition. The Wallpeckers destroy segments of the Wall but also preserve the Wall as a folk memory in the atomized global "museums without walls" of individual mantelpieces, curiosity cabinets, and shoe-boxes. Fragments of the Wall will be heirlooms passed down through family genealogies, an unofficial personal alternative to public museums. Very few monuments are as physically large as the Berlin Wall, so few allow such a pluralism of preservation and interpretations; it is atypical. It is exactly this exceptional magnitude which allows such insight into the complexity of people's interaction with and use of the material culture they perceive to be part of the past: a complexity not exclusive to the Wall.

References

Aanderud, K.-A. & G. Knopp. 1991. *Die Eingemauerte Stadt: die Gescbichte der Berliner Mauer*. Recklinghausen: Georg Bitter.

Asmuss, B. 1987. *Berlin, Berlin: Materialien zur Geschichte der Stadt*. Berlin (West): Berliner Festspiele.

Assion, P. 1986. Historismus, Traditionalismus, Folklorismus: zur musealisiereden Tendenz der Gegenwartskultur, in Utz Jeggle et al. (ed.), *Volkskultur in der Moderne*: 351–62. Reinbek bei Hamburg: Rowohit Taschenbuch.

Baker, F. 1988a. History that hurts: excavating 1933–45, *Archaeological Review from Cambridge* 7: 93–109.

1988b. Museums without walls. Unpublished M.Phil. dissertation. Department of Archaeology, University of Cambridge.

1990a. Archaeology, Habermas and the pathologies of modernity, in Baker & Thomas 1990: 54–62.

1990b. The problems of conservation in a unifying Berlin, *Archaeological Review from Cambridge* 9: 167–9.

1992a. Mauerspechte, in *Wörter, Sachen, Sinne, eine kleine volkskundliche Enzyklopädie Studien und Materialien* 9: 113-15. Tübingen: Tübinger Vereinigung für Volkskunde.

Baker, F. & G. Korff. 1992a. National, Heimat and Active museums: an outline of the development of the German museums into the 1990s, in *New Research in Museum Studies* 3: *Museums in Europe*. London: Athlone Press.

1992b. Nacionaini, domozanski in aktivni muzeji: oris razvoja nemskih muzejev na poti v devetdeseta leta, *Ethnolog, Glasnik Slovenskega Ethnografskega Muzeja* 2(2).53. Ljubljana.

Baker, F. & J. Thomas (ed.). 1990. *Writing the past in the present*. Lampeter: St. David's University College.

Balfour, A. 1990. *Berlin, the politics of order*. New York (NY): Rizzoli.

Bausinger, H. 1986. *Volkskultur in der technischen Welt*. Frankfurt am Main: Campus Verlag. (First edition 1961.)

Bayley, S. 1989. *Commerce and culture: from Pre-industrial art to Post-industrial value*. London: Design Museum.

Berliner Zeitung. 1989. Erich Honecker, *Berliner Zeitung* (20 January).

1992a. Geheimplan: Berliner Mauer sollte schon 1961 wieder gesprengt werden, *Berliner Zeitung* (2 January).

1992b. Mauer-Rest als Expo-Stück, *Berliner Zeitung* (22 April).

Biermann, W. 1991. *Über das Geld und andere Herzensdinge: Prosaische Versuche über Deutschland*. Köln: Kiepenheuer & Witsch.

Bohn, R., K. Hickethier & E. Müller (ed.). 1992. *Mauer-Show: Das Ende der DDR, die deutsche Einheit und die Medien*. Berlin: Sigma Medienwissenschaft Rainer Bohn.

Bredow, J. 1992. Wall Hawkers say "Buyer Beware!" *Checkpoint* 11.

Buford, B. (ed.) 1989. *New Europe*. Cambridge: Granta Publications. *Granta* 30.

Chippindale, C. 1990a. Editorial. *Antiquity* 64: 705–7.

1990b. Contributions to Thames 1990.

Cleven, T. 1993. Es gibt keinene Grund, die Mauer zu vergessen, *Ostsee-Zeitung* (13 August).

Corner, J. & S. Harvey (ed.). 1991. *Enterprise and heritage: crosscurrents of the national culture*. London: Routledge.

Craig, G. A. 1982. *The Germans*. Harmondsworth: Penguin.

Darnton, R. 1991. *Der letzte Tanz auf der Mauer: Berliner Journal 1989–1990*. München: Carl Hanser.

Diemer, G. (ed.). 1990. *Kurze Chronik der Deutschen Frage*. München: Olzog. Geschichte und Staat Band 288.

Dobberke, C. 1992. Die Mauer läßt ihn nicht los, *Die Welt* (2 August).

Draecker, J. 1990. 2 Millionen aus dem Mauer-verkauf fur Denkmalpflege und Gesundheit, *Berliner Morgenpost* (18 October).

Drews, A., U. Gerhard & J. Link. 1985. Moderne Kollektivsymbolik: eine diskurstheoritisch orientierte Einfuhrung, *Internationales Archiv fur Sozialgeschichte der deutschen Literatur*, Sonderheft 1. Tübingen: Niemeyer.

Drosdeck, A. et al. 1989. *Grenze als Stadtebauliche Aufgabe: Berlin*. Darmstadt: Technische Hochschule Darmstadt-Fachbereich Architektur.

Eckhardt, U. 1987. *Der Moses Mendelssohn Pfad*. Berlin (West): Berliner Festspiele.

Edelmann, M. 1975. Die symbolische Seite der Politik, in W.-D. Narr & C. Offe (ed.), *Wohlfahrtsstaat und Massenloyalität*: 307–22. Köln: WestDeutscher Verlag.

Enzenberger, H. M. 1989. The state of Europe, in Buford 1989: 136–42.

Escaut-Marquet, M. T. 1990. *Die Mauer. The Berlin Wall Special Auction*. Monte Carlo: Galerie Park Palace.

Fischer, G. & F. Von der Schulenburg. 1990. *Die Mauer: monument of the century*. Berlin: Ernst & Sohn.

Garton Ash, T. 1990. *We the people: the revolution of 89 witnessed in Warsaw, Budapest, Berlin and Prague*. Cambridge: Granta Books.

Geisler, M. E. 1992. Mehrfach gebrochene Mauerschau: 1989–1990 in den US-Medien, in Bohn et al. 1992: 257–75.

Gerig, U. 1986 *Barrieren aus Eisen und Beton: in Berlin und quer durch Deutschland*. Krefeld: Rohr.

Gewis. 1990. Wollen die Berliner die Mauer wieder? Trailer um die Mauer, *Prinz* (8 November): 20–26.

Gonzsalez-Marcen, P. & R. Risch. 1990. Archaeology and historical materialism, in Baker & Thomas 1990: 94–104.

Gorbachev, M. 1988. *Perestroika: new thinking for our country and the world*. London: Fontana/Collins.

Gow, D. 1991. Wall artists help to fill state coffers, *Guardian* (6 February).

Grant, R. G. 1991. *The rise and fall of the Berlin Wall*. Leicester: Magna Books.

Hartung, K. 1989. Der Fall der Mauer, *Tageszeitung* (6 November).

Hildebrandt, R. 1988a. *The Wall speaks/Die Mauer Spricht*. Berlin: Haus am Checkpoint Charlie.

    1988b. *It happened at the Wall*. Berlin: Haus am Checkpoint Charlie.

    1993. *Die Deutsche Teilung: Todlichegrenzfalle und Schwerverletzte*. Berlin: Haus am Checkpoint Charlie.

Hildebrandt, R. et al. 1990. Grenzen durch Berlin und durch Deutschland. Zablein-material. Berlin, *Arbeitsgemeinschaft* (13 August). Berlin: Haus am Checkpoint Charlie.

Honecker, E. 1980. *Aus meinem Leben*. Berlin (East): Dietz.

Jameson, F. 1984. Post-modernism, or the cultural logic of late Capitalism, *New Left Review* 146.

Korff, G. 1990. Rote Fahnen und Bananen: Notizen zur politischen Symbolik im Prozess der Vereiningung von DDR und DDR, *Schweizerischen Archiv fur Volkskunde* 3/4: 130–60. Basel.

Korngiebel, W. & J. Link. 1992. Von einstürzenden Mauern, europäischen Zügen und deutschen Autos in Bildern und Sprachbildern der Medien, in Bohn et al. 1992: 31–53.

Kugler, A. 1991. Später Sieg des Dollars, *Tageszeitung* (9 December).

Kuzdas, H. J. 1990. *Berliner Mauer Kunst*. Berlin: Elephanten Presse.

Lapp, P. J. 1987. *Frontdienst im Frieden: Die Grenztruppen der DDR*. Koblenz: Bernard & Graefe.

Lübbe, H. 1990. Zeit-Verhältnisse: über die veränderte Gegenwart von Zukunft und Vergangenheit, in W. Zacharias (ed.), *Der Verschwinden der Gegenwart und die Konstruktion der Errinerung*: 40–49. Essen: Klartext.

Lusebrink, H.-J. & R. Reichardt. 1990. *Die Bastille: zur Symbolgeschichte von Herrschaft und Freiheit*. Frankfurt am Main: Fischer Taschenbuch.

McCauley, M. 1983. *The origins of the Cold War*. London: Longmans.

Malzahn, C. C. 1988. Asbest-Alarm: Die Mauer unter Glas!, *Tageszeitung* (2 December).

Mander, J. 1962. *Berlin: the hostage of the West*. Harmondsworth: Penguin.

Mehls, E. & H. Mehls. 1979. *13 August: illustrierte historische Hefte 17*. Berlin (East): VEB Deutscher Verlag der Wissenschaften.

Miller, D. 1987. *Material culture and mass consumption*. Oxford: Basil Blackwell.

Möbius, P. & H. Trotnow. 1990. *Mauern sind nicht für ewig gebaut: zur Geschichte der Berliner Mauer*. Berlin & Frankfurt am Main: Propyläen.

1991. Das Mauer-Komplott, *Die Zeit* (Hamburg) (9 August).

Nürnberger, D. 1992. Der letzte Wachtturm Passender Ausstellungsort, *Berliner Zeitung* (14 August).

Petschull, J. 1990. *Die Mauer*. Hamburg: Stern Bucher.

Pokatzy, K. 1990. Ostler gegen Wessie-sicht, (Hamburg) *Die Zeit* (29 June).

Ribbe, W. & J. Schmaedeke. 1988. *Kleine Berlin Geschichte*. Berlin (West): Landeszentrale fur politische Bildungsarbeit.

Robins, K. 1991. Tradition and translation: national culture in its global context, in Corner & Harvey 1991: 21-45.

Rühle, J. & G. Holzweißib. 1988. *13 August 1961. Die Mauer von Berlin*. Köln: Verlag Wissenschaft und Politik.

Rürup, R. (ed.) 1989. *Topography of terror*. Berlin (West): Verlag Willmuth Arenhövel.

Samson, R. 1992. Knowledge, constraint and power in inaction: the defenceless medieval wall, in P. Schackel & B. Little (ed.), *Historical Archaeology* 26: 26–44.

Scheub, U. 1992. Geschichte auf der Straße, *Tageszeitung* (29 February).
Schneider, P. 1983. *The Wall jumper*. New York (NY): Pantheon.
Smith, K. 1990. *Berlin: coming in from the cold*. Harmondsworth: Penguin.
Spiegel. 1990. Auch das noch!, *Spiegel* 28: 156–8.
Stahl, J. 1989. *An der Wand: Grafitti zwischen Grafitti und Anarchic*. Köln: DuMont.
Thames Television. 1990. In search of the Berlin Wall, film in series *Down to Earth*, broadcast on Channel 4, London, 8 November.
Wagner, H. 1990. Die Innendeutsche Grenzen, in A. Demandt (ed.), *Deutschlands Grenzen in der Geschichte*: 235–76. München: C. H. Beck.
Walser, M. 1989. *Über Deutschland Reden*. Frankfurt am Main: Edition Suhrkamp 1553.
Warnecken, B. J. 1992. "Aufrechter Gang" Metamorphosen einer Parole des DDR-Umbmchs, in Bohn et al. 1992: 17-29.
Weber, H. 1985. *Geschichte der DDR*. Munchen: DTV-Wissenschaft 4430.
——— 1990. *Kleine Geschichte der DDR*. Köln: Edition Deutschland Archiv.
Wedow, J. 1992. What happened to the Wall?, *Checkpoint* 11.
Weissler, S. 1990. *Rettet die Mauer!* Berlin: Presseerklarung det Al-Fraktion im Abgeordneten Haus (10 October).
Wenders, W. & P. Handke. 1989. *Der Him mel über Berlin: ein Filmbuch*. Frankfurt am Main: Suhrkamp.

4

Sahuayo, Mexico, and Its U.S. Colonies

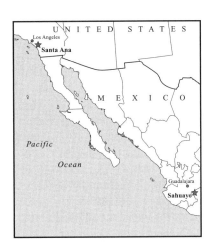

David Fitzgerald

This study explores the relationship between the community of Sahuayo—in the central west part of Mexico—that has been sending migrants north to the United States for almost a century, and Santa Ana, California, one of the communities these migrants established in the United States. The linkages include Santa Ana residents sending home cash, sponsoring annual fiestas, conducting periodic personal visits, and creating a website for Sahuayo residents in the United States as well as efforts by Catholic priests in Sahuayo to establish closer ties with migrants. Sahuayo and its migrants living in the United States constitute, in effect, a transnational community. This type of connection across borders is typical of many areas around the world where migrants maintain contact with their places of origin. Transportation and modern communication technologies characteristic of the globalizing world enable people to overcome the traditional barrier functions of many borders.

David Fitzgerald is a doctoral student in sociology at the University of California, Los Angeles. His research and publications are on international migration and Mexican politics.

Sahuayo, Michoacán, and Its Migrants

Sahuayo rises on a hillside 15 kilometers southeast of Mexico's largest lake—Chapala. A century ago the lake reached Sahuayo, but over the years the

Excerpts from David Fitzgerald, "Sahuayo and Its 'Colonies,' " in *Negotiating Extra-Territorial Citizenship: Mexican Migration and the Transnational Politics of Community*, Monograph Series 2 (La Jolla: Center for Comparative Immigration Studies, University of California, San Diego, 2000), 49–73. Reprinted by permission of David Fitzgerald.

shoreline has receded, extending a swath of fertile farmland called the Ciénega of Chapala. Some of the first international emigrants from the region began their trip north by steamship across Lake Chapala to Guadalajara, 125 kilometers to the northwest (Ochoa Serrano 1998), but today it is only an hour and a half by car from Sahuayo to the Guadalajara airport and a three-hour flight from there to Southern California. Alternately, a Sahuayan bus company offers daily departures and US$85 one way fares to two destinations on the California border—Mexicali and Tijuana.

I arrived in Sahuayo on a bus, several hours after the overnight flight from Los Angeles landed in Guadalajara. My wife and I were standing on a street corner finding our bearings when a man in his twenties approached and offered us a ride. Luis Manuel had just arrived from Compton, near Los Angeles, where he had lived for the past eleven years. As he maneuvered his mini-van down Sahuayo's main street, we joked about how traffic in Sahuayo was worse than in Los Angeles. Like the van, at least a quarter of the cars had license plates from California, Illinois, and other U.S. states. Shoppers bustled in every imaginable kind of retail shop and strolled past travel agency windows posting the lowest fares to Los Angeles and Chicago. Every few blocks, there was an automated teller machine behind gleaming glass or Mexican and American flags advertising a *casa de cambio* (exchange house). This was not the economically depressed community one might expect to find in an area of such high emigration. Luis Manuel dropped us off in the plaza and gave us his telephone number, urging us to call him if we needed anything. I wondered how he was received by strangers on his first day in Compton.

Not surprisingly, the plaza is the center of Sahuayo's social life. An arcade around its fountain and wooden kiosk dates to 1910. During the day, straw-hatted men who are almost as old as the arcade stake out their turf in one corner of the plaza. Rubén, age 74, swam the Rio Grande in 1946 to pick grapefruit in Pecos, Texas, with dozens of other Sahuayans before returning to the United States twice as a bracero. Now he sells snacks and newspapers to pedestrians. On Sunday evenings, hundreds of Sahuayans gather to hear free concerts sponsored by the city hall. A statue of Miguel Hidalgo shakes a fist toward young elites in fashionable clothes who lounge on the steps outside a nightclub, watching their friends speed past on mopeds. Pickup trucks cruise past, blaring *rock-en-espanol, banda,* or Kenny G. Behind the plaza, the illuminated twin spires of the cathedral "soar like white doves," in the words of "Sahuayo, Mi Tierra," a song I first heard in Santa Ana.

Sahuayo has been the source of sustained emigration to the United States for almost a century, despite its position as the economic capital of the Ciénega for even longer. Its economic strength in the region stems largely from its strategic positioning on the old road between Mexico City and Guadalajara (González 1979). Sahuayo has much stronger social and economic links to Guadalajara than to the Michoacán state capital of Morelia 210 kilometers to the east. Throughout the 1700s, the giant hacienda of Guaracha absorbed the available land around Sahuayo, reducing Sahuayo's opportunities for agricultural production and leading to a focus on commerce and artisan production in its stead. Sandal manufacture dates back to the mid-1800s in Sahuayo (Forbes Adams 1994). By 1990, Sahuayo produced 2 million pairs of sandals (guaraches) a year. The industry supports an estimated one in four Sahuayans; these artisans work in scores of small workshops and homes (Zepeda Patterson 1990:153).

Sahuayo's relationship to agriculture today is primarily in the sale of agricultural inputs and, to a lesser extent, in the sale of agricultural products. By the mid-1980s, Sahuayo was attracting customers from throughout northwest Michoacán and southeast Jalisco. Among the primary goods sold were animal fodder, wholesale grains, furniture, groceries, pharmaceuticals, shoes, and electric goods. Small factories made ceramic tiles, clothing, and shoes (Forbes Adams 1994). Sahuayo was once famed for its sombrero production as well, but this industry is declining. To this day, there are no large factories in any sector, even in the thriving sandal industry.

The economic and political history of the region in the early twentieth century continues to reverberate in Sahuayan politics. During the Cristero War in the 1920s, in which Catholic rebels fought the central government and the Agrarian Reform, Sahuayo was an important regional base for the Cristeros (González 1979). Conservative Catholicism and anti-*cardenismo* continued to reinforce each other as Lázaro Cárdenas's Agrarian Reform expropriated local haciendas and ranches (Vargas González 1993). A strong rivalry grew between Sahuayo and its smaller but more politically powerful neighbor, Jiquilpan, 10 kilometers to the south. Jiquilpan was the hometown and political base of Lázaro Cárdenas and his brother, Dámaso, who dominated Ciénega politics for more than thirty years (Ochoa Serrano 1999, Zepeda Patterson 1989).

The Church throughout Michoacán, but especially in the Ciénega, has sought to keep the population immune from cardenismo. While the Church does not attempt to assume direct political power, it is an extremely influential pressure group (Zepeda Patterson 1990: 76). Sahuayo is still known throughout the region as a bastion of Catholicism and opposition to the secular state (Forbes Adams 1994, González 1979, author interviews 1999). As in many Michoacano communities, social life revolves around religious festivals, and priests are among the most important community leaders. The Church also penetrates civil society through its hospitals and charity organizations (Zepeda Patterson 1990, author interviews 1999).

The direct exercise of political power in Sahuayo historically has been restricted to a business elite whose interests have been served regardless of the party in office. From 1963 to 1986, every municipal president, with one exception, was a businessman. The PAN has been a strong presence in Sahuayo since the 1940s, and it was able to elect a municipal president in 1962, one of the earliest PAN municipal victories in the entire country. A coalition elected PAN candidate Salvador Múgica Manzo after the PRI candidate openly confronted the Church over control of a secondary school. However, the 1962 election was considered less a sign of *panista* strength than evidence of the power of the Church. The election did not threaten the PRI, which soon co-opted Múgica Manzo (Vargas González 1993).

The PAN lay relatively dormant in Sahuayo until the early 1980s, when the Sahuayan commercial class perceived that Michoacán's governor, Cuauhtémoc Cárdenas, was threatening its interests (Vargas González 1993). Over the last fifteen years, the PAN and PRI have alternated power in Sahuayo. Two panistas have been elected municipal president in this period, though the current municipal president is a *priísta*. The PRD has never won a municipal election, though it runs candidates in major elections. Sahuayo's historical antagonism with cardenismo and the widespread perception in Sahuayo that the PRD is an agent of secularism and even atheism have limited the PRD's success. The opposition Green Party of Mexico (PVEM) ran a candidate in the 1998 municipal elections, although the party has little support and is rumored to have been financed by the PRI to split the opposition vote. The PVEM candidate left to live in Orange County following the election.

Sahuayo has extremely high rates of emigration and has been a source of migrants to the North[1] for at least eighty years. It was impossible to find a single person who did not have at least one close family member in the United States. The majority of men questioned had been to the North at least once. Most Sahuayans who were interviewed perceived that the rate of female migration also is increasing, a finding in line with survey research elsewhere in west-central Mexican communities with high migration rates (Massey et al. 1994: 1512, Durand 1994: 157). Despite Sahuayo's active commercial life, there are not enough well-paying jobs to keep Sahuayans from migrating to the United States and cities like Guadalajara and Mexico City. The culture of migration is so strong that even children express a desire to go to the United States, at least to experience the adventure. Educators complain that their students do not apply themselves in their studies because they expect to leave as soon as they become adults.

The first ten Sahuayan migrants to the United States went to Galveston, Texas, and Chicago in 1917. Contracted braceros began arriving in Santa Ana in the 1940s (author interviews with surviving family members 1999). Today there are four large concentrations of Sahuayans in California. After Santa Ana, the largest populations are in Los Angeles, Merced, and Hayward. There is also a concentration of Sahuayans in Chicago and northern Indiana.

The population of Sahuayans living in Santa Ana is difficult to estimate.[2] The number of residents of Mexican origin is only measured in the decennial U.S. census which typically undercounts immigrants, especially the undocumented (*Binational Study* 1997). Data about hometown origin are only available from self-reporting to the Mexican consulate. Despite the limitations of the data, an estimate can be made using 1996 voluntary registration data from the Mexican consulate in Santa Ana and the 1990 U.S. census.[3] Twenty percent of Orange County residents—480,000 people—described themselves as Mexican-origin in 1990 (*Hispanic Databook* 1994). Approximately 43,000 Mexican nationals registered with the consulate in 1996. Using the 1990 census figures for the Mexican population, we can conservatively estimate that approximately one of eleven Mexican-origin residents was registered with the consulate in 1996. Three of the five Mexican cities most represented in the consulate register are in Michoacán—Jiquilpan, Sahuayo, and Morelia. The register lists 287 Jiquilpenses and 283 Sahuayans. It is impossible to know how registration rates vary by town of origin, but if we assume that Sahuayans follow the average registration rate, we can estimate a 1996 population of roughly 3,000 Sahuayans in Orange County.

Ample evidence from interviews suggests that the vast majority of Sahuayans in Orange County live in Santa Ana. Sahuayans live throughout the city and are not especially concentrated in any neighborhood. Neither are Sahuayans concentrated in any economic niche. Most are blue-collar workers, but a number own restaurants and small businesses. There are no reliable data on the proportion of Sahuayans living in Santa Ana or elsewhere in the United States who have legal status, but interview data and the estimates of migrants suggest that neither legal nor illegal status is overwhelmingly dominant.

The municipio of Sahuayo estimates that 50 percent of Sahuayan families receive remittances from family members in the United States (*Plan de Desarrollo* 1999). The circulation of dollars in the economy is impressive. In 1999, there were eighteen casas de cambio. The owner of four of the casas estimated that he exchanges an average of over $100,000 a day, including cashing U.S. money orders, U.S. pension checks, and exchanging cash. It is impossible to know what portion of these dollars is from remittances and what portion is due to the use of dollars as a common currency in Mexico for large transactions, but the importance of remittances as an economic pillar of Sahuayo is unquestioned.

Remittances in Sahuayo are typically used for personal consumption or housing construction, as researchers have found elsewhere in Mexican communities with high rates of emigration (Massey et al. 1987). Housing construction and furnishings provide a sustained source of employment in Sahuayo. For example, the owner of a chain of four hardware stores with forty years in business estimated that 40 percent of his sales are to norteños. A carpenter who employs ten men in his workshop said that most of his business is with norteños, who pay top prices for custom furniture and fittings. The U.S.-based migrant portion of their businesses has increased in the last ten years, unlike the decrease in migrant investment in housing and furnishings found in other high-emigration communities as many migrants settle in the United States (Cornelius 1998).

Sahuayan businessmen and political leaders agree that only a small share of remittances is directly invested in businesses. Still, there is survey and anecdotal evidence that suggests that many small businesses in Sahuayo are started at least in part with capital earned by migrants who worked in the North and then returned to settle in Sahuayo. In her study of sandal production in the 1980s, Forbes Adams found that between 1950 and 1985, 6.2 percent of sandal workshops and 11.7 percent of subcontractor sandal workshops were formed primarily with capital saved from migration (1994). In 1999, I found a variety of businesses started with earnings from the North, such as clothing stores, restaurants, an agricultural seed store, a sporting goods store, a printing business, and an avocado distributorship. Entrepreneurial former migrants may themselves underestimate the influence of migrant investment by neglecting to consider indirect investment mechanisms. For example, one businessman said that he did not start his beverage distribution franchise with capital he raised as a wage laborer in the United States. Yet he went on to describe how he used his savings to buy two pieces of property in Sahuayo. Upon returning from Chicago, he built a house on one property and sold the other to raise the capital to start his business.

Migration is also an emergency debt-relief strategy that enables entrepreneurs to bail themselves out in hard times. For example, a sandal workshop owner went bankrupt in the 1980s economic crisis. He went to work in Chicago and saved enough money to pay off his debts in Sahuayo. When he returned, he was able to obtain a loan with his clean credit and start a new workshop that today employs sixty workers (author interview 1999). Forbes Adams found that the same emergency strategy was used by sandal makers in the 1970s (1994).

"We are like ants who go out and bring food back home," explained a Sahuayan who worked as a merchant in Mexico City for ten years before returning to build a two-story home in Sahuayo. Wandering and a commercial instinct are important elements of Sahuayo's collective self-identity. According to a local joke, when Neil Armstrong stepped from the Eagle lunar landing module and was about to drive the North American flag into lunar soil and proclaim himself the first man on the moon, he heard a Sahuayan pass by with his herd crying, "Pigs for Sale! Pigs for Sale!"[4]

The New Transnational Media: "Sahuayo, California"

The long-term migrants who tend to be the most active leaders of Sahuayans in the United States did not live in Sahuayo during the period of political liberalization in the late 1980s and the 1990s. Living in California exposes migrants to alternative worldviews and political practices (Castañeda 1993), but it also may isolate migrants from political changes in their communities of origin. However, new technologies allow absent migrants to become better informed members of their communities of origin. "Real time" access to information is especially important to our understanding of extra-territorial citizenship, because it addresses one of the main complaints of those who reject the principle of extra-territorial citizenship—namely, that absentees are ignorant of the daily public life of the community. While the transnational migration literature is replete with references to the effects of new technologies such as telephones and jet travel (R. Smith 1995, Sontag and Dugger 1998), the Internet is a new means of transnational communication. There are now three grassroots Internet Web sites created by Sahuayan migrants that truly create a transnational community where social and political information is exchanged in ways that compress space and time.

The captain of a Sahuayan soccer club in Orange County launched a bilingual Internet site in 1998 called "Sahuayo, California."[5] In two years of operation, it has received over 12,000 "hits" and messages from Sahuayans as far away as Argentina, Spain, and Japan. A directory of electronic mail addresses and telephone numbers lists sixty-five Sahuayans all over the United States and one in Sahuayo. There is a page with gossip and news from Sahuayo and its satellite communities, a chat room, general background information about Sahuayo, and a handful of advertisements for Sahuayan businesses in Orange County and Sahuayo.[6] The soccer captain works at a wrecking yard whose Anglo owner employs four Sahuayan workers and has hired other Sahuayans in the past. The owner pays the $20 monthly cost to operate the Web site. The site has a link to a commercial used-autoparts Web site operated by the owner, but the owner's reasons for designing and paying for the Sahuayo site appear to be more paternalistic than motivated by economic self-interest. He has encouraged the Sahuayan who provides the information used in the Web site to take computer classes, learn to manage the site himself, and find employment outside the wrecking business.

Several months after the site was established, the Sahuayan worker traveled to Sahuayo to solicit help from the local Internet service provider. After several months of inactivity, the site now has a stream of listings from Sahuayans, mostly but not exclusively in the United States. Sahuayans post listings of births, report soccer club scores from Sahuayan teams in Santa Ana, solicit information about traveling to Sahuayo, and even post personal ads seeking a mate. A message posted on the night of the July 2, 2000, elections crowed, "Sahuayo is with the PAN! Congratulations, Vicente Fox! Out with the PRI rats! Rats out! Out with the PRI!" Use of the Internet is growing steadily in Sahuayo, though it is still primarily used by the elite and university students. In July 1999, there were 150 regular subscribers with the local Internet service provider. An Internet café opened in July 1999 with ten computers and has attracted a steady stream of users. A similar Internet café has been open since 1998 in Jiquilpan, and a third opened in Sahuayo in 2000.

The transnational media also include newspapers. One of the three weekly newspapers in Sahuayo prominently lists a correspondent in Anaheim, Orange County. In six months as a correspondent, he has not sent a single article to the editor of the newspaper (his brother-in-law), though he did arrange a weekly advertisement for an Orange County charter bus company. The correspondent is one of the paper's financial supporters. The editor suggests that perhaps when the correspondent retires in three years, he will have more time to write. Clearly, the correspondent's position is a status symbol for the newspaper more than a reader service. Yet even symbolic correspondents build prestige for the editor in Sahuayo, underlining the interdependence of migrants and non-migrants. In December 1999, the editor met with Sahuayan migrant representatives living all over the United States to encourage them to write articles for the paper and find an economical way for Sahuayans in the United States to subscribe. He suggested sending a bundle of newspapers by an express courier service to migrant representatives in selected U.S. cities who would then distribute the paper.

The editor of a regional newspaper in Jiquilpan that also covers Sahuayo has met with members of the Inglewood Jiquilpense association to promote subscriptions to his newspaper. He cites the example of an entrepreneur in neighboring Venustiano Carranza who sends weekly issues of the local newspaper to the satellite community in Hawaiian Gardens near Los Angeles. Through these new media, migrants are able to diversify the kinds of information they receive about their communities of origin and remain engaged in local Mexican politics. They illustrate how new technologies such as the Internet, jet travel, the cheap international telephone call, and courier services allow migrants to maintain contacts with their communities of origin in ways that were impossible for migrants in previous eras.

A Transnational Collection Plate? Networks of Migrants and Priests

Considering the pervasive influence of the Catholic Church in Sahuayo, it is not surprising that the Church is also one of the most important institutional actors in the relationship between Sahuayo and its migrants. The Church's role is even more significant because it is one of the few transnational organizations that has the capacity to interact directly with migrants on both sides of the border. During the first waves of mass migration at the turn of the century, priests throughout Mexico feared that contact with the United States would contaminate migrants. Returning migrants were seen as potential agents of Protestantism, secularism, and moral decay. Many priests encouraged their congregations to stay in Mexico. As it became clear that mass migration would continue, Mexican priests forged closer relationships with migrants and began offering them special masses, often celebrated during a designated Day of the Absentees (Hernández Madrid 1999, Durand 1994).

The Church in the United States has encouraged migrants to maintain or develop ties with both sending and receiving areas. Lone migrants who are not rooted in a community are considered more likely to engage in behaviors, such as infidelity, that the Church proscribes. The Church hopes that by encouraging migrants to associate with other migrants from their hometowns, they will maintain their cultural and religious traditions and be less likely to fall prey to secularism and moral turpitude. One Sahuayan priest encourages Sahuayans in the United States to approach priests in Sahuayo if they feel that clergy in the United States are not responsive to their needs. Sahuayan priests can then address the problem in the North through official Church channels. At the same time as the Church encourages transnational ties, its efforts also integrate migrants into their receiving communities by making their lives more comfortable and building their social networks (Levitt 2000, author interviews 1999).

Two churches in Santa Ana are gathering points for Sahuayans, and many of the networks of collective migrant participation in Sahuayan public life are based on relationships between migrants and priests. Yet even these religious networks are multistranded and can reflect divisions. There is a long history of priests traveling to the United States to ask for financial contributions for churches in Sahuayo or to officiate rites such as first communions or baptisms. Sahuayans living in the United States frequently finance these visits. The visits are not only welcomed by Sahuayan migrants; they are expected. "If he is a good priest, he will come to visit the people," said one Sahuayan community leader in Los Angeles.

Yet clergy on both sides of the border are sensitive to the perception that some Mexican parish priests only visit migrants to pass a transnational collection plate. Several current priests and migrants angrily refer to former priests who went to Sahuayan satellite communities primarily to collect money rather than officiate rites or offer spiritual succor. A leading Sahuayan priest who actively promotes a stronger relationship between migrants and the Church in Sahuayo—without the fund-raising component—emphasizes, "It's not right that we go and exploit people who are already exploited." Some priests also feel that even if it is legitimate to raise funds among Sahuayan migrants, those funds should be spent on productive projects or charities rather than fiestas.

Leaders of the Church in Orange County are concerned that there are Mexican priests who officiate rites in the United States without requesting permission from U.S. parish priests. Performing marriages without sanction from the parish priest is illegal according to California law, while performing unauthorized rites such as baptisms violates Church rules. Church leaders see these practices as worse yet if there is an appearance of the transaction of rites for financial contributions. Officially, the Church leadership discourages any secondary fund-raising outside standard Church channels. Some U.S. parish priests ignore the fund-raising of Mexican priests if the latter do not perform rites. U.S. parish priests may also turn a blind eye if visiting Mexican priests officiate masses in private homes, as long as there is no quid-pro-quo fund-raising. Sahuayan priests generally do not contact their counterparts in U.S. parishes when they visit. Some of the Sahuayan clergy feel that North American priests have different communication styles and maintain such hurried schedules that interaction is uncomfortable. There is also a perception among some Sahuayan clergy that Spanish priests in the United States disrespect Mexicans. Most importantly, the transnational personal networks of Sahuayan priests obviate the need to work directly with U.S. parish priests.

One of the functions of migrant-priest networks is to encourage migrant participation in Sahuayan religious festivals such as the fiestas of the Virgin of Guadalupe and the patron saint, Santiago Apóstol. Veneration of the Virgin and Santiago are two of the essential markers of Sahuayan identity. Religious fiestas are important in many towns in Michoacán and elsewhere in Mexico, but they are especially central to the public life of Sahuayo (González 1979, author interviews 1999). Migrant participation in these two fiestas is one of the strongest ways to assert a moral extra-territorial citizenship rooted in a specific place. Migrant-funded church projects also demonstrate migrants' financial commitment to Sahuayo. The Church's encouragement of Sahuayan solidarity through migrants' expressions of Mexican religious and cultural traditions legitimates migrants' claims to extra-territorial citizenship. The stamp of the Church on these activities is the strongest possible mark of the participants' Mexican Catholic morality, which demonstrates that despite residence in the United States, migrants remain Mexicans and Sahuayans of good moral standing.

The Colonia Sahuayense

The most visible and long-lived transnational Sahuayan network is a loose formation called the Colonia Sahuayense, which sponsors one of the twelve days of the annual fiesta of the Virgin of Guadalupe in Sahuayo. Each day of the fiesta is sponsored by a different *gremio* (guild), such as the sandal makers or the merchants from the marketplace. Since the late 1950s, Sahuayans who live in the United States have sponsored the fiesta on December 5th. By the early 1960s, Sahuayan migrants had organized Colonias in Santa Ana, Merced, and Los Angeles to sponsor the fiesta. Several years later, Sahuayans in Chicago organized a Colonia. Accounts of the Colonia's formation vary. Some priests and current Colonia leaders claim that the Colonia Sahuayense was a migrant initiative, while others assert that the idea originated with a Sahuayan priest. All agree that individual priests with contacts in the North were crucial for the motivation and organization of the Colonia.

Annual fiesta in Sahuayo, Mexico, in which migrant groups from the United States participate. *Photograph by David Fitzgerald*

The Colonia raises funds in the United States throughout the year, usually by sponsoring dances and dinners where raffles and sales of food and drink are the main source of income. Colonia leaders contact other Sahuayans through telephone calls or at venues where Sahuayans concentrate, such as churches, Sahuayan-owned businesses, and soccer or baseball games where Sahuayan teams play. A diverse group of Sahuayans and their friends from other parts of Mexico attend Colonia events. Three hundred people attended a typical monthly fund-raiser held in 1999 at the home of a Sahuayan community leader in Pico Rivera, halfway between Santa Ana and Los Angeles. The host owns a pet shop in Los Angeles and a furniture factory in Sahuayo. After he first came to California in 1979, he rarely returned to Sahuayo, but now he flies there almost once a month on business. He explained that at the same time as the community raises money to help Sahuayo, fund-raising parties make life more enjoyable in the United States by bringing Sahuayans together. The fund-raisers allow Sahuayans to exchange information about business and job opportunities. Carlos González Gutiérrez, one of the architects of the consulate's Communities Abroad program, argues that the main function of many Mexican HTAs [hometown associations] is to create a sense of community among migrants in the United States and that projects in Mexico are secondary (1995). These two functions reinforce each other in the case of Sahuayo.

The Colonia Sahuayense proclaims its identity in the December 5th fiesta through inclusive and exclusive identity displays. Identity displays are directed outward at an audience of non-migrants and other migrants, but they also strengthen a sense of belonging among the participants. Performances of belonging call forth the same reaction in the performers as they do in the audience (Austin 1975). On December 5, returning migrants parade through the streets as a group to assert their Sahuayan identity publicly. Family members sometimes march to represent absentees. Former migrants now settled in Sahuayo may also march in place of friends who cannot attend. During the procession, the participants display symbols of Mexico and Sahuayo, such as a Mexican flag emblazoned with the name of the "Colonia Sahuayense Residente en Indiana," banners of the Virgin of Guadalupe, and a banner showing the twin towers of the main cathedral in Sahuayo. Each Colonia has a separate banner that announces the specific satellite community of the residents parading behind it. Mariachis and school-aged dancers accompany the procession as fireworks explode in the background.

The Colonia serves as a representative of a corporate body of Sahuayans abroad. In 1999, the priest presiding over the parade explicitly recognized the marchers as representatives of all Sahuayans who live in the United States. He declared over the microphone to the crowd of thousands that lined the parade route, "I extend a welcome to the Colonia del Norte. These people have given up their work and time to come here. Not all in the North could come, but the Colonia represents them." Migrants in the North can vicariously experience the parade through videos that are filmed at the yearly fiestas of the Virgin and Patrón Santiago by a Cuban-American and sold to Sahuayans in greater Los Angeles.

The leaders of the Colonia tend to be middle-aged men who have lived in the United States for twenty years or more. The current 48-year-old president is a permanent U.S. resident who since 1973 has lived in the Los Angeles area, where he owns a home and works as a janitorial supervisor. He returns to Sahuayo at least once a year and owns another home there. As soon as his youngest child graduates from high school in three years, he intends to return to Sahuayo. One of the striking features of contemporary migrant associations studied in New York City and in California is that they are often formed by long-term settlers. The level of transnational practices is not necessarily a declining function of the length of U.S. residence. Settlement does not presuppose a rejection of the country of origin. For some, transnational practices are much more important than brief transitory phenomena as migrants settle in the United States. Conversely, transnational associational life may actually integrate migrants into their receiving communities by strengthening their social networks in the United States (Glick Schiller et al. 1992, Basch et al. 1994, Portes 1999).

Several of the leaders are blue-collar workers with well-paying jobs, but they can raise their class position dramatically by returning to Sahuayo as benefactors. Marginalization in the United States has been noted by other researchers as one of the most important reasons that migrants organize transnationally. Rouse argues that migrants from Aguililla, Michoacán, living in California maintain their transnational links as a means of circumventing their subordinate class and racial positions in the United States (1992). While the Sahuayan migrants in this study do not frame their participation in these terms, they often emphasize that they feel much freer in Sahuayo from the control of the U.S. government and that society's rigid social norms. The freedom to litter, drive after drinking, and have loud parties without being ticketed by the police is praised frequently and contrasted to a restricted life in the United States.

Motivations for transnational activities partly depend on diverse experiences in the North, but the identity displays themselves (such as the Virgin of Guadalupe procession) are claims to inclusion in that they assert a shared concern for Sahuayo that is not mitigated by physical absence. At the same time, inclusive identity displays may be purposefully or unintentionally exclusive. Returnees have set themselves apart from other Sahuayans by organizing themselves as the Colonia del Norte and spending thousands of dollars on the fiesta. Paradoxically, migrants are able to sidestep their marginalization in the United States by displaying in Mexico the wealth they could only earn in the North. A 30-year resident of California who skins chickens at a processing plant led one of the Colonias in the procession wearing a fashionable new suit and jewelry. Vacationing returnees buy rounds of drinks and throw street parties for their neighborhoods. Even when their savings are minimal, returning migrants assert material success to the point that some are bankrupt by the end of their vacation and must borrow money to return to the United States.

When one former migrant who owns a business in Sahuayo was asked if norteños in the United States invest in the Sahuayan economy, he snorted that "they invest in drinking" when they come for vacation. "They come in their nice cars, but people here say they are conch shells—pretty on the outside, ugly inside. . . . They were born in Mexico, but they don't like anything here. They are no longer Sahuayans. They are Michoacanos of convenience so they can buy land, but they don't have any love for their country. . . . In practice, they are from neither here nor there." Although he underlined the importance of family remittances to the Sahuayan economy, he prefers that migrants stay in the United States and only send money, because they drive up the prices of housing when they return.

Many other Sahuayans do not share his resentments, and they welcome returning migrants with open enthusiasm. Yet displays by migrants that set them apart from non-migrants create a common impression that long-term migrants have adopted what are widely perceived as the consumerist, ostentatious values of the United States. Thus identity displays are a double-edged sword. A parade that is ostensibly an inclusive identity display may have the unintended consequence of delegitimating the Sahuayan-ness of migrants in the eyes of some non-migrant Sahuayans.

Sahuayans tend to reserve their harshest criticisms for migrant youths. Norteño youths are widely blamed for a perceived wave of gang crime and drug use in Sahuayo over the last ten years. During one interview, a Sahuayan businessman and community leader lashed out at migrants and the influence of American culture more generally. He blamed drugs, new attitudes, new religions, and delinquency on U.S. influences transmitted by return migrants, television, and tourists. "There were practically no bad people in Sahuayo before!" he said. While his comments are hyperbolic, the perception of a Sahuayo corrupted by norteño youths is a common concern. Sahuayans point to graffiti from Santa Ana gangs such as the Lopers, which is scrawled on walls around town. As quoted by a local newspaper, the ranking priest in Sahuayo blamed returning emigrants for contaminating the fiesta of the Patrón Santiago by wearing grotesque masks and dressing as pregnant women. Inclusive identity displays such as the procession of the Colonia become even more important as migrants seek to counter the image that they have been corrupted by America and have lost their Sahuayan morality.

The Colonia has recently tried to project another image of norteño youths through the selection of a "Queen of the North." The use of young women to represent their (or their parents') communities of origin is a ubiquitous feature of HTAs in the United States, and it is usually discussed by HTA leaders and researchers in the context of encouraging the second generation of immigrants to identify with the community of origin (R. Smith 1995, Zabin and Escala Rabadán 1998). The use of hometown queens should also be examined as an attempt by migrants to demonstrate to their communities of origin that their children are not gangsters and that they continue to hold the moral values of their Mexican communities. It is not coincidental that women are used to symbolize moral purity and tradition, in contradistinction to the negative images of norteño youths that primarily revolve around young men. Women are often the bearers of notions of tradition and morals.

The Colonia Sahuayense in Los Angeles selected a Queen of the North in 1998 from among five candidates who sold tickets for the competition. The winner was born in Sahuayo but left to live in Los Angeles when she was one year old. She returned to Sahuayo after her selection to ride in an open car during the December 5th parade and to attend the Colonia-sponsored fiesta at the town jail. Although she had regularly visited Sahuayo for summer vacations, she said the act of returning as the Queen made her feel even more proud to be Sahuayan. She said she did not take offense when she was teased in Sahuayo as "The Queen of the Cholos." The $900 she raised selling tickets to support her candidacy was spent mostly on her airfare and special clothing. The 1999 contest was canceled partway through because the six candidates did not raise sufficient funds to pay for a queen's expenses. However, HTA pageants can be an important source of income for developing transnational projects.

When the Colonia raises excess funds, it donates them to a church in Sahuayo for renovation expenses or to a home for the elderly. The Colonia is currently raising $4,000 on its own initiative for a new front door to one of the churches. When a priest balked at putting a plaque on the door in recognition that it was a contribution of the Colonia, a Colonia leader threatened to withdraw the funding. Only after securing a promise of recognition did fundraising continue. In the 1970s and 1980s, the Colonia also raised funds for a Catholic dispensary, the construction of classrooms at a Catholic school, and donations of food and blankets to poor Sahuayans. The Colonia no longer dispenses goods in public, however, in part because of an incident several years ago in which some Sahuayans waiting in line for donations scuffled with norteños when the supply was exhausted. The Chicago Colonia gave charity aid to some of Sahuayo's poorest neighborhoods several years ago (Espinosa 1999), but in 1999 it was not developing any new projects.

For the last seven years, the Colonia as a whole has sponsored musical groups that perform on December 5th in the courtyard of the town jail. In 1999, about fifty migrants joined over one hundred prisoners in an hour-long fiesta. While some prisoners danced to the music, others circulated among the migrants selling handmade crafts and soliciting cigarettes. The Colonia also sponsored a free lunch for the prisoners the day before. Migrant patronage of these activities is well publicized; Colonia leaders, followed by a brass band playing at high volume, lead a procession through the streets to the jail.

Collective migrant patronage of processions and projects goes beyond displaying shared community symbols. Migrant economic participation in the community through projects and remittances is another potential legitimization of extra-territorial citizenship claims. Among Sahuayan politicians who accept the principle of extending suffrage in Mexican presidential elections to Mexicans living abroad, migrant remittances are one of the most frequently cited reasons for this right of citizenship. Non-migrant Sahuayans who support local forms of extra-territorial citizenship for absent Sahuayans also cite the importance of remittances. Both family remittances and group remittances by an organization such as the Colonia are considered a sign of continued interest and involvement in the community.

Economic participation as citizenship legitimization has its limits, however. Many non-migrant Sahuayan elites take an instrumental view of extra-territorial citizenship. They are willing to accept absent migrant participation in Sahuayan public projects insofar as migrants provide funding, but they reject a fuller measure of extra-territorial citizenship, such as the extension of the vote abroad. For this large segment of elites, migrant economic participation is not the legitimization of full citizenship, but rather the *object* that explains their grudging acceptance of a truncated extra-territorial citizenship. Migrant economic participation also must appear altruistic if that participation is to legitimate migrant citizenship. Migrants must avoid the appearance that they are attempting to "buy" citizenship, because the perception of buying citizenship would violate the moral dimension of citizenship based on affective ties and a shared community identity.

The economic participation of the Colonia throughout the United States is weakening, however, for external and internal reasons. There were no development or philanthropic projects under consideration in 1999. The current president of the Colonia says that the needs of Sahuayo's poor are so great that the Colonia could never help all of them. Twenty years ago, the Colonia raised an average of $20,000 a year in Santa Ana and thousands more from the Colonias in other U.S. cities. In 1999, all of the Colonias together raised only $16,000. Most of this money is spent on mariachis, flowers, firecrackers, and other costs of the December 5th fiesta. Over the last ten years, fewer norteños have returned to Sahuayo to march in the parade. In 1999, less than fifty people marched, even though many more norteños returned to Sahuayo for the fiesta.[7] Norteños who have not contributed financially to the Colonia are often embarrassed to march, underlying the way that expenditure legitimates participation in the public expression of a Sahuayan identity. Migrant children born in the North tend to be less enthusiastic about the fiesta than are their parents, and new absenteeism policies in Santa Ana schools are a deterrent for parents to take their children out of class in early December. The Sahuayan priests traditionally most active in making trips to the United States to raise funds and motivate Sahuayans to continue participating in the fiesta have died or been reassigned to other posts.

Sahuayans in the United States who were once involved in the Colonia are now sometimes reluctant to give their time and money because of the widespread perception that former Colonia leaders in Santa Ana and Chicago-Indiana misappropriated funds for their personal use. Current leaders of the Colonia in Chicago warn that if norteño interest in the fiesta does not increase, 1999 will have been the last year that money was raised. The Colonia is almost moribund in Santa Ana, and many Sahuayans who live there are not sure if it still exists. The current president of the Colonia in Santa Ana was appointed by a priest in Sahuayo following the annual mass for migrants in May 1999. The appointment deviated from the normal procedures of the Colonia, in which each satellite community elects the board of directors of the Colonia by secret, democratic vote.[8] When the leadership structure of the Colonia falters, Sahuayan priests assert their influence to rebuild the organization.

Nevertheless, Sahuayan priests have not assumed control over the finances of the Colonia to create greater confidence among supporters. This is a departure from procedures elsewhere in the region, such as Francisco Sarabia, a village of 2,200 inhabitants three kilometers from Sahuayo. In Sarabia, a transnational network between migrants in Santa Ana and the Sarabia church relies on the priest to control funds raised for projects in Sarabia. The priest travels to Santa Ana to raise money for donations of food and blankets, church renovation, and a meeting hall that is owned by the church but used for all kinds of community functions. A lay coordinator in Santa Ana gathers Sarabians at public parks, private homes, and restaurants for masses or fiestas when the priest visits. The priest gives contributors receipts and then returns with the cash to Sarabia, where he reads aloud a list of donors at the end of mass.

The priest claims that Sarabian migrants are more likely to initiate or support projects with practical concerns for daily life rather than church renovations. In working to develop projects with municipal authorities and migrants, however, the priest is concerned that the municipal government will lower its public works budget in proportion to rising group remittances. The danger in projects financed by migrants from Sarabia and elsewhere is that group remittances will replace, rather than supplement, government spending. The unintended consequences of such projects would be to make governments less accountable to the demands of the citizenry by eliminating a measure of government responsibility for social welfare and development.

Although Francisco Sarabia is only three kilometers from Sahuayo and has a large satellite community in Santa Ana, the collective action networks of the two towns are separate. Sahuayans married to Sarabians living in Santa Ana may attend Sarabian events there, but there are no cooperative projects between the two towns or their migrants. The current Sarabian priest was formerly based in Sahuayo. During his 17-year stint, he raised practically all of the funds to build a new church from Sahuayans in the United States, mostly in Santa Ana. Since leaving Sahuayo, he has not contacted Sahuayans in Santa Ana, even when he goes to Santa Ana to visit Sarabians.

Sahuayan transnational religious networks also are fractured. In the 1980s, a 64-year-old blue-collar Sahuayan worker who has lived in Santa Ana since 1972 organized fund-raising for the July fiesta of the patron saint. He already was active in the Colonia Sahuayense and used the same personal networks to solicit funds directly for an informal group called Devotees of the Patrón Santiago Living in Santa Ana. Leaders of the Colonia saw his efforts as competing with their own project, and the two networks did not cooperate. For sixteen years, the Devotees raised funds for the Patrón Santiago fiesta and dispensed free meals to the poor, but the founder abandoned the effort because he felt there was a lack of interest among migrants and because the work was too time-consuming. He also suspected that funds he raised for a new church devoted to the Patrón Santiago were not used for their stated purpose, and he differed with a Sahuayan priest over the organization of the fiesta. Although he is a naturalized U.S. citizen, he holds dual Mexican nationality and returns to Sahuayo every July for the patron saint festival. He once thought that he would eventually return to Sahuayo but has now decided to stay in Santa Ana, where he no longer has much contact with other Sahuayans.

Many individual Sahuayan migrants continue to return for the fiesta of the Patrón Santiago and participate in the elaborate parades, but there is no longer any collective migrant presence.[9] More migrants return for the Patrón Santiago fiesta now than for the fiesta of the Virgin of Guadalupe, because the Santiago fiesta has a more carnival-esque atmosphere, and it is easier for migrants with established jobs or families in the North to take vacations in the summer. Domestic migrants have decreased their support for the fiesta of the Virgin as well. The Colonia Sahuayense in Guadalajara and Ocatlán, Jalisco, continues to organize a parade on December 12th, but the Colonia Sahuayense in Mexico City has not participated since the leaders of the gremio died. A former director of the government cultural center in Sahuayo derogatorily refers to Sahuayans in Mexico City as "*pinches chilangos*" who no longer care about Sahuayo. The negotiation of extra-territorial citizenship on the local level extends to domestic Mexican migrants.

A new generation of Sahuayan priests is trying to reestablish links with Sahuayan migrants in the United States. One priest recently took two month-long tours of Sahuayan communities in the North.[10] At least two North American parish priests in Orange County have visited Sahuayo. Mexican Catholics are being recruited to serve in Orange County, where there is a need for priests who speak fluent Spanish and understand religious customs in Mexico. In June 1999, 32-year-old Ramón Cisneros became the first Michoacano ordained in the county. Like 90 percent of his high school class in Sahuayo, he had migrated north. He crossed the border illegally and headed to Orange County, where he worked as a cook. Eleven years later, he had become a priest and U.S. citizen (Godines 1999). Scores of Sahuayans attended his ordination and a reception where mariachis sang Sahuayan songs and the hall filled with cries of "*Arriba Sahuayo!*"[11] A replica of the Patrón Santiago figured prominently in the procession through the church. After the transnational priest officiated his first mass in Santa Ana at another church with a large congregation of Sahuayans, he returned to Sahuayo as a triumphant native son. He led a procession of two hundred people from his parents' home to the cathedral, where he gave mass to a crowd of 1,500. Migrants and priests are still negotiating their economic and pastoral relationship, but there appears to be a consensus among parish priests and higher Church authorities in both Orange County and Michoacán that the clergy must learn to be as mobile and transnational as its congregations.

Notes

1. In Michoacán, *el Norte* refers to the United States, and migrants living in the United States are called *norteños*. While norteño is not considered a derogatory term by most migrants and non-migrants, I met one long-term migrant who disliked the term because he said it suggested he was "less Sahuayan."

2. I do not have access to consular data from other cities in the United States with high concentrations of Sahuayans. Sahuayan municipal officials do not know how many Sahuayans live in the United States.

3. This method is derived from Zabin and Escala Rabadán's calculation of the number of Mexicans in Los Angeles by state of origin (1998).

4. I am grateful to Álvaro Ochoa Serrano for sharing this joke.

5. www.gr8net.net/sahuayo/. Other Sahuayan sites are www.sahuayense.com and http://members.tripod.com/Sahuayo_Michoacan/.

6. A similar Internet site and electronic mail bulletin board for the high-emigration town of Jerez, Zacatecas, generates a steady flow of information about the political, cultural, and social life of Jerezanos all over the United States and Zacatecas. The bulletin board allows Zacatecanos in the United States to coordinate visits to Jerez and to plan reunions of Jerezanos in the North. It is often used by Zacatecanos born in the United States who are interested in visiting or learning more about Jerez.

7. In all diasporas, a small core has an influence greater than its numbers for representing the diaspora to others and creating a sense of diaspora among potential diasporans (Tölölyan 1996).

8. In addition to the board of directors of each city's Colonia, there is a president of the Colonia for the entire United States. The current general president is the president of the Los Angeles Colonia, though in past years the general president has been the president of the Colonia in Santa Ana or Merced.

9. Another organization of Sahuayans in Santa Ana is moribund as well. For six years during the 1980s, the Club Sahuayense sponsored an annual marathon in Sahuayo. It gave out prizes and T-shirts and attracted runners from all over the republic. When the California economy declined in the late 1980s, the Club was disbanded.

10. Earlier in his clerical career, the priest went north (without legal papers or permission from Church authorities) for a month-long vacation in which he saved up money for a car by washing dishes at a Los Angeles restaurant during the week and officiating mass at a local church on the weekends.

11. "Up with Sahuayo!"

References

Austin, J. L. 1975. *How to Do Things with Words*, edited by J.O. Urmson and Marina Sbisa. Oxford: Clarendon.

Basch, Linda, Nina Glick Schiller, and Cristina Szanton Blanc. 1994. *Nations Unbound: Transnational Projects, Postcolonial Predicaments and Deterritorialized Nation-States*. Langhorne, Penn.: Gordon and Breach.

Binational Study on Migration between Mexico and the United States. 1997. Commission on Immigration Reform, U.S.A./Secretaría de Relaciones Exteriores, Mexico. Mexico City: Regina de los Ángeles.

Castañeda, Jorge. 1993. "Mexico and California: The Paradox of Tolerance and Dedemocratization." In *The California-Mexico Connection*, edited by Abraham Lowenthal and Katrina Burgess. Stanford, Calif.: Stanford University Press.

Cornelius, Wayne A. 1998. "Ejido Reform: Stimulus or Alternative to Migration?" In *The Transformation of Rural Mexico: Reforming the Ejido Sector*, edited by Wayne A. Cornelius and David Myhre. La Jolla: Center for U.S.-Mexican Studies, University of California, San Diego.

Durand, Jorge. 1994. *Más allá de la línea: patrones migratorios entre México y Estados Unidos.* Mexico City: Consejo Nacional para la Cultura y las Artes.

Espinosa, Victor. 1999. "La Federación de Clubes Michoacanos en Illinois: construyendo puentes entre Chicago y Michoacán." Chicago: Heartland Alliance for Human Needs and Human Rights.

Forbes Adams, Victoria. 1994. "Profit and Tradition in Rural Manufacture: Sandal Production in Sahuayo, Michoacán, Mexico." Ph.D. dissertation. University College, London.

Glick Schiller, Nina, Linda Basch, and Cristina Szanton Blanc, eds. 1992. *Towards a Transnational Perspective on Migration: Race, Class, Ethnicity and Nationalism Reconsidered.* New York: New York Academy of Sciences.

Godines, Valeria. 1999. "O.C. Catholic Churches Look to Mexico to Help Supply Priests," *Orange County Register*, August 31.

González, Luis. 1979. *Sahuayo.* Monografías Municipales del Estado de Michoacán. Morelia: Gobierno del Estado de Michoacán.

González Gutiérrez, Carlos. 1995. "La organización de los inmigrantes mexicanos en Los Angeles: la lealtad de los oriundos," *Revista Mexicana de Política Exterior* 46: 59–101.

Hernandez Madrid, Miguel J. 1999. "Iglesias sin fronteras. Migrantes y conversos religiosos: cambios de identidad cultural en el noroeste de Michoacán." In *Fronteras fragmentadas,* edited by Gail Mummert. Zamora: El Colegio de Michoacán.

Hispanic Databook of U.S. Cities and Counties. 1994. Milpitas, Calif.: Toucan Valley Publications.

Levitt, Peggy. 2000. "Two Nations Under God? Latino Religious Life in the U.S." Typescript.

Massey, Douglas, Rafael Alarcón, Jorge Durand, and Humberto González. 1987. *Return to Atzlán: The Social Process of International Migration from Western Mexico.* Berkeley: University of California Press.

Massey, Douglas, Luin Goldring, and Jorge Durand. 1994. "Continuities in Transnational Migration: An Analysis of Nineteen Mexican Communities," *American Journal of Sociology* 99 (6): 1492–1533.

Ochoa Serrano, Álvaro. 1998. *Viajes de michoacanos al norte.* Zamora: El Colegio de Michoacán.

_____. 1999. *Jiquilpan-Huanimban: una historia confinada.* Morelia: Morevallado.

Plan de Desarrollo Municipal: Sahuayo 1999–2001. 1999. Sahuayo, Michoacán: H. Ayuntamiento Constitucional.

Portes, Alejandro. 1999. "Conclusion: Towards a New World: The Origins and Effects of Transnational Activities," *Ethnic and Racial Studies* 22 (2): 462–77.

Rouse, Roger. 1992. "Making Sense of Settlement: Class Transformation, Cultural Struggle, and Transnationalism among Mexican Migrants in the United States." In *Towards a Transnational Perspective on Migration: Race, Class, Ethnicity and Nationalism Reconsidered,* edited by Nina Glick Schiller, Linda Basch, and Cristina Szanton Blanc. New York: New York Academy of Sciences.

Smith, Robert Courtney. 1995. "Los Ausentes Siempre Presentes: The Imagining, Making and Politics of a Transnational Migrant Community between Ticuani, Puebla, Mexico and New York City." Ph.D. dissertation, Columbia University.

Sontag, Deborah, and Celia W. Dugger. 1998. "The New Immigrant Tide: A Shuttle between Worlds," *New York Times,* July 19.

Tölöyan, Khachig. 1996. "Rethinking Diaspora(s): Stateless Power in the Transnational Moment," *Diaspora* 5 (1): 3–35.

Vargas González, Pablo. 1993. *Lealtades de la sumisión. Caciquismo: poder local y regional en la Ciénega de Chapala, Michoacán.* Zamora: El Colegio de Michoacán.

Zabin, Carol, and Luis Escala Rabadán. 1998. "Mexican Hometown Associations and Mexican Immigrant Political Empowerment in Los Angeles." Nonprofit Sector Research Fund Working Paper Series. Washington, D.C.: Aspen Institute.

Zepeda Patterson, Jorge. 1989. "Sahuayo y Jiquilpan: génesis de la rivalidad por una región 1880–1930." In *Estudios Michoacanos III,* edited by Sergio Zendejas. Zamora: El Colegio de Michoacán.

_____. 1990. *Michoacán: sociedad, economía, política y cultura.* Mexico City: Universidad Nacional Autónoma de México.

5

Migration from Lesotho, Mozambique, and Zimbabwe to South Africa

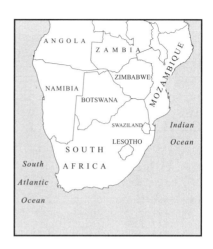

David A. McDonald, Lovemore Zinyama, John Gay, Fion de Vletter, and Robert Mattes

When a country receives large numbers of documented and undocumented immigrants, negative stereotypes often develop. Immigrants are viewed as arriving in hordes, bringing crime and disease and threatening the social and economic stability of the host nation. Some of these issues were alluded to in the previous selection on Sahuayo. This chapter examines many of these perceptions through thousands of interviews with residents of Mozambique, Lesotho, and Zimbabwe, the countries that send most of the migrants to South Africa.

David A. McDonald, a political scientist, is in the Geography Department at Queen's University, Kingston, Canada; Lovemore Zinyama is a professor in the Department of Geography at the University of Zimbabwe, Harare; John Gay is with Sechaba Consultants, an indigenous Lesotho consulting company with experience in the socioeconomic, rural development, and natural resources management fields. Fion de Vletter, a private consultant working for international organizations and an expert on microfinance programs, was formerly a professor at the Department of Economics, University of

From David A. McDonald, Lovemore Zinyama, John Gay, Fion de Vletter, and Robert Mattes, "Guess Who's Coming to Dinner: Migration from Lesotho, Mozambique and Zimbabwe to South Africa," *International Migration Review* 34, no. 3 (Fall 2000): 813–41. Tables omitted. Reprinted by permission of Center for Migration Studies of New York Inc.

Swaziland. Robert Mattes is associate professor of political studies and director of the Democracy in Africa Research Unit, Centre for Social Studies, University of Cape Town. He is also an associate with the Institute for Democracy in South Africa (Idasa) as well as a co-founder and co-director of the Afrobarometer, a regular survey of Africans' attitudes toward democracy, markets, and civil society.

Cross-border migration in Southern Africa has a long and complex history. Originating with the need for large pools of cheap labor for the mines and farms of South Africa in the late nineteenth century, hundreds of thousands of contract workers from as far away as Malawi—but predominantly from Lesotho and Mozambique—have been recruited to work in South Africa as mining and agricultural laborers. Although some changes have been made to this contract migrant labor system over the years, there is little sign of it changing dramatically in the foreseeable future. In fact, recent trends have shown an increase in the percent of the mining workforce that is from outside of South Africa—largely as a result of increasing retrenchments of South African nationals.[1]

By far, the most significant change in cross-border migration in South Africa in the 1990s has been the dramatic increase in noncontract migration. Africans from other parts of the continent—mostly from the region but now from as far away as Ghana and Somalia—are entering South Africa in increasing numbers to look for work, to visit friends, to sell and buy goods, and so on. Documented border crossings from countries in the Southern African Development Community (SADC) alone have increased almost seven-fold to over 3 million visitors a year since 1990, and there are also significant increases in the number of visitors from Eastern Europe and Asia.

Undocumented migration would appear to have increased dramatically as well. Estimates range from 2.5 to 12 million undocumented migrants living in the country at any one time (out of a total South African population of approximately 38 million people), and although these figures are most likely grossly exaggerated there can be little doubt that there has been a significant increase in the number of people overstaying their visas and entering the country without proper documentation (Crush, 1997).

In response to these changes in cross-border migration activity, and as part of the broader legislative changes taking place in post-apartheid South Africa, immigration policy is in the process of being redrafted in the country. The release of a "White Paper on International Migration" in April of 1999 followed by a migration Bill by the South African Department of Home Affairs mark a radical departure from the current, apartheid-era Aliens Control Act. As the name implies, the current immigration act is styled in the tradition of control-and-expulsion and is a legacy of South Africa's reliance on short-term, contract labor from the region. When needed, labor could be re-

The South Africa-Mozambique border with barbed wire and an electric fence to deter unauthorized crossings, 1999. *Photograph by Paul Ganster*

cruited; when not, it could be expelled. The Bill and White Paper are a first attempt at making South Africa's immigration policy more consistent with the country's human rights legislation as well as recognizing South Africa's important role in the regional labor market (RSA, 1999). A White Paper on refugees was released in July 1998 (RSA, 1998).

Needless to say, this policy reform process has not been without contro-versy. Immigration issues have been hotly contested in policy circles and in the popular press, and public sentiment towards foreigners of African origin has a decidedly negative streak in South Africa. Although not as negative or as widespread as one would be led to believe by reports in the popular press, anti-immigrant sentiment is, nevertheless, a real concern (Mattes et al., 1999). Physical attacks on foreign street vendors in Johannesburg by South African traders, xenophobic press coverage, and prejudiced comments by senior poli-ticians about the "flood of illegal aliens" into the country are indicative of the kind of rhetoric that permeates the public debate on foreigners of African origin living in South Africa (Peberdy and Crush, 1998). There is also a large cadre of apartheid-era civil servants still working within the Department of Home Affairs (the ministry responsible for immigration issues in South Af-rica) and as border officials. Not surprisingly, these bureaucrats often have very conservative and racist views of people from other African countries and represent a major obstacle to more democratic modes of immigration governance.

This is, therefore, a crucial and sensitive time in the development of immigration policy in South Africa, and it is essential that policymakers, academics and the general public have as much reliable information on the causes and consequences of cross-border migration as possible. In an attempt to help fill this informational gap, the Southern African Migration Project (SAMP) has been conducting research on a wide range of cross-border mi-gration activities in the region.[2] This current article summarizes key findings from national surveys conducted in Lesotho, Mozambique and Zimbabwe. The surveys were designed to gauge people's experiences with, and attitudes towards, migration to South Africa and are the most comprehensive and meth-odologically rigorous surveys conducted on issues of cross-border migration in the region to date. The same surveys have been conducted in Namibia and Botswana but were not available at the time of writing.

The article begins with a brief discussion of research methodology to allow the reader to better assess the credibility of the data and its significance in comparison to related research. In light of some rather questionable research methodologies employed recently in South Africa on issues of un-documented migration, it is all the more important to define our method-ological framework.

We then present the research data in three sections. The first section provides an overview of the migration histories of the sample population in an attempt to give readers a better sense of the quantitative and qualitative nature of out-migration from these three countries. The second section high-lights peoples' attitudes to migration and immigration policy and discusses how these attitudes are shaped by their perspectives of South Africa and of their home country. And finally, we look at the significance of these findings for future cross-border migration trends. The article concludes with a discussion of the policy relevance of the research and makes some general policy recommendations.

Methodology

The first point to make about research methodology is that the surveys represent a coordinated effort across the three countries surveyed and the data is entirely compatible. Beginning with a planning workshop in Harare, Zimbabwe, in October of 1996, and continuing through every stage of design work, sample selection, data input and report writing, the principal researchers worked together and were in constant contact with one another.

It should also be noted that these surveys are only one part of a larger public opinion survey cluster which included interviews with 3,500 South African citizens about their attitudes towards immigrants and immigration policy, as well as 500 interviews with migrants currently living in South Africa.[3] These additional surveys were coordinated by the same research team and correspond with the questionnaire and methodologies used in the research being reported here. The results of all of these surveys can be found in McDonald (2000).

For reasons of space, the current article deals strictly with the interviews conducted in Lesotho, Mozambique and Zimbabwe. In this respect, we do not purport to present the "full picture" of attitudes and practices with respect to cross-border migration in Southern Africa. What we will discuss here are interviews with people who are currently living in their home country and who may or may not have been to South Africa. It is important, therefore, to note that this gives us a somewhat biased sample insofar as it does not include residents from the three countries who are currently living in South Africa. It can be said, however, that results from the 500 surveys with migrants who are living in South Africa are remarkably similar to the results presented in this article. In fact, the only notable exception is that foreign nationals living in South Africa are slightly more likely to say that they want to stay in South Africa on a permanent basis. These caveats notwithstanding, the surveys provide us with a reliable and representative sample of the in-house populations of the three countries in question and offer some invaluable insights into people's attitudes towards, and experiences with, cross-border migration in the region.

The reasons for choosing Lesotho, Mozambique and Zimbabwe are twofold. First, these are by far the largest source countries in terms of documented migration into South Africa and by all accounts would appear to be the three largest source countries of undocumented migration as well. Second, popular perception in South Africa is such that these are the largest and most problematic source countries for migrants—Mozambique in particular

—and perception is just as important as reality when dealing with public policy. It should also be noted that the interviews in Mozambique only covered the southern half of the country—in part because this is where the overwhelming majority of Mozambican migrants originate, and in part because of the logistical challenges of including the northern half of the country (the population of the provinces covered is approximately 6.5 million).

The surveys themselves consisted of a lengthy questionnaire of approximately 200 questions ranging from basic demographics to people's attitudes to immigration policy and their migration plans for the future. Given the volume of interviews, Likert and scaled questions as well as pre-defined response options were the only feasible options for data analysis and comparability across countries. This form of closed-option responses limited the scope and depth of answers that interviewees could provide, but this is a trade-off that had to be made in order to capture nationally representative samples. The wide range of questions that were asked and the complex layering of issues also helped to offset the shortfalls in this quantitative method and in the end provided an extraordinarily rich set of data.

In total, 2,300 interviews were completed—692 in Lesotho, 661 in Mozambique and 947 in Zimbabwe—over a four-month period beginning in February 1997. Fifty-six percent of the interviewees were men and 44 percent were women,[4] with the minimum age for interviewees set at 15 years.

Sample lists were initially compiled using census data and/or aerial maps (depending on what was most available and reliable) to form a list of enumerated areas. In Zimbabwe, equally weighted enumerated areas were randomly selected within various desired substrata (e.g., the proper portion taken from a list of urban and rural enumerated areas). In Lesotho and Mozambique, the census data was used to weight the probability of drawing an interview point (from which five interviews were done) from given geographic areas (using the smallest geographic unit for which we had reliable data). Once this random list was drawn, interviewers would go to every *nth* dwelling in a given direction starting at a certain point. A card selection procedure was then used to select household members. Some sampling points in particularly remote or dangerous areas were substituted with a point chosen from a geographic unit taken from a second, randomly selected list.

This random selection procedure was, in and of itself, an enormous undertaking given the dearth of reliable census material in some areas and the logistics of sending researchers to remote parts of each country, and we cannot overemphasize the effort that was made to ensure that sample selection was as representative and random as possible given the circumstances. Random field visits by the principal researchers in each country served to further ensure that these procedures were being followed by field staff. The same kind of detailed and coordinated planning also applied to translations (and back-translations) of questionnaires, training of researchers, pilot tests, and data input procedures.

It is impossible to present all the data from the research in a single paper. What follows is a summary of the key findings with an emphasis of the important similarities and differences between the three countries and between different demographic variables. The data also allows us to debunk some of the negative stereotypes around cross-border migration into South Africa from the three countries concerned and to "de-demonize" the migrants themselves.

Past Experiences with Cross-Border Migration

As noted earlier, there is a long history of movement from Lesotho, Mozambique and Zimbabwe into South Africa, and this history shows up clearly in the interviews. Fifty percent of respondents have parents who have visited or worked in South Africa and 34 percent have grandparents who have done the same. But more important to our discussion here is the number of residents in the countries surveyed who have themselves been to South Africa, who they are, their reasons for going, how often they go, and what methods of entry they use. We look at each of these questions below.

Profile of Visitors to South Africa

Clearly, cross-border movement into South Africa remains a widespread phenomenon from all three countries, with 42 percent of respondents saying that they have visited South Africa at least once in their lives.[3] There are significant variations, however, in both the scale and make-up of visitors from the different countries. In Lesotho, fully 81 percent of the population has visited South Africa, while the figures for Mozambique and Zimbabwe are only 29 percent and 23 percent, respectively. Of these totals, there are also variations in terms of gender and socioeconomic indicators. First, women make up a much larger part of the mobile population in Lesotho and Zimbabwe than they do in Mozambique. In the case of Zimbabwe, this reflects the large number of women traveling to South Africa to buy and sell goods, while in Lesotho it is more of a reflection of the number of women traveling to South Africa to visit relatives, go for medical care and go to work. Second, the overwhelming number of people crossing the border from Zimbabwe are from urban areas, while the majority of those from Mozambique are from rural areas. This difference may also account for the fact that average education levels of Zimbabweans who have been to South Africa are slightly higher than those for the other two countries.

There are also a number of important similarities between the three countries. Of particular interest is the type of people who have visited South

Africa. Far from being the kind of rootless drifters that they are often portrayed to be in the South African media, the majority of visitors from the
countries surveyed would appear to be well-established, family-oriented citizens. Almost three quarters of those who have visited South Africa are married, over half are heads of household, over 80 percent own their own homes,
over half have annual incomes per household member of at least R1200 (this
is slightly higher than the sample as a whole), almost half have full- or part-
time work, and at least one third have a minimum of some high school education—hardly the stuff of desperate, uneducated criminals threatening South
African society.

Frequency of Visits to South Africa

The surveys also illustrate the short-term and temporary nature of these respondents' visits to South Africa. This temporality is particularly pronounced
in Lesotho, where respondents have been to the country an average of 68
times in their lives—with some people having been to South Africa hundreds
of times. These figures are significantly lower for Mozambique and Zimbabwe (with averages of 5 and 6 visits, respectively), but there is clearly a regular and quite frequent cross-border movement from these countries as well.

   Moreover, the length of each visit is quite short, with 60 percent of respondents staying in South Africa for less than a month at a time. There are
important variations here, however, with people from Lesotho staying the
shortest amount of time and people from Mozambique staying the longest.

Reasons for Going to South Africa

Not surprisingly, a large portion of those respondents who have been to South
Africa in the past cited work, or looking for work, as the reason for their last
trip to the country. But work is not the only reason people go to South Africa.
Shopping, visiting friends and relatives, taking holidays, receiving medical
treatment, and an assortment of other, non-job related activities constitute a
majority of the cross-border traffic. There are important differences between
the three countries, once again, with Mozambicans citing work (or looking
for work) and Zimbabweans citing "buying and trading goods" as the most
common reasons for last being in South Africa, but for all three countries
there is a significant amount of non-work related activity.

   More important, perhaps, is the fact that for an overwhelming majority
of respondents there was both a freedom of choice and a desire to return to
their home countries. Contrary to popular opinion in South Africa, most visitors from Lesotho, Mozambique and Zimbabwe return home of their own
free will when their planned visit is over. And, with the notable exception of
Mozambique, very few of the respondents were deported from the country.

The figures do not capture the residents of these countries who have decided to stay in South Africa, of course, but the survey results do suggest that much of the cross-border activity from Lesotho, Mozambique and Zimbabwe is highly circular and that a large percentage of the residents from these countries who do visit South Africa do so for non-work related purposes.

It is important, therefore, to distinguish between short-term, purpose-oriented migration that happens on a regular basis and long-term or permanent immigration. Even the term "migration" is somewhat misleading here given that much of this cross-border movement is for very short-term trips to shop, visit friends or go to doctors, in which case "visitors" or "tourists" would be a more apt description. Nomenclature aside, the important point to keep in mind here is that people from the countries surveyed are not only going to South Africa to work or look for work and most return home of their own free will.

Methods of Entry into South Africa

Of equal interest to the current debates on cross-border migration in the region is the question of how people enter South Africa. As the following quote attests to, there is a popular image in South Africa that most cross-border migration from neighboring countries is clandestine:

> Various methods are used by illegals to enter South Africa. The most common is simply to cross the border clandestinely. In the case of Mozambican and Zimbabwean borders this may be difficult where there are border fences (some electrified) and other obstacles to cross first—not to mention crocodiles in the rivers that need to be swum, the lions in the game reserves and even land mines (Minaar and Hough, 1996:134).

Electric fences, crocodiles and lions are seen by many to be South Africa's only hope for keeping out the ravenous hordes, with the Minister of Defense even threatening at one point to turn the fence on the Mozambican border up to "lethal mode" if clandestine border crossings were not significantly reduced. There is also a perception in South Africa that border officials are irretrievably corrupt and that noncitizens gain entry into the country en masse with false passports, bribes and other forms of corruption (see, e.g., Minaar and Hough, 1996:153–9).

There can be no doubt that clandestine border crossings occur in South Africa on a regular basis and that corruption exists within the immigration system—no country is immune to this. The question that needs to be asked is "How serious are these problems?" Our findings in Lesotho, Mozambique and Zimbabwe (as well as preliminary results from the surveys in Namibia and Botswana) would suggest that "illegal" cross-border movement is relatively minor and that the general picture is one of a highly organized and regularized movement of people. As a case in point, of the 971 respondents who said that they had been to South Africa in the past, 49 percent crossed the border on their last visit by car or minibus, 22 percent by bus, 14 percent by train, and 4 percent by plane or other formal modes of transportation. Of the remaining 8 percent that crossed the border "on foot," many of these people took a bus or minibus to the border, went through immigration on foot, and then took another bus or minibus to their destination in South Africa—a particularly common phenomenon at the Zimbabwean border posts. In other words, there are relatively few people sneaking into the country under fences or swimming across rivers.

Moreover, 89 percent of these respondents had official passports from their home countries before entering South Africa, and 72 percent had the appropriate South African visas. Admittedly, this means that a significant number of people crossed the border without proper documentation on their last visit, but the figures are not nearly as high as one would suspect from anecdotal reports in the press in South Africa.

It is worth noting that the majority of respondents without proper visas were from Zimbabwe, due in part to the fact that it is so difficult and time consuming to get visas for South Africa in that country. At the time this research was conducted, there were only two places in Zimbabwe to get a South African visa (Harare and Bulawayo) and these two offices had to process up to 30,000 visas a month (personal interview with Mr. JNK Mamabolo, South African High Commissioner, Nov. 19, 1996). For those who made the trek to these two locations (a rather expensive and time consuming task for those in rural areas—especially those in the southern part of the country who have to travel north before traveling south again to South Africa), queues at the visa offices begin well before dawn each day. The fact that so many Zimbabweans make the effort to get the proper visas—despite all the costs and obstacles involved—serves to reinforce the argument that clandestine border crossings are very much the exception rather than the rule.

This image of the "law-abiding citizen" is also apparent in people's perceptions of the South African border (including those who have never been to South Africa). When interviewees were asked a series of questions about whether they would know how to get across the border and stay in South Africa without the proper travel documents if they had to, over three quarters said they "did not know about this and do not know how to find out about it." Only 10 percent of respondents said they "know about this," with another 12 percent saying they "do not know about this but could [or might be able to] find out about it" if they tried.

When asked how concerned they would be about getting caught by the police and sent home if they went to South Africa without the proper travel documents, there was a similar level of concern among the respondents—

suggesting once again that people from the countries surveyed take borders seriously and are not wantonly violating immigration rules and regulations. There are differences between the countries, with people from Lesotho being most concerned about border regulations, but the differences are really a matter of degree with citizens in all of the countries surveyed clearly wanting to operate within the bounds of the law.

It must be stressed, once again, that these interviews cover only a few key countries and that "illegal" border activities take place with nationals from other parts of Africa, Asia, North America and Europe (in fact, some of the worst visa offenders are from Europe and North America, with 10,910 Germans, 12,593 Britons and 3,149 Americans overstaying their visas in the first four months of 1996 alone (Crush, 1997:19). Nor do we know for sure exactly how many undocumented migrants are currently in South Africa and what their methods of entry were. What the data do suggest is that we need to reassess the popular perception that most Africans from other countries enter South Africa illegally and/or overstay their visas.

Attitudes towards Migration to South Africa

We next explore people's attitudes towards South Africa and their home countries, and towards cross-border migration in the region in general. These opinion-based questions allow us to better assess the rationale for migrating (or not migrating) to South Africa from the countries in question and to gauge the potential for people to migrate in the future. The findings also allow us to compare the actual attitudes of people from the region to the commonly held stereotypes of these attitudes in South Africa.

Comparing South Africa to the Home Country

Immigrant-receiving countries like South Africa often develop a very distorted view of migration. People are coming to their country for what they believe to be clear and obvious reasons: for economic opportunity and for a better quality of life. Residents of the receiving country assume that everyone in the world would want to come to their country, first because the large number of newcomers reinforces that impression, and second because residents of receiving nations, like anyone else, are proud of their country and biased in their beliefs about its virtues: Wouldn't everyone want to live here?

Not surprisingly, then, South Africans have the impression that residents of neighboring countries are all anxious to leave their homes and come to South Africa. It is assumed that Africans from other countries are either pulled to South Africa by the country's superior social, economic and political climate, or pushed from their home countries by poverty, chaos and a lack of opportunity. The perception that South African borders are relatively porous adds to the belief that the country is the destination of choice for the continent as a whole.

The results from our surveys present a much more complex picture. When asked to compare their home countries with South Africa, the majority of those interviewed identified their home countries as a better place to raise a family, with access to basic resources like land, water, and housing seen to be much better than in South Africa. Levels of crime and safety were also seen to be better at home, and even South Africa's much-vaunted democratic reforms would appear to carry little weight with people in the countries surveyed, with over two-thirds of respondents saying that they find "peace," "freedom" and "democracy" to be as good, or better, in their home countries as in South Africa.

Not surprisingly, job opportunities were deemed far better in South Africa than at home, as were opportunities for buying and selling goods, but this perception of job opportunities does not necessarily translate into a flood of migration. As we shall see, only a small percentage of those interviewed said it was likely that they would go to live in South Africa for even a short period of time. In other words, not everyone in the countries surveyed wants to move to South Africa just because job opportunities are better, suggesting that the actual number of people wanting to settle in South Africa is much lower than one would be led to believe by the popular press.

There are two other revealing points about people's attitudes towards their home countries that should be highlighted here. First, it is clear that the overwhelming majority of respondents are proud of their home countries. No less than 95 percent of respondents said that they "agree" or "strongly agree" when asked if they are "proud to be called a citizen of [their home country]," and 92 percent responded in this way when asked if "being a citizen of [their home country] is a very important part of how [they see themselves]." Second, although respondents were more circumspect when asked whether they approve of the way their government has performed over the past year and whether or not they can trust their governments "to do what is right," the approval ratings are still reasonably high (47% and 40%, respectively). Moreover, disapproval of the government should not necessarily be seen as a sign of being "unpatriotic" or desiring to emigrate.

Nevertheless, jobs and social services like health care and education are perceived to be better in South Africa and would appear to be an important part of what pulls people to South Africa from the three countries surveyed. But the would-be push factors tell a different story, bringing into doubt the explanatory value of any simple push/pull model of cross-border migration in the region. The pull factors are counterbalanced by a very strong set of factors that would work to keep someone at home (or at least push them out).

Perceived Impacts of Migration

We were also interested in knowing people's perceptions of the impacts of migration on themselves, their families, their communities and their country. At the risk of over-simplifying a long history of scholarly research on the subject, it can be said that the bulk of the literature on cross-border migration in the region paints a very negative picture of the consequences of migratory labor and apartheid-era immigration laws. From exploitative labor practices and deferred pay systems to the transmission of AIDS and the splitting up of families, there is ample evidence to suggest that cross-border migration has served to undermine the social, cultural and economic integrity of SADC states. This is not to suggest that all cross-border movement has been seen to be negative or that it affects all people in the same way, but the overwhelming sense from the literature is that cross-border movement has had a deleterious impact on individuals, families, communities and states in the region (see, eg., Bundy, 1979; Lacey, 1981; Murray, 1981; First, 1983; Packard, 1989; Crush et al., 1992).

Given the scholarly evidence, one would assume that our interviews would also be full of negative attitudes towards migration. And yet, we received an overwhelmingly positive response from interviewees when they were asked about the impact of migration. Important variations between the three countries notwithstanding, over half the people interviewed see cross-border migration as having a positive (or at least neutral) impact on them personally, on their families, on their communities and on their countries as a whole. Interestingly, the most positive responses came at the personal and family level, where a majority see the impact as positive.

Even more surprising is that women also have a largely positive outlook on migration—despite the enormous impact that the migrant labor system has had on family life and relationships in these countries in the past. Even on a personal level, 14 percent of the women interviewed said cross-border migration has had a "very positive" impact on them personally, 39 percent said "positive," and 27 percent said "no impact." These responses are balanced somewhat by the fact that 26 percent of women (and 23% of men) identified "having an affair" or "having a second family" in South Africa as one of their three main concerns about a family member going to work or staying in South Africa, but the fact remains that a majority of women gave positive responses. Despite the many negative impacts that cross-border migration has had in the region, people also see benefits for themselves, their families, their communities and their countries. The fact that people say they like something does not necessarily mean it is in their best interest to be doing it, but it is important not to represent individuals in Southern Africa as mere "victims" of a migratory system.

Immigration Policy Preferences

We have already discussed the myth that everyone in the region wants to live in South Africa. Equally problematic, however, is the popular stereotype in South Africa that everyone in the region expects the South African government to throw open its borders to migrants. The South African press is full of articles which imply—directly or indirectly—that South Africa must "hold the line" on border controls and not fall prey to the entry demands of other SADC states. The rather vitriolic reaction of the South African media, as well as some policymakers and academics, to the 1996 SADC proposal (SADC, 1996) to gradually phase in a "freer movement" of peoples in the region illustrates this fear and has heightened suspicions that there is a concerted effort to undermine South Africa's border controls on the part of neighboring states.

Once again, our data challenges these stereotypes. Although citizens of Lesotho, Mozambique and Zimbabwe would like to see a relaxation of border regulations and consider it a "basic human right" to be able to move from one country to another, they do not expect the South African government to abandon border controls altogether. Most people would like to see policies in place which make it easier to move from one country to another, and many question the legitimacy of borders that were created during the colonial era, but respondents do not advocate a radical dismantling of current border systems.

Approximately one-third of respondents disagree with the suggestion that people should be able to move "freely" across borders and over half feel that borders are an important part of defining who they are. Even more important is the fact that a majority of respondents feel that the South African government should be able to restrict the number of (im)migrants allowed into the country and that they should also have the right to deport people who are there "illegally," are "not contributing to the well-being of the country," or have "committed serious criminal offences." Respondents would like to see the South African government define these restrictions and categories in a humane and rational manner, but do not reject the idea of selective (im)migration and do not expect the government of South Africa to grant amnesty to every non-South African currently living in the country. Nor do the majority expect preferential or privileged treatment for people from their own countries—despite their history of cross-border relations and proximity to South Africa.

It must be noted, however, that there are significant differences in attitudes towards borders between Lesotho and the other two countries surveyed and that Lesotho is, in many ways, a "special case." This difference is perhaps best illustrated by the fact that 41 percent of Basotho said that Lesotho and South Africa should simply join as one country (as opposed to 7% and 9% of Mozambicans and Zimbabweans, respectively). The reasons for this are no doubt rooted in the exceptionally high number of contract workers from Lesotho (by far the largest of all the SADC states) as well as the close cultural, linguistic and familial ties between Basotho and a large section of the South African population (i.e., Sotho and Tswana speakers). The fact that Lesotho is completely surrounded by South Africa also contributes to the image of Lesotho as more of a province of South Africa than an independent state.

Another interesting finding is that respondents do not necessarily expect to have all the same rights and privileges as South African citizens. Although the majority of respondents feel that noncitizens should have the same access to jobs and basic resources like education, medical services and housing as South African citizens, they were much more hesitant when it came to questions of a more political nature: the right to vote; the right to become a permanent resident or a citizen of the country; and the right to request amnesty for nonnationals. In other words, people from the countries interviewed want the same basic human rights and the same economic opportunities as South African citizens, but they do not necessarily expect (or want) the political rights of citizenship—with the notable exception, once again, of Basotho.

It is also interesting to note that these attitudes to immigration policy are largely reciprocal. To the extent that respondents would like to see South Africa relax its immigration laws, people from Lesotho, Mozambique and Zimbabwe are also willing to allow a freer movement of people and goods from South Africa into their own country (with the exception, in Lesotho and Zimbabwe, of a reluctance to make land available to foreigners for farming no doubt due to the critical shortage of arable land in both countries. The fact that Mozambicans were significantly more agreeable on this point may, in turn, be due to the fact there is a considerable amount of arable land still available in that country).

Far from expecting the South African government to throw open its doors to whoever wants to enter, a majority of people in the region have a strong respect for the sanctity of borders. Even in Lesotho—where independence of the nation is itself in question—there is a pragmatic and selective approach to questions of sovereignty, immigration and border controls with South Africa.

The Attitudes of Women

A full discussion of the gender dimensions of the research is beyond the scope of this article but it is worth noting that women's attitudes to migration and their perspectives on life in South Africa are remarkably similar overall to the men interviewed (for a more detailed analysis, see Dodson, 2000). Almost to a percentage point, women gave the same responses as men on virtually every opinion-based question in the survey. Their perceptions of South Africa, their reasons for going to South Africa (or for not going), their expected treatment by South African authorities and citizens, and their comparisons of South Africa with their home country were almost identical to that of the men interviewed. And although women were slightly less knowledgeable and slightly less sure of themselves in terms of their ability to get into South Africa and to find accommodation and work if they so desired, the differences were not enormous. Women outlined a similar pattern of family and friend networks in South Africa as did men, and they expressed a similar understanding (or lack thereof) of how one lives as a foreigner in South Africa. In other words, women have the same general perceptions of South Africa vis-à-vis their own countries, and they have a very similar sense of what it takes to be a migrant in the Southern African context.

Interestingly, these similarities exist despite the very different first-hand experiences that men and women have with respect to migration to South Africa. As might be expected, more men have been to South Africa than women, men tend to stay for longer periods of time, and men tend to work in more formal, pre-arranged occupations than women (e.g., mining, manufacturing). More men claimed to be the "head of the household" than did women (57% versus 18%), more men claimed to be the person who "makes the final decision as to whether to go to South Africa or not" (57% versus 29%), and more men claimed that they "would be able to go to South Africa if [they] wanted to" (76% versus 61%). The questionnaire did not, unfortunately, capture the dynamics of joint decision making between men and women—often an important part of the decision-making process in African households—but the statistics clearly imply that men are more in control of decision making about cross-border migration than women. Nevertheless, the data do raise some counter-intuitive questions about women's attitudes to cross-border migration and would appear to challenge the notion that women necessarily see migration in a negative light.

What Does the Future Hold?

It is impossible to say for sure what the future of migration from Lesotho, Mozambique and Zimbabwe to South Africa looks like given the uncertainties around the broader political and economic context within which cross-border migration will take place. What can be discussed is people's propensity to migrate or immigrate to South Africa based on their stated intentions in the interviews. Although by no means a foolproof measure of future migratory patterns, we can nevertheless make some defensible comments on likely migration trends in the region—trends which once again challenge the stereotypes of gloom and doom.

We have already discussed the fact that not everyone in the region wants to live in, or even visit, South Africa. The popular notion that South Africa is an island of tranquility and prosperity in a sea of grief and poverty does not bear itself out in the minds of the majority of respondents—that much is clear. There are concerns about safety in South Africa and finding affordable housing and jobs, and there are concerns about leaving family and assets at home. Unless these underlying concerns change dramatically over the next several years, one can expect people's opinions about migrating to South Africa to remain much the same.[6]

There were also questions in the survey which asked people directly about their "desire" to go to South Africa (for a short and long period of time) and the "likelihood" of their going to South Africa in the future. It is apparent from the responses to these questions that the majority of respondents are not interested in living in South Africa—at least not for an extended period of time. When asked "to what extent do you want to leave [your home country] to live in South Africa permanently," two-thirds of respondents said "not at all" and another 12 percent said "not much." Only 13 percent said that they wanted to leave their home countries "to a great extent" (despite the fact that 69% of respondents said they would be able to go to South Africa if they wanted to). When asked how "likely" it was that they would go to live in South Africa permanently, only 6 percent of respondents said "very likely."

Responses were slightly more positive when people were asked if they would like to go and live in South Africa for a "short period of time (up to 2 years)," with 18 percent saying they would definitely "want" to go and 12 percent saying it was "very likely" that they would go, but 41 percent of respondents said it was "unlikely" or "very unlikely" that they would live in South Africa for even two years.

Further indication of the lack of desire to emigrate to South Africa can be found in a series of questions that were asked about how permanently people would want to stay in the country—with the number of negative responses increasing with the "degree of permanence." Not surprisingly, Basotho are more inclined than Mozambicans and Zimbabweans to say that they would like to take up permanent residence (33% versus 14% and 13%, respectively), but the overwhelming majority of Basotho do not even want permanent residence. Moreover, the percentages drop significantly as the stakes increase, with only 27 percent of Basotho saying they would like to retire in South Africa and only 17 percent saying they would like to be buried there. For Mozambique and Zimbabwe, these figures are lower yet, with only 1 percent of Mozambicans and 4 percent of Zimbabweans saying that they would like to be buried in South Africa. Clearly, "home is where the heart is" for the majority of the people interviewed.

This is not to deny the fact that a significant number of those interviewed do want to live or work in South Africa for a period of time. The point being made here is simply that the stereotype that everyone in the region wants desperately to get into the country is not borne out in the surveys and that this is unlikely to change drastically in the near future.

In the end, the decision about whether or not to migrate will not be made easily. Although economic opportunities are deemed to be much better in South Africa, the quality of life on other dimensions is less positively perceived. Indeed, there are many aspects of life that are deemed to be much better at home than in South Africa. These are not the kinds of circumstances that are associated with people leaving their homes in droves to go to South Africa, which may help to explain the fairly large discrepancies noted earlier between those who said they want to go and those who said they will go.

Policy Implications

Immigration Management

The first, and perhaps most important, conclusion to be drawn from the research is that cross-border migration into South Africa (at least from the three countries surveyed) would appear to be much less chaotic and overwhelming than has been previously thought. Both the volume of traffic and the methods of crossing the border, as well as the type of people crossing the border and their stated plans for the future, present a much more regularized, decriminalized and manageable picture of the migratory process than reports in the press and other research initiatives on undocumented migration would indicate.

The upshot of these findings is that a humane, management-oriented approach to immigration is not only a feasible option in South Africa, but there is a highly regularized migration process already in place upon which to build. To create a more onerous, control-and-expulsion oriented approach to migration at this point in time in South Africa risks forcing people underground (quite literally) and therefore eroding the good will and legal practices that currently exist as well as undermining efforts to build on this regularized movement in the future.

This is not to suggest that there should be no border controls at all. Effective border monitoring and immigration law will always be needed at some level. Nevertheless, the fact remains that South Africa is at a crossroads in its immigration policy, and it can either take the path of "fortress South Africa" or it can recognize both the need and the feasibility of managing the growing levels of cross-border migration in a humane and rational manner.

Immigration and Human Rights

Concurrent with the previous point is the need for the South African government to address human rights issues within the immigration system and to create immigration legislation that is consistent with the new Bill of Rights in the Constitution (for a more detailed discussion, see Crush, 1998). The increasing criminalization of migrants from the region lends itself to the kinds of human rights abuses that continue to plague South African security and immigration authorities—not to mention the abuses that take place on the farms and factories that employ both documented and undocumented laborers from the region—and aggravates what could be a very civil and regularized movement of people. If the profile of visitors from our surveys is any indication of the kind of person visiting South Africa from the region, there would appear to be little grounds for the paranoia and xenophobia that continues to permeate parts of the South African immigration system.

Regional Integration

As Southern Africa moves towards an era of greater integration, effective management of cross-border migration can strengthen and build on existing regional linkages. From the personal to the national, from the familial to the regional, cross-border migration is an integral part of the social, political and economic lives of people in Southern Africa.

This research has demonstrated many of these linkages, but it is perhaps at the economic level that we can draw our most concrete conclusions. As discussed earlier, the buying and selling of goods, working in South Africa, and sending remittances home are some of the core motivations for cross-border migration. Although difficult to quantify in absolute terms, these cross-border economic activities (both formal and informal) make up an important part of the national and household budgets in the three nations surveyed. In Mozambique, for example, official remittances in the form of "deferred payments" from Mozambicans working in South African mines alone make up 55 percent of the non-aid budget of the Mozambican government (Personal Communication, Mozambican Minister of Labor H. E. Guilherme Mavila, Nov. 11, 1996) and are an essential part of the household budgets of most miners' families (De Vletter, 1998). If one were to include goods brought back from South Africa, as well as other formal and informal income, the importance of cross-border movement on the economy of Mozambique would be difficult to overstate (for a discussion of informal cross-border trading, see Peberdy and Crush, 1998).

In terms of informal remittances, we found that 67 percent of the people who had worked in South Africa in the past had sent money home—an average of R321 per month (which worked out to over half the average monthly income). It is impossible to estimate an aggregate value for these remittances due to the different lengths of time that people worked in South Africa, but with close to a third of the entire national sample saying that they have worked in South Africa in the past and having sent money home, this is a significant source of revenue. We also found that 85 percent of the respondents said they would send money home if they were to work in South Africa in the future. Forty-five percent said they would send money to their parents, 26 percent said they would send money to their spouses, and 18 percent said they would send money to their children (with the final 10% divided between other family members and friends).

We are not saying anything particularly new here, of course. We are simply reinforcing the point that immigration policy must take into account not only the macro-economic linkages in the region, but also the ground level, micro-economic connections that are an essential part of building a robust regional economy. If handled properly, cross-border migration can work to the economic benefit of everyone in the region—South Africans included.

Having said this, it is also essential that policymakers understand the dynamics of these micro-economic linkages. Recent trends in South Africa towards the blaming of noncitizens for stealing jobs and competing for scarce resources are not only disturbing in terms of their implications for violence against foreign workers and residents, but also because they do not necessarily represent the realities of noncitizen participation in the South African economy. As noted earlier, research by SAMP has demonstrated that noncitizens in South Africa also create jobs and that competition for scarce resources like housing need not be a conflict-ridden process.

Migration versus Immigration

We have already noted the need to distinguish between short-term, purpose-oriented cross-border migration of the sort described by the majority of respondents in this research and long-term permanent immigration. The "White Paper on International Migration" in South Africa also makes a point of differentiating between these two forms of cross-border movement and discusses the implications of these differences on immigration policy and management at some length, and there is no need to go into further detail here. What should be noted, however, is that the empirical evidence from our research supports the need for this distinction and lends credence to the argument that managing short-term migratory flows is feasible.

Special Status for Lesotho?

The South African government has already made special concessions to noncitizens from SADC countries by granting amnesties in 1996 to foreign miners and unauthorized migrants from these countries, and by granting amnesty to certain refugees from Mozambique. As we have seen here, there is good reason for this special treatment: citizens of SADC states make up the overwhelming majority of visitors to the country (both authorized and unauthorized); there are important social and economic linkages in the region; and colonial boundaries have little to do with the geographic and ethnic realities of the subcontinent (Crush and Williams, 1999).

But what about Lesotho? With 81 percent of Basotho having visited South Africa an average of 28 times in their lives, and 41 percent of Basotho saying that the two countries should simply join under one government, there is clearly a need to at least recognize the uniqueness of Lesotho's relationship with South Africa. What this means in practical terms is beyond the scope of this article, but one can easily envision an easing of visa and passport restrictions between the two countries and perhaps an extension of certain employee benefits (e.g., pension plans) and other social welfare benefits (e.g., access to housing subsidies for homes built/purchased in South Africa).

Although a majority of Basotho (63%) disagreed with the statement that "people from Lesotho should receive special treatment" when it comes to immigration policy in South Africa (compared to 29% in Mozambique and 51% in Zimbabwe), the number of Basotho who visit South Africa, the frequency with which they visit the country, their stated desires to see an easing of border restrictions, and their stated desires for equal rights and benefits in South Africa (significantly higher, on all accounts, than Mozambique and Zimbabwe) would suggest that it is indeed time for a new—and perhaps "special"—immigration compact between South Africa and Lesotho.

Conclusion

In conclusion, the findings from these national surveys both reinforce and challenge some commonly held conceptions of cross-border migration from Lesotho, Mozambique and Zimbabwe into South Africa. The results reinforce the impression that cross-border migration is an integral part of the political, social and economic landscape of the region and that cross-border migration will continue to be an important part of regional linkages for many years to come. But the data also challenge some rather negative, and disparaging, stereotypes of cross-border migration that must be addressed by policymakers. Most importantly, migration into South Africa from the three largest source countries is not the chaotic, criminalized and overwhelming activity it is made out to be in the popular press and in much of the recent academic work on the topic in South Africa. South Africa can, and should, build on the highly regularized and legalized process of cross-border migration that is already taking place. South African immigration policymakers need to capitalize on this opportunity to manage the cross-border migration process in a humane and rational way rather than forcing people underground.

Notes

1. South African mining companies claim that they retain foreign workers because foreign workers tend to occupy skilled positions, while critics claim that foreign nationals are retained because they are less likely to be unionized and/or are less

militant in the workplace due to a fear of deportation. The reasons for this imbalance are not entirely clear, however, and more research is required to provide a detailed profile of downsizing (on this point, see Crush, 1995).

2. Detailed information on SAMP can be found on the Project website at http://www.queen su.ca/samp.

3. The survey of South African citizens was a nationally representative, random sample of adults 18 years of age and older with over-sampling in key demographic and geographic areas. The survey of (im)migrants living in South Africa posed a difficult methodological challenge given that the total sample size is unknown (and perhaps unknowable). We therefore targeted a broad cross-section of migrant communities based on anecdotal knowledge of the likely sample composition of migrants in the country and the policy significance of certain migrant groups and used trained researchers to do snowball sampling in these communities. The study is therefore not a "representative" sample, per se, but it is the most comprehensive survey of migrants conducted to date.

4. This overall bias in favor of men is largely a result of a gender imbalance in the Mozambican subsample where the male/female ratio was 61/39. Although this bias can be attributed, in part, to the fact that many Mozambican women were away from their homesteads for an extended period harvesting in the fields, it is not entirely clear why this should have produced such an imbalance.

5. With sampling error this figure could range from 38.5% to 45.5%.

6. The fact that there has not been a mass exodus, or any significant exodus at all, from Zimbabwe during the turmoil in that country since these interviews were conducted attests to the deep-seated nature of these attitudinal profiles.

References

Bundy, C. 1979. *The Rise and Fall of the South African Peasantry*. Berkeley: University of California Press.

Crush, J., A. Jeeves and D. Yudelman. 1992. *South Africa's Labor Empire: A History of Black Migrancy to the Goldmines*. Boulder: Westview Press.

Crush, J. 1997. "Covert Operations: Clandestine Migration, Temporary Work and Immigration Policy in South Africa." *SAMP Migration Policy Series*, No. 1. Cape Town: Idasa/SAMP.

Crush, J. 1995. "Mine Migrancy in the Contemporary Era." In *Crossing Boundaries: Mine Migrancy in a Democratic South Africa*. Ed. J. Crush and W. James. Cape Town: Idasa/IDRC.

Crush, J., ed. 1998. *Beyond Control: Immigration and Human Rights in a Democratic South Africa*. Cape Town: Idasa/SAMP.

Crush, J., and V. Williams. 1999. *The New South Africans?: Immigration Amnesties and Their Aftermath*. Cape Town: Idasa/SAMP.

De Vletter, F. 1998. "Sons of Mozambique: Mozambican Miners and Post-Apartheid South Africa." *SAMP Migration Policy Series*, No. 8. Cape Town: Idasa/SAMP.

Dodson, B. 2000. "Women on the Move: Gender and Cross-Border Migration to South Africa." In *On Borders: Perspectives on International Migration in Southern Africa*. Ed. D. A. McDonald. New York/Cape Town: St. Martin's Press/SAMP.

First, R. 1983. *Black Gold: The Mozambican Miner, Proletarian and Peasant.* New York: St. Martin's Press.
Lacey, M. 1981. *Working for Boroko: The Origins of a Coercive Labour System in South Africa.* Johannesburg: Ravan Press.
Mattes, R., D. M. Taylor, D.A. McDonald, A. Poore and W. Richmond. 1999. "Still Waiting for the Barbarians: SA Attitudes to Immigrants and Immigration." *SAMP Migration Policy Series*, No. 14. Cape Town: Idasa/SAMP..
McDonald, D. A., ed. 2000. *On Borders: Perspectives on International Migration in Southern Africa.* New York/Cape Town: St. Martin's Press/SAMP.
Minaar, A., and M. Hough. 1996. *Who Goes There?: Perspectives on Clandestine Migration and Illegal Aliens in Southern Africa.* Pretoria: Human Sciences Research Council.
Murray, C. 1981. *Families Divided: The Impact of Migrant Labour in Lesotho.* Cambridge: Cambridge University Press.
Packard, R. 1989. *White Plague, Black Labor: Tuberculosis and the Political Economy of Health and Disease in South Africa.* Berkeley: University of California Press.
Peberdy, S., and J. Crush. 1998. "Trading Places: Cross-border Traders and the South African Informal Economy." *SAMP Migration Policy Series*, No. 6. Cape Town: Idasa/SAMP.
RSA (Republic of South Africa). 1999. "White Paper on International Migration." Pretoria: Government Printer.
RSA. 1998. "Refugee White Paper." Pretoria: Government Printer.
RSA. 1997. "Draft Green Paper on International Migration." Pretoria: Government Printer.
SADC (Southern African Development Community). 1996. "The Draft Protocol on the Free Movement of Persons in the Southern African Development Community." Mimeo. Gaborone, March 16.
Sechaba Consultants. 1997. "Riding the Tiger: Lesotho Miners and Permanent Residence in South Africa." *SAMP Migration Policy Series*, No. 2. Cape Town: Idasa/SAMP.

6

West African Boundary Making

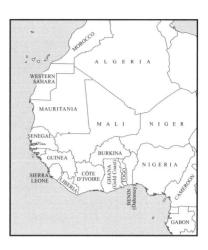

J. D. Hargreaves

Many border regions are characterized by the division of cultural groups by international boundaries. This partitioning of peoples is evident, for example, along the U.S.-Mexican border with various Native American tribes and along the Russian-Finnish border in Karelia. However, nowhere is the fraction of ethnic groups by borders more evident than in Africa. This article describes how the boundaries were created in West Africa without regard to existing human settlement patterns. By the late nineteenth century, the focus of England, France, and other European colonial powers had evolved from protecting trading rights to actual control and administration of extensive territories. But the process of drawing the new boundaries was influenced by lack of knowledge of local conditions, geography, and peoples. The result is the present network of arbitrary partitions that separate many African peoples.

John D. Hargreaves was Burnett-Fletcher Professor of History at the University of Aberdeen, Scotland. He is the author of numerous books on colonialism and West Africa.

Explanations of historical development can be broadly classified in three groups: the determinist, the conspiratorial and the accidental (or, more vulgarly, the "cock-up") theories. So many African boundaries appear arbitrary and irrational that it seems impossible to explain their demarcation (as distinct from the wider historical context of the European partition) by any

From J. D. Hargreaves, "The Making of the Boundaries: Focus on West Africa," in *Partitioned Africans: Ethnic Relations across Africa's International Boundaries, 1884–1984,* ed. A. I. Asiwaju (Lagos: University of Lagos Press, 1985), 19–27. Reprinted by permssion of University of Lagos Press.

determinist hypothesis. Conspiracy theories are more tempting; surely only positive malevolence can explain some of those geometrical constructions through the centres of living communities. But to what end? Explanation seems difficult without ample recourse to H.A.L. Fisher's formula of "the contingent and the unforeseen." Yet study of the records usually reveals a certain short-term rationality within the narrow horizons of the respective European negotiators; it was the accidental convergence of these, with the ensuing conflicts and compromises, which determined the final outcome. The roads along which accidents take place have usually been constructed with some purpose; and the aim of this essay is to sketch the changing historical context within which those durable boundaries were provisionally fixed. It will involve one more look at the behaviour of the fighting elephants, though it will suggest that their behaviour was not unaffected by events in the grass beneath their feet.[1]

During most of the nineteenth century Europeans were able to pursue their purposes in tropical Africa—usually as traders or as missionaries—without needing, or desiring, to make major encroachments on the territorial sovereignty of African states. The object of "free-trade imperialism" was to extend the area open to European activity, rather than to establish national reservations; most of the small coastal colonies originated as leases held at the pleasure of an African landlord. What the Europeans needed, said Guizot in 1843, were "strong and secure maritime stations . . . to support our commerce";[2] this coincided with the perception of African rulers like Al Haj 'Umar that "the whites are only traders." In Senegambia, one area where inland penetration seemed feasible, the Vienna settlement of 1815 confirmed a de facto partition of waterways, not land; the French controlled access from the ocean to the Senegal river, the British held a dominant position in the Gambia, the Portuguese were left a consolation prize in the Rio Grande. Inter-European conflicts did occur but to the chagrin of the home governments, which assumed there was plenty of room for all. "Friendly European nations ought to avoid elbowing each other . . . in such countries as Africa," wrote a British official in 1866.[3]

By that date, it is true, elbowing was becoming more frequent: British and French officials were claiming incompatible rights by virtue of treaties with African rulers, or of their own military and naval action. Sometimes (for example, during Faidherbe's governorship in Senegal, 1854–61 and 1863–65) this can be attributed to imperialistic ambition—the conscious desire to assert power, or to promote specific economic interests. More often, the immediate cause was the need of governors of the small coastal colonies, obliged as they were to finance their own administration out of local revenue, to collect customs duties on European trade. Although initially their right to do this usually rested on treaties, wittingly or unwittingly signed by African rulers, this form of indirect taxation was not welcomed by those engaged in commerce (of whatever nationality, European or African); not surprisingly, the establishment of a customs house was commonly followed by a displacement of trade to coasts where taxes were payable only to the African ruler. Thus, when heavy liquor and tobacco duties were imposed at Lagos in 1863, French and Brazilian importers switched much of their business to Porto Novo, where a fierce Anglo-French struggle for power began.

This particular local confrontation was in many ways typical of a new phase in international rivalry on the West African coast, not least because African rulers joined in to exploit the situation to their own short-term advantage. Although French and British objections were initially confined to the shores of the coastal lagoon, the line along which they finally partitioned south-west Yorubaland in 1889 largely reflected the territorial and dynastic objective of King Tofa.[4] During the 1860s, '70s and '80s the British, French, and later German governments, without any initial intention to extend their colonial empires over African populations, repeatedly claimed fiscal sovereignty over strips of coast. By 1884 this coastal "scramble" had extended to Eastern and South-Western Africa, and the Berlin Conference was convened to bring a little order into the inter-European rivalries which had been engendered. Henri Brunschwig emphasises that even now European statesmen did not intend to partition Africa into colonial dependencies; "they were not talking of partitioning Africa but rather of ensuring the continuation of the traditional free-trading system on its coasts and its great rivers."[5] Only in a few exceptional areas, such as the Senegal valley and the southern Gold Coast, could one talk of colonial administration in 1884.

The following year, however, saw wide extension of "jurisdictional imperialism" through the elastic device of the Protectorate.[6] This nebulous legal concept acquired a new popularity because it seemed to offer a method of asserting rights which other European governments could recognise without extending the protector's administrative obligations in the countries which were being exploited commercially. The early partition treaties were essentially allocations of fiscal resources, and of responsibility for maritime police; their negotiators were not envisaging problems of administering the African interior. Nevertheless, colonial governors were increasingly led to expand their political power, not only through economic pressure and patriotic fervour, but to support the interests of African collaborators on whose consent the fiction of Protectorate depended.

It emerged that the territories within which Africans pursued their interests rarely corresponded to the allocated spheres of European influence. Thus an agreement of 1882 concerning the Northern Rivers of Sierra Leone (which were also the Rivières du Sud of Senegal) allocated the basin of the Mellacouric to France, that of the Scarcies to Britain; this bisected not only the Samu chiefdom, but the commercial, religious and political unities of a wider historical arena within what has been called "the Sierra Leone-Guinea system."[7]

(This was not exactly a "culture area," since Susus, Temnes and Limbas spoke different languages and were bound together by conflicts as much as by communities of interest.) Had the European negotiators been able to envisage the future problems of government in their region, they might have sought some wider arrangement, which could have done less violence to African trade-routes, and enabled them to evolve more coherent policies towards their African neighbours; but by the time the disadvantages of the line became apparent, interests and attitudes had hardened and any substantial revision of what had been agreed proved beyond the range of European statecraft.

The Anglo-French "Arrangement" of 10 August 1889 marked a reluctant recognition that the old system of free trade imperialism in West Africa would have to be replaced by one involving fixed colonial boundaries. Recognising "the practical impossibility of putting timely and adequate checks upon the acquisitive energies of officers employed in remote and unexplored countries,"[8] British and French diplomatists sat down in Paris to draw lines which would keep them apart in four areas of colonial conflict. From purely metropolitan viewpoints, it did not matter greatly where the boundaries were set, although the French were anxious to exclude all British influence from the upper basin of the Niger while the British (apart from their important interests in Nigeria, which they believed to be already secure) wanted to place a substantial territorial buffer around Freetown harbour. The more progressive imperialists, like Augustus Hemming of the Colonial Office, favoured a comprehensive partition, following the 10th parallel from the mouth of the river Pongos to 4° West and thence going directly north-east to a place called Burrum on the Niger, with British settlements on the Gambia exchanged against the French outposts in Dahomey and the Ivory Coast. Such a crude carve-up would have greatly reduced the number of African peoples doomed to partition; ironically it was British ministers' fears that one African community, the Creoles of Banjul, might create political difficulties which preserved the identity of British Gambia, and ensured the eventual fragmentation of colonial West Africa.

Failing such a simple and radical allocation of responsibilities, it was necessary to draw many boundaries. An Anglo-French Commission of diplomatists and colonial experts was formed for this purpose, but the limits of its expertise soon became evident. Lord Salisbury sardonically explained how, in the cause of international peace,

> We have been engaged in drawing lines upon maps where no white man's feet have ever trod; we have been giving away mountains and rivers and lakes to each other, only hindered by the small impediment that we never knew exactly where the mountains and rivers and lakes were.[9]

Although geographers were available to advise, European knowledge of the physical, let alone the human, geography of Africa was still rudimentary.

Although a famous epigram defines geography as being about maps rather than chaps, its value is always defined by the knowledge of the chaps who draw the maps. In 1889 the French geographical expert, a Foreign Ministry official called Desbuissons, relied on a map drawn up five years earlier by Captain P.L. Monteil to define a line which seemed to meet the objective of excluding Britain from the upper Niger basin. Later, on comparing the location of Timbo as fixed by other travellers, he concluded that this line had had a precisely contrary effect.[10] Fortunately, the British were prepared to agree to an alteration; but this only made Desbuissons more determined to uphold his own interpretation of such questions as the route traversed by E.W. Blyden in 1872, which had somehow become one of the criteria for defining the boundary under that 1889 Arrangement. The British, however, had their own experts, officers of the War Office, Military Intelligence, who remained equally confident in their own back-room topography.[11]

Faced with this combination of ignorance and intransigence among the colonial experts, diplomatists whose concern was with the wider relationships of European nations groped for some criterion which, in each individual case, would point to an unambiguous line of partition. Although it may seem that this could have been best provided by following existing African boundaries, well-defined territorial sovereignty had not become a general rule in Africa, as it had in Europe. The experts of the British Military Intelligence Department crudely simplified this problem of assigning firm boundaries to mobile populations, and in multi-ethnic areas:

> The tribes themselves have as a rule no idea of territorial limits, their locations are constantly changing, and there often exist small tribes between the large ones which owe allegiance sometimes to the one and sometimes to the other.[12]

Rather than attempting to follow the boundaries of states whose rulers might not be able to describe them accurately, the French preferred to allocate territory along some natural feature like a watershed.[13] But often even topographical features could not be identified on the ground in the form envisaged; the classic case was the Rio del Rey, accepted as the Nigeria-Cameroon boundary in an Anglo-German agreement, which proved to be an estuary receiving several small streams.[14] The safest way to avoid ambiguity and consequent conflict might thus be to use lines of latitude and longitude, which ought to prove capable of objective survey; "it is a question if a wrong line is not better than no line." Provided that the Demarcation Commissioners charged with applying diplomatic texts to African terrain were authorized to recommend minor deviations to accord with "ethnological divisions," it seemed that no great difficulty should arise.

This expectation proved unduly sanguine. The arduous task of trekking through the tropical bush to lay down boundary markers by agreement with a foreign colleague usually fell to ambitious young patriots, often military officers with some knowledge of surveying, who might regard it as their duty not merely to define their national claims, but to extend them as far as was conceivably compatible with the agreements they were supposed to be executing. One way of doing this was to uphold such territorial claims by Africans as coincided with the interests of the power in question. Captain Lang, appointed to demarcate the western frontier of the Gold Coast in 1892, espoused the claims of the Appolonians and other Akans who had for years been moving westwards, while his French colleague Captain Binger defended the territorial integrity of Kinjabo, Indenie, and other states of the lower Comoe and Bia valleys whose rulers had accepted treaties with France.[15] Meanwhile, in the Sierra Leone-Guinea Boundary Commission, Captain Lamadon, hoping to consolidate African opposition to Samori, was maintaining close relations with Karimu, whose political influence remained strong in the British sphere in the Scarcies valley, while his British colleague Captain Kenny relied on the advice of Alimami Sattan Lahai, one of the Temne chiefs most involved in the politics of the area claimed by France. European intervention was not the sole or even the principal cause of these African conflicts, and there was no possible frontier which could have kept the antagonists apart: but the proceedings of Lamadon and Kenny seem to have inflamed relations between Temne and Susu, as well as between French and British.[16]

Hence, although the Boundary Commissions established to apply the 1889 Agreement to Lagos and Senegambia were able to fix boundaries of some sort, the attempts to do the same with Sierra Leone and the Gold Coast actually made things worse. The diplomatists could only return to their inadequate maps, and try to devise less ambiguous instructions. "Far away from an African sun and its notoriously irritating influences, unexposed to the narrowing advice of naturally jealous local authorities, one might arrive at a solution which now seems hopeless." Unfortunately the conciliatory disposition of this particular diplomatist went far beyond what his colleagues in temperate London would accept.[17] And during the mid-1890s the freedom of detached negotiators to accept rational compromises was complicated by the intensification of European—particularly, Franco-British—colonial rivalries.

The years between 1894 and 1898 marked the high-point of popular colonialism in Europe, and pressure-groups in France and Britain competed in demanding strong action to protect supposed national interests on the Niger and the Nile. In this climate diplomatists concerned to avoid international conflict could not give much weight to the complaints of Africans, or even of colonial Governors, about the deficiencies of colonial boundaries. When in May 1894 the energetic new Governor of Sierra Leone proposed a revised boundary with Guinea, affecting the section already agreed as well as that still under discussion, which would pay greater attention to African political alignments and trade routes and respect the integrity of Samu and Luawa chiefdoms, officials recoiled from the thought of further protracted negotiations. Secretary Ripon wrote:

> I sympathize strongly with Col. Cardew's desire not to divide the territories of Native Chiefs. It is a wretched system, unjust to the chiefs and their people, and a fruitful source of disputes and trouble to the dividing Powers. But of course we cannot now deal with these matters as if the negotiations were to be entered upon for the first time.[18]

In fact, diplomatists under pressure were even then drawing new border-lines just as arbitrary as the old.

Most African boundaries still reflect the arbitrary compromises of the two decades when the chauvinistic forces of the European nation-states were most closely focussed upon colonial rivalry. Exceptionally, subsequent diplomacy might secure some minor adjustments. In 1904 a particularly tortuous piece of political geometry redefined the Anglo-French frontier in Sokoto so as to facilitate the movement of caravans with Niger.[19] Seven years later an adjustment of the Anglo-Liberian border partly restored the unity of the Luawa chiefdom—a rare example of an African ruler, Fabunde, being able to influence a boundary change.[20] But in general, the early provisional frontier settlements endured.

Thus study of European archives supports an accidental rather than a conspiratorial theory of the marking of African boundaries. The only logic which can be discerned in the record is that untidy form of historical rationality which derives from the interaction of conflicting interests and objectives. Primarily, of course, this meant the interests of certain European nation-states which had temporarily become dedicated to territorial empire in Africa; but sometimes African rulers were able to play minor roles in settling actual boundaries. The populations of the frontier areas were envisaged, if at all, only as dim and inarticulate presences in the background—which did not mean that they were unable to influence the manner in which the imposed boundaries subsequently operated.

African experience in this respect, however, represents only an extreme example of contemporary international practice. Until the Paris Peace Conference of 1919 attempted to apply Wilsonian principles of self-determination, with no great success, European boundaries too were commonly settled by interacting ambitions of remote potentates. The partitions and repartitions of Poland, the drawing of the Franco-German frontier through Lorraine in 1871, the tripartite division imposed on the "Big Bulgaria" of 1878, gave no more weight than African boundary agreements to the wishes and interests of the populations involved. In both continents, the inhabitants of the grass had to learn to endure the trampling of contending elephants—and to cope with other predators as well.

This essay has been deliberately focussed upon the West African region, with which the author's studies have been primarily concerned. Some of the features described clearly affected boundaries elsewhere in Africa—the predominant imperatives of European "national interests," the high degree of geographical ignorance on the part of negotiators and their consequent desire to avoid ambiguity by defining lines capable of objective survey, the growing tendency of the 1890s for European politicians to identify African territory with national "prestige."

However, Afro-European relations on the West Coast had distinctive historical characteristics which may limit continent-wide generalisations. To start with, the longer period of contact meant that African rulers in general played more active and more sophisticated roles in pre-partition politics than in much of Eastern and Southern Africa—the obvious exceptions being Ethiopia, Buganda and Lesotho. The activities of Egypt and Zanzibar present further complications. Secondly, the larger number of European leases, settlements, colonies and related claims on the West African coast before 1800 meant that there were more frontiers to settle, some enclosing very small territories indeed. Finally, because the Foreign Office, not the Colonial Office, was responsible for British interests in Eastern Africa while Germany had no independent Colonial Office until 1907, diplomatic negotiations were usually conducted by a single government department. This made the process of delimitation much simpler than in the West African Joint Commissions, where the British and French delegations had to reconcile the conflicting priorities of Foreign and Colonial Office—of diplomacy and colonial administration. But by and large, the "accidental hypothesis" seems likely to hold up on a continental basis.

Notes

1. This metaphor is based on the Igbo proverb which states that when two elephants fight, it is the grass beneath the two that suffer. Here the elephants are the partitioning European powers, and the grass the defenceless Africans, especially those in the area through which negotiated boundaries were drawn.

2. Speech by Guizot, 31 March 1843, quoted B. Schnapper, *La Politique et le Commerce français dans le Golfe de Guinée de 1838 à 1871* (Paris, 1961), p. 13.

3. C.O.267/287, Minute by T.F. Elliot, 14 Nov., on Blackall, 72, 11 Oct. 1866.

4. See N.S. Senkomago, "The Kingdom of Porto Novo, with special reference to its external relations, 1862–1908," unpubl. Ph.D. thesis, University of Aberdeen, 1976.

5. H. Brunschwig, *Le Partage de l'Afrique noire* (Paris, 1971), p. 51.

6. See W. Ross Johnston, *Sovereignty and Protection: A Study of British Jurisdictional Imperialism in the Later Nineteenth Century* (Durham, NC, 1973).

7. A.M. Howard, "The relevance of spatial analysis for African economic history: the Sierra Leone-Guinea system," *Journal of African History*, XVII, 1976, pp. 365–85.

8. Salisbury Papers (Christ Church. Oxford) A57, Lytton to Salisbury, 12 Dec. 1888. For the context of this negotiation, see *West Africa Partitioned*, pp. 230–46.

9. Speech by Salisbury, 6 Aug. 1890, *The Times*, 7 Aug.

10. Archives Etrangères, Paris (AE), Mémoires et Documents, Afrique 129, Note sur la Délimitation entre les Possessions françaises et britanniques . . . 1890.

11. For this controversy, see C.O.267/399, F.O. to C.O., 16 Nov. 1892; also the correspondence with W.O. in C.O.267/397.

12. F.O.84/1899, Memo by Lake and Darwin (M.I.D.), 16 July 1889.

13. AE, Afrique 129, Note, 13 Jan. 1891.

14. See J.C. Anene, *The International Boundaries of Nigeria* (Longman, 1970), Chap. 3.

15. Archives Nationales, Section d'Outre-mer, Paris, Côte d'Ivoire III/S. Binger's report on Boundary Commission, esp. fo. 8.

16. Kenny's report of 24 May 1892 in C.O.879/35, C.P. African 422, No. 81; Lamadon's is in AE, Afrique 130. I hope to treat this question more fully in Vol. II of *West Africa Partitioned*.

17. C.O.879/35, C.P. African 422, No. 88, Phipps to Differin, 30 May 1892; cf. C.O.267/399, Minute by Hemming on F.O. to C.O. 16 Nov. 1892 and on Phipps to Anderson, Phe 15 Nov.

18. C.O.267/409, Minute by Ripon, 27 June, in Cardew to Ripon, Conf. 38, 23 May 1894.

19. Anglo-French Convention of 8 April 1904, *British Documents on the Origins of the War*, II. pp. 381–82.

20. M. McCall, "Kai Lundu's Luawa and British rule," unpubl. D.Phil. thesis, University of York, 1974, ch. IV; A.J.G. Wyse, "The Sierra Leone/Liberian boundary: A case of frontier imperialism," *Odu*, n.s. 15, 1977, pp. 5–18.

7

The Jívaro People between Peru and Ecuador

Catherine Elton

Borders that restrict or prohibit movement of human populations due to national policies or military hostilities often have a severe impact on those ethnic or cultural groups that are divided by the international boundary. The following essay examines the Peru-Ecuador border where members of the Jívaro tribe were separated from friends and relatives for nearly a half-century due to conflict between Peru and Ecuador. The signing of peace accords in 1998 at last enabled families to reunite to preserve a shared culture.

Catherine Elton is a freelance writer and photographer now living in Guatemala. She often writes about conservation and the environment in Latin America.

When Tukup Wampui was a child living in the Ecuadoran jungle near the border with Peru, his father would tell him of their family members living on the other side. They too were Shuar Indians, although in Peru they now went by the name Huambisa. Tukup was curious about these mysterious family members whom he'd never met. His father explained that because of the border conflict between Peru and Ecuador they could no longer visit their family as he and the elders had always done in the past.

Tukup's father also told him that when he was grown up and when the conflict was over that he should try and find his family from the other side. Tukup kept his promise to his father, making attempts to contact his family even during the years of conflict. He would go to the offices of the Federation

From Catherine Elton, "Bonds beyond Borders," *Américas* 5, no. 1 (1999): 6–13. Reprinted by permission of Catherine Elton.

of Shuar Indians, where Radio Shuar was broadcast, stand in line to buy his ticket, and leave messages to be broadcast in that day's address.

His messages would sail freely over the airways unobstructed by the border that separated him and his family. Somewhere on the other side, in soft, crackly radio tones, his message would fill a thatched riverside hut where his family members lived. "I said that I hoped they were well and in good health and that we are alive here in Ecuador and that the day they give us freedom to cross we will meet."

Many Shuar people sent messages to family and loved ones in Peru as Tukup did. But these were times of conflict; two-way radio contact was forbidden, and without a radio station of their own the Huambisa were unable to send the types of messages the Shuar did. Tukup's messages were probably heard, but he never heard back.

It was not until this past January that Tukup, now forty years old, was able to fulfill his now-deceased father's request. Last October [1998], Peru and Ecuador signed a peace accord delineating the border between the two nations and agreeing to a future of cooperation and integration, a moment Tukup doubted he'd see in his lifetime. Scarcely three months later a group of Huambisa Indians landed on the shores on the Ecuadoran side of the Santiago River. They were in transit to the second of two binational reunions of the Jívaro language family, which includes Huambisa and Shuar among other indigenous people who straddle this stretch of the border.

The Huambisa delegation stopped for a while in the spare wooden community hall in Tukup's village. The Shuar and Huambisa mingled and conversed, tracing the tangled paths of long overgrown family trees, discovering for the first time cousins and uncles, brothers-in-law and great-aunts. Passing a bowl of *masato*, the traditional yucca drink of the Amazon, they toasted to the peace accord and to a closer future for their people.

The signing of the peace accord brought to an end the nearly 170-year border dispute that resulted in one war, two armed conflicts, and a handful of smaller skirmishes. The signing extinguished the only border flashpoint in the Hemisphere and was internationally hailed as an act that would bring more stability and progress to the region. But one of the lesser known benefits of the peace will be enjoyed by the Jívaro people who had been separated since 1941 by a border they never even knew existed before. For them this peace accord heralds an end to the suffering of separation and the start of renewed relations.

Jívaro is the name that linguists and anthropologists have assigned to the Amazon tribes Shuar, Huambisa, Aguaruna, and Achuar, who share the same language with slight variations in dialect. The historical center of the Jívaro was in Macas, Ecuador. Over the years after the Spanish conquest they migrated south, eventually occupying territory in what is now Peru.

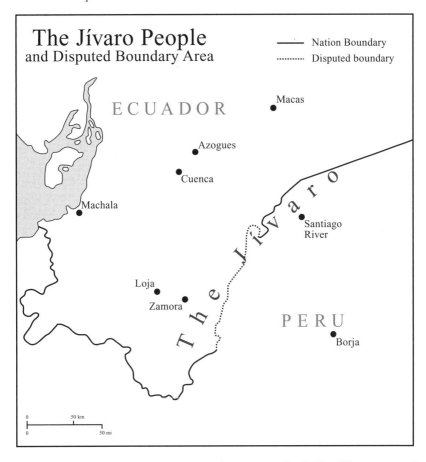

The Jívaro People
and Disputed Boundary Area

—— Nation Boundary

·········· Disputed boundary

ECUADOR

Macas

Azogues

Cuenca

Machala

Santiago
River

Loja

Zamora

PERU

Borja

0   50 km

0   50 mi

Currently the Jívaro occupy nearly seven-and-a-half million acres of jungle land along the Peru-Ecuador border. The Shuar have a population of around seventy-three thousand, while the Huambisa in Peru have a population of around fifty-five hundred; both tribes occupy the basins of the Santiago, Yaupi, Zamora, and Morona rivers. Another smaller tribe, the Achuar, occupies borderland east of the Shuar and Huambisa along the Pastaza River. They number around seven thousand in Ecuador and forty-eight hundred in Peru. The Aguaruna, who total around forty-five thousand, are found today only in Peru, along the Cenepa and Marañón rivers. (Peruvian population figures are from the most recent government census in 1993; Ecuadoran figures are from the indigenous organization Confenie.)

Before the war between Peru and Ecuador in 1941, the Achuar, Shuar, and Huambisa traveled freely from one side of the border to another to fish, hunt, trade, and visit with family. "We always had very friendly relations with our brothers. And there were no controls," recalls Huambisa elder Juan

Flores Nawech, who estimates his age to be between eighty and ninety years old. "We didn't know what Peru was or what Ecuador was. We didn't know what the border was. We were upper Shuar and lower Shuar, but we were one family." According to Nawech there was also trade between upper and lower Shuar, who bartered *itip*, the traditional skirts for men made from tree bark or cotton; *tiwaz*, or crowns made from toucan and wild turkey feathers; *chaquiras*, or beads; and the poison they used for hunting with blow darts.

But life the way Nawech had always known it suddenly and surprisingly changed. In 1941 the territorial disputes that had plagued Ecuador and Peru ever since they gained independence from Spain in the early 1820s came to a head and the two nations clashed in a brief border war. After this war the two countries signed the Protocol of Peace, Friendship, and Limits in Rio de Janeiro in 1942, commonly called the Rio Protocol. In this accord both countries agreed to a border for the first time. But disputes soon arose over seventy-five miles of this 1,054-mile border. Nearly fifty miles of mountainous jungle in the heart of Huambisa-Shuar and Aguaruna territory were left open or unmarked. This stretch of the border was the source and the site of two more armed conflicts, in 1981 and 1995.

After the 1941 war, military bases were erected near the border and controls were established. Shuar, Huambisa, and Achuar could not travel freely to hunt and fish in places they had hunted and fished from time immemorial, nor could they cross the line to visit each other.

"The Shuar and Huambisa people are very integrated in terms of family and have close and affectionate relationships. We love each other. The separation was very significant. There was no way to communicate. We didn't know how they lived; we didn't even know if they were alive or dead. It was as if the family on the other side didn't exist. This affected us emotionally on both sides of the border," says Shapiom Nomingo, a Huambisa Indian who is the president of the Santiago River branch of the Aguaruna-Huambisa Council.

Despite the controls and the military presence, over the next half-century some broke the lines on occasion to visit family members. Both the upper Shuar and the lower Shuar had always hunted nocturnal birds in the cave of the Tayos, just over the border in Peru's territory. The mouth of this vast cave soon became a secret meeting place where family members would visit and catch up on recent events.

But a cloud always hung over these stolen moments among family. These meetings, as innocent as they were, were forbidden, illegal events, and those who attended them feared being found out. It turns out this fear was warranted. According to Wrays Pérez, a Huambisa Indian who is secretary of the Interethnic Association for the Development of the Peruvian Amazon, there were a number of cases over the years of people caught by the military for crossing the border. In one high profile case, in 1986, Tito Yagkur, a Huambisa, was arrested and accused of spying after coming back from Ecuador. He was taken all the way to Lima, where the military intended to try him for treason. He was released after indigenous organizations rallied to his defense.

Over the years in a few isolated moments—depending on how hot the conflict was at the time and depending on the benevolence of the military officers in charge—military leaders would allow short reunions of Huambisa and Shuar on military grounds. But these types of meetings too left a lot to be desired. Despite the fact that one of these military-supervised reunions in 1979 enabled Pedro Uvijindia to meet his Peruvian half-brother for the first time, he talks of these meetings with a tinge of bitterness in his voice. "It was something we felt a little nervous about. It wasn't anything legal, and you always thought something could happen to you. There was no way to talk freely with family members from the other side. There were military officers who observed us."

Beyond the physical separation, there was another, perhaps even more damaging, if less tangible, form of dividing a people. "Since primary school we studied that we were invaded by Peru in 1941, that they robbed us of however many square kilometers of land, and that we were made to sign the Rio Protocol by force. This caused a lot of indignation to Ecuadorans," says Uvijindia, who is now an educator in Santiago, Ecuador. "This feeling of indignation grew and grew in many Shuars from Ecuador and even more so when we would go to do our military service and we were inculcated with this feeling with more force. It is something psychological that has been our conditioning ever since elementary school."

And viewing brothers as enemies, in some cases, also meant taking up arms against them. Today many Huambisa and Shuar regret participating in armed conflicts and feel that they were used by the militaries as "cannon fodder." But during times of conflict many people felt differently. Huambisa and Shuar both fought in the conflicts of 1981 and 1995, and many felt that they were defending their nations. "When we joined the military we had different instructions and incentives, which changed us a lot. It didn't matter to us that we had family on the other side; they were simply considered an enemy. They told us they were our enemies regardless if they are brothers," recalls Clovis Pérez, who served two years of obligatory military service in the 1980s.

The specter of fratricide became all too real for the elder Nawech in 1995. After the 1941 war, he was taken by force to Peru by the military, who accused him of belonging to that side of the border. Most of his family and his wife's immediate family were left behind in Ecuador. Years later his wife took advantage of a relatively relaxed era in Peru-Ecuador relations and arranged with local military officials to move back to Ecuador with four of their sons. She never came back to Peru. Nawech stayed in Peru, with his sons from another marriage. Nawech remembers listening to Radio Shuar one evening and hearing a message reporting that one of his sons who lived in Ecuador was participating in the 1995 conflict. Any parent would be worried and saddened to hear such news, but for Nawech the news was especially hard to take. For not only was his son in Ecuador marching off to war, so was one of his sons in Peru.

"My son who lives in Peru fought in 1995 and so did my son on the other side. I was so saddened to think that brothers would fight against each other. I cried thinking that my sons would die in this war. Many people from my community fled to other communities farther from the border because they were scared of the sounds of war. But I stayed here in my house thinking, crying, and grieving for my sons," Nawech says. Luckily, both of his sons lived through the conflict.

Now that a definitive accord has been signed, the suffering of armed conflicts, separation, and confusing messages of "brothers are our enemies" are now behind the Jívaro people. Since the October signing, the two nations have been busy in the delicate but urgent task of removing the roughly 100,000 land mines sewn into the border's earth and placing twenty-three waist-high, cement border markers that finally "close" the unmarked stretch of border, which was officially demarcated last May. Ironically, closing this border will actually open it. The nations agreed to take measures to facilitate travel across the border at the official border crossings by not requiring passports, and plans are being made to build three more roads connecting the two countries. Government officials have been courting international donors and lenders to contribute to the U.S.$3 billion binational development program the two nations agreed to as part of the accord.

As soon as the peace was signed, indigenous organizations from Peru and Ecuador began meeting to plan reunions. They held one in Peru in December and one in Ecuador in January. The day of the first reunion, in San Juan de Morona, Peru, started out like a perfect summer day, but just as the Ecuador delegation was about to arrive the sky was covered over by a thick blanket of clouds, pierced by lightning, and rattled by thunder. But no one lamented that a perfect day for a picnic had been ruined. Quite the contrary; for the Jívaro this was a symbolic message, called Arutam. In their lore, when someone who has the vision or who will have a great impact comes to visit, lightning, thunder, and rain always accompany them.

The reunion lived up to its ominous beginnings. For many it was the first time they met family members. As people arrived, they wandered around searching for family in the faces of strangers. Guido López was not on the limited list of those who would be transported by military helicopter to this first reunion, but that didn't stop him from going. Nor did the very pronounced limp he has from a childhood sickness. López walked two days through jungle and over mountains to get to the reunion. But according to him his trek was worth it.

Arriving at the reunion, he approached two men walking together and asked if they knew his family. ' "Who are you?' they asked. I said I was Peruvian, and my father is Santiago López. They stood there staring at me. 'Son,' they said, 'are you really Santiago's son?' When I said yes, one of them said, 'you are my son.' He called me son instead of *compañero*. They hugged me and cried. And I cried too. They were my family. They didn't know me at all, and I didn't know them. I was born here, and they didn't even know I'd been born. And then at twenty-four years of age without ever having seen their faces, I met them and they hugged me. I felt like I was with family."

For those who were seeing family members they'd already met during secret or military-supervised meetings, it was still an emotional and landmark experience. Pedro Uvijindia saw the half-brother he'd met only once nearly ten years before at a military-arranged meeting. At the reunion, "I felt so different because I could talk freely with my brother and there was total confidence. I could speak freely in front of the Peruvian soldiers who were walking around and say that this is my brother, he is Peruvian and I am Ecuadoran. I was able to talk to my brother without fear."

After meeting and reacquainting, the delegations of Shuar, Huambisa, Aguaruna, and Achuar from either side got down to business. The members of the Jívaro language family wanted to make sure that their unified voice would be heard when government officials sit down to designate the U.S.$3 billion worth of development programs for the border. Together at the two reunions they drafted agreements and proposals for the future.

To many of the leaders, the separation put their people at a developmental disadvantage, and they are eager to work together now that the accord has been signed. "By separating our people and by not having contact there we were at a disadvantage in many respects," Shapiom Nomingo says. "It would have been much different without the separation. We could have maintained our culture more intact. We could have exchanged concrete experiences in education and health, and we would have had a stronger political presence before our respective governments."

At the reunion the delegations agreed, among other things, to cooperate on improving already existing bilingual cultural education programs and work together to establish a native health system. They want to plan together how to protect their natural resources, which are coveted by logging, petroleum, and mining interests. They also want to establish trade between these two economically depressed border areas that once bartered together and lobby their governments to approve transit across the border for family visits in Jívaro territory.

During the years of separation, once unified people followed different trajectories of development on either side of the border. In Ecuador the native communities are connected to cities and other towns by roads. They participate in more trade and commercial activity. They have more access to clothing and medicines, health care, and education. They even have an indigenous university located in Puyo.

On the Peru side, life for the Huambisa is still centered around the rivers, as there are no roads and only fluvial transport. Clothing and medicines are scarce; universities are far away. But being isolated has also meant being insulated. In Peru the indigenous people have better protected their natural resources and have been better able to fend off the incursion of the western way of life and land-grabbing colonists. They have been able to preserve more of their customs and traditions. According to indigenous leaders, these differences mean that there are lessons to be learned and remembered on either side.

But despite the differences time has created, indigenous people on both sides face the same overall problems: extreme poverty, threats to the delicate and diverse ecosystems in which they live, and threats to their culture. Most of the government attention these regions have received in the past half-century has been military, and they lag behind the rest of their respective nations in terms of development.

"Peru has never been our enemy; it is a brother country that has the same problems and lives in the same situation that all the people of Latin America live. How could we live fighting with the same people who have the same problems?" Uvijindia asks.

The reunions were hailed a great success. Unfortunately, due to limits on the numbers of those who could obtain government permission, only about two hundred people were able to attend the reunions. This has left many people waiting to see family. For even though the peace has been signed, the transit across the border is still restricted in the Jívaro territory, as Shuar Indian Fernando Nawech found out at the end of the second reunion. He traveled to the border with the Huambisa delegation, hoping to cross over with them to visit his father, the elder Nawech, who was too frail to make the trip to either of the reunions. He was denied passage but is sure that the moment will come when he will cross to the other side and visit his father in his home, drink *masato*, and rekindle their relationship.

About a year ago, while partaking in the religious rite of Ayahuasca, the younger Nawech had a vision. In his vision he was in the home on the shores of the Santiago River where he grew up and left as a teen never to return. Despite the years that have passed, he says he remembers the place in vivid detail. He remembers the spots on the bank of the river where his father took him as a boy to dig for turtle eggs in the soft, sun-baked sand. He remembers the lushly vegetated mountains where they hunted and the fishing holes they traveled to in their dugout canoes. In his vision it was all there but most importantly so was he—reunited with his father and his half-brothers, who live on the other side. "I am sure that one day that visit I saw in my vision will become a reality, that it will happen just like I saw in my vision," says Fernando with an air of total confidence. But then he hesitates, cocks his head to the side, and corrects himself, for there is one detail of his vision he says he is also sure will not come true: "in my vision I crossed the border in fear, hiding myself because it was the time of conflict. But when I really go I won't have to hide. Because now we are in times of peace."

8

Boundaries as
Social Practice
and Discourse
The Finnish-Russian
Border

Anssi Paasi

Using the case of Finland and Russia, geographer Anssi Paasi suggests that borders need to be viewed as more than lines marking the territorial limits of a nation. It is important to examine their significance to regional and national populations, particularly in a world where traditional borders are breaking down in some places and hardening in others. Paasi reviews the history of this border from a closed one that defined the limits of the Soviet Union in northern Europe to a more open one that marked the division between the European Union and Russia. He pays particular attention to how once-separated local rural and urban populations have fared with a more open border.

Anssi Paasi is professor and head of the Department of Geography at the University of Oulu in Finland. His research interests include social construction of regions and territorial identities, theories of region and place, and the links among territories, boundaries, and individual/social consciousness. He is the author of numerous articles and books on these subjects.

Introduction

Boundaries have become objects of substantial interest within various academic fields since the early 1990s. Scholars from various disciplines are studying intensively not only the material functions of boundaries but, increasingly, also their symbolic and metaphoric meanings and their roles in the constitution of identities. Simultaneously, several new border research institutes have

From Anssi Paasi, "Boundaries as Social Practice and Discourse: The Finnish-Russian Border," *Regional Studies* 33, no. 7 (1999): 669–80. Figures omitted. Reprinted by permission of Taylor and Francis.

been established and new journals launched (Newman and Paasi, 1998). Many interdisciplinary books have been published on borders in general (e.g. Anderson M., 1996; Welchman, 1996; Shapiro and Alker, 1996; Michaelsen and Johnson, 1997) and on the meanings of boundaries in various spatial contexts, mainly in Europe (Eger and Langer, 1996; O'Dowd and Wilson, 1996; Anderson and Bort, 1998).

The main background to this current interest has doubtless been the collapse of the rigid post-World War Two dichotomy between eastern and western blocs. The disappearance of the "Iron Curtain" has profoundly altered the world's geopolitical landscape and created a number of new boundary disputes. The simultaneous rhetoric of globalization and the increase in various flows—cultural, economic and human (migrants, refugees)—have made boundaries, border crossings and questions of identity particularly topical. Some authors have been ready to announce the "death of the nation-state" in a "borderless world" (Ohmae, 1995) while others have called for more analytical approaches to scrutinize the changing roles of the state, boundaries and sovereignty in a globalizing world (Anderson J., 1995, 1996; Hirst and Thompson, 1996). Despite the effects of globalization, the changing meanings of sovereignty, environmental problems and post-nationality arguments, the state—as the key medium in the governance of the international system—will apparently remain the ideal form of organization for most "nations" in the near future. Therefore, rather than mechanically repeating the arguments regarding the disappearance of states and boundaries, the challenge for border scholars is to develop new approaches for understanding their changing meanings (Paasi, 1998).

Political geographers, in particular, created the language of border studies at the turn of the current century in order to depict a modern world that was becoming territorialized along rigid boundary lines that characterized a state-centred system. Formerly loose frontiers were replaced by exclusive lines. Thus state territoriality came to be crucially shaped by the ideas of boundedness and exclusion. Political geographers, too, were involved in the creation of a "territorial trap": an image of the world as divided into distinct territorial units (Agnew, 1994). This rigid, modernist boundary language has maintained its position in political geography up to recent years (Paasi, 1998). Traditional border studies in political geography have typically regarded boundaries as lines that shape and modify all forms of interaction and make cross-border links possible. The major context for these studies has been the border area or border landscape itself, and many descriptions of those local contexts have been produced and their meanings compared.

In this paper, boundaries will be understood not merely as static lines but as sets of practices and discourses which "spread" into the whole of society and are not restricted to the border areas. The production and reproduction of boundaries is part of the institutionalization of territories—the process in

Finnish–Russian
Border Crossing Points
1998

NORWAY

Crossing Status

>—< Operational
>–< Proposed
— Temporary

Raja-Jooseppi >—< Lotta

Kelloselkä >–< Salla

S W E D E N

RUSSIA

Vartius >—< Lyttä

F I N L A N D

Niirala >—< Värtsilä

Imatra >—< Svetogorsk
Nuijamaa >—< Brusnitshnoje
Vainikkala >—< Luzhaika
Vaalimaa >—< Torfjanovka

Gulf of Bothnia

Gulf of Finland

St. Petersburg

0   100 km
0   100 mi

which their territorial, symbolic and institutional "shape" is determined (Paasi, 1991). Therefore boundaries manifest themselves in numerous social (economic, cultural, administrative and political) practices and discourses that may be simultaneous and overlapping. Power and governance are part and parcel of the construction of boundaries, and this is particularly obvious in the case of state borders. Boundary discourses may also become materialized, as can be seen in the "iconographies of boundaries" that manifest themselves in legislation, memorials, films, novels and education, for example, all of which produce, express and reproduce territoriality, as well as in the concrete boundary landscapes (Paasi, 1996; Newman and Paasi, 1998). Boundaries exist and gain meanings on different spatial scales, not merely at the state level, and these meanings are ultimately reproduced in local everyday life. Boundaries are rarely produced in the border areas themselves, however, since these are usually national peripheries in an economic sense and their essential meanings as far as foreign policy, the national economy and politics are concerned are typically produced in centres. This means that many competing discourses usually exist on the roles of boundaries.

The present paper analyses the Finnish-Russian border as a set of social practices and discourses. This border is a fitting illustration of the de-territorialization and re-territorialization processes occurring in Europe and elsewhere, as well as of the recent increase in cross-border activity. During Soviet times it was the longest border between a western capitalist state and the leading socialist state, a much-used example of a closed ideological border but, since the collapse of the Soviet Union, cross-border activities have vastly increased. On the other hand, with Finland's entry into the European Union in January 1995, it became the only border between the EU and Russia. I will scrutinize the meanings of this border both on the scale of the Finnish state and on a local scale.

First, a historical overview of the development of the border is presented, evaluating both its pre- and post-World War Two meanings. This is followed by a discussion of the roles of the border in the post-Soviet context, evaluating in particular the current forms of cross-border co-operation. Finally, the meanings of the border for the local population will be discussed by considering the case of Värtsilä, a small Finnish community that was divided between Finland and the Soviet Union as a consequence of World War Two. The paper draws on diverse materials such as historical documents, statistics and media discourses. Local experiences are illustrated using mainly interview materials collected in the Värtsilä area between 1987 and 1992. As Finland's entry into the EU in 1995 changed the international, national and local meanings of the border still further, the information received from these interviews was filled out in spring 1998 by means of telephone interviews with some key actors in local enterprises, administrative organizations and voluntary associations in the Värtsilä area.

The Establishment of the Finnish-Russian Border

The meanings of boundaries are not constant but may change crucially according to social and political situations. The "truths" and arguments regarding a state, its relations to other territories and the consequent meanings of boundaries are historically contingent. This is obvious in the case of the Finnish-Russian border. The Finnish state gained its independence in 1917 after being an autonomous Grand Duchy of Russia since 1809, and before that an administrative part of Sweden from the 12th century onwards. During the autonomy period Finland did not have a foreign policy of its own, even though it had a national economy and a customs border with Russia. Before 1917 this border was an open one and very much a formality, and there was intensive economic and cultural cross-border interaction (Paasi, 1996). After 1917 Finland's territorial strategy changed, however, as it tried to secure its boundaries and use them to signify the territoriality of an independent state. The eastern border of the state was finally confirmed, in effect created, three years later, in the Peace of Tartu (1920). Before that—and in practice up to 1922—even its location generated conflicts between Finland and Russia because of a Finnish-speaking population remaining on the Soviet side, and becoming part of the Workers' Commune of Karelia in 1920 and the Autonomous Republic of Karelia in 1923.

For Finland, the construction of exclusive political boundaries was a crucial part of the process of nation-building and strengthening the state, and this found expression in many ways. One aim was to develop the living conditions in border areas—to "nationalize the peripheries" in order to increase the political reliability of the inhabitants. The border also became an economic one; whereas in 1910 almost 30% of Finnish exports had gone to Russia, in the 1930s only 0.5% went to the Soviet Union (Michelsen and Kuisma, 1992). The orientation of public policy in the 1920s and 1930s was to create economic connections with Western Europe and the U.S.

Foreign policy and popular discourses regarding the Soviet Union also changed. Before World War Two, Finnish publicity and education painted a dark view of the Soviet Union as the "Other." The border became a mythical manifestation of the "eternal opposition" between two states and a crucial constituent of Finnish national identity (Paasi, 1997). Finland's refusal to cede some parts of its territory to the Soviet Union led to the Winter War of 1939–40; and in the subsequent Continuation War of 1941–44 justifications were sought for the extension of Finland's territory towards its "natural boundary" in the east, when Finnish troops moved over the old border to occupy Russian areas in Eastern Karelia (Paasi, 1996). As a consequence of the war, however, Finland had to cede huge amounts of its territory to the Soviet Union. The border was confirmed in the Treaty of Paris in 1947, along a line that had already been established in the Peace Treaties of Moscow in 1940 and 1944.

The Post-Soviet Geopolitical Order and Contested Border Discourses

Foreign policy can partly be seen as a set of boundary-producing discourses that are exploited in the creation of territorial identities (Campbell, 1992). The boundary discourses of foreign policy experts may differ radically from those prevailing in civil society and those outside the state. This is clear in the Finnish case. In the Cold War geopolitical order, Finland, defeated in the war but still an independent state, belonged to the neutral but disputed camp between the Eastern and Western blocs. The "neutrality" which formed the cornerstone of Finland's official foreign policy discourse up to the time of the collapse of the Soviet Union formally placed Finland outside the blocs, but in practice international images were strongly coloured by the pacts which Finland had concluded with the Soviet Union after the war. The Soviet Union also tried to exert influence on Finnish foreign and security policy in many unofficial ways. Finland had been a "western" country in the geopolitical literature of the period before World War Two, but many post-war representations placed it in Eastern Europe—one famous manifestation of this was the idea of "Finlandization" (Paasi, 1996). Finland's entry into the EU and western links in security and defence policy have once more altered its location in the geopolitical imagination. The EU, in particular, has become an important instrument in Finnish security policy.

A modern state usually has several territorial strategies (Taylor, 1994). As a "power container" it tends to preserve the existing boundaries, whereas as a "wealth container" it strives towards larger territories. Furthermore, as a "cultural container" it tends towards smaller territories, even though national representations of a homogeneous culture are crucial in most narratives of nationhood. Taylor's ideas also apply to the meanings of the Finnish-Russian border. During the Soviet period the border was closed and it became a taboo subject with co-operation formally organized and controlled at the state level. But since the collapse of the Soviet system the border has become a significant topic in economic, political, military and cultural discourses. These have found many forms and modes of expression, including entry into the EU (and the decision to join the European Economic and Monetary Union, EMU), speculations on possible NATO membership and the future of national identity in relation to a general European identity.

One theme draws together many recent Finnish discourses: the question of the location of the border. Its roots lie in the debates over the Karelian territories that Finland had to cede to the Soviet Union after the war. This area amounted to 12.5% of Finland's territory, and its loss led to the resettlement of 420,000 people to other parts of the country. This created a national trauma that has come out into the open only since the demise of the Soviet Union. Before that, during the 1970s and 1980s, the ideological interests of the organizations for resettled Karelians, the economic interests of local authorities and the emerging heritage industry all combined to give rise to a kind of "reconstructed Karelia" in the border areas of eastern Finland. War memorials, houses built in the Karelian style, the symbols of Orthodox religion, and events exploiting the Karelian heritage mushroomed in this part of the country and created a symbolic space that provided the Karelians with cultural representations that perhaps partly compensated mentally for their lost territory, while at the same time stimulating tourism (Paasi, 1996).

This substitute was not enough for all Finns, however, and during the 1990s some organizations began actively promoting debates on the future of the ceded areas. The intention was to interest the leading politicians and apparatus of "statecraft" in the Karelian issue, which was regarded by these associations as a problem (Karelian Association, 1996). The Peace of Tartu Movement, in particular, has been very active in promoting such views, mainly in newspapers, and has openly challenged the prevailing statecraft. It has called for these areas to be restored to Finland, at times using Ratzelian, organistic rhetoric when describing the "sufferings" of the "wounded body" of the state which could be healed only by re-establishing its organic connection with the ceded areas. Some muted discussion along these lines had been going on in civil society since the war, but the Soviet collapse turned these demands into a public debate which has at times been a very lively one, particularly in 1997 when President Yeltsin asked the Finnish media to put an end to it.

Official foreign policy and the Finnish Border Patrol Establishment have been thinking along different lines. The current boundaries have been confirmed in three peace treaties and no territorial claims exist. This stance is also linked to the broader geopolitical framework of the EU, where one criterion for new members is that they should not have any border disputes. Official foreign policy in Finland coincides with that of the Russian authorities, and surveys among the Finns also show that the great majority (80% in 1995) would not demand any reopening of negotiations with Russia on these matters. Similar surveys have also been carried out in Russia, where 70% of the people answered in 1998 that the ceded areas should not be returned to Finland (Mikkola, 1998).

Whereas the discourses calling for restoration of the ceded areas have been aimed at the de-territorialization of the current territorial frame in a very concrete way—or re-territorializing it by moving the border—foreign policy as such has tried to maintain the current framework while also de-territorializing it in a very different way. There are several examples from the last few years that point to a de-territorialization of the traditionally exclusive forms of foreign policy. Since the collapse of the Soviet Union, Finnish foreign policy has taken long strides towards the west—principally through membership of the EU and EMU—but simultaneously it has struggled to keep its ties with the east and even strengthen the links that would integrate

Russia into this larger European space. The first effort was perhaps the "neighbouring area co-operation" agreement of 1992, aimed at promoting peaceful, stable development, strengthening economic relations and minimizing environmental problems. In this context a whole new discourse has emerged, not only on Finnish-Russian relations but also on the new "regionalizations" in the Baltic Sea and Barents regions (Forsberg and Vaahtoranta, 1993). It should be noted that border questions are not included in this agreement. Later, the Finns adopted a visible role in preparations for Russian membership of the Council of Europe. Current discussion of the "Northern Dimension" in EU policy is also illustrative, since this initiative came originally from Finland. Its aims are complex ones: firstly, to emphasize co-operation and economic benefits in order to lower the old barriers between west and east based on traditional power politics; and secondly, to bring the energy resources of the Barents region and North-western Russia within the reach of the EU. The effort to create co-operation with Russia is, therefore, not just a matter of economy and co-operation but also one of security policy.

Concomitantly with this relative de-territorialization of the border, foreign and security policy practices and discourses are continually evaluating the limits of sovereignty, which in turn imposes limits on deterritorialization. In 1997 President Yeltsin suggested to Finland's President Ahtisaari that the two states could undertake "common border control," but Ahtisaari reminded him that "sovereign states always take care of border control independently"! Finland's entry into the EU and resulting responsibility for the EU's only border with Russia actually points towards organizing a more effective patrolling system, since customs operations are now carried out on behalf of the whole EU area. Border surveillance has become increasingly technical in nature—with cameras and electronic monitoring systems adopted during the 1990s—which makes control over the boundaries of the national space more effective and less visible. The nature of the patrolling operations has also changed. Whereas this action was very formal in Soviet times, it is now characterized by increasing co-operation and exchange of information with the Russians, e.g. on criminal activities. On the other hand, border controls are very strict, and the number of refugees who have entered Finland by crossing this boundary has been very low, varying from seven to 45 per year between 1994 and 1997. The number of people turned back from the border has been increasing continually, though the total, some 800 in 1997, is still low relative to the intensity of passenger traffic over the border.

De-Territorialization, Flows and Cross-Border Activities

Even though there had been extensive trade between Finland and the Soviet Union, the border was strictly controlled and cross-border activity was permitted only in certain controlled places, which facilitated some tourist traffic and joint construction projects. Cooperation was thus regulated and organized at the state level. The Finnish economy was highly dependent on this bilateral trade, with more than 20% of Finnish exports going to the Soviet Union in 1985—86, for example. But with the decline of the Soviet system this export market collapsed, so that the above proportion was only 13% in 1990 and less than 3% in 1992 (Sweedler, 1994). Now it is rising again, however, so that 6% of exports went to Russia in 1996 and 7.1% of its imports came from there. Thus Russia ranks fifth among both the countries of destination and origin in the Finnish foreign trade statistics (Suomen Tilastollinen Vuosikirja, 1997).

Guard towers and tight controls marked the Finnish-Russian border, 1995. *Photograph by Paul Ganster*

As far as the whole border area, almost 1,300 km in length, is concerned, 70 years of almost no activity across the border itself had made the peripheral areas on both sides highly dependent on their own national political and economic centres, typical "alienated borderlands" (Martinez, 1994). However, cross-border traffic began to intensify in many places around 1990. Finnish travel to Russia became increasingly a matter of business and shopping trips and visits made by people of Karelian origin to their former home areas. A new phenomenon was Russian travel to Finland. Where 8,500 Russian cars came across the border in 1991, the figure was almost 170,000 in 1996, while Russian visitors spent a total of 455,000 nights in Finland in that same year, which puts them in third place after Swedish and German visitors (Suomen Virallinen Tilasto, 1997). Local attitudes towards Russian tourism have also become more favourable, as they spend a lot of money, and it is now becoming increasingly popular to study the Russian language, e.g. in southeastern Finland (Arolainen, 1996).

Since the signing of the "neighbouring area co-operation" agreement in 1992, local authorities on both sides have actively promoted cross-border schemes to open up routes, establish connections and develop the economy of the border area. This agreement arose from the break-up of the Soviet Union, and it gave more power to the republics to look after their own foreign relations, for instance, provided their actions were not in conflict with central government policy. The total number of crossing-points is now 26, including six that are open to international traffic, the other 20 crossing-points being for goods traffic—mainly timber transport—and/or crossings by Finnish and Russian citizens only. Two new international border stations (Imatra and Kelloselkä) are being financed through the EU TACIS programme (Siukonen, 1998). Total border crossings by passengers rose from 0.96 to 4.1 million between 1990 and 1996, the number of Russian passengers having increased rapidly since 1994 to almost 2 million in 1997, while the number of Finns seems to be decreasing after the initial boom. The increased flows of people have also led to images of undesirable elements, with smuggling, organized crime and the control of alcohol flows among the popular themes in media discourses (e.g. Österberg, 1996; Naulapää, 1998).

The partial de-territorialization of the border has not only given rise to various "flows" but has created new social practices that are gradually turning the border areas into "interdependent borderlands" (Martinez, 1994). Cross-border interaction is becoming more diverse, varying from cultural to environmental, from economic development to humanitarian projects. Actors in Finnish border communes are looking forward to shedding their peripheral location and opening up communications with areas in Russia, with an optimism that is partly motivated by the chance to obtain resources through the EU INTERREG programme and from the TACIS programme, which was founded specifically to foster co-operation between EU and CIS (Commonwealth of Independent States) countries. Several TACIS-based projects are in progress in the Finnish-Russian border area, and much effort has been concentrated on developing the infrastructure for border crossings (customs houses, services). In addition to actual land use planning and construction activities, the opening of the border has encouraged the "place-marketing" (Kearns and Philo, 1993) of border-crossings. Finnish local authorities and consulting firms have been active and many plans have been produced or are under development to realize the potential of the prospective corridors, gateways and regionalizations.

The Russian area beyond the border is divided between three larger territories: the St. Petersburg region; the Republic of Karelia; and the Murmansk region. These areas are perceived by the Finns as offering different opportunities. The future international crossing point at Kelloselkä, for instance, has been represented in the media as a "ventilation hole" for north-eastern Finland, not only opening up links for business travel and goods transport but facilitating the passage of European tourists to the Kola Peninsula and of Russian shoppers to Finland. Local actors are also placing their trust in the future exploitation of the gas and oil fields in the Barents region (Välimaa, 1997). In south-eastern Finland expectations are high because of the potential represented by two large Russian cities, St. Petersburg and Vyborg. Russian trade and visitors are seen as being increasingly important to this area although, alongside the beneficial effects, there are social and health worries about increasing rates of crime, alcohol consumption, prostitution and venereal diseases, topics which have been very visible in the media.

However, in spite of the increasing cross-border activity and optimism, serious obstacles persist. The border continues to run between two completely different societies, and the gap between the standards of living on the two sides is among the largest in the world—often likened to the situation prevailing on the U.S.-Mexico border (Sweedler, 1994). Recent surveys show that one in four of the Russian Karelians see their personal economic situation as catastrophic. As Jussila et al., 1997, point out, the vast majority of Russian Karelians have experienced a huge deterioration in purchasing power since the Soviet collapse, even though some people have managed to accumulate enormous wealth. This simply means that most Russians are not "happy border-crossing consumers," nor will they become such for a long time. It is thus very unlikely that this area will become an "integrated borderland" (Martinez, 1994), where people, goods and ideas flow without restriction.

The location of the border areas was strategically important during the Soviet period, and thus their territorial structure was shaped to a crucial extent by the strategic thinking and regional and production policies of those times. The Russian population areas beyond the border are largely urbanized, with urban dwellers accounting for 93% of the total population of the Murmansk region (approximately 1.1 million) and 74% of that of the Karelian Republic (approximately 0.8 million). Whereas the strategy in Finland was to "nationalize" the peripheries of the territory after 1917, the Soviet idea was to peripheralize and "de-nationalize" the border area because of a fear of the emergence of Finnish border communities (Lynn and Fryer, 1998). This process continued after World War Two and took place both ideologically and in terms of settlement policy, as a result of which the population of Russian Karelia, for instance, finally consisted predominantly of non-Karelian people. People from Russia, the Ukraine and Belorussia began to settle in the area soon after the war, and the proportion of the Finnish population is today some 2.6% (Paasi, 1996).

The Russian border also has become more open to economic flows. The number of firms with foreign investments has increased rapidly, so that where the number of foreign firms registered in Russia in 1987 was only 23, they numbered nearly 2,000 in 1990 and almost 15,000 in 1995. About 85% of these were joint venture companies usually with a partner from an industrialized western state, chiefly the U.S. or Germany (Eskelinen et al., 1998, p. 21).

The economic policy of the Karelian Republic relies on its border location and natural resources, and legislation has been established to encourage foreign investments (Lynn and Fryer, 1998). The Republic stresses resource-based industries (timber, fishing and mining) but activities related to the border such as tourism, transport and communications are also important (Kortelainen, 1997). The number of firms with foreign investments has also increased in Russian Karelia. Whereas there were 20 registered firms of this kind in 1990, they numbered 170 in 1992 and more than 400 in 1995. Eskelinen et al., 1998, p. 23, remind us, however, that the distinction between registered and operational firms is a crucial one, since only 211 of the 400 firms were actually operative in 1995, i.e. they reported having employees and pursuing actual business activities. The proximity of Russian Karelia to Finland is reflected in the number of small investments and other local forms of co-operation across the border. This activity has taken many forms (Eskelinen et al., 1998). Firstly, companies in eastern Finland have subcontracted assembly work to Russian Karelia; secondly, various civil and public organizations have been involved in numerous local projects; and thirdly, numerous training and development schemes have been launched. One motive behind these activities is the belief that they will improve the physical and social infrastructure for future interaction.

Nevertheless, a certain scepticism has infused the hope and enthusiasm prevailing on either side of the border since the collapse of the Soviet Union. In eastern Karelia, for instance, debate soon arose as to whether the aim of the Finns was "neo-colonization" of the Karelian areas in an economic sense and exploitation of their natural resources (Sykiäinen, 1993). From the viewpoint of foreign capital, Karelia has been seen primarily as a source of raw materials, mainly because of its huge forest resources, making up 70% of the surface area of the Republic. More recently, as far as the EU Structural Funds are concerned, the lack of information has at times led to suspicions that the Finns are using their Russian partners in order to benefit from the programmes. The actors in the border communes in both Finland and Russia have organized joint seminars to promote trust among the partners and to clarify the aims and possibilities of the EU programmes. Co-operation over the boundary works quite well at the political level, but the practical situation is different, because the Russians lack financing capital and many cultural and institutional factors prevent real commitment to co-operation (Siukonen,

1998). On the other hand, surveys carried out among the Russian business partners show that they feel that their western counterparts are being passive (Eskelinen et al., 1998).

Finnish foreign policy during the post-war period stressed good relations with the Soviet Union; feelings in civil society were more complicated, mainly because of the violent history of the border areas. A lack of trust still characterizes the current situation and may prove an obstacle to future cross-border activities. Social representations are often galvanized by old, deeply embedded visions and judgements, and this is perhaps still the case on this border between a western capitalist state and the former leading socialist state (Paasi, 1996). Surveys carried out among local people on both sides of the border (Kinnunen, 1995) indicate that the Finns and the Russians do not know much about each other, and that the Russians have a more favourable opinion of the Finns than the Finns do of the Russians. Also, Finnish opinions are polarized, so that some people favour co-operation while others have deep prejudices and suspicions. As far as the development of cross-border activities is concerned, only about half the Finns see this as a good thing, whereas two-thirds of Russians are of this opinion. One-third of the Finns do not approve of the opening of the border, but only a small percentage of the Russians think in this way. This survey was carried out in northern Finland and Russia in 1994 (ibid.) but it is obvious that, at least in Finland, the results are indicative of a broader band of opinion that prevails in civil society. Kinnunen, 1995, writes that the attitudes of Finns and Russians regarding the opening of the border perhaps reflect the readiness for social change in these states. He points out that the Finnish media, in particular, have tended to stress the problems in Russia, thus painting a negative image, whereas Russians are more or less forced to seek contacts with the West, and Finland is their nearest western neighbour.

Not all members of the security elite have been unreservedly delighted at the post-Soviet developments either, or at the challenges to infrastructures, for instance, presented by the new de-territorializations. Some military leaders have been worried about the strategic changes that might take place once new road connections have been built over the border, particularly in northern Finland. This infrastructure is crucial for organizing any kind of cross-border activity, however. No explicit threat from Russia is experienced in military circles, but old images of an enemy still existed after the Soviet collapse, even though not explicitly directed at Russia (Joenniemi, 1993). The comment made by General Hagglund, Commander-in-Chief in the Finnish Army, is perhaps indicative of a new era: "The Finns should not turn their backs on Russia, but keep up their links" (Koivisto, 1996). All the above examples illustrate the fact that boundaries are not only lines in the forest but also meaningful symbols and institutions which are deeply sedimented in various social practices and discourses.

Life in a Divided Community: The Perspective of Local Experience

Narratives constructed on national identities and threats, and on bounded, exclusive national spaces, are expressions of national socialization processes and boundaries usually play a crucial role in these narratives (Paasi, 1996, 1997). Questions of identity, culture and memory become complicated, fragmented and diversified in daily life, depending crucially on where people live—space makes a difference. Shils, 1981, argues that individual histories always include elements of the history of a "larger self"—a family, neighbourhood, locality or nationality. This collective memory unites individuals as parts of the histories of these entities. In daily life on the local scale, questions of distances, well-being, culture, economics and administrative practices become very concrete ones, and in border areas the social control of people in relation to the border is typically very strict, i.e. the local scale and the state coincide in very concrete terms.

During the Soviet period it was impossible to visit the ceded territories freely. The loss of these home areas was therefore a bitter experience for the spatial identities of evacuees. The Karelians preserved their lost landscapes and homes in their collective memory, their literature, collective action and myths. A return to their homes and the past became the major goal for most of them. A visit to the ceded areas became a Utopian dream (Paasi, 1996).

Värtsilä was a rapidly developing community before World War Two and was located some 100 km from the border. It was the main centre of the iron industry in Finland, with about 1,000 of its approximately 6,000 inhabitants employed in the iron works. The locality had emerged during the 19th century as a typical product of the rise of industrial capitalism. People living in the community often had a long local family history and therefore had a strong identity with the place and the industrial milieu. After World War Two, Värtsilä was split by the new border which ruined the whole infrastructure of the commune; the iron works, the central built-up area and all services were on the Soviet side, and in 1947 a frontier zone was established on the Finnish side which considerably restricted movement in the border area. Foreigners, for instance, needed permission from the Finnish security police to visit the zone. The border became a closed, controlled, mystic phenomenon. The ceding of the area also destroyed the population base. Värtsilä had had some 6,000 inhabitants before the war and was left with some 3,000 afterwards, but since the area could not provide jobs, out-migration continued at a rapid rate, so that the population was 2,000 in 1950, about 1,700 in 1960 and 922 in 1980. Today there are about 700 inhabitants (Paasi, 1996). The population of the Russian community of Värtsilä beyond the border was some 3,000 around 1990 (Paasi, 1996). The iron works that employed 1,000 during the Soviet era today provides work for some 600 people (Tykkyläinen, 1998).

In practice all Finns were evacuated to Finland from the areas that were ceded to the Soviet Union as a consequence of World War Two. The Finnish-speaking population is a small minority in the ceded areas today, representing the descendants of people who moved to Russia from the 17th century onwards, those who remained on the Soviet side when the border was established in 1920 and those who moved there on ideological grounds in the 1930s. The inhabitants are therefore mainly Russian speaking. A further reason for this lies in the settlement policy of the Soviet authorities after World War Two, in that the people who were first allowed to move to the ceded areas of Karelia were mainly Belorussians and Ukrainians (Paasi, 1996). This was also evident in Värtsilä. New inhabitants and factory workers were recruited from other parts of the Soviet Union, being chosen by the Party, which allowed only reliable communists to become members of the border community.

The complete closure of the border destroyed the spatial basis of the traditional local identities. It took almost 50 years after the war before the Finns were allowed to visit their old homes beyond the border. Russian Värtsilä, which became part of the larger administrative area of Sortavala, could still be seen from the hills on the Finnish side. It was formally forbidden to even look across the border to the Russian side, but people did so, anyway, to keep their memories alive. All activities in the Finnish commune of Värtsilä were directed towards Finland, and only a rail connection for the transport of timber joined the two sides of divided Värtsilä. The period of 50 years was long enough to produce many overlapping territorial identities among the people living in the locality, and the in-depth interviews carried out on the Finnish side in 1987–89 showed that attitudes towards the boundary varied a lot between the generations (Paasi, 1996). Those who had experienced life in the old, ceded community, the creation of the new border and the loss of their homes seemed to be living in a world where memories of the lost community still formed a crucial part of their regional identity, whereas the younger generations who had not experienced the war years seemed to live their daily lives in a context which had always been limited by geopolitical facts. For these people the boundary had always been there and the rules for acting in border areas had always been part of their daily routines. These people simply did not have any experience of a different situation or of the former territorial disputes. There was also another important difference between the generations. It was typical for the older people to be afraid of the new border after the war, but for younger generations the boundary had been rather a neutral phenomenon, part of what was taken for granted in everyday life.

When the border was gradually opened for personal travel, the number of border crossings increased rapidly since it became possible for the older people to bring their Utopian dream alive and visit their old home areas in the ceded territory. The opening of the border came at an opportune moment, for there were some 180,000 former refugees still alive who had been born there, and an immediate boom in nostalgic journeys to Karelia ensued. The total number of border crossings increased rapidly, and this was also the case at the Niirala crossing point in Värtsilä. The number of border crossings had already reached 26,000 by 1989, and in 1997 it was about half a million. Most Finns soon became familiar with pictures depicting former refugees searching Karelia for something that might bring back their local memories and identities from the past which had been broken off 50 years previously.

Like many Karelians, those born in Värtsilä also established associations, one in Joensuu in eastern Finland and one in Helsinki. The Värtsilä Association in Joensuu today has less than 200 members and scarcely 30 of these are active. It has concentrated on maintaining local forms of identity and heritage and on organizing visits to their former home area beyond the border. As with the Karelian people in general, the number of nostalgic trips has now decreased, largely due to the fact that the Utopian land they were looking for no longer exists; if the war did not destroy everything, the Sovietization of landscape and infrastructure did away with the rest (Paasi, 1996). The first visits were enough to demonstrate the huge gap in standards of living, and one new form of local participation has been to take clothes and other forms of aid to the children and elderly people in Russian Värtsilä.

Värtsilä was one of the first localities where cross-border activities were seen as a serious challenge for the future and it is still one of the major routes to the east. Soon after the opening of the border, plans for a great future to be achieved by co-operation were laid down and the idea of Värni, an industrial estate, was devised and soon registered in 1992. The partners were Finnish, Karelian and Russian firms together with five local authorities in eastern Finland. The idea was to provide Finnish, Russian and other firms with the opportunity to operate in a context that would open the way to exploiting the "enormous eastern markets" (Oksanen, 1994). Economic success has not been forthcoming, however, even though the number of border crossings has increased enormously The early expectations and plans that followed the opening of the border were perhaps too optimistic, in Värtsilä as elsewhere. Local Finnish entrepreneurs criticize the Finnish and Russian bureaucracy, the lack of financial resources and Russian investments and, finally, cultural and institutional differences. One example of a more successful project is a small sawmill company, Karlis Ltd., owned by four Russian partners and one Finnish one. This project—a real example of the emerging capitalism rather than an initiative from the local authorities—employs some 35 people, only one of whom comes from Finland. The Finnish co-owner's office, from which he conducts his business, is just on the Finnish side of the border; 90% of the sawn timber is supplied to customers outside Finland. The wage level is about

1/8th-1/10th of that prevailing in Finland, but for the local people it provides a clear alternative to unemployment (Tykkylainen, 1998).

Cross-border interaction has also had an effect in shaping the forms of local culture. According to the telephone interviews that the author carried out in spring 1998, the number of people who are able to use a combination of the Russian and Finnish languages is increasing continually and friend-ships have grown up between Finnish and Russian families. Local inhabit-ants often have long-term visas which allow them to go shopping in Russia, where motor fuel and cigarettes are cheaper. Increasing interaction can also be seen in the fact that mixed marriages between Finns and Russians are becoming more common. The opening of the border has had its effect on the local "moral landscape" also, as became obvious in my interviews at the be-ginning of 1998. Seven Finns, mostly men, had recently divorced their Finnish spouse and married a Russian, causing quite a stir in a small commu-nity of some 700 inhabitants. The processes of de-territorialization and re-territorialization of the border are thus also manifesting themselves in a reshaping of the borders of social and personal spaces as well.

Conclusion

Much of the recent discourse concerning the roles of the nation-state and boundaries has suggested that both are fading away in the post-modern, glo-balizing world. Territoriality is still explicitly linked with nation-states in the current world, however, and with the socialization processes aimed at the continual production and reproduction of the national social space. Bound-aries play a major role in the symbolization of this space. While the current world is becoming increasingly characterized by flows, boundaries still exist as symbols of the sovereignty of states, even if they do not have such a dra-matic role in distinguishing territories as they had in earlier times.

This paper has illustrated the complexity of boundaries by analysing the changing meanings of the Finnish-Russian border. The collapse of the Soviet Union radically altered the formerly closed, peripheral position of the border area, and Finland and Russia now share a motivation for cross-border inter-action and co-operation. The implications of the Russian transition and the opening of the border have been understood in similar ways on both sides, and the strengthening of economic ties is an important challenge for local and regional development. The problem is that the infrastructural prerequi-sites for cross-border co-operation are weak in the area. Much of the effort to strengthen co-operation has been concentrated on creating these prerequi-sites (buildings, roads, customs houses, education of the population). The challenges are substantial ones, as Eskelinen et al., 1998, p. 47, remind us; since transport routes towards the border were not fostered during the Soviet era, the border regions are sparsely populated and the urban centres with their service facilities are usually located considerable distances apart. The political separation of neighbouring regions also has produced remarkable cultural and institutional differences. All these problems are structural ones, which makes their eradication very difficult.

The collapse of the Soviet Union transformed not only Finnish economic policies but also political, security and military practices and discourses regarding the border areas. The political role of the border has changed now that it serves as the border between the EU and Russia. In Finland this larger institutional space is used both as a new scale for identification and as a resource for organizing cross-border activities. The military, border guarding and foreign policy elites maintain traditional national narratives of sovereignty, but the new security policy discourses are also characterized by different forms of de-territorialization. One example of these is the fact that Finland has been very active within the context of the European Union in opening up new connections with Russia and including that country in a larger European space. Finnish political elites were very active in efforts to have Russia accepted as a member of the Council of Europe, and their efforts to develop a "Northern Dimension" in EU policy have the same aims of creating economic links with Russia, integrating Russia into the larger European space and preventing environmental problems. These new connections are therefore not only economic ones but also illustrate the changing strategies of the security policy elite (Paasi, 1999).

All these examples show that the traditional interpretations of political geography regarding boundaries as lines are perhaps too narrow for our contemporary world, which is characterized by processes of de-territorialization and re-territorialization. Boundaries are complicated, historically contingent phenomena that are concomitantly both contextual social institutions and symbols and are constituted on various spatial scales in various institutional practices and discourses.

References

Agnew J. (1994) The territorial trap: the geographical assumptions of international relations theory. *Rev. Int. Pol. Econ.* 1, 53–80.

Anderson J. (1995) The exaggerated death of the nation-state, in Anderson J., Brook C. and Cochrane A. (Eds) *A Global World? Re-ordering Political Space*, pp. 65–112. Open University, Oxford.

Anderson J. (1996) The shifting stage of politics: new medieval and post-modern territorialities? *Environ. Plann. D* 14, 133–53.

Anderson M. (1996) *Frontiers: Territory and State Formation in the Modern World*. Policy Press, Cambridge.

Anderson M. and Bort E. (Eds) (1998) *The Frontiers of Europe*. Frances Pinter, London.

Arolainen T. (1996) Kaakonkulman onnenpäivät, *Helsingin Sanomat*, 11 February.

Campbell D. (1992) *Writing Security: United States Foreign Policy and the Politics of Identity*. Manchester University Press, Manchester.

Eger G. and Langer J. (Eds) (1996) *Border, Region and Ethnicity in Central Europe*. Norea Verlag, Klagenfurt.

Eskelinen H., Haapanen E. and Izotov A. (1998) The emergence of foreign economic activity in Russian Karelia, Publications of Karelian Institute No. 119, University of Joensuu.

Forsberg T. and Vaahtoranta T. (1993) Lähialuepolitiikan tuleminen, in Forsberg T. and Vaahtoranta T. (Eds) *Johdatus Suomen ulkopolitiikkaan*, pp. 232–60. Gaudeamus, Helsinki.

Hirst P. and Thompson G. (1996) *Globalization in Question*. Polity Press, Cambridge.

Joenniemi P. (1993) Euro-Suomi: rajalla, rajojen välissä vai rajaton? in Joenniemi P., Alapuro R. and Pekonen K. (Eds) *Suomesta Euro-Suomeen*, pp. 17–48. Rauhan-ja Konfliktin-tutkimuslaitos, tutkimustiedote 53, Tampere.

Jussila H., Bertolini J., Hünerkoch A., Rautio S. and Webber J. (1997) Price levels and purchasing power in Finnish and Russian Karelias, in Kortelainen J. (Ed) *Crossing the Russian Border*, pp. 127–36, Publication No. 3, Department of Geography, University of Joensuu.

Karelian Association (1996) *The Karelian Issue*. Karelian Association, Helsinki.

Kearns G. and Philo C. (Eds) (1993) *Selling Places*. Pergamon Press, London.

Kinnunen P. (1995) A look across the border: the views and expectations of the people in Northern Finland and Northwest Russia, in Dahlström M., Eskelinen H. and Wiberg U. (Eds) *The East-West Interface in the European North*, pp. 45–56. NST, Stockholm.

Koivisto P. (1996) Venäjälle ei saa kääntää selkää, *Kaleva*, 4 June.

Kortelainen J. (Ed) (1997) *Crossing the Russian Border*, Publication No. 3, Department of Geography, University of Joensuu.

Lynn N. J. and Fryer P. (1998) National-territorial change in the republics of the Russian North, *Pol. Geogr.* 17, 567–88.

Martinez O. (1994) The dynamics of border interaction: new approaches to border analysis, in Schofield C. H. (Ed) *Global Boundaries, World Boundaries*, vol. 1, pp. 1–15. Routledge, London.

Michaelsen S. and Johnson D. (Eds) (1997) *Border Theory: The Limits of Cultural Politics*. University of Minnesota Press, Minneapolis, MN.

Michelsen K. and Kuisma M. (1992) Nationalism and industrial development in Finland, *Bus. & Econ. Hist.* 21, 343–53.

Mikkola P. (1998) Alueita ei takaisin Suomelle, *Kaleva*, 8 February.

Naulapää R. (1998) Itärikollisuuden uhra on torjuttavissa, *Helsingin Sanomat*, 13 February.

Newman D. and Paasi A. (1998) Fences and neighbours in the postmodern world. Boundary narratives in the postmodern world, *Progr. Hum. Geogr.* 22, 186–207.

O'dowd L. and Wilson T. M. (Eds) (1996) *Borders, Nations and States.* Avebury, Aldershot.

Ohmae K. (1995) *The End of the Nation-state.* Free Press, London.

Oksanen K. (1994) Värni, teknologiakylä rajan takana Värtsilässä, *Rajaseutu* 71, 22.

Österberg E. (1996) Alkoholia virtaa itärajan takaa, *Helsingin Sanomat,* 8 January.

Paasi A. (1991) Deconstructing regions: notes on the scales of spatial life, *Environ. Plann. A* 23, 239–56.

Paasi A. (1996) *Territories, Boundaries and Consciousness: The Changing Geographies of the Finnish-Russian Border.* John Wiley, Chichester.

Paasi A. (1997) Geographical perspectives on Finnish national identity, *Geojournal* 43, 41–50.

Paasi A. (1998) The political geography of boundaries at the end of the millennium: challenges of the de-territorializing world, in Eskelinen H., Liikanen I. and Oksa J. (Eds) *Curtains of Iron and Cold: Reconstructing Borders and Scales of Interaction,* pp. 9–24. Ashgate, Aldershot.

Paasi A. (1999) Boundaries as social processes: territoriality in the world of flows. *Geopolitics* 3(1), 69–88.

Shapiro M. and Alker H. (Eds) (1996) *Challenging Boundaries.* University of Minnesota Press, Minneapolis, MN.

Shils E. (1981) *Tradition.* University of Chicago Press, Chicago.

Siukonen T. (1998) Tacis-rahojen viipyminen hidastaa raja-asemien tekoa, *Helsingin Sanomat,* 27 January.

Suomen Tilastollinen Vuosikirja (STV) (1997) *Statistical Yearbook of Finland.* STV, Helsinki.

Suomen Virallinen Tilasto (SVT) (1997) *Statistics Finland: Tourism Statistics. 1997, Transport and Tourism.* SVT, Helsinki.

Sweedler A. (1994) Conflict and co-operation in border regions: an examination of the Russian-Finnish border. *J. Borderland Studies* 9, 1–13.

Sykiäinen R. (1993) Itä-Karjalassa tehdään Suomesta hirviötä, *Kaleva,* 10 June.

Taylor P. J. (1994) The state as container: territoriality in the modern world-system, *Progr. Hum. Geogr.* 18, 151–62.

Tykkyläinen M. (1998) The emergence of capitalism and struggling against marginalization in the Russian North, in Jussila H., Majoral R. and Mutambirva C. (Eds) *Marginality in Space: Past, Present and Future,* pp. 48–69. Ashgate, Aldershot.

Valimaa S. (1997) Sallaan 50.000 ylittäjän raja, *Kaleva,* 15 December.

Welchman J. C. (Ed) (1996) *Rethinking Borders.* University of Minnesota Press, Minneapolis, MN.

9

The Attitudes of Youth toward the Other Side

The Finnish-Swedish and Finnish-Russian Borders

Pirjo Jukarainen

This essay analyzes how young people living on the Swedish-Finnish and Finnish-Russian borders view both the boundaries and the people on the other side. In addition, this article repeats the thinking of young border residents about nation and nationalism. It also includes comments on significant differences in attitudes on Finland's eastern and western borders. The study makes the point that perceptions and attitudes are important parts of border regions.

Dr. Pirjo Jukarainen is a senior researcher at the Tampere Peace Research Institute and a lecturer in the Department of Regional Studies and Environmental Policy at the University of Tampere, Finland. For more information about the complexity of the Finnish-Russian border see her internationally available co-authored book: Pirkkoliisa Ahponen and Pirjo Jukarainen, eds., Tearing Down the Curtain, Opening the Gates: Northern Boundaries in Change *(Jyväskylä, Finland, 2000).*

Introduction

This paper examines the cultural and national attitudes of young people living in two different border regions: the Finnish-Russian Karelia borderland and the Finnish-Swedish Tornio River Valley. The analysis is based on the author's survey of young people (ages 12 to 16) who live close to these national borders.

From Pirjo Jukarainen, "National Divisions and Borderland Youth," in *Cooperation, Environment, and Sustainability in Border Regions,* ed. Paul Ganster (San Diego: Institute for Regional Studies of the Californias and San Diego State University Press, 2001), 355–66.

At first glance, it might seem that Finland's eastern and western borders are absolute antipodes: the western borderland exudes peace and harmony and the other still resembles an Iron Curtain. The Finnish-Swedish borderlands (like the Swedish-Norwegian) are often cited as examples of soft, invisible borders, areas with an inner Nordic sense of togetherness. When examined from a sociocultural perspective, however, Finland's eastern and western border regions share many similarities. In the spatial and cultural views of young residents, both eastern and western national borders are culturally demarcating and limiting. On the western border, there is a sense of "Finns versus Swedes," in which Finnish youth, in particular, set themselves in opposition to their neighbors. In the east, the border is more sharply demarcated, with one interesting difference. Along the Finnish-Swedish border, both countries' young people have similar attitudes toward the culture and nation across the boundary. Finnish and Russian youth, however, have very different attitudes toward one another. Finns want to more or less close the border to prevent Russians from entering their hometowns, while Russians want to keep the border open to guarantee at least their own opportunities to cross the boundary. Interestingly, young Finns are more reserved and suspicious about cross-border activity in both the east and the west. The Finnish youth puts up a severe national-cultural barrier that is not easy to break through.

The Tornio River Valley

Although Finland's western border has been open for most of its history, a peculiar type of national-cultural divide exists between young Finns and Swedes. One teacher from the Finnish-Swedish twin-city of Tornio-Haparanda aptly stated that every cross-border cooperative activity is hindered by an underlying spirit of national battle (*maaotteluhenki*). National interests too often take precedence over regional or local needs. Despite Nordic harmony (the Finnish-Swedish border has been named by the media the most peaceful border in Europe) and border permeability, the last 200 years of national politics have created nationalist and separatist consciousness in its youth. Given these mental and national borders, it seems inevitable that there will be serious barriers to cross-border cooperation and the development of border region identities in the near future.

Another indicator of nationally divided consciousness in the area was a vote against a cross-border united city infrastructure in a referendum held in the fall of 2002. Despite an active campaign by local authorities and entrepreneurs, slightly more than half of the voters said no to the project called "Rajalla/På Gränsen/At the Border" (see http://www.pagransen.com/). The municipal actors did not give up, however. The Haparanda municipal council decided to continue to build the city centers of the two border-towns, Swedish Haparanda and Finnish Tornio, together. The authorities justified their decision to move ahead with the project because voter turnout was only about 50 percent of registered voters, which meant that only about a quarter of the Haparanda population could be counted as opponents.

Tornio-Haparanda

The Tornio-Haparanda area was composed of a single town (Tornio) until 1809, when the border was established between Sweden and Russia and Finland was incorporated into Russia. Tornio had been an important northern trading center since the Middle Ages and in order to guarantee the continuation of trade and communication, it was deemed necessary to build another town (Haparanda) on the Swedish side of the new border. Haparanda achieved city status in 1842. After Finland's independence in 1917, and even more so after Finland and Sweden joined the European Union (EU) in 1995, the two towns managed to overcome administrative barriers in many fields of activity. Today, administratively and logistically, they are run more like one city than two. The latest effort is the already mentioned infrastructure project called At the Border, which started in 1996 and is to be completed in 2015. The aim of this project is to retain expenditures of local people more in the twin-town area, of which 60 percent now flows elsewhere. The project budget is 200 million euros (approximately U.S.$200 million), and is funded by the local and regional authorities and by the EU through the Interreg Programme. One of their cooperative organizations or forums is called "Provincia Bothniensis" (northern province). The twin-city (also called a "Eurocity") has about thirty-five thousand inhabitants, two-thirds of whom live on the so-called Finnish side.

Interviews and information from this area were collected primarily from a "cross-border school" (really a language school) where the classes are a mixture of pupils from both sides of the border. The respondents had daily contact with young people of another nationality and were being educated to be bilingual and bicultural. Nonetheless, they had not lost their national identities, although their nationalism was strangely ambiguous. The majority of the students were unable (or unwilling) to define what kind of fundamental differences there are between Finns and Swedes. Often, the differences they recognized were practical variations rather than fundamental cultural issues: some goods were said to be cheaper, better, or more easily available across the border; there is a one-hour time difference; or the other side was said to have a better public swimming pool, a taller city hall, more or better shops or cycling routes, and so on. The few who were able to define cultural and national differences spoke about the "others" in a negative fashion and used a variety of social and national stereotypes. They described the "other" as being worse than them in some ways and grouped them together by making generalizations: "they" were said to be snobbish, dumb, lazy, poorly dressed, proud, always complaining, too loud, badly behaved, and so on.

This attitude prevailed on both sides of the border. Both young Finns (from Tornio) and young Swedes (from Haparanda) found far more to complain about than to cherish in their neighbors. Only one minor difference was revealed, as there seemed to be a bit of jealousy underlying the remarks the Finnish youth made when criticizing their Swedish neighbors. They mentioned with some envy that the Swedes were more extroverted, better ice hockey players, or better musicians. The Swedes showed no signs of jealousy. In fact, three students from Swedish Haparanda, aged 15 to 16, sarcastically wished a "happy return to the Finnish side" to those Finns that complained about Swedish society, but lived in Haparanda nonetheless. These young Swedes had enough self-esteem to defend their own side of the border; they had pride in their homeland and wanted the Finns to know it.

The nationalist attitudes of these young people seem mild and ambiguous, but they were clearly there. They were not grounded in any deep or fundamental ethnic antagonism, but in a more postmodern cultural differentiation, contextually sensitive and complex rather than strong, deterministic, or coherent. This nationalistic ambiguity is best illustrated by the young people's general attitudes toward the border and their descriptions of their own everyday lives close to the border. They took the openness of the border for granted and liked the flexibility and ease they are accustomed to when crossing the border. At the same time, however, they saw many things through a "national lens." They talked about national points of interest and advantages, never forgetting their own nationalities. Their "sides" were central elements of their spatial "mind maps," even though most crossed the border weekly, almost without noticing.

From an administrative and logistical standpoint, the students viewed the border more positively than negatively. The majority on both sides of the border considered the current openness of the border either good or satisfactory. Some even appreciated it for introducing positive multiplicity and variety into the local milieu. In this respect, it could be said that they had a sense of borderlander mentality as far as everyday life was concerned. The border was there to be crossed and benefitted from; it was not thought of as a hindrance.

> A good thing about living near the border is that if one does not find nice clothes at home, one just has to cycle over [the border bridge] and see if one finds something over there. And then if one goes out, then it is good that they are so close to each other. It is good to go to Tornio if there are only a few people around in Haparanda.
> —Girl, age 16, Haparanda

> Border traffic should increase because Finnish people buy things from
> Sweden.
> —Boy, age 13, Haparanda

> Just now it is good that Haparanda lies close to the border. This way one
> has more opportunities.
> —Girl, age 15, Haparanda

The uncontrollable aspects of the border worried some students. Pollution from traffic, drug imports, and the transport of other illegal goods were named as reasons that border crossings should diminish. Their feelings about other, more social aspects, however, were mixed. They expressed patriotism in conjunction with a notion that the border would naturally continue to be open; they assumed that the border would always remain open in the future, but nevertheless wished to preserve and protect their own nations and nationalities.

> It can be very tough to live here on the border, especially when Finland
> wins the ice hockey games. But if the winner is Sweden, it is pretty cool.
> —Girl, age 16, Haparanda

> I don't care whether the border traffic increases or diminishes, as long as
> the Swedes stay on their side.
> —Boy, age 13, Tornio

> I think that Haparanda is getting bigger with inhabitants from Finland cross-
> ing over . . . on the other hand, I hope that Haparanda stays Swedish.
> —Boy, age 13, Haparanda

Some young people worried about cultural segregation, but generally, they took the cultural/national borders for granted. They, too, felt that there were two sides, two nations.

> It is bad when, for example, Sweden and Finland meet in a hockey game.
> Then it becomes almost a competition between us [Haparanda and Tornio].
> —Girl, age 13, Haparanda

> I don't know whether the border traffic should increase or diminish, since
> there are Swedes in Tornio and Finns in Haparanda anyway.
> —Girl, age 13, Haparanda

> It is good that there is traffic. From both sides. There is nothing strange in
> that.
> —Girl, age 15, Tornio

> Isn't it beneficial for Finland and Sweden if there is more traffic crossing
> the border?
> —Boy, age 15, Tornio

Finnish Pello and Swedish Pello

Although they bear the same name and society and culture across the border over the delineating Tornio River, the two Pellos have no established twin-city practices as Haparanda and Tornio do. The population is much larger on the Finnish side than on the Swedish side. The Finnish municipality of Pello has approximately five thousand six hundred inhabitants, half of whom live in the city itself. Its tiny neighbor, Swedish Pello, is a village of 498 people.

Young people's opinions in this region were very similar to those expressed in Tornio-Haparanda as far as national differences were concerned. Most young people described "us" and "them" in quite similar terms, but still found the identifying terms "Finnish" and "Swedish" natural and legitimate. One difference became evident when students from Finnish Pello were interviewed. They were rather disinterested in contacting their Swedish neighbors or finding out more about their everyday lives. Of those interviewed, 26 percent (11 of 42) held negative attitudes toward the Swedes and Sweden in general, 45 percent (19 of 42) showed no interest in their neighbors whatsoever, and only 29 percent (12 of 42) expressed any kind of interest—some even thought that increased social communication would be beneficial for both sides. This should not be taken to mean that the students never cross the border; quite the contrary, in fact. Even those with the most negative attitudes said that they visited the other side at least once a month. The reasons for doing so, however, were pragmatic: for cheaper candy, better skiing and skateboarding, and so on. Only three of the respondents from the Finnish side mentioned relatives or friends on the other side as reasons for crossing the border.

Finnish-Russian Karelia

The Karelian situation was studied by conducting two local case analyses: one with a pair of cities, Russian Vyborg (population 80,000) and Finnish Lappeenranta (population 57,000); and another with a pair of towns, Russian Haapalampi (approximate population 2,000), and Finnish Tohmajärvi (population 5,700). All lie close to the border established by the Soviet Union and Finland in 1944. The contemporary population of both Vyborg and Haapalampi is mostly Russian speaking, as its predecessors were from different areas of the former Soviet Union. The original Karelians, literally a borderland population between the so-called Western and Eastern spheres of influence, are now a tiny minority (approximately 10 percent of the total population). Most of the Karelian population in the south was evacuated to Finland after the final peace treaty in 1944 and extensive practices of Sovietization (in the USSR) and Finlandization (in Finland) took place in Karelia. As a result, Karelian culture, including the language, slowly lost its importance.

The nationalistic attitudes of the youth living along this eastern border were quite similar to those held by their western counterparts. One major difference was that the Russians expressed a great deal of curiosity about and willingness to cross into Finland. Their interest, however, was connected to Russian patriotism in Vyborg and to feelings of regional belonging in Haapalampi. Young people from Vyborg wanted to cross the border for social and economic reasons, while remaining culturally and linguistically Russian. Those from Haapalampi were even more open to cross-border activities, but still wished to retain and protect their Karelian regional culture. The young Finns in the area were more distrustful and reserved about cross-border activities, making openly protectionist statements. Many had little or no respect for Russians, wanted more extensive border controls, or were even willing to change the location of the border. The following examples show the strong national-political opinions expressed by young people on both sides of the Finnish-Russian border.

The Finns

> The Finnish-Russian border shouldn't stay the same as it is now. It should go far forward into Russia because Russia is many times bigger than Finland has ever been . . . Finland can never give up to Russia. If that would happen, Russia would run the whole country, and at least the food economy would go bankrupt. Russians should stay on their side of the border and they should live as they can on their own. They have no reason to come here.
> —Boy, age 13, Lappeenranta

> This is just that kind of border town [marginalized] and you are not able to make yourself known that much here—in order to become famous, for instance. Maybe it is the castle that I like the most here, although the Russians will probably take it over sooner or later, as they have taken our jobs already.
> —Girl, age 14, Lappeenranta

> I kind of hope that Karelia will be taken back, as I think its natural resources would benefit Finland. If this does not happen, I think the border will remain the same as it is now. Good luck to efforts to buy Karelia back.
> —Girl, age 15, Lappeenranta

> I will never learn the Russian language, even if I have to die.
> —Boy, age 13, Tohmajärvi

> It really bothers me that the Russians' tactic is to buy weapons with all their money, then they ask for food supplies from other countries, and if the others won't give them, then they conquer that country.
> —Boy, age 13, Tohmajärvi

The border traffic should diminish since there are now almost more Russians than Finns here.
—Girl, age 14, Tohmajärvi

The Russians

I believe in the rebirth of our home district, and it means that in the year 2020 everything will be well. In the twenty-first century, people of many nationalities will live here, but everybody will speak Russian. . . . I think that if I went abroad I would not be able to live there. Russian people are different. We have a different soul and a different humor. When I went to Finland, I met a Russian lady there; I was so happy when I understood that I could live here and still be in Russia.
—Girl, age 15, Vyborg

[In the year 2020] people here will speak Russian. In Russia everybody has to speak the same language, and no one can prohibit that.
—Girl, age 16, Vyborg

In the future, I think the border with Finland will be open. In my opinion, people will then speak Russian, and only Russian, here. Living in the neighborhood with Finland is no excuse for the Finnish language to invade our home.
—Boy, age 15, Vyborg

Tohmajärvi and Haapalampi

In the Russian village of Haapalampi in the Karelian Republic, young people enthusiastically described the beauty of their immediate surroundings and the nearby natural features of Karelia. Almost all of them showed personal affection for the rich flora and fauna of their area. Their positive praise of their homeland was overwhelming. It seemed that the young people from Haapalampi wanted to prove to this Finnish researcher that Karelia (their Karelia) was doing just fine.[1] The majority supported an increase in border crossings, stating idealistically that people should live peacefully, get to know each other, and be friends. Only four of 43 surveys turned in by respondents showed negative attitudes towards the "other side." Indeed, many even said they "love" the Finnish language and expected to use it a lot in the future, either at work, with their friends, or even with new relatives. For the most part, they saw Finland positively as a nation (one 15-year-old boy mistook Finland for a city), admiring its beauty and cleanliness.

I study Finnish because I live in Karelia, next to Finland, and here the Finnish language is more popular. It will be easier to find a job and get a profession.
—Girl, age 15, Haapalampi

I study the Finnish language because lots of Finns visit us and Finland lies next to our country. . . . I would like it if Russians would learn Finnish and we would visit them more often and be in contact with them, and they visit us. Let them spend their vacation here, and ours there.
—Girl, age 14, Haapalampi

I decided by myself to study the Finnish language because I wanted to know more about life there on the other side of the border. I wonder why it is so clean there. No garbage anywhere, pure paradise.
—Boy, age 13, Haapalampi

In the small municipality of Tohmajärvi in the Finnish province of North Karelia, ideas about the border and those who live on the "other side" were quite different. Young people found a great deal to criticize in Russian society. They wondered, for instance, how Russian houses could be so dilapidated, why the roads are so poor, the economic system so wrought, and people's salaries unpredictable. To them, Russia means the nearby Karelian Republic, which some of them had firsthand experience with and knowledge about. Still, they talked about Russia and Russians in general terms, not about Karelia or Karelians. This was an interesting contrast to their Russian counterparts' strong sense of their own regional Karelian identity. The young people from the Finnish town of Tohmajärvi did not acknowledge or endorse this regional identity.

Very few of those from Tohmajärvi found anything negative to say about Russians themselves. One girl stated that she does not trust Russians; others used the pejorative wartime name "ryssä"[2] for Russians. Almost all critiques and complaints focused on the Russian social and political system, not the Russian culture or people. In fact, some expressed a sort of pity and sympathy for the Russians, laying the blame on an abstract system rather than on individual persons.

Finnish Lappeenranta and Russian Vyborg

In this area, cultural differences were quite clear between Russians and Finns. The students on both sides were very attached to their cities. They described and analyzed the current and future development of their cities in a national framework, not a regional one. The "border region" of Karelia was hardly mentioned at all. Many young people from Russian Vyborg were more interested in learning Central European languages than Finnish.

I think Finland may have lots of very interesting things, but not as much as Russia and the former Soviet Union. I think this because Finland has been part of Russia, and has been very influenced by it.
—Boy, age 15, Vyborg (never been to Finland)

I study English, German, and I started (but didn't continue) to learn Finnish. Language is a tool for communicating with people from other countries. English is an international language. I will need English in my work and then I will be able to read English literature.
—Girl, age 15, Vyborg (visited Finland once)

Attitudes toward the border varied greatly on both sides. The majority of young people interviewed in Vyborg saw the increase in border crossings as useful and fruitful. Finns were once again more negative and skeptical about cross-border connections and the majority was against an increase in border traffic.

The Russians

In my opinion, border crossings should increase. From the Russian side it [the ability to cross] is a kind of sign of welfare. On the Finnish side, it is more a matter of tourist curiosity and economic benefit. It also helps communications between Russia and Finland.
—Boy, age 15, Vyborg

Border crossings should increase because Russia needs cooperation with Finland in many areas.
—Boy, age 16, Vyborg

To me, borders are not needed at all. Although a border is financially profitable (collecting money), it is not needed in this century. Borders bring only problems.
—Girl, age 16, Vyborg

I think border crossings should diminish as this would ease and hasten the crossing procedure because there would be less crowds. A border, however, cannot be invisible. It is a difficult question and Russia now has too many problems to fully open the border.
—Girl, age 16, Vyborg

[Ironically] Border crossings should increase as everybody should see the huge and almighty Finland.
—Boy, age 15, Vyborg

The Finns

Border crossings should decrease because horrible, rattling cars cross from Russia.
—Boy, age 13, Lappeenranta

Border crossings should be reduced a bit, and control of drug smuggling should be strengthened.
—Boy, age 13, Lappeenranta

There should be more frequent border crossings, especially when seen from an administrative perspective, so that the customs practices would be better organized. It is not fun to sit in a car for a couple of hours just for nothing.
—Boy, age 13, Lappeenranta

Border traffic should increase, as it would just bring more money to Finland.
—Boy, age 14, Lappeenranta

At the moment, one-third of all people in Lappeenranta are Russian, at least almost. The good thing is that they bring lots of money here, but there are bad sides as well. For example, in the hardware store, they serve Russians first. It is the priority and not in the service of us locals. Of course they want to create a good image of us, but in my logic, it is inconsistent. In my opinion, there should be fewer Russians in Lappeenranta.
—Girl, age 15, Lappeenranta

Russians should come less to Finland and Finns should go more to Russia, as the Russians are not needed here stealing all kinds of stuff and driving like crazy, but Finns should go to Russia and bring CDs, spirits, and tobacco from there.
—Boy, age 15, Lappeenranta

Conclusion

Nationalist attitudes are certainly evident among young people living close to the Finnish-Swedish border, despite efforts to obliterate boundaries in the area. Even those who showed the most positive attitudes toward the culture and society across the border used nationalist terms (Finland, Sweden, Finnish, Swedish, and so on) and did not speak of a common borderland, such as the Tornio River Valley.

We should appreciate Swedish people and Sweden more, likewise the Swedes should appreciate Finland and Finnish people. We are similar and equal (although Finns are better in ice hockey).
—Girl, age 13, Finnish Pello

Language is traditionally one of the most (if not the most) important issues in modern nations and the concept of nationalism. The youth in the Tornio-Haparanda borderlands, however, regarded language in a very postmodern manner. These young people presumed (and even hoped) that the two sides to the border would remain in the future and that both sides would be bi- or multilingual, without clear linguistic divisions.

In Tornio, both Finnish and Swedish are—will be—spoken, since here we "live on the border."
—Boy, age 15, Tornio

The youth of Pello, however, seemed more reserved about being bilingual. The following statement crystalizes this attitude:

> In Sweden, they speak some Finnish, but in Finland people hardly speak Swedish at all. In the year 2020 people might speak Swedish here in [Finnish] Pello.
> —Girl, age 13, Pello

It is interesting that not one young person mentioned the existing borderlands language of the Tornio River Valley, meän kieli ("our language"), which is a kind of creole hybrid of Finnish and Swedish. Even more strange is that even those few who used this borderlands language when answering the questionnaire did not mention it as a future language of the area, but spoke about national ones instead.

On the Karelian border, most young Russians (both from Vyborg and Haapalampi) were proud of their language and wanted to protect it, although they were also very interested in learning other languages—mostly English, but also German, French, and even Finnish. This great interest is understandable. For a long time it was not possible for many Soviet citizens to learn foreign languages. Even now, there are problems finding fully qualified language teachers and learning opportunities.

Most Finns had a rather passive attitude toward learning other languages. Their most common answer to why they studied a particular language was that it was required by their school. To them, learning languages was an unavoidable task somewhat taken for granted.

In general, the national-cultural divide between Finns and Russians was most evident in the way the young people felt about so-called security issues. (Security issues here are understood broadly as anything based on perceptions of threat.) In Russian Haapalampi, in the Karelian Republic, main security issues involved environmental problems, forest industries in particular. The "other side" was heavily blamed for environmental contamination or devastation. The environment was, above all, perceived as national property to be protected from influences from across the border.

> In my mind, the border should not be crossed so often and we should have less tourists. In Karelia—my home country—we cut our forests and then send them to you, to Finland. There you grow your own trees and have beautiful forests. But now we have only empty places, we do not have full forests. You cannot walk anywhere and hear the birds sing.
> —Boy, age 15, Haapalampi

> There is plenty of forest in Karelia. Forests are very beautiful, but now lots of wood is taken away from Karelia. Why does everybody like our nature, our forests, and yet destroy them? Why does one appreciate only the riches one owns him- or herself? Why aren't the other's riches appreciated?
> —Girl, age 15, Haapalampi

On the Finnish side, and especially in Lappeenranta, young people felt that the main security problem was illegal traffic in the form of smuggling, drug dealing, and criminals crossing the border. In Vyborg, the students were more concerned with their cultural (mostly linguistic) unity and survival. They were proud of their Russian culture and language and wanted to protect them from external invasions.

> It really bothers me that in their own country Finns are very well behaved and obedient, but if they come to Russia they show all the signs of an uncivilized people. This hurts us deeply.
> —Girl, age 15, Vyborg

> Our two nations (Russia and Finland) should help each other. . . . But borders should never be "invisible," because of our centuries-old regional independence. Cultural development should not be united because it is important for every nation to keep up its own traditions. Mutual cultural relations should develop harmoniously, without national conflicts. The language should not be common because two cultures should not be mixed together.
> —Girl, age 15, Vyborg

> Finns are an interesting people, but they lack the kind of soulfulness, ingenuity, and resourcefulness that we Russians or their neighbors the Swedes have (I know from personal experience as I have been both to Finland and Sweden). But we have lots to learn from the Finns. Sometimes I am disturbed by misunderstandings due to our psychological differences.
> —Boy, age 15, Vyborg

> I believe that in the year 2020 Russian people will still live here and they will speak Russian. Rude and drunk Finns will finally feel ashamed of themselves and will respect both us (the whole of Russia) and me personally, as I will stay and live here also in the year 2020.
> —Boy, age 15, Vyborg

Notes

1. In Karelia, words have many meanings, depending on who is speaking. Some Finns use the term, "lost Karelia" or "Russian Karelia," when referring to the ceded and evacuated areas now belonging to the Russian Federation, including areas that have never been under Finnish rule. The Karelian Republic excludes areas of the administrative region of Leningrad (Leningradskaja oblast) in the south, which Finns consider to belong to Karelia.

2. During World War II, the derogatory term, "ryssä," was commonly used by Finns to refer to the Russian enemy. Today, it has a more explicitly negative and racist connotation.

10

Meaning and Significance of the Canadian-American Border

Roger Gibbins

Borders are often not only on the geographic margins of national life, but they are on the political and social margins as well. The Canadian-U.S. boundary, however, is somewhat different. While this border is far from the centers of power in the United States, most of Canada's population is located along its length. Thus, it has a huge impact on Canadian life, but a small impact on the United States. This article explores these issues, providing a useful comparison with the U.S.-Mexican border, the other major boundary in North America.

Roger Gibbins is head of the Canada West Foundation, a nonpartisan public policy research group based in Calgary, Alberta, Canada. He is also professor of political science at the University of Calgary. He has published nineteen books and over one hundred articles and book chapters, most dealing with western Canadian themes and issues.

Introduction

In any comparative study, there is a risk in stressing the idiosyncratic features of one's own case. To argue, for example, that the Canadian-American borderlands are unique could diminish their comparative appeal. . . . At the same time, it may be the very distinctive aspects of this particular North American experience that best characterize the Canadian-American borderlands and

From Roger Gibbins, "Meaning and Significance of the Canadian-American Border," in *Borders and Border Regions in Europe and North America*, ed. Paul Ganster et al. (San Diego: Institute for Regional Studies of the Californias and San Diego State University Press, 1997), 315–31.

that have the greatest impact on the interplay between the international border and transnational regional integration.

This paper has a straightforward architecture. The first section examines the nature of the Canadian-American border and identifies some of its unique characteristics. The second section briefly discusses a number of ways in which the border has been eroded in recent years, ways which in most respects are not peculiar to the Canadian-American experience but which instead reflect more global patterns. The third section explores the complexity and asymmetry of the border region, and shows how the American border region differs quite dramatically from its Canadian counterpart. The fourth discusses the interplay of the international border with the dynamics of transnational regional integration. In conclusion, a tentative examination of the extent to which the Canadian-American experience sheds useful light on the more general comparative experience with borders, borderlands, and transnational regional integration will be offered.

The Canadian-American Border

The Canadian-American border stretches almost 8,000 kilometers from the Atlantic Ocean to the Pacific Ocean, and then runs along the northern boundary between Alaska and both British Columbia and the Yukon Territories. Its very length has given the border a mythological significance, at least within Canada, where it is lauded as the world's longest undefended border.[1] This phrase reflects the lack of significant geographical, racial, linguistic (except in the case of Québec), or religious barriers between the American and Canadian populations, barriers which a political boundary might reinforce under less fortunate circumstances. It also reflects the fact that there has never been a need for Americans to defend themselves against Canada, and that Canadians would be unable to defend themselves against an American invasion.[2] At the same time, Canadians have made a concerted effort to defend the border through political and economic means, a defense that does not take place along the border as such but that extends backwards into the national community to incorporate a variety of barriers to American economic and cultural intrusions. For example, the tariff wall between the two countries provided the foundation of the national economic policy for more than 100 years, and there have been multitudinous restrictions on foreign investment and American content on Canadian radio and television. Indeed, debates over the need to protect Canada from American intrusions have formed one of the fundamental axes of Canadian political life (Smiley 1980). In short, the border has been of great significance to the historical unfolding of Canadian politics, a significance *not* shared in the American experience.[3]

The national asymmetry with respect to the historical importance of the border is more generally characteristic of the Canadian-American experience. The American population, which is approximately ten times that of Canada,[4] is relatively evenly dispersed throughout the country whereas three-quarters of the Canadian population live in a narrow band within 150 kilometers of the international border. Unlike the situation in Canada, where major cities—Fredericton, Québec, Montreal, Toronto, Winnipeg, Regina, Vancouver, Victoria—are strung out in close proximity to the border, few major American cities are located near the border. Those that are, owe their location to the proximity of important geographical features, such as the Great Lakes, rather than to the magnetism of the border itself. While the Mexican-U.S. border may have been "a line that attracted people" (Hansen 1981: 34), this has not been the case with the Canadian-American border. As a result of all of these factors, the border has a much more limited impact on American life than it has on Canadian life; even its impact on American communities physically proximate to the border is slight.

For Canadians, however, the border looms large because the United States has been such a pervasive factor in virtually all aspects of Canadian life. As previously noted, the bulk of the Canadian population lives in close proximity to the international border, although this demographic distribution may stem from a desire to move as far south as possible rather than from the pull of the border per se. The border itself is very porous; it is spanned by extensive family and friendship ties, corporate structures, media networks, trade unions, social and religious organizations, and professional sports leagues.[5] Although it would be an exaggeration to say that the northern two-thirds of North America is seamless, the seam created by the international border is all but invisible in many respects. In the words of McKinsey and Konrad (1989: 1), "the border acts more like a sieve than a shield."

The influence of the United States is felt not only in communities proximate to the border but throughout Canada. In this sense, the border penetrates the Canadian consciousness, identity, economy, and polity to a degree unknown and unimaginable in the United States. Thus, although Canadians and Americans may share the same international border,[6] they share it in very different ways. Only Canada can be described as a "borderlands society" (Gibbins 1989). If we think of the "borderlands" as a region in which the international boundary is blurred at the same time that its saliency is heightened, then the term fits Canada remarkably well. Despite a persistent Canadian search for national differences, "things American" are so extensively woven into Canadian life that the national boundary all but evaporates. As a consequence, Canadian-American comparisons, slights both real and imagined, and undercurrents of anti-Americanism play prominent roles in the Canadian political culture and broader social fabric.

Finally, it is worth noting here that the Canadian-American border is Canada's only border of any significance, whereas the Mexican-American border has been far more important to Americans, and to the American culture and media, than has the international border to the north. (Just try to find an American restaurant specializing in "Canadian food"!) The Arctic border has not been a significant part of the Canadian public consciousness, except perhaps during the 1950s and 1960s when there was a possibility of Soviet bomber attacks.[7] Thus, Canada stands in sharp contrast to a country such as Germany, which borders on nine different nation-states. Canada has but a single point of national comparison, and that happens to be the wealthiest and most powerful country in the world. As novelist Margaret Atwood (1982: 380) points out: "One of Canada's problems is that it's always comparing itself to the wrong thing. If you stand beside a giant, of course you tend to feel a little stunted."

The Erosion of the International Border

The Canadian-American border, like international borders everywhere, is under pressure from a variety of continental and global forces that are eroding the "lines on maps" demarcating the international state system (Gibbins 1991). These forces include economic globalization, borderless financial markets, technological change with respect to the mass media, and transnational social movements such as environmentalism and feminism, which challenge nationally idiosyncratic approaches to social values and public policies. This pattern of change was both symbolized and reinforced in the North American context by the 1990 Free Trade Agreement (FTA) between Canada and the United States, and by the 1993 North American Free Trade Agreement (NAFTA) among Canada, Mexico, and the United States.[8] While neither the FTA nor NAFTA fully replicates the corrosive impact of the European Union on international borders, both move North America down the same road.

The erosion of the border has often been cast in normative terms by Canadian scholars who see it as a threat to Canadian cultural values, to social programs such as national health insurance, to the remnants of domestic control within the national economy and, more recently, to environmental standards. In short, the erosion of the border has been seen as a threat to Canadian sovereignty, and to the distinctive national values sheltered by that sovereignty.[9] American scholars, however, have not identified a reciprocal threat to American sovereignty or values stemming from the erosion of the international border between Canada and the United States. Although the NAFTA debate evoked some faint undertones of the Canadian debate in the United States, the American fear was directed toward Mexico rather than Canada, and toward an economic rather than cultural threat. This difference in national perspectives is rooted in the reality that should the erosion of the border lead to the convergence of cultural values or social policy, it is Canadians rather than Americans who will do the converging. As Smiley observed (1988: 442) in the context of the FTA debate:

> The thrust of any free trade agreement between Canada and the United States will be towards the harmonization of the public policies of the two countries. It is overwhelmingly likely that the direction of the harmoniza- tion will be to bring Canadian policies into harmony with U.S. norms rather than the reverse.

The border crossing at Huntingdon between Washington state and British Columbia on the U.S.-Canadian border, 1995. *Photograph by Paul Ganster*

It is also worth noting that debates over national sovereignty are a more pressing and immediate concern in Canada than they are in the United States, a difference that again makes Canadians more sensitive to the international border. This comes only in part from the fact that Canada is the smaller and weaker partner in the continental relationship. It also reflects greater internal instability in the Canadian case. The chronic national-unity crisis, and the continued uncertainty about Québec's future within the federal state, have made Canadians more alert to threats to sovereignty and national survival. In addition, the internal-unity debates have been explicitly linked to the evolu- tion of the Canadian-American relationship. It has been argued, for example, that continental free trade may make the sovereignty option more attractive for Québec by diminishing the importance of the Canadian economic union. For the same reason, it has been argued that free trade may increase the inher- ently centrifugal forces of regionalism by increasing north-south trade while at the [same] time reducing east-west trade within Canada.

For better or worse, there is little doubt that both international borders and the internal borders of federalism in North America are being eroded, as they are being eroded elsewhere in the world. But what does this mean for the immediate Canadian-American borderlands and for transnational patterns of regional integration? To address such questions, we must begin with a closer look at the border regions.

The Border Regions

It might seem reasonable to expect that the border regions of Canada and the United States would be a rich and extensively exploited area of comparative research. As previously mentioned, the border has been of central importance in the evolution of Canadian political life, and the bulk of the Canadian population lives reasonably close to the border. Moreover, there have been numerous border disputes between the two countries involving such things as acid rain, fishing rights, tanker traffic, and water pollution, disputes which could provide, and in a few cases (Lemco 1991) have provided, the fodder for academic discourse.

In general, however, the borderlands region has not generated a great deal of research,[10] nor has it played a significant role in the comparative literature on borders and borderlands.[11] Certainly there has been a marked indifference among American scholars, whose research has focused almost exclusively on the Mexican-American border. Canadian scholars, for their part, have focused on the more general penetration of American business, culture, and politics into Canada; the borderlands, per se, have been of little interest. (Of course, given that such a large proportion of the Canadian population lives so near the border, this distinction can get blurred.) There have certainly been comparative studies of Canada and the United States,[12] and there have even been a few comparative studies of regionalism in Canada and the United States (Gibbins 1982). However, there have been very few comparative studies of contiguous regions in the two countries.[13]

Regional contiguity is important because the Canadian-American borderlands are a collection of very different regional communities that reflect the sheer length of the border and the geographical complexity of the two transcontinental societies. On the eastern side of the continent, the border cuts through the forests and hills of New England and the upper Gaspé before hitting the St. Lawrence River just southwest of Montreal. It follows the St. Lawrence to Lake Ontario, and then threads for almost 1,600 kilometers through the Great Lakes before running aground on the western shore of Lake Superior. (At its southernmost extension, near Windsor, Ontario, and Detroit, Michigan, the border dips below the latitude of the state border between Oregon and California.) From the Ontario-Manitoba boundary, the international border follows the 49th parallel west across the Great Plains, the

Rocky, Selkirk, and Cascade mountain ranges, and into the Pacific just south of Vancouver. At that point, it dips south to follow the Strait of Juan de Fuca around the tip of Vancouver Island.

The international border follows geographical boundaries for some of its length. Thus, the St. Lawrence River and Great Lakes provide a natural boundary of sorts between the two national communities. However, there is no natural logic to the international border west of the Great Lakes; it is a political line sketched across unbroken prairie and mountain terrains. As has been so frequently noted in the Canadian literature, the natural lines of the continent run north and south rather than east and west, as the border runs. The border, therefore, tends to sever natural geographical regions and communities such as the prairies and the west coast. At the same time, we must be careful not to exaggerate the integrity of those severed communities, or hypothetically severed communities. While it is true, for example, that Vancouver has had a good deal in common with Pacific Coast communities stretching south to San Francisco, the sense of an integrated coastal community has not penetrated very far into the British Columbia interior.

Niles Hansen (1981: 19) defines border regions as "subnational areas whose economic and social life is directly and significantly affected by proximity to an international boundary." Within this context, the American border region is both thin and insignificant. The relatively few substantial American communities in the region stand with their back to Canada; their economic, social, and cultural lifelines all flow south into the American heartland (Gibbins 1974). By comparison, the Canadian border region is thicker and more significant; the Canadian communities stand with their faces to the United States and their backs to the wilderness stretching northwards to the pole. However, it is not clear that the Canadian communities form a border region in the terms that Hansen suggests, for the most important impact comes not from the proximity of the international boundary itself, but from the more general proximity of the United States.

This difference is not just one of semantics, but is fundamental to an understanding of the North American border experience. Canadian values, culture, and economic activity may wash across the international boundary to a degree, but they do so with limited impact on the immediate border region and with negligible impact on the larger American society. By contrast, American values, culture, and economic activity wash across Canadian communities irrespective of their proximity to the border. American magazines, television, products, and services are as much a feature of life in Edmonton or Saskatoon as they are in communities closer to the border. Even environmental issues seem to follow this pattern. The problems of acid rain, for example, are asymmetrical: the United States is the major contributor to a problem whose effects are disproportionately felt in Canada (Menz 1992: 48–49), and the effects are by no means limited to the immediate border region but are carried deep into the Canadian countryside. It is for these reasons that Canada at large can be seen as a borderlands society.

The vitality of the immediate borderlands is limited by the fact that there are relatively few incentives for Canadians or Americans to cross just over the border. When Canadians go south, they are likely to go deep into the United States, to Miami, Palm Springs, Phoenix, San Diego, and Los Angeles rather than to Detroit or the small border communities in Montana, Idaho, or Maine. Canadians travel in large part to flee the weather, and this cannot be accomplished by slipping across the border. There was, admittedly, a brief flare-up of cross-border shopping when the federal government imposed the seven percent Goods and Services Tax (GST) in 1990, but this has not persisted and has not left much of a mark on the borderlands. There have also been few incentives for Americans to slip north across the border where prices are generally higher, the climate is just as harsh, and standards of public and private morality, at least in the past, have been even stricter. (For most Americans, a "weekend of sin" in Canada was an oxymoron.) In short, there has been little to support a flourishing borderlands economy. Whether the falling value of the Canadian dollar and recent provincial initiatives to build gambling casinos in locations easily accessible to American visitors will change this picture remains to be seen.[14]

It is useful, in the context of the borderlands economy, to compare briefly the immediate Canadian-American borderlands with the Mexican-American borderlands to the south. The latter are remote from the American and Mexican heartlands (Hansen 1981: 156), whereas the Canadian border region in many respects *is* the Canadian heartland. (Neither border, however, is close to the American heartland, which is dispersed across the continent.) Until recently, the Mexican-American borderlands were a relatively unpopulated region. As Hansen notes (1981: 159): ". . . the great westward surge of population following the Civil War tended to bypass the borderlands," and until quite recently the Mexican government actively discouraged settlement in its northern states. By contrast, the center of gravity of Canadian settlement has always been very close to the international border although, and as noted earlier, there is little reason to believe that the border itself served as a population magnet. The pattern of urbanization along the Mexican-American border is characterized by paired cities straddling the border: San Diego and Tijuana, El Paso and Ciudad Juárez, and Brownsville and Matamoros come to mind. There is little evidence of any similar pattern in the Canadian case and, to the extent that contiguous border communities such as Detroit and Windsor do exist, there is little evidence that they were created in response to the border itself. The Mexican border communities have been and remain economically dependent upon the United States, whereas the border communities in Canada, to the extent that they can be distinguished from other Canadian communities, are no more dependent than the national norm. Hispanics are increasingly important players in the politics of the American border-lands and border states (Ganster and Sweedler 1990: 423; Fernandez 1989: 2), a role that has no parallel among Americans living in Canada or Canadians living in the United States.

For all of these reasons, then, the Mexican-American borderlands constitute a distinctive and relatively integrated cultural environment with trans-border cultural institutions. As Ganster and Sweedler (1990: 423) explain:

> The presence of Hispanic populations on both sides of the international boundary, stimulated by important transboundary economic linkages, has encouraged strong social and cultural linkages. Although difficult to quantify, these social and cultural aspects of interdependence are nonetheless real and growing. In a number of areas along the border, binational cultural events are prospering. Transboundary cultural events in the fine arts, classical and contemporary music, and literature are ubiquitous.

By contrast, the Canadian-American border regions do not form a distinctive cultural environment; there is nothing in the linguistic or ethnic mix, cultural traditions, or even cuisine to set the regions apart from their neighboring national communities.[15] McKinsey and Konrad (1989: 4) maintain that "borderlands can be said to exist when shared characteristics within the region set it apart from the country that contains it: residents share properties of the region, and this gives them more in common with each other than with members of their respective dominant cultures." Once again, this description does not seem characteristic of the Canadian-American border regions.

Ganster and Sweedler (1990: 419) also note that the Mexican-American border region is "where the asymmetries between the two countries are most apparent," but also where "interdependence and integration between the two nations are most visible." Neither condition holds in the case of the immediate Canadian-American borderlands where asymmetrical examples of American wealth are relatively rare and where the economic interdependence of the two countries departs little from the national norms. In short, the international boundary does not demarcate significantly different economic spheres. Certainly it does not mark "a significant division between the First World and the Third World, between the developed world and the developing world," as does the boundary between Mexico and the United States (Ganster and Sweedler 1990: 440). In most respects, then, the Canadian-American and Mexican-American borderlands have little in common, and thus it is perhaps not surprising that the extensive research enterprise that has grown up around the latter borderlands has not prompted parallel lines of enquiry with respect to the former. The two borderlands share the United States, but not much else.

It should also be noted that the complexity of the borderlands is reinforced by the fact that the international boundary is between two federal states. Thus, for example, the border between Canada and the United States is also the border between Alberta and Montana, and between Maine and New Brunswick. Seven of the ten Canadian provinces abut the international border, as do 14 of the 50 American states. (Four American and six Mexican states are strung out along the Mexican-American border.) As will be discussed below, it is in the federal character of the international border that we find some potential for cross-boundary regional integration and collaboration.

One unique feature of the Canadian-American borderlands is the number of First Nation, or Native American Indian, reserves that straddle the border or lie in close proximity to it. The best example is the Akwesasne reserve that spans five political jurisdictions: Canada and the United States, Ontario and Québec, and New York state. Approximately 8,000 aboriginal persons live on the Canadian side of the international boundary, while another 5,000 Mohawks live on the American side. There are no longer immigration or custom controls on border crossings within the reserve, but a host of jurisdictional problems remain. It is not clear, for instance, which residents are entitled to Canadian health-care coverage, or where motor vehicles should be registered. As has been seen in recent years, effective law enforcement is virtually impossible when the jurisdictional confusion is coupled with the constraints imposed by the recognition of aboriginal sovereignty.

These borderland reserves are of considerable contemporary importance as a point of entry for goods smuggled from the United States to Canada.[16] It has been estimated that by late 1993 more than 60 percent of the cigarettes purchased in Québec were bought on the black market, and most of those entered Canada through reserves.[17] Because the Canadian governments were unwilling to risk confrontations with the reserves by moving to block smuggling, the cigarette black market created intense pressure on federal and provincial taxes. High taxes led to greater consumer demand for black-market products, and the demand led to more smuggling. Finally, in February 1994, the federal government and four provincial governments—Ontario, Québec, New Brunswick, and Prince Edward Island—substantially reduced the level of taxation on cigarettes in order to reduce black-market demand; the price of a carton of cigarettes in Québec, for example, dropped from 47 to 23 dollars. Thus, this peculiar feature of the Canadian-American border led to a direct reversal of decades of high-tax policy with respect to smoking, much to the horror of the anti-smoking lobby. It also led to an estimated loss of 450 million dollars in federal tax revenues at a time when the government was battling a 45 billion-dollar deficit. This was a significant impact indeed, and there is some indication that reserve-based smuggling of alcohol may have the same impact on federal and provincial taxation policy.[18]

In many ways, the reserve communities are the most interesting aspect of the contemporary borderlands, at least in the Canadian context. Part of this interest, however, arises from the fact that economic barriers still exist between Canada and the United States, barriers that can be circumvented through the reserves and thereby provide the principal economic impetus for smuggling. It is interesting to ask, then, what impact continental free trade might have not only on the reserve communities but on the more general borderlands. In all likelihood the FTA and NAFTA should further diminish the importance of the border regions as the international boundary becomes progressively less relevant for the movement of goods and services, and less important as a factor in determining where businesses locate. In short, proximity to the border should be of reduced economic importance. If there is indeed free trade, then there is little reason for American entrepreneurs to try to develop the border market. Why should Canadians be lured across the border when Walmart will come to them? At the same time, there has never been much incentive for Americans to cross the border to shop in Canada, and there is nothing in the FTA or NAFTA that will increase the incentive.

If the economic relevance of the Canadian-American borderlands is in decline, and if the borderlands are not a distinctive cultural region, then we might be tempted to conclude that the borderlands will remain of limited research interest. Before reaching such a conclusion, however, we should consider the potential impact of the border and borderlands on patterns of transnational regional integration.

Transnational Regional Integration and the Border Regions

In their work on the Mexican-U.S. border, Ganster and Sweedler (1990) identified a number of factors that can be expected to promote transnational regional cooperation:

- a shared "security community"[19]
- economic interdependence
- relatively easy transboundary labor flows
- a shared cultural environment
- a shared remoteness of the border regions from the centers of economic and political power in their respective national communities.

The existence of all five factors in the case of the Mexican-U.S. borderlands has created an extensive and growing network of regional arrangements that span the border, and that have developed independently from the national relationship between Mexico and the United States. Regional integration in the Mexican-American borderlands, Ganster and Sweedler argue, has followed dynamics that, until recently, have had little to do with the larger international and binational relationship. While the dynamics of regional integration may be accelerated by larger developments such as NAFTA, they are likely to retain a significant measure of autonomy.

However, the situation with respect to the Canadian-American border-lands is quite different. While both borderlands are part of a continental security community, three of the remaining four factors promoting regional integration are relatively absent in the Canadian-American case. Although economic interdependence characterizes the larger national relationship between Canada and the United States, interdependence is not brought into bold relief within the borderlands. There is not, in other words, a robust borderlands economy that is a direct consequence of the international border. Labor flows between the two countries in general, and between the border regions in particular, are relatively constricted. The labor mobility often characteristic of border regions (Hansen 1981: 28) does not apply in this case. It is uncommon, for example, to find Canadian day workers in the United States, or American day workers in Canada, and there are no American plants built along the border to capture a mobile Canadian work force. As previously noted, there is little indication that the Canadian and American borderlands share a distinctive cultural environment. To the extent that they have a common culture, it is because they are both thoroughly enmeshed in a continental culture that sweeps across the border. The residents of the neighboring communities of Coutts, Alberta, and Sweetgrass, Montana, may indeed have a common cultural environment, but it is not an environment that is distinct from that shared by most of their respective national compatriots.

The situation with respect to the fifth factor—a common remoteness of the border regions from the centers of economic and political power in their respective national communities—is somewhat more complex. In their discussion of the Mexican-American borderlands, Ganster and Sweedler state (1990: 424) that "the two parts of this region are far from Washington, D.C., and Mexico City, and people on the border often feel neglected by the national capital when dealing with transboundary issues of local, but vital, concern." For the most part, this observation has little applicability to the Canadian-American case. The Canadian borderlands lying to the east of Manitoba are by no means remote from the national centers of economic and political power and, if the corresponding American borderlands are somewhat more remote from Washington, D.C., this remoteness has seldom been linked to the presence of the international boundary or to the neglect of transboundary issues.

Where the observation by Ganster and Sweedler rings a more responsive chord is in the western provinces and northwest states, where perceived neglect by the national governments has been a persistent theme in regional alienation. Certainly *western alienation* has been a characteristic feature of the political culture in the prairie provinces and British Columbia, and it can be detected, albeit in a much less virulent form, in the northwest states. It is interesting to note in this context that the tariff defense of the international border by the Canadian government was one of the historical mainstays of regional discontent among western Canadians. Western Canadians believed that the benefits from the *national policy* of tariff protection accrued for central Canadians while the agricultural community in the West carried a disproportionate share of the costs. It would seem, therefore, that the fifth factor is present to a degree on the western edge of the continent.

However, Ganster and Sweedler go on to note (1990: 424) some important consequences stemming from the remoteness of the Mexican-U.S. borderlands:

> Thus, over the years, border residents have evolved a whole range of informal arrangements to deal with transborder aspects of their daily lives. Examples that come to mind are seen in the informal, but regular, cooperation of fire departments, health authorities, and police to deal with emergencies without the intervention of either federal government.

While the border between Canada and the United States would not preclude such community cooperation in an emergency situation, there is no evidence that it is more generally characteristic of even the western borderlands. Hostility toward the central authorities has seldom been linked to transborder issues, and has not promoted the evolution of transborder institutional collaboration. The absence of paired cities straddling the international boundary has also removed both the necessity of and opportunity for such collaboration. The importance of such paired cities in the Mexican-American case is stressed by Hansen (1981: 156): "Economic, social, and cultural relations between the twin-cities have been more marked by increasing symbiosis than by the confrontation of differing systems. On both sides, formal and, perhaps even more influential, informal institutions have supported a permeable boundary." To the extent that the Canadian-American boundary is permeable, it has little to do with the twin-city phenomenon.

The general pattern, then, is clear: There has not been a great deal of transnational regional integration across the Canadian-American border. Even in the West, where the condition of remoteness from national centers of power is best met, there have been few concrete manifestations of regional integration. At the same time, the door for such integration has been held open by the fact that both Canada and the United States are federal states. This means, in turn, the existence of provincial and state governments with the capacity to pursue autonomous initiatives of regional integration, autonomous, that is, from the actions or predispositions of the respective national governments. Indeed, there is some evidence of such initiatives. The Pacific Northwest Economic Region (PNWER), headquartered in Seattle, has been formed to bring together public- and private-sector leaders from Alaska, Alberta, British Columbia, Idaho, Montana, Oregon, and Washington, and to explore opportunities for economic cooperation.[20] PNWER has a population base of more than 16 million people—six million Canadians and ten million Americans—

and its organizers claim a GNP that would place it tenth among the nations of the world. While the PNWER initiative has yet to generate formal intergovernmental institutions, it appears to enjoy broad and growing governmental support across the region.

PNWER may also reflect what can best be described as the subterranean "Cascadia" movement for regional integration. The movement taps a nascent regional consciousness, a history of regional alienation, and a common perception that the key to regional prosperity is to be found in the Pacific rim rather than in the continental economy. It is a response to globalization, to the diminished importance of national communities signaled by FTA and NAFTA, and to continued unease with the federal governments in Ottawa and Washington, D.C. However, it is not yet a movement with any institutional coherence or leadership, or with much public recognition or political support. It is more likely to find expression, and even then only occasional expression, in talk shows and pubs than it is in formal political arenas.

If interest in the Canadian-American borderlands is to grow in the years ahead, it will likely be in response to developments like Cascadia. If regional communities in the United States, and particularly those in the Northwest, feel estranged from the national community, then movements such as Cascadia may gain some momentum. If the American experience begins to replicate the Canadian experience with respect to territorial alienation, then the ground may be laid for the more extensive development of a transnational, regional community in the West. This could also happen if globalization makes national economic communities less important while enhancing the importance of regional trading links. Finally, support for a transnational regional community could grow in the face of renewed constitutional conflict and deadlock in Canada. However, while one can see glimmers of developments such as Cascadia, they are not yet a significant factor in either country.

The Canadian-American Border in Comparative Perspective

For those interested in borders and borderlands, the international boundary between Canada and the United States should have a natural appeal. The sheer length of the border, its historical continuity, and its importance to the unfolding of Canadian if not American political life all suggest that it should provide a rich research venue. It should also provide an opportunity to explore the corrosive impact of trade liberalization and new social movements such as environmentalism and feminism on international boundaries. In these latter respects, the Canadian-American experience could offer some useful comparative insight into recent European developments.

At the same time, however, it is difficult not to be struck by the unique features of the Canadian-American borderlands. The region is asymmetrical in a critically important sense: It is shallow and of relative insignificance on the American side of the international boundary, and deep and of great significance on the Canadian side. The underlying similarities of the Canadian and American societies have rendered the border of little importance in the United States, and of great importance in Canada. As the larger society, Americans have little to fear from the absence of a significant boundary between the two countries, whereas Canadians, as the smaller society, have much more to fear from cultural homogenization and economic domination. This asymmetry suggests that the real comparative value of the Canadian-American borderlands will be greatest with respect to other asymmetrical situations. Yet even here, the lack of significant parallels between the Canadian-American and Mexican-American borderlands suggests that asymmetry alone does not ensure comparative value. In the final analysis, the Canadian-American border and its regional communities may indeed be a unique case.

Notes

1. By comparison, the Mexican-American border is approximately 3,200 kilometers long.

2. The thought of an American invasion may seem bizarre in contemporary times. It is worth noting, however, that the United States is the only country to have invaded Canadian soil—at the time of the American Revolutionary War, during the War of 1812, and briefly at the end of the American Civil War—and that fear of invasion played a decisive role in the confederation of the British North American colonies into the single colony of Canada in 1867.

3. To the extent that the border has registered in the recent American political experience, it has been with respect to debates in the American Congress over tariff and nontariff trade protection.

4. The Canadian-American comparison in this respect is somewhat analogous to that between Finland and Russia, or between Denmark and Germany.

5. Eighteen of the 26 National Hockey League franchises in Canada's "national sport" are located in the United States.

6. As I have argued elsewhere (Gibbins 1989: 11), the Canadian-American border is "international" only in a formal sense. There is little feeling on either side that one's *neighbours* (or *neighbors*) are "foreign" in any significant way. The relationship between the two countries is more familial than international; the international environment begins offshore.

7. However, the defense of the Arctic border has been a major preoccupation of Canadian military policy. The defense of Canadian sovereignty in the area has also led to significant diplomatic tension between Canada and the United States.

8. NAFTA was signed in 1993 and entered into force on January 1, 1994.

9. Somewhat ironically, those who bemoan the erosion of the international border often bemoan the strength of jurisdictional boundaries within the Canadian federal state.

10. The most notable exception here is the Borderlands Project orchestrated by Lauren McKinsey and Victor Konrad, and anchored by the Canadian-American Center at the University of Maine. The project initially involved more than 100 scholars on both sides of the border. For a selection of the published research, see Lecker (1991). For an earlier study of the Windsor border region, see Lajeunesse (1960).

11. Duchacek (1986), for example, dismisses the applicability of the general borderlands literature to the Canadian-American case.

12. Duchacek (1986).

13. An important exception is Stephen J. Hornsby, Victor A. Konrad, and James J. Herlan, eds. (1989). For a more recent exception, see George Melnyk (1993).

14. In May 1994, Ontario's first gambling casino opened in Windsor, which is Canada's busiest point of entry with 42,000 border crossings a day. It is anticipated that 80 percent of the casino's 12,000 daily visitors will come from the United States. Jane Coutts, "Windsor Feeling Pretty Lucky these Days," *Globe and Mail*, April 28, 1994.

15. Perhaps the closest the Canadian-American borderlands come to having a distinctive cultural character is in the appeal by American PBS television stations for pledges from Canadian viewers who receive PBS programming through cable television. Thus, for example, Calgary and Edmonton are two of the most important funding sources for the PBS station in Spokane, Washington. However, the two Canadian cities, which respectively lie 300 and 600 kilometers north of the international boundary, can be considered part of the *borderlands* only if, as suggested above, we think of Canada as a whole as a borderlands society.

16. In the case of cigarette smuggling, it should be pointed out that the cigarettes are almost entirely *Canadian* products that are exported to the United States and then smuggled back into Canada in order to avoid Canadian taxes. American cigarettes have not been smuggled in any significant quantity.

17. Royal Canadian Mounted Police Commissioner Norman Inkster asserted that 70 percent of all contraband cigarettes entered Canada through the Akwesasne reserve (*Macleans*, February 21, 1994, p. 11). The Jay's Treaty, signed in 1794 by Great Britain and the United States, allowed Indians to cross the international border with "their own proper goods and effects."

18. It has been estimated that almost half of the hard liquor bought in Québec comes from the black market. Lysiane Gagnon, "A Perfectly Sensible Solution to Smuggling by Indian Reserves," *Globe and Mail*, March 12, 1994, p. D3.

19. A security community exists when policymakers and the public in adjoining countries do not contemplate the possibility of mutual warfare, and when no significant resources are devoted to defensive capabilities against one another. As Holsti explains (1983: 441), Canada and the United States constitute a security community, as do Mexico and the United States.

20. PNWER's formal mandate is to bring together "legislative, government, and private sector leaders to work toward the development of public policies that promote the economies of the Pacific Northwest region and respond to the challenges of the global marketplace."

References

Atwood, Margaret. 1982. *Second Words: Selected Critical Prose*. Toronto: Avanti.

Duchacek, Ivo D. 1986. *The Territorial Dimension of Politics: Within, Among, and Across Nations*. Boulder: Westview Press.

Fernandez, Raul A. 1989. *The Mexican-American Border Region: Issues and Trends*. Notre Dame: University of Notre Dame Press.

Ganster, Paul, and Alan Sweedler. 1990. "The United States-Mexican Border Region: Security and Interdependence." In *United States-Mexico Border*

Statistics since 1900, David Lorey, ed. Los Angeles: UCLA Latin American Center Publications, University of California at Los Angeles.

Gibbins, Roger. 1974. "Nationalism: Community Studies of Political Belief." (Ph.D. diss., Stanford University.)

Gibbins, Roger. 1982. *Regionalism: Territorial Politics in Canada and the United States*. Toronto: Butterworths.

Gibbins, Roger. 1989. *Canada as a Borderlands Society*. Borderlands Monograph Series #2. Orono: The Canadian-American Center, The University of Maine.

Gibbins, Roger. 1991. "Ideological Change as a Federal Solvent: Impact of the New Political Agenda on Continental Integration." In *The Nation-State versus Continental Integration: Canada in North America, Germany in Europe*, Leslie A. Pal and Rainer-Olaf Schultze, eds. Bochum: Universitatsverlag Dr. N. Brockmeyera.

Hansen, Niles. 1981. *The Border Economy: Regional Development in the Southwest*. Austin: University of Texas Press.

Holsti, K. J. 1983. *International Politics: A Framework for Analysis*. 4th edition, Englewood Cliffs: Prentice-Hall.

Hornsby, Stephen J., Victor A. Konrad, and James J. Herlan, eds. 1989. *The Northeastern Borderlands: Four Centuries of Interaction*. Fredericton, NB: Acadiensis Press.

Lajeunesse, Ernest J., ed. 1960. *The Windsor Border Region: Canada's Southernmost Frontier*. Toronto: University of Toronto Press.

Lecker, Robert, ed. 1991. *Borderlands: Essays in Canadian-American Relations*. Toronto: ECW Press.

Lemco, Jonathan, ed. 1992. *Tensions at the Border: Energy and Environmental Concerns in Canada and the United States*. New York: Praeger.

McKinsey, Lauren, and Victor Konrad. 1989. *Borderlands Reflections: The United States and Canada*, Borderlands Monograph Series #1. Orono: The Canadian-American Center, The University of Maine.

Melnyk, George. 1993. "Magpie and Tortoise: Regionalism in the Two Wests." In *Beyond Alienation: Essays on the West*, George Melnyk, ed. Calgary: Detselig.

Menz, Fredric C. 1992. "Transboundary Acid Rain: A Canadian-U.S. Problem Requires a Joint Solution." In *Tensions at the Border: Energy and Environmental Concerns in Canada and the United States*, Jonathan Lemco, ed. New York: Praeger.

Smiley, Donald V. 1980. *Canada in Question: Federalism in the Eighties*. Toronto: McGraw-Hill Ryerson.

Smiley, Donald V. 1988. "A Note on Canadian-American Free Trade and Canadian Policy Autonomy." In *Trade-Offs on Free Trade: The Canada-U.S. Free Trade Agreement*, Marc Golden and David Leyton-Brown, eds. Toronto: Carswell.

11

Northern Ireland

Michael Ignatieff

The historic junction of many borders, as we know, was to separate different ethnic and cultural groups. However, in a number of regions in the world, some groups share the same space through accidents of history or processes of globalization such as migration. This selection explores the cultural-ethnic-religious complexities of people who compete for the same territory. The case is Northern Ireland, where Protestants (900,000) and Catholics (600,000) have been locked in a struggle either to remain "British" or become independent or link with the neighboring Catholic country of Ireland. One result has been the formation of informal internal borders that segregate the two faiths.

Michael Ignatieff is Carr Professor of Human Rights Practice and director of the Carr Center of Human Rights Policy in the John F. Kennedy School of Government at Harvard University. His recent essays examine the moral connection created by modern culture with distant victims of war, the architects of postmodern war, the impact of ethnic war abroad on thoughts about ethnic accommodations at home, and the junction of memory and social healing.

The shutters are run down on the butcher shops and the betting shops, and crowds gather silently on the pavements. In the distance, from the tight warren of streets off the Shankill Road, comes the skirl of pipes and the tread of feet. A flatbed truck appears first, bearing wreaths with the initials of the Ulster Volunteer Force picked out in red, white, and blue flowers; then comes

Excerpts from Michael Ignatieff, "Northern Ireland," in *Blood and Belonging: Journeys into the New Nationalism*, 213–23. © 1993 by Michael Ignatieff. Reprinted by permission of Farrar, Straus and Giroux, LLC.

a hearse with a flower-decked coffin, followed by a silent army of men. There are perhaps two hundred of them, wearing big-shouldered, double-breasted suits, white shirts, black ties. Their dark glasses glint as they turn to scan the crowd. When they see a camera, a posse breaks ranks and comes over to pass the word. "Now, don't be filming. Wouldn't be wise."

The Shankill is paying its last respects to Herbie McCallum. He had been providing protection for a Protestant parade, armed with a pistol and a grenade, when the police tried to reroute the march away from the Catholic Ardoyne. Scuffles broke out between Loyalists and the police. Some say the grenade was intended for the Catholics, others for the police, but the person who took the full force of the explosion was twenty-nine-year-old Brian "Herbie" McCallum, father of two, paramilitary hero to his friends, Protestant terrorist to his enemies.

Before the rifles were fired into the air in the graveside salute, one of Herbie McCallum's commanders gave a speech in which he said:

To stand for capitulation. To stand silent, immobile in the face of treachery. To suffer ignominiously the malignment of our people, our culture, our history. To bow to the whims of mere pragmatists—is cowardice. Volunteer Brian Herbie McCallum and many, many Ulster Volunteers who have made the ultimate sacrifice are testimony that this Nation will be defended. . . .

No place in Europe has carried ethnic division as far as Belfast. The peace walls, put up in the 1970s to keep people in the same street from firebombing and murdering each other, are now as permanent as the borders between nation-states, twenty feet high in some places, sawing working-class Belfast in two.

Ethnic apartheid does reduce the death toll. In the mid-1970s, between 250 and 450 people were dying every year. Now the figure is under 100. At the same time, community segregation is growing. Sixty percent of the population now live in areas that are more than 90 percent Protestant or Catholic.

The segregation grows in molecular fashion: a tire is slashed, a child is beaten up, petrol is poured through a letter box, by one side or the other, and another family decides to choose the safety of numbers. Belfast likes to talk about "ethnic cleansing"—but molecular nastiness bears no comparison to genocide in Bosnia. If Sarajevo could look like Belfast one day, it would consider itself lucky.

In Northern Ireland, as in Croatia and Serbia, as in Ukraine, ethnicity, religion, and politics are soldered together into identities so total that it takes a defiant individual to escape their clutches. On one side, people who have never been to a church in their lives have to live with the tag of "Protestant." On the other, people who have no desire for a united Ireland but happen to be Catholic get labeled, once and for all, as "nationalists."

These labels imprison everyone in the fiction of an irreducible ethnic identity. Yet Northern Ireland's is not an ethnic war, any more than the Serb-Croat or Ukrainian-Russian antagonisms are ethnic. In all three cases, essentially similar peoples, speaking the same or related languages, sharing the same form of life, differing in religions which few actually seem to practice, have been divided by the single fact that one has ruled over the other. It is the memory of domination in time past, or fear of domination in time future, not difference itself, which has turned conflict into an unbreakable downward spiral of political violence.

I am in Ulster to find out what Britishness looks and feels like when it has been put on the rack of a dirty war. In mainland Britain, Britishness is a casual puzzle, a subject for after-dinner conversation. In Ulster, it can be a matter of life and death. Loyalism, I thought, would serve as a mirror that would show me what the British might look like if their nation's life was on the line. I've chosen to visit in July because the great festival of Loyalism, the marching season, is about to begin. But after Herbie McCallum's funeral I'm already unsure as to what the mirror of Loyalism reveals. Protestant paramilitaries now kill more people in Northern Ireland than the IRA. Their victims range from innocent Catholics to British soldiers and members of the police. Here is a Britishness at war with Britain, a Britishness that swears allegiance to the Crown and the Armalite rifle.

The illusion that Britain is an island of stability in a world of troubles does not survive a day on the streets of Belfast. In reality, there is more death by political violence in Great Britain than in any other liberal democracy in the world. Since 1969 there have been three thousand political killings and more than fifty thousand people have been seriously injured. More people have died, per capita, of political violence in Great Britain than in India, Nigeria, Israel, Sri Lanka, or Argentina, all nations which the British regard as more violent than their own.

There is nothing especially mysterious about this level and intensity of violence. Nationalism by its very nature defines struggles between peoples as struggles for their honor, identity, and soul. When the stakes are raised this high, conflict is soon reduced to a zero-sum game. Victory for one side must mean total defeat for the other. When the stakes appear to involve survival itself, the result is violence. Such is the case in Northern Ireland. Two nation-states lay claim to the province. Nine hundred thousand Protestants or descendants of Protestants wish to remain British. Six hundred thousand Catholics or descendants of Catholics mostly, but not invariably, wish to become Irish. Since one wish can be satisfied only at the expense of the other, it is scarcely surprising that the result is unending conflict.

What is more surprising than the level of violence is the willingness of the mainland to continue to pay the price. A relatively poor liberal democracy spends £3 billion a year and deploys twenty thousand troops to back up a local police force in a struggle which can be contained but which cannot be won.

Such commitment would be unthinkable if the territorial integrity of the British state and the legitimacy of its authority were not both on the line. One might have expected that such a cause would rouse the deepest nationalist feeling. Yet all that seems to sustain the British presence is a weary cross-party consensus that terror must not be seen to pay and that the troops cannot be withdrawn lest civil war ensue.

If the cause in question in Northern Ireland is defense of the Union, then already Ulster is not treated like a part of mainland Britain. There is an imperial proconsul, the Northern Ireland Secretary, who runs everything from negotiations with Dublin to the allocation of council housing. The currency is the British pound, but the Northern Ireland banknotes are not'tradable as legal tender on the mainland; British political parties do not compete for votes in the province. Local democracy has been all but eliminated by twenty-five years of direct rule from Westminster. Ulster knows it is already semi-detached.

Loyalists bitterly note the curious disparity between the outpouring of nationalist feeling when Argentina invaded "British sovereign territory" in the Falklands and the indifference about Ulster. Mainland Britain would give Ulster away if it could. Opinion polls give greatest support to options that entail relinquishing British sovereignty over Northern Ireland or sharing it with Ireland.

And the British commitment to Ulster is hedged with conditions. Since the Anglo-Irish Agreement of 1985, Britain is committed to remain in Northern Ireland only so long as a majority of its people wish it. Thus the province is the only part of the Union with an entrenched right of secession. For Loyalists, it is an outrage that the British government should portray itself increasingly as a "neutral" peacekeeper between one community which wishes to stay British and another which wishes to become Irish.

If the cause in question in Ulster is the defense of the Union, then it is a cause that moves few British hearts. Yet this is paradoxical. British nationalism has always been of the civic variety: an attachment to the institutions of a state—Crown, Parliament, rule of law, the Union itself—rather than to a nation. Yet like Canada, India, Belgium, and other multi-ethnic states, it is discovering that attachment to the state may prove weaker than commitment to the nations that comprise it. The Union, after all, is a constitutional contrivance, and who can feel deep emotion about constitutional contrivances?

Ethnic nationalism attaches itself to the defense of a tradition and way of life, and all of this could survive a redrawing of the Union. The British could cede Northern Ireland and few on the mainland would feel the sting of shame or the twist of remorse. Whether they should do so is another matter. But what exactly does this tell us about Britain—that it has lost the nationalist impulses which might once have rallied to Ulster's defense, or that it never had them in the first place?

The English have always made the comparison between their own tolerant moderation and the nationalist delusions of other peoples a touchstone of their identity. Living on an island, having exercised imperial authority over more excitable peoples, priding themselves on possessing the oldest continuous nation-state in existence, the English have a sense of a unique dispensation from nationalist fervor. An ironic, self-deprecating national character that still prizes the emotional reserve of its officer class approves of itself for declining the strong drink of nationalist passion.

Hugh Seton-Watson, a great English historian of Eastern European nationalism, was convinced that there was no such beast on his own soil. A people who have never been conquered, invaded, or ruled by others, he believed, could not be nationalistic. "English nationalism never existed, since there was no need for either a doctrine or an independence struggle." A Scottish nationalism perhaps, a Welsh nationalism, too, but never an English nationalism.

After 1707, and the Union of the Scottish and English Crowns, a British national identity was forged which allowed the British to develop their unique double affiliation—to their nations of origin, and to the nation-state and empire. As the original multi-ethnic, multinational state, Britain was perhaps the first country where patriotism was directed to the imperial state, not to the nations that comprised it. In its imperial heyday, British civic nationalism focused on the image of Britannia, ruler of the seas.

Imperialism was the form and expression of such British nationalism as there has been, and Britain's colonial peoples were never in much doubt about the incorrigible self-regard of their masters. Yet the masters themselves believed that their patriotism was by its nature different from the nationalism of other peoples. This view of nationalism as an illness that infected only foreigners provided a rationale for centuries of British imperial rule. Bringing the lesser breeds within the law meant freeing them from lesser tribal fanaticisms and teaching them the civil temper of the English race. Even when it proved that colonialism, far from extinguishing ethnic loyalties, actually helped to solidify them into nationalist consciousness, the British believed themselves confirmed as a people raised "above" the tribal emotions of others. Hadn't they acquired the Empire, according to a celebrated phrase, "in a fit of absence-of-mind," and didn't they relinquish it with a degree of dispatch which proved that they were free of grasping nationalist ambition? Imperialism may have been the face of Britishness for two centuries, but by its own reckoning, imperialism was a unique form of disinterestedness, a "burden" diligently borne and willingly renounced.

As the British adjusted to a new post-imperial era of genteel relative decline, they could find reasons to praise themselves for being immune to the lure of the kitsch of national self-regard. The stridently patriotic self-confidence of the Americans served as a perfect foil for the elaboration of a post-imperial national identity that regarded any form of British national self-regard as a comic turn.

The Cold War also acted to repress national self-definition, not just in Britain, but across Europe. The normal national self-assertiveness and competitiveness of the Western European states were suspended for fifty years by the agreed necessity to present a united front against the Soviet threat.

At the same time, the relative prosperity of the 1950s and 1960s eroded British provincialism and began to weaken the British confidence in the charming and incorrigible distinctiveness of their way of life. A new black and Asian population arrived whose simple presence began to expose how very white and imperial were the symbols of collective belonging. The old national rituals began playing to a new audience; and in the process both the audience and the spectacle had to change. Even the monarchy ceased to be specifically British: it became the fairy-tale family romance for the entire planet.

Out of decolonization, immigration, and genteel economic decline there emerged a new style of national identification which enjoyed and celebrated Britain precisely because it was essentially post-nationalist, because the demands it placed upon individuals were mild and fluid enough to enable each to be as British as he pleased.

I arrived in Britain from Canada in 1978. I rather liked Britain in supposed decline. It was relatively free of the provincialism of those nations which take themselves to be the center of the world. It was less self-important than the United States; less complacent than West Germany; less self-enclosed than France. It was in trouble, and that made it an interesting place to live.

I both disliked and disbelieved the ambient rhetoric of national decline. It struck me mostly as a suppressed form of imperial nostalgia. Almost everything that was taken as a symptom of decline and decay—loss of Empire; a new African, Asian, and Caribbean population; traumatic economic restructuring—seemed a sign of health to me. Postwar Britain had been forced to change as radically as any society in Europe, and it had done so without falling apart, without ceasing to function as some kind of liberal democracy.

But as I have lived here longer, I have come to see that the space for a multicultural, multiracial, post-national cosmopolitanism in Britain was much narrower than I had supposed. Those who speak on behalf of that kind of identity remain locked in a battle of ideas with those who still imagine a Britain on its own, safe from the incursions of Europe, defined by its monarchy and the sovereignty of its Parliament. This is the cause at the heart of the thirty-year war over Britain's place in Europe, and only a fool would suppose that history is on the side of the cosmopolitans.

The depth of the resistance to Europe led me to suspect that I had been taken in by the British image of themselves as beyond the lower nationalist emotions of the Continentals. This is just another of Britain's stylish affectations. In reality, the British are among the most fiercely nationalistic of all peoples. Indeed, modern nationalism is an English invention.

The very idea of the "nation" acquired its modern meaning during the Protestant Reformation in England. In the 1530s, the Tudor state, under Henry VIII, led a nationalist revolt in the name of "the English nation" against the Papacy and the Catholic Church. At the same time, the Tudor state initiated the conquest of Catholic Ireland. From the very outset of its nationhood, Englishness was defined antagonistically as the creed of an Anglo-Saxon Protestant nation locked in battle with continental Europe, the Papacy, and the Catholic Irish. From the Marian persecutions of the 1550s, through the Spanish Armada of 1588, to the execution of Charles I in the Civil War, the English nation defined itself against Catholic invaders from abroad and Catholic despots at home.

One of the turning points in the formation of English identity occurred when the Catholic King James II ascended the throne in 1685 and set about challenging the authority of Parliament and persecuting the Protestant faith. A national rising in 1688 appealed for deliverance to the Dutch ruler, William of Orange, who arrived in England, put James to flight, and established both the sovereignty of Parliament and the supremacy of the Protestant religion.

James retreated to his Catholic domains in Ireland and began reconquering it as a prelude to an invasion of Britain. At the same time his ally and patron, Louis XIV of France, invaded Protestant Holland. The fate of Protestant Europe hung in the balance. All of Ireland was soon in James's hands, except the Protestant north. In 1689, the Jacobite armies laid siege to Londonderry, and for 105 days it held out, giving time for William of Orange to disembark and commence the reconquest of Ireland. In June 1690, William of Orange himself came ashore at Carrickfergus. At the Battle of the Boyne, fought on July 12, 1690, he decisively defeated the Catholic pretender.

William of Orange's victory has entered British myth as the Glorious Revolution, inaugurating the imperial high noon of parliamentary sovereignty, religious toleration, and constitutional monarchy. In Ulster, William's triumph became a founding myth of ethnic superiority. For Ulstermen, the Battle of the Boyne is exactly what the Battle of Kosovo is for the Serbs—the moment when a small people, in battle with mortal foes, defended Christendom for all of Europe. (While the Protestants won at the Boyne, and the Serbs lost at Kosovo, both cultures came to see themselves as heroic and misunderstood defenders of the faith.) The Ulstermen's reward, as they saw it, was permanent ascendancy over the Catholic Irish, whom they now conceived, once and for-ever, as potential rebels against the British Crown.

From 1688 until 1912 at least, the Ulster Protestants believed that their founding myth was also the founding myth of the British state—defeat of King James guaranteed a Protestant ascendancy in Ireland and constitutional monarchy in Britain. Yet this was not to be. Ireland proved to be the great failure of British state and nation building. The Protestantism at the very heart of the British identity made it impossible to assimilate successfully the Catholic Irish into the Union. When, in 1912, the British conceded Irish Home Rule, Ulstermen, led by Sir Edward Carson, rose in fury to resist, believing that the most loyal of all the Crown's subjects had been rewarded with a betrayal of the essential element of Britishness itself, its Protestant core.

The inability of the British to think of Ulster as an essential part of Brit-ain has much to do with British awareness that their nation building met its greatest failure in Ireland. The Troubles have reinforced in the British mind the conviction that Ulster is, after all, paradoxically and impenetrably Other, i.e., Irish.

Since Irish independence in 1920, Catholic Ireland has ceased to be one of the mirrors in which the British define who they are. Ireland and Britain are no longer brother enemies. Protestantism, once the very touchstone of what differentiated Britain both from Ireland and from Catholic Europe, is now a vestigial element of self-definition in a secularized country in which only 15 percent of the population define themselves as regular church attenders. Not so in Protestant Ulster, where 65 percent of the population attend services on Sunday. They, alone of the British people, remain face-to-face with the Other which has defined Britishness for centuries. No wonder theirs is the fiercest British nationalism on these islands; no wonder to visit Ulster is to travel down through the layers of historical time that separate mainland Britain from a Britishness that once was its own.

12

The Fault Line
between Israelis
and Palestinians

Thomas L. Friedman

After the 1967 war, Israelis occupied the West Bank and Gaza Strip and integrated those territories into the state of Israel. Palestine was reconstituted as a geographical entity within the borders of Israel; this change had the effect of creating an ongoing struggle within the political boundaries instead of across them. The threat perceived by Israel was no longer from outside its borders, but rather from inside, with no area immune from violence. The ongoing conflict between the Palestinians and the Israelis is reminiscent of the long history of violence in Northern Ireland.

Thomas L. Friedman won the 2002 Pulitzer Prize for commentary (his fourth Pulitzer for the New York Times*). In the 1980s he was the bureau chief for Beirut and for Jerusalem. He became the paper's foreign affairs columnist in 1995.*

The first thing one notices after walking across the Lebanon border into Israel is how straight everything looks. In contrast to the chaotic farm fields of Lebanon, the Israeli banana groves are planted in perfectly parallel rows, and the kibbutz family houses are built in symmetrical patterns that smoothly and gently carry the eye along. The roads are straight and the white lines down the middle all seem freshly painted. Indeed, the whole vista exudes a sense of planning and order. Even Israel's coastline looks straighter than Lebanon's.

For a while after I arrived there, Israel's straight lines fooled me. It took my eyes several months to penetrate the forest of right angles and to discover

Excerpts from Thomas L. Friedman, "The Fault Line," in *From Beirut to Jerusalem*, 322–65. © 1989 by Thomas L. Friedman. Reprinted by permission of Farrar, Straus, and Giroux, LLC.

the jagged and volcanic fault line that lurked just beneath the surface of Israeli society. Whereas Lebanon was built on many different fault lines, separating the seventeen different Christian and Muslim sects that make up the country, Israel and the occupied West Bank and Gaza Strip are built over just one, which separates Israeli Jews and Palestinian Arabs. In Lebanon, the government was constantly being shaken by tremors which exploded along its sectarian fault lines. Eventually, a tremor came along in 1975 that was powerful enough to open them all at once and send the whole country crashing into an abyss.

In Israel, the government was much stronger and more cohesive. For twenty years, from June 1967 to December 1987, the Israeli government was able to absorb all the shock waves and tremors that built up along the fault line dividing Palestinians and Jews—so much so that many Israelis, and even some Palestinians, forgot that it was even there. But living in Beirut had made me very sensitive to geological disturbances; like any earthquake survivor, I never stopped feeling them.

Whenever I told Israelis that their country reminded me of Lebanon much more than they might have thought, they bristled with indignation. "What are you talking about," a prominent Hadassah Hospital neurologist sputtered at me when I made such a comparison at a Jerusalem dinner party. "Civil war in Jerusalem? Gaza is like Beirut? You have spent too much time in Lebanon."

Indeed I had.

On Friday, November 6, 1987, the *Jerusalem Post* ran the following item about the Palestinian owner of the Dallas restaurant in East Jerusalem, one of the city's more popular purveyors of Arabic food:

"If Mohammed Hussein has his way, observant Jews may soon be able to grab a bite in [Arab] East Jerusalem. Last month Hussein applied to the local religious council to receive a kashrut certificate for his restaurant Dallas . . . in the heart of the city's main Arab shopping district. According to Hussein, there is a great demand for a kosher restaurant in East Jerusalem. 'Jews come here all the time and ask if we have a certificate,' he said. Hussein believes that the restaurant—a stone's throw from Salah e-Din Street, the courts, and the Justice Ministry—will attract a kashrut-observing clientele. A religious Muslim, Hussein understands the burden of dietary restrictions; 'I look at this as a chance to help people observe their religion.' "

Mohammed Hussein's plans to make his Arabic restaurant kosher were not the mad antics of an isolated Palestinian quisling trying to curry favor with his occupiers. To the contrary, they were emblematic of the extent to which Israelis and Palestinians from the occupied West Bank and Gaza Strip were inexorably melding together into a single binational society during the twenty years that followed the 1967 war.

From their side, the Israelis integrated the West Bank and Gaza Strip into their own systems of municipal government, zoning, town planning, road signs, and transportation. When you drove from pre-1967 Israel into the West Bank, there was no WELCOME TO THE WEST BANK sign to tell you where you were, and there was no change in the road or physical scenery. The two regions blended together in a way that was seamless, which explains why Israelis who grew up after 1967 often don't have a clue where the border runs and would be hard-pressed to draw the outlines of the West Bank on a map. By the late 1980s some 70,000 Israelis had moved into towns and settlements in the West Bank (not including East Jerusalem). Most of them were not gun-toting religious zealots in search of the Messiah but Israeli yuppies in search of a house with a yard and armed with nothing more dangerous than briefcases stuffed with the commuting schedules to Tel Aviv and Jerusalem. Indeed, roughly 85 percent of the Jewish settlers living in the occupied territories today reside in ten urban centers within a 30-minute commute of Tel Aviv or Jerusalem. Maybe that was why few Israelis seemed to take notice when a Hebrew version of Monopoly was issued in which players could buy houses and hotels in the West Bank towns of Hebron, Bethlehem, and Nablus as easily as in Haifa and Tel Aviv.

Shopping for bargains in Arab villages and markets on Saturday became a weekly routine for many Israelis. In fact, I knew a very senior Israeli military intelligence officer who told me that every Sunday, after giving a top-secret briefing to the Israeli Cabinet on the week's intelligence developments, he would drive directly from the Prime Minister's office to his favorite Arabic restaurant in the West Bank town of Bethlehem to sate his appetite for grilled lamb and Arabic salads.

But while all the world seemed to be focusing on how Israel was sinking roots into the occupied West Bank and Gaza Strip, few paid attention to how much the Palestinians living in these areas were sinking their own roots—voluntarily and unconsciously—into Israeli society. No one observed this process of Palestinian integration with more insight and honesty than Palestinian philosopher Sari Nusseibeh, who teaches at the West Bank's Bir Zeit University. The son of a prominent Palestinian politician, Anwar Nusseibeh, Sari, now in his late thirties, was born and raised in Jerusalem in the days before 1967, when it was under Jordanian control, and he watched every step of the way as his Palestinian compatriots slowly became "Israelified."

"It all began with an Egged bus," said Sari, referring to the Israeli national bus cooperative. "After the 1967 war, Palestinians would not get near an Egged bus. It looked like a terrifying monster from outer space, transporting aliens from one foreign place to another. Some people said we should never ride the Israeli buses because it would be recognizing the Israeli occupation. But slowly, Palestinians started using the Egged buses; they figured out where they were going and where they were coming from. The Israeli system is the Egged bus, and we have learned to use it."

The Palestinians felt they had no choice: either they learned to ride the Egged buses and did business with the Israelis on Israeli terms or they resisted and didn't eat. Israel controlled all the means for importing raw materials and exporting finished products and would not allow them to develop their own industrial infrastructure that might compete with the Israeli economy or serve as the basis for an independent state. The Israelis did, however, encourage Palestinians to work as laborers in Israel, to trade with the Israeli economy, and to export their surplus agriculture to Jordan. In this way, Israel hoped that the Palestinians would prosper as individuals but remain impoverished as a community. The Palestinians chose to play the game by Israel's rules, while all the time denouncing the Israeli occupation. It was their version of moral double bookkeeping and it enabled them to survive, and in some cases thrive, without feeling they had abandoned their claims to independence.

Observed Nusseibeh: "If you look at our workers and trade over the past twenty years, you'd have to say that the salient feature was how we integrated and assimilated into Israel. We were, in a word, co-opted, and our whole economic well-being and existence became parasitic on our being co-opted. Whatever form of Palestinian activity you saw, it required some kind of assent from the Israeli authorities and we, ourselves, went out and got it. Although as individuals we talked about Palestinian independence and uniqueness, as a community we behaved just the opposite."

Indeed, by the late 1980s roughly 120,000 Palestinians living in the West Bank and the Gaza Strip would wake up each morning and drink their Israeli-made Tnuva milk and Israeli Elite coffee, slip on their Israeli-made jeans, tuck their Israeli-issued identity cards in their back pockets, hop into a pickup truck belonging to an Israeli contractor, factory owner, or shopkeeper, and spend their day working in an Israeli town and speaking Hebrew. Later on, these same Palestinian workers would pay their income taxes to the Israeli government, maybe bribe an Israeli official for a building permit, read their Israeli-censored Arabic newspaper, and then drive to the airport with their Israeli-issued licenses to fly abroad on their Israeli-issued travel documents. While the parents were abroad, their children would use Israeli Tambour paint to spray anti-Israeli graffiti on the walls outside their homes. After sunset, some Palestinians, bought and paid for by the Israeli Shin Bet domestic intelligence agency, would inform on their neighbors. The next morning they would rise again at dawn to build with their own backs every Israeli settlement in the West Bank and Gaza Strip. In some cases, Palestinians even worked on settlements that were built on their own confiscated land.

In the Old City of Jerusalem, in Bethlehem and in Jericho, Palestinian merchants would sell yarmulkes, menorahs, "I Love Israel" T-shirts and other

Jewish items—most of them made by Palestinian labor—right alongside kaffiyehs and Korans and other traditional Arabic souvenirs. A Palestinian-owned pasta factory in the village of Beit Sahur, a tahini factory in Nablus, and an RC Cola factory in Ramallah were among the dozens of Palestinian food manufacturers which arranged to receive kosher certification from rabbis hired from adjacent Jewish settlements; it was their only way of gaining access to the lucrative Israeli market. By 1987, some 800 West Bank and Gaza Palestinians who had worked officially in Israel for more than ten years, and then turned sixty-five, were receiving old-age pensions from the Jewish state they did not recognize.

I was once visiting Rabbi Jonathan Blass and his wife, Shifra, two Jewish settlers who live with their children in the West Bank Jewish settlement of Neve Tzuf, about twenty miles north of Jerusalem. In the course of interviewing them about life on their settlement, they mentioned with pride the fact that their fourteen-year-old son, Shlomo, had gone into business with the son of the muezzin of the neighboring Palestinian Arab village of Deir Nizam. (The muezzin is the Muslim cleric who traditionally calls other Muslims to prayer five times daily from atop the mosque's minaret.)

And what did they do together?

"They make yarmulkes," said Mrs. Blass. "Well, not exactly. The muezzin's son has a group of women working for him in the village and they knit the yarmulkes. Shlomo, our son, gets them the orders and sells them. Many of the yarmulkes worn by Gush Emunim settlers were sewn by the women of Deir Nizam. They just exported a shipment of five hundred to a group of observant Jews in South Africa. The muezzin's son gets the patterns to sew on them from a book that we gave him that was put out by B'nai Akiva [the religious Zionist youth movement]. He knows the colors and the styles that the different groups of Jews like to wear. He makes a beautiful one with the skyline of Jerusalem sewn on it. He does Hebrew letters, too—whatever you want."

The Palestinians did such a brisk commerce under the ever-vigilant eye of the Israeli tax collectors that Israel started to make a profit from occupying them. A study done by the West Bank Data Base Project, an independent research organization focused on the occupied territories and headed by former Jerusalem Deputy Mayor Meron Benvenisti, concluded that "the occupied territories never constituted a fiscal burden on the Israeli treasury. On the contrary, the Palestinian population contributed large sums to the Israeli public consumption." According to Benvenisti's study, the Israeli government raised tax revenues from West Bankers and Gazans through two means. One was by local income, property, and value-added taxes collected in the occupied territories. These funds were used to support the Israeli military administration and its capital expenditures on roads, hospitals, and municipal infrastructure in the West Bank and Gaza. The other was through value-added taxes on goods purchased by Palestinians while in Israel, as well as excise taxes, import duties, and payroll deductions. Any West Banker or Gazan who worked officially in Israel had about 20 percent of his salary withheld to cover National Insurance payments. But since most of the insurance benefits were applicable only to Israelis, the Palestinian contributions were transferred directly to the state treasury. Some of these funds went to make up the deficit between the cost of the Israeli occupation and the amount of taxes collected locally from Palestinians. What was left over—roughly $500 million during the first twenty years of the occupation, according to Benvenisti—was used by Israel for its own development.

At the same time, the Palestinians—as a community—were so well be-haved under the Israeli occupation that between 1967 and 1987 Israel had to deploy only about 1,200 soldiers a day, along with a few hundred Israeli Druse Border Police and a few hundred Shin Bet agents, to control all 1.7 million Palestinian inhabitants of the West Bank and Gaza Strip. Israel maintained its occupation so cheaply and efficiently by using a network of contact points to which they got the Palestinians to voluntarily submit, hence little brute force or manpower was required to keep them in line.

"For 95 percent of these contact points to be effective in controlling the Palestinians they required our consent and cooperation," said Nusseibeh. "For example, you were sent an order telling you to come to the military governor's office in Beth El, and you knew that they were going to arrest you, yet you came anyway, on your own, instead of just ignoring the order and forcing the Israelis to send a whole army unit to your village to get you. You were told you needed a building permit to add a wing to your house. Instead of just building the wing and ignoring the Israelis, most people went down and waited in line for a permit, without anyone holding a gun to their heads. The same was true with press censorship. Even the most radical Palestinian papers went to the Israeli censor every day. We were once sent an order to close Bir Zeit University. We read about it in the newspaper, and instead of everyone turn-ing out at the university and challenging the Israelis to throw them out, we all just sat home. The symbol of the Palestinian acquiescence to the Israeli occu-pation was our willingness to hold [Israeli-issued] identity cards. The Israeli ID was the cornerstone of the occupation. It told the Israelis where you were from and who your family was and where they could find you. The Israelis set things up so that we could not travel, drive, trade, import, or go to a hos-pital without presenting our ID card, and we cooperated. I would say that only 5 percent of the Israeli occupation involved brute force—Israeli troops physically forcing Palestinians to comply with some order or regulation. Ninety-five percent of the time we did it ourselves."

While the Palestinians in the West Bank and Gaza constantly complained about the symptoms of the Israeli occupation—the land confiscations, the arbitrary arrests, the house demolitions, and the curfews—as a community they did very little to undermine the system of occupation. There would be an occasional strike or demonstration by lawyers or students—those highly politicized elements of the society—and an occasional casualty from a confrontation with Israeli troops, but rarely anything sustained or widespread. Mass civil disobedience that would have shaken the system of occupation was constantly discussed in the PLO literature that was distributed throughout the occupied territories in the 1970s and '80s, but it was virtually never implemented. When in 1980 the military government issued Order 854, which would have put all the university curricula and teaching under the authority of the Israeli army, the Palestinian universities and students banded together and rejected it; eventually the Israelis backed down. That was real communal resistance, but it was the exception, not the rule.

Why didn't the Palestinians get themselves organized, resist more as a community, and disengage from the Israeli system? To begin with, they had no stable independent economic base to fall back on and they were not willing to endure the economic and personal hardships that mass civil disobedience on the scale required to really bring pressure on Israel would have entailed. Second, Israel used its military power and its Shin Bet domestic intelligence service to disrupt any Palestinian attempts at mass organization and to arrest any Palestinian who remotely behaved like a local leader; Israel would tolerate Palestinian spokesmen, but any spokesman who got more than three people to follow him was eventually arrested, expelled, or harassed into submission. Third, with the PLO guerrilla leadership in Beirut, and later Tunis, claiming to have responsibility for confronting Israel and making all political decisions, it became very convenient for the Palestinians in the West Bank and Gaza Strip to accommodate themselves to the Israeli system, even profit from it, while declaring that liberation was the PLO's responsibility. Whenever I would ask West Bankers when their liberation would start to become their own responsibility, they never really had a convincing answer.

Fourth, as in Lebanon, Palestinian society was riven with ethnic, clan, sectarian, and regional divisions, which always made concerted popular action difficult to organize. Palestinian Christians suspected Palestinian Muslims, Muslim fundamentalists suspected Communists, pro-Jordanians suspected pro-PLOniks, Hebronites suspected Jerusalemites, the members of one extended family in a village refused to cooperate with those of another. These rivalries also explain why the Shin Bet never had any problem recruiting what they called "Shtinkers"—Palestinian informers who kept them abreast of who was saying what to whom in every village and refugee camp in the West Bank and Gaza Strip.

Finally, the Palestinians in the West Bank and Gaza had so convinced themselves that the Israeli occupation was being carried out by brute force—and not by their consent and cooperation—that they did not believe they had within themselves the power to challenge the Israeli system. . . .

One of the most popular fads among West Bank Palestinian youths in the early 1980s was to wear T-shirts emblazoned with the words *I Love Palestine* over an olive tree. They would usually wear them, though, under their regular shirts, so the Israeli soldiers couldn't see them. If Israeli soldiers caught Palestinians dressed in such attire, they were under orders to strip them and then arrest them. I always wondered what the charge would be. Inflammatory underwear? Seditious skivvies? This Israeli crackdown on T-shirt terrorism only served to produce some imaginative alternative tactics by the Palestinians. One favorite ploy was to lasso the tops of small supple trees, tie a red, white, green, and black Palestinian flag to the treetop, and then let the tree spring back up, leaving it for Israeli soldiers to figure out how to get the flag down. Usually the Israelis just took an ax and chopped down the whole tree. In recent years it was hard to find a laundry line in the West Bank or Gaza Strip that did not have some item of clothing hanging on it in the colors of the Palestinian flag, and few Palestinian youths did not own at least one scarf, key chain, necklace, or bracelet in the shape or colors of Palestine that was made in a secret underground factory.

This was no idle West Bank fad that would fade away after a season, to be replaced by mini-skirts and pet rocks. Rather, it was an expression of a process of Palestinian nation-building and identity-building, which took place as a direct result of the Israeli occupation which began in 1967. Men are as often defined by their enemies as by themselves and this was particularly true of the Palestinians in the West Bank and Gaza.

How so? It must be remembered that after 1948 Palestine was broken up into three different pieces—one chunk had been taken over by the Jews, another chunk in the Gaza Strip had been seized by the Egyptians, and a third chunk, the West Bank, had been carried off by the Jordanians. Palestine as a geographical entity was done for, which was one reason the whole Palestine question went into remission between 1948 and 1967. After all, an evicted people might be able to get its land back from one nation, but not from three. Paradoxically, Israel's occupation of the West Bank and Gaza in 1967 put Palestine back together again as a geographical entity and put the Palestinians from the West Bank, Gaza, and Israel back together again as a single community. As a result, the whole Palestine issue came back to life: once again the exact same communities—Jews and Palestinian Arabs—were fighting over the exact same territory—British Mandatory Palestine—that their forefathers had fought over twenty years earlier. The only difference was that the British were not around anymore to oversee things; the Jews were now in charge.

At the same time that Israel's victory in 1967 enabled the Palestine issue to be reborn, it also created the conditions for a rebirth of Palestinian identity as well. The process began with the young generation of Palestinians who came of age after the 1967 war and spread upward to their parents. The older generation of Palestinians grew up between 1948 and 1967 when the West Bank was under Jordanian rule and the Gaza Strip was under Egyptian rule. Because Egyptian and Jordanian cultures were in many ways similar to that of the Palestinian Arabs, the older generation did not feel compelled to constantly assert their uniquely Palestinian identities—not politically and not culturally. In fact, many members of the older generation of West Bankers and Gazans actually became "Jordanized" or "Egyptianized" between 1948 and 1967. Since Jordan granted Palestinians citizenship (Egypt did not) many Palestinians of this pre-1967 generation came to look upon the Bedouin King Hussein as their leader more than any Palestinian.

But the Palestinian youths from the West Bank and Gaza Strip who were born under Israeli occupation had their identities shaped in an entirely different atmosphere. They never had the chance to inherit the world of their fathers. Jordan was not around when they came of age in the West Bank, or Egypt in the Gaza Strip. Israel had supplanted both and had brought with it its own unique blend of Western and Hebrew culture, which was not an option for Palestinians growing up in the occupied territories in the way Egyptian or Jordanian culture had been an option for their parents. To the contrary, these youths despised the Israelis and wanted to emphasize how different they were from them. Since Jordanian or Egyptian identities were no longer available, it was natural for Palestinians to fall back on their own roots and to emphasize more than ever before their uniquely Palestinian political and cultural heritage.

It would not be an exaggeration to say that it took the pressure of a truly foreign, non-Arab community like Israel to provoke Palestinians in the West Bank and Gaza into fully asserting their own distinctive identities. Munir Fasheh, the dean of students at Bir Zeit University, who grew up in the West Bank when it was under Jordanian control and continued to live there after it fell to Israel, once remarked to me that "between 1947 and 1967 whenever anyone asked me what I was, I always hesitated. Legally I was Jordanian, but emotionally I was Palestinian. Now there is no kid on the West Bank under the age of twenty-five who has ever experienced anything other than being a Palestinian. When you consider that 60 percent of the West Bank population is under the age of twenty, it means that for three-quarters of them Jordan is something that doesn't exist."

At the same time, it took a Western-style democracy such as Israel to allow Palestinians the liberty to establish ostensibly non-political trade unions, universities, newspapers, theater groups, and other cultural associations—with a level of free expression that while not equal to that of Israelis was far greater than anything Palestinians had ever enjoyed in Jordan or Egypt. Yasir Arafat's picture and name probably appeared in the Israeli-censored Palestinian Arabic press in East Jerusalem more frequently than it ever did in Amman.

These Palestinian cultural institutions became the vessel and rudimentary framework for their national aspirations. . . .

The 1967 war also created the conditions for those Palestinian refugees living outside the area of Palestine—in Lebanon, Jordan, and Syria—to be transformed from poor forlorn refugees into a political force. In the wake of the '67 defeat, the Arab regimes for the first time allowed the Palestinian refugees to take control of their own destiny after having monopolized the Palestinian cause and made it an exclusively pan-Arab issue between the years 1948 and 1967. Having been vanquished by Israel, the Arab regimes needed some time to regroup, and while they did, they gave the Palestinians and the PLO free rein to carry on the war with Israel. It was this opening, this emancipation, which [Yasir] Arafat and his PLO exploited to the fullest.

In short, the biggest victors of the 1967 war turned out to be the Palestinians, both the refugees outside and the West Bankers and Gazans inside. But while these two different Palestinian communities shared the same objectives, they developed along very different, parallel tracks. Instead of being shaped by Israel, the PLO and its followers in Beirut were highly influenced by inter-Arab politics, Lebanon, and the whole late 1960s revolutionary mood. Arafat and the PLO came on the scene at the same time as students in Paris were manning the barricades and the Vietcong were challenging the American superpower.

The West Bankers and Gazans, however, were shaped by a very different history and in a very different furnace. To begin with, because they were confronted with Israeli culture, which they could not and did not want to be a part of, they became more and more Palestinian in their minds and in their communal institutions. But because Israel absorbed the West Bank and the Gaza Strip, and because many Palestinians living there physically assimilated into the Israeli system for economic reasons, they became less and less Palestinian in their bodies. This put them into an identity bind. From the head upward they swore allegiance to Yasir Arafat, and from the shoulders downward they paid allegiance to the Prime Minister of Israel. The T-shirts Palestinians from the West Bank and Gaza wore under their sweaters, the Palestinian calendars they put on their desks, and the key chains they hid in their pockets were not meant for the Israelis; they were meant for themselves. They were their own identity cards, issued by themselves to themselves—the tangible proof that they really were Palestinians, as their minds declared, and not Israelis, as their bodies seemed to suggest.

I first detected this identity bind listening to Palestinians living in the occupied territories talk about how they no longer felt at home in their own houses and their own villages—even though they were feeling more and more Palestinian in their heads. Sometimes, Palestinians would say, it was just the little things that made them feel not at home—like dialing a number some-where in Israel or the West Bank and getting a recording in Hebrew, which they could not understand. Sometimes it was the road signs, with Hebrew and English letters spelling out place names, sandwiching the smaller Arabic in between. In Ramallah, an exclusively Arab town north of Jerusalem, for example, the local Israeli police station sign spells out "Police" in Hebrew and English, but not in Arabic—as if police protection were not something meant for Palestinians. Sometimes it was the little indignities. A Palestinian teenager in the Kalandia refugee camp outside Jerusalem told me how one hot summer day the residents of his camp were on a political strike. That afternoon, he said, an Israeli soldier stopped him, took away his watch and his bicycle, and told him he would not get either of them back until he got a shopkeeper to open and give the soldier and his unit some ice cream. And sometimes it was the big things: the insecurity of never knowing when your land might be confiscated—Israel has seized or restricted use of more than 50 percent of the land in the West Bank and 30 percent of the Gaza Strip since 1967—or not knowing when your son might be arrested in a security sweep after a bombing, or when your father might be slapped before your eyes for saying the wrong thing to an Israeli soldier at a checkpoint.

I was once interviewing an Israeli infantry soldier, Moshe Shukun, about his work in the Gaza Strip. He said the strangest missions he had to go on were always those that involved arresting Palestinians in their beds at night—which is standard Israeli procedure, since that is when they have the best chance of finding someone home.

"When we go into homes, we surprise people at night," Shukun explained to me. "Sometimes you burst in at delicate times. One time we came in on this couple in Gaza and it was either just before or just after—ah, well, you know. And this Palestinian woman was wearing a very see-through night-gown. I mean it was something that did not leave anything to the imagina-tion, and this lady was beautiful. And there we were—four guys with machine guns pointed at her husband. He got out of bed and asked us if he could go out back to take a piss. So we said okay, and then the four of us just stood there watching over this girl with our guns pointed at her. I have to tell you, they had to practically drag us out of there."

Listening to this story, I could not help but wonder how terrifying, not to mention humiliating, it must have been for that Palestinian man and woman—guilty or not—to have had their most private sanctum and moment violated in such a way.

Not surprisingly, for many young West Bank Palestinians "home" has become the most frightening place in the world. Mohammed Ishteyyeh, a short, curly-haired, Bir Zeit University political-science graduate in his early thirties, came from a village near Nablus and had been arrested at home three times for political agitation. Home is not where his heart is any longer.

"I don't feel at home when I am at home," Ishteyyeh told me. "Actually, my family's home is the most dangerous place for me, because that is the address where the Israelis will come to find me. When the Israelis came to arrest me in 1979, it was at night and the dogs in the village started barking. Ever since then, I hate that sound. When I am at home and the dogs bark at night, I spend hours sitting in front of the window watching who is coming. I wish the daylight could be for twenty-four hours. I don't feel comfortable sleeping in my own bed. I always sleep better out of the country. It is really sad for my mother. When I am home she is afraid. But when I am not home, she wants me there."

Johar Assi, a twenty-five-year-old Palestinian from a village near Ramallah, whom I met while interviewing Palestinian inmates at Israel's Dahariya prison near Hebron, took me by surprise when I asked him whether he was anxious to get out and return home.

"How can I feel at home," he growled, "when I have five uncles in Jordan who are not allowed to travel here? When I am in my village I am afraid to go for a walk outside the village because I might run into an Israeli soldier who will ask me for my ID card and want to know where I work and then tell me to come to the military headquarters tomorrow so they can try to talk me into being a collaborator. If I go for a walk in the village and someone sees Johar talking quietly to Mohammed, there will always be some informer around who will tell the Israelis, and a week later I will get called in by the army and they will say, 'Why were you and Mohammed whispering to each other last week?' So I just keep to myself and to my house and talk a lot to my father."

But Israelis didn't only make it so Palestinians didn't feel at home in the West Bank and Gaza; they made it so that at times the Palestinians didn't feel at home in their own skin—even when they were far away from Israel. As I noted earlier, the PLO, in order to grab the attention of the world when it emerged in the late 1960s, engaged in some spectacular acts of terrorism and airplane hijacking. This gave the Israelis an opportunity to brand the entire Palestinian national movement and cause as a criminal "terrorist" phenomenon. Eventually, the two words "Palestinian" and "terrorist" became fused together in the minds of people the world over. Although 99 percent of the Palestinian people have never been involved in terrorist activity, this label—"terrorist"—became a heavy cross they all had to bear wherever they traveled.

Its weight was felt the minute the immigration officer, the customs inspector, the airline official, or the hotel clerk looked at their travel document: the black ink said only *Palestinian* under nationality, but the invisible ink said *terrorist*. The reading of it was often followed by a suspicious stare and then the words "Could you please step over here." I came to appreciate how upsetting this could be when a Palestinian friend, Jameel Hamad, a prominent West Bank journalist from Bethlehem, told me of the bitter end to a journey he had made to the United States.

"I was in Frankfurt Airport, coming home from New York," said Hamad, who, with his neatly trimmed mustache, glasses, and salt-and-pepper hair, looks more like a grocer without his apron than a potential hijacker. "I was in transit to Tel Aviv. After I went through security in New York, they checked my bags all the way through to Tel Aviv. When I went up to the Lufthansa gate in Frankfurt to get on the flight to Tel Aviv, they asked for my ticket and passport. I was traveling on an Israeli Laissez Passer [a special travel document Israel issues for Palestinian refugees]. The man at the gate said to me, 'You are flying to Tel Aviv?' I said, 'Yes.' So he said, 'Where are you coming from?' I said, 'New York.' Then he said, 'Where are your bags?' I said, 'I already checked them through in New York.' He said, 'Please stand over here.' They let all the passengers get on the airplane. Then they took me outside to the runway. They took all the luggage off the plane, and I was asked to identify my bags. All the passengers were sitting on the plane watching me out the window. It took about an hour for them to get all the bags off and for me to find mine. Then they took me to a room and told me to take all my clothes off—everything. They checked my groin area even—everything. Then they finally let me on the plane. The people had been waiting inside for ninety minutes, so they were really angry with me. I said to the people seated around me, 'Ladies and gentlemen, I am very sorry. I wasn't in the bar, I wasn't getting drunk; my problem was very simple: I am a Palestinian.'"

How did you feel at that moment? I asked.

"I have never felt like such a stranger, like such an outsider before," Hamad said through clenched teeth. "I was just not part of the symphony. I was mad at everyone, the whole world. At that moment, if I had had a bomb, I would have dropped it on the world.". . .

For some Israelis, the 1967 war expanded their sense of home spatially, thanks to the addition of the West Bank and Gaza Strip. Israelis, who felt as though they had been living in a tiny room for twenty years, could finally stretch their legs, put their cars into fifth gear, and really let out their breath. For the first time they enjoyed a feeling of space, of a back yard with a lawn and garden. For other Israelis, the occupation of the West Bank, Jerusalem, and Gaza deepened their sense of home spiritually. Coming back to Hebron, the Old City of Jerusalem, Nablus, and Jericho was, as we've seen, the real return to Zion for many spiritually minded Israelis; up to 1967 they felt as though they had only been living on the doorstep, peering into the house through the front window. "For me to live in Judea and Samaria is to return home in the deepest sense," Jewish settler leader Israel Harel told me one day at his West Bank home in Ofra. "The attachment to the land is almost erotic."

Sometimes on the Passover holiday when you walked through the Jewish markets in Jerusalem you could smell matzo baking. On Friday evenings in Jerusalem a siren sounds across the city to herald the coming of the Sabbath. On Sabbath mornings there are often so few cars on the road in Jerusalem that residents returning from synagogue, often still draped in their prayer shawls, walk down the middle of the streets. Where have Jews ever felt so much at home?

Yet, there was a catch. These very territories—these additional rooms— that expanded and deepened the Israelis' sense of being at home came with a population which constantly made the Israelis feel unable to relax. The new rooms contained 1.7 million Palestinians whose own national identity and claim to ownership of the house was sharpened by their contact with the Israelis.

What bad luck! Just at the moment when Israelis were really beginning to believe they had ended their exile, that they had more power than any Jewish collective in history, they found themselves constantly reminded by the Palestinians that they could not take their shoes off.

While the Palestinian challenge to Israelis—both political and military— had existed from 1948 to 1967 as well, in those days it was primarily viewed as an external threat. The Palestinians were seen by Israelis as part of a general Arab horde challenging their existence, and the Palestinians' own unique identity was submerged to some extent in that pan-Arab coalition. But once the Palestinians in the West Bank and Gaza fell under Israeli authority, they were no longer an external threat that Israel could just build a fence against or unleash its air force on; they were no longer an enemy that lived behind a clearly delineated borderline, with barbed wire and guard towers, which, if you avoided it, meant you could go through the day without giving security much of a thought. Instead, they became an internal threat that made the lives of every Israeli uncomfortable wherever they went in their own country.

This internal threat was accompanied, as was noted, by the rise of the PLO after 1967 as an international representative of the Palestinian people and as a guerrilla force based in Beirut. With the PLO working from the outside and the West Bankers and Gazans from the inside, the Palestinians as a whole were able to shadow the Israelis as never before. Whether it was at home or abroad, at the United Nations or at women's conferences in Nairobi, around every corner Israelis bumped into their Palestinian shadow, which by word and deed was always whispering: "It's not your home. Palestine is not yours. It's ours."

This constant challenge, like a continual poke in the ribs, really got to Israelis. Palestinians planted bombs in Israeli supermarkets, on their airplanes, under the seats of their buses, and even in an old refrigerator in the heart of Jerusalem. They hijacked their airplanes, murdered their Olympic team, and shot up their embassies. None of this threatened Israel's national existence in the way Egypt or Syria could. But in some ways it was worse. It destroyed the

Israelis' sense of belonging, of feeling fully at home, just when they most wanted to feel at home, and it introduced a frightening unpredictability to their daily lives. It was like living in a beautiful mansion on a beautiful plot of land that was constantly being burglarized. Every time an Israeli walked on the street, went to a movie, got on a bus, or stepped inside a supermarket, his eyes were on the lookout for unattended packages and objects. When the *New York Times* has empty space on a page it will often run a tiny filler advertisement for the Fresh Air Fund, a New York charity that sends inner-city youth to summer camps. When the *Jerusalem Post* has empty space, it runs a filler ad that reads: "Suspicion saves! Beware of suspicious objects!"

Dalia Dromi, the spokeswoman for the Israeli Nature Preservation Society, was born and raised in Netanya, a coastal town just north of Tel Aviv. Before the 1967 war Netanya was considered, strategically speaking, one of the most dangerous spots in Israel, because it was situated at the narrowest point in the bottleneck between Tel Aviv and Haifa—only nine miles from the nearest Jordanian West Bank military outpost in the town of Tulkarm. After the 1967 war, though, Dalia discovered that her whole sense of home had changed in a way she never would have predicted.

"In Netanya before the '67 war, if you put your car in fifth gear you could find yourself across the border," explained Dromi. "Yet, in a funny way, in those days I never felt the border. What I mean is that Israel was a narrow country then, but I never felt personally threatened. You knew where the border was, you knew that there was an army there protecting you from the enemy on the other side, and you just went about your life. Now I feel threatened all the time. I don't know where the border is or where the enemy is coming from. Before 1967, I would go to the beach by myself all the time; now I would never go by myself. If I go to the beach, I never sit with a crowd where someone might put a bomb. Before 1967, I never remember being afraid. Since 1967, I am always afraid. Israel was very small before 1967, but it is only now that I feel I am in a small country. Whenever anyone talks to me about 'strategic borders,' I laugh. Today the border is everywhere. It is in the village of Wadi Ara when I drive past and get a stone from a Palestinian, and it is on the road to Haifa when I pass [the Israeli Arab village] Jisr a-Zarqa and I get a stone. You see now the border is really in my own bed. It goes home with me at night and gets up with me in the morning. Before, when Israel was nine miles wide, I felt as though it was my country alone. Yes, there were Arabs living here, but they were not thought of as Palestinians who threatened you personally. They were thought of as Israeli Arabs, citizens of the state. I felt free to go everywhere without feeling threatened. Fear came to me only after 1967.". . .

The silent majority of Israelis in the middle simply learned to live with the situation, because it was usually quite livable. Most of them rarely visited the occupied territories. Whenever I came back from Gaza or Nablus, Israelis would always quiz me as though I were Mark Twain describing some distant land. "Is it really like that?" people would say. At most, they shopped at some West Bank marketplace on Saturdays, went to Bethlehem occasionally for Arabic food, had their cars repaired in the low-cost Palestinian-owned garages, hired cheap Palestinian labor to build additions to their houses, or used the roads through the West Bank as shortcuts on the drive from Jerusalem to the Galilee. They saw the Palestinians, but they did not view them as members of another legitimate national community inhabiting the same space; they saw them either as Arab terrorists, who should be shot or jailed, or, more often, as objects—waiters, carpenters, maids, and cooks—who could be ordered around. When Ann and I moved to Jerusalem from Beirut, we looked at an apartment next to the King David Hotel that had a very small living room. When we asked the Israeli real-estate agent whether we could knock down a wall to make the living room larger, she answered without hesitation, "Sure, no problem. Just get an Arab and knock down the wall." It wasn't get a hammer. It wasn't get a workman. It was get an Arab. . . .

This relationship turned Israelis and Palestinians into intimate neighbors and bitter enemies at the same time. On any given day, one could find the Israeli army arresting all Palestinian males ages eighteen and over in one West Bank village, while in the next village an Israeli contractor would be hiring all Palestinian males eighteen and over to build a new Jewish town. As for the Palestinian, on the same day he could be installing the bus stop at a new Jewish settlement in the West Bank in the morning and in the evening leaving a parcel bomb under the seat of that same bus stop in order to kill or maim any Jew who sat there. Meron Benvenisti termed this crazy conflict a "twilight war"—a half-war, half-peace kind of existence in which there were no trenches, no front lines, no barbed wire separating the two sides, and no accepted distinctions between civilians and soldiers, enemies and neighbors. It was a war, as Benvenisti liked to say, "between two peoples who shared the same sewers."

But then Benvenisti should have known. He lived in a sprawling old stone house in one of the few mixed neighborhoods of Arabs and Jews in Jerusalem. A few years ago, one of his Palestinian neighbors planted a bomb in the front garden of a Jewish home a couple of doors down from Benvenisti's. It wasn't a big bomb, just a small plastic bag filled with a little dynamite and a crude detonator—maybe enough to blow apart a small person.

The police soon arrested Zuhair Qawasmeh, the eldest son of Benvenisti's next-door neighbor, who confessed to planting the bomb. He was sentenced to eighteen years in jail, but was released after only four years as a result of a prisoner exchange between Israel and Palestinian guerrillas in Lebanon.

Shortly after gaining his freedom, Zuhair Qawasmeh got married and, like a good neighbor, invited Benvenisti to his wedding. He invited him in Hebrew, which he had learned during his stay in prison.

"So there I was at the wedding," Benvenisti remarked to me one day, "and I am asking myself, Who is he? My enemy or my neighbor? He is my neighbor, but he is a man who could have killed my children. In America you can have a neighbor who is also your enemy, but not in this sense. He is my mortal enemy. He is a soldier. He is fighting for his own people against my people, like in war—but he is my neighbor."

Precisely because this twilight war involved two entire communities, two peoples, two tribes, two nations, fighting each other without a frontline, neither one really made any distinction between civilians and soldiers. Each side viewed the members of the other community as the potential enemy, and hence as potential soldiers in the enemy army. Relations between Israelis and Palestinians became so thoroughly politicized that after a while there was no such thing as a crime between them, and there was no such thing as an accident between them—there were only acts of war.

There was also no such thing as death between them; there was only martyrdom. Ofra Moses, a thirty-five-year-old mother of three, lived in the West Bank settlement of Alfei Menashe, fifteen minutes from the suburbs of Tel Aviv. On April 11, 1987, she was riding with her family to buy matzo for Passover when a Palestinian hiding in an orange grove threw a firebomb through the window of her Ford Escort and burned her alive. Mrs. Moses thought she was an innocent civilian, but many Palestinians saw her, by her very existence as a West Bank settler, as an occupier, a perpetrator of violence, a soldier, and therefore a legitimate target. The most moderate West Bank Palestinian lawyer I know said to me with great indignation, "I heard on the Israel Arabic radio that the mayor of the Arab village next to Alfei Menashe went to the settlement to express his people's sorrow at Mrs. Moses's death. They weren't sorry. She was a settler, the root of all evil, and they expect us to believe that people are sorry she was killed? I'm not sorry one bit."

Two days after Mrs. Moses died, Musa Hanafi, a twenty-three-year-old Palestinian from Rafah, in the Gaza Strip, was shot and killed by Israeli troops during a Palestinian nationalist demonstration at the West Bank's Bir Zeit University. Mr. Hanafi may have thought he was at Berkeley in 1968, taking part in a campus protest, with a little harmless stone-throwing and tire-burning, but that is not how the Israeli soldiers receiving the stones viewed him.

Lieutenant Colonel Yehuda Meir, the Nablus area commander, was not in Bir Zeit that day, but he has faced many similar demonstrations. I asked him what his men saw when they looked through their gunsights at the Palestinian student demonstrators.

"They see soldiers without uniforms or ammunition," said the Israeli officer. "But if [the Palestinian demonstrators] had ammunition they would use it. This is not Berkeley. They are not protesting for books or tuition. These students are motivated to do what they do by a nationalist cause."

The lack of distinction between civilians and soldiers carried right through to the graveyard. Normally, civilians who are killed in a war get a civilian burial. But not in this twilight war. In Israel and the occupied territories, civilians who died in any way remotely connected to the conflict were buried as martyrs and war heroes, and each community used these deaths to reaffirm the rightness of its cause and to justify revenge against the other. Palestinian and Israeli funerals were so similar it was uncanny. Each side stood over its coffins and drew out the old familiar slogans like pistols from a holster.

At Mrs. Moses's funeral, Minister of Transportation Chaim Corfu delivered the eulogy. And what did he say of this woman who was killed buying matzo?

"Just as the soldiers who fell yesterday [in Lebanon] were killed defending the security of the Galilee, so you, Ofra, fell in the defense of the security of Jerusalem," declared Corfu. "You, Ofra, you are our soldier."

Within a week of her burial, Mrs. Moses had a monument erected to her on the spot where she was immolated.

As for Hanafi, his funeral was more problematic. Israelis understand the power of the memorial, so when Palestinian students are killed, the army usually impounds the body, conducts an autopsy, and then compels the relatives to bury the corpse at midnight, with only immediate family present. (A month before Hanafi's death, Awad Taqtouq, a money changer from Nablus, was "accidentally" killed by Israeli soldiers. That evening 500 of his friends and family hid in the Nablus cemetery after dark, taking Israeli soldiers totally by surprise when they showed up with the corpse at midnight for a quick burial.) Hanafi's friends went further. They brought a car to Ramallah hospital and slipped his body out the back door before the Israeli troops got to it. His friends then kept the body packed in ice at a house in the West Bank. Finally, a few days later, they got hold of a car with Israeli license plates and used it to take Hanafi's corpse back to his home in the Gaza Strip, undetected by Israeli troops. The family quickly put out the word that Musa was back, and 5,000 people turned up to watch his body, draped in a Palestinian flag, lowered into its grave.

"It was kind of a political festival," said Mohammed Ishteyyeh, who attended the funeral. "People praised Hanafi as a 'bridge to liberation.' It was a real push for new sacrifice. You could feel the anger in the young boys there. I was watching them. They had lost the smile of childhood. Everybody was ready to die."

The next day Israeli troops were reported to have dug up Hanafi's body and brought it to Tel Aviv for an autopsy. Two days later it was returned and buried again—at midnight.

It seemed as though this situation would continue forever, with Israelis and Palestinians living their strange twilight existence: not exactly war, not exactly quiet; never really friends, but not always enemies; always longing for peace, but never really sacrificing to achieve it.

Most Israelis certainly thought it would last. In June 1987, on the twentieth anniversary of the Israeli occupation, the Civil Administration—the Israeli euphemism for the military administration which runs the West Bank and Gaza Strip—published a glossy booklet, with colored photographs on very expensive paper, entitled *20 Years of Civil Administration*. Its cover showed a golden wheat field with a West Bank Arab village off in the distance. At first glance, I thought the booklet was an annual report for an international commodities firm. It included page after page of all the good things the Israelis were doing for the Palestinian natives, from improved public services and hospitals to the installation of modern telephones. In the introduction, Shiomo Goren, who holds the title Coordinator of Government Operations in Judea, Samaria, and the Gaza District, a rather nice name for a former senior intelligence officer who runs the occupied territories from his bureau in the Ministry of Defense, concluded by saying, "All the achievements of the past twenty years could not have come about without the devoted work of the staff, both civilian and military, of the Civil Administration. To them we extend our deepest gratitude. I am sure that the population of the areas join me in thanking them."

One aspect of the arrogance of power is that it presumes knowledge. Goren was an Israeli "expert" on the Palestinians, but he did not have a hint of what was brewing in their souls on the twentieth anniversary of the Israeli occupation.

Paradoxically, though, neither did many Palestinians. On a warm afternoon in July 1987 I sat on the patio underneath the pomegranate tree of Sari Nusseibeh's parents' house and asked him where the Palestinians were headed. How much longer could they lead their twilight existence? The Nusseibeh family home is situated right on what used to be the Green Line dividing Israeli-controlled West Jerusalem and Jordanian-controlled East Jerusalem. A Jordanian army pillbox could still be seen jutting through the twenty-year-old brush and foliage that had grown over it since June 1967. It was an apt metaphor for our discussion about Palestinians being absorbed by Israel yet remaining in their minds distinct and separate. Unlike Goren, Sari was certain that a radical change was in the wind, but he didn't know what.

"The only thing that is missing is the consciousness, the self-awareness of what we have been doing," said Sari of the Palestinian assimilation into

Israel. "While our Palestinian bodies are now immersed in the Israeli system, our heads are still above water. Our bodies integrate with it, while our consciousness rejects it. But when consciousness and reality are so far apart, sooner or later either reality will be made to fit the consciousness, or the consciousness made to fit the reality."

Either the Palestinians will stop paying taxes, stop talking about joining the Jerusalem city council, stop building Jewish settlements, and stop riding the Egged buses, as their heads tell them they should do, said Sari, or their national strategy will be made to fit their assimilation. That is, they will stop trying to wage a twilight war against Israel and demand instead to be made citizens of the Israeli state—with rights equal to the Jews'. Sari thought it was going to be the latter. He told me he had the feeling that the Palestinians were going to wake up one morning soon, realize that they have been in bed with the Israeli system for twenty years, and demand a marriage certificate. And when they did, predicted Sari, the real moment of truth for Israel would arrive.

Sari was wrong. The Palestinians did wake up and find themselves in bed with the Israeli system—but instead of a marriage they demanded a divorce.

13

Environment, Development, and Security in Border Regions

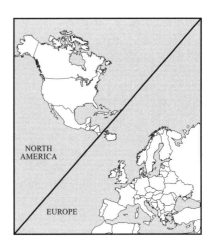

Perspectives from Europe and North America

Norris Clement, Paul Ganster, and Alan Sweedler

As its title indicates, this article is concerned with the issues of environment, development, and security in border regions. It reviews the changing functions of international boundaries in the context of the global economy and addresses the multidimensional nature of the transborder relationship. The study relies on perspectives from European and North American borders but offers suggestions for understanding border regional development everywhere.

Norris Clement is professor emeritus of economics at San Diego State University; Paul Ganster, a historian, directs the Institute for Regional Studies of the Californias at SDSU; and Alan Sweedler is professor of physics at SDSU and has worked on security and energy issues in border regions.

From Norris Clement, Paul Ganster, and Alan Sweedler, "Development, Environment, and Security in Asymmetrical Border Regions: European and North American Perspectives," in *Curtains of Iron and Gold: Reconstructing Borders and Scales of Interaction*, ed. Heikki Eskelinen, Ilkka Liikanen, and Jukka Oksa (Aldershot, England: Ashgate, 1999), 243–81. Reprinted by permission.

Introduction

As the number of international boundaries and border regions multiply and are transformed by changing local, national, and international political-economic circumstances, the need for understanding them in a public policy context has grown accordingly.[1] While the literature in this area has expanded rapidly in recent years, most of it is directed at specific geographic regions and/or specific functional areas, largely neglecting the methodological aspects of borderlands studies. By addressing economic, environmental, and security issues jointly, we hope to contribute to the development of a comprehensive, multidisciplinary conceptual framework for analyzing border regional development issues.

The major thesis to be developed here has two components. First, that the changing functions of international boundaries in the context of the New Economy (more open, globalized, high-tech economy) dictate that the regionalization of decision-making accomplished through transboundary collaboration can have positive benefits in terms of reducing conflict and attaining higher levels of prosperity and quality of life. Second, that any analysis of regional development requires an analysis of transboundary collaboration which, in turn, requires a multidisciplinary or systems approach in order to understand the multidimensional nature of the transborder relationship and the complex interdependence between those relationships.

The emphasis here will be on those borders that are significantly asymmetrical and draw mainly from the authors' experiences and analyses of the United States–Mexican border region with some comparisons with external European Union border regions. While it can be argued that all border regions are asymmetrical, these borders are generally characterized by much larger differences between living standards, technological development, and institutional patterns than are, say, the nations within the EU or between Canada and the United States.

The essay is organized into four major sections. In the first we examine the changing economic functions of international boundaries that define the unique character of, and condition the potential for, the development of border regions. In the second section, we explore the relationship between economic development and the environment, noting particularly the environmental costs associated with development and the need to create transboundary environmental management systems. In the third section we examine the changing nature of security issues in the North American and European contexts and the relationship between border regional development and security. Finally, we discuss the implications of the first three sections for developing a conceptual framework for analyzing border regional development and transboundary collaboration.

Economic Development of Border Regions

The Changing Economic Functions of International Boundaries

Traditional economic theory does not provide us with a general theory of international boundaries nor of border region development (Hansen 1981: ch. 2). In general, traditional economic analysis views international boundaries as barriers to trade, which, like tariffs and quotas, tend to reduce the volume and value of trade, and its associated benefits such as production efficiencies and lower prices for consumers. Additionally, to the extent that international boundaries are disputed and/or politically unstable, they introduce a higher level of risk and therefore tend to discourage investment and legal economic activity in adjacent regions.[2]

Another view of boundaries is that they serve as screening agents or permeable membranes that regulate what can *legally* flow from one political jurisdiction to another and under what conditions. Commodities and persons that cannot legally pass through the ports of exit or entry are either excluded from international trade, or are compelled to utilize illegal means if they are to get to the other side. Thus, informal and illegal markets develop for smuggling items of high value and low volume such as drugs, exotic animals, or persons while crossing costs vary according to the degree of risk and the severity of penalties, which, in turn, depend mainly on the strength and effectiveness of the law enforcement capabilities of the adjoining countries.

Historically, restrictions on cross boundary flows varied significantly between countries in accordance with national political, economic, and cultural norms and policies. In many cases it was, and still is, these differences between national norms and policies that create many of the opportunities for international trade and investment flows such as U.S. direct foreign investment in Mexico during the period of industrial protectionism, or, prohibition of alcoholic beverages in the United States during the 1920–1933 period, which was an important factor in the development of Mexican border cities due to increased border transactions.

In summary, international boundaries are viewed, in the case of market oriented economies, as barriers to transactions of goods and services (both inputs and outputs), technology, and people that flow across borders in response to a constellation of market and nonmarket (i.e., social/cultural) conditions.[3] The driver of the market-based interactions is, in the case of firms, the expectation of maximizing profits or, in the case of consumers, maximizing real income by shopping on both sides of the border. The differences in price, quality, and availability of goods and services emanating from the resource and production complementarities and aysmmetries between countries is a powerful force for generating transborder flows of goods, services, finances, technology, and people.[4] However, in order for international sales/

purchases to be realized, all commodities and persons must somehow pass the thorough screening processes carried out by the appropriate authorities at ports of exit/entry in accordance with the customs and immigration regimens of both countries. Both countries allow goods, services, and people to enter/ exit only upon payment of required fees, presentation of necessary documentation, and compliance with elaborate sets of regulations, all of which are usually formulated at the national level in accordance with national interests.

In the last decade, due to a rapidly changing set of economic, political, and strategic factors, Western European and North American boundaries have become less significant as economic barriers than at any time since the Great Depression of the 1930s, when tariffs were at the highest level of the 20th century. Tariff rates and non-tariff barriers have been reduced significantly, largely due to negotiations carried out in the context of the General Agreement on Tariffs and Trade (GATT), the new World Trade Organization (WTO), and regional trade blocs such as the European Union (EU) and the North American Free Trade Agreement (NAFTA).

In Western Europe, where the process of regional economic integration has advanced the most, restrictions on the mobility of goods and services, capital, and labor within the EU have been dramatically reduced, creating two significantly different types of borders. These are internal between EU member states and external between EU member and nonmember states. Thus, with the free movement of people and goods, customs and migration inspections between EU countries on internal borders have largely disappeared, reflecting the relatively homogenous living standards and levels of development among member states. These borders are increasingly viewed as contact points that will bring together EU countries into a united Europe. EU external borders, however, are quite traditional in the sense that inspections are still carried out and at many ports of entry long waiting times, especially for commercial transport vehicles, signal the growing volume of trade between East and West and attest to the bureaucratic procedures that are required to pass into and out of the EU.

Additionally, the disintegration of the Soviet Union and the reduction of Cold War hostilities have resulted in dramatic changes between those nations that were previously on different sides of the Iron Curtain. However, within Eastern Europe an increased number of independent countries and borders has not resulted in a uniform easing of restrictions between nation states. In many places, as old regimes suddenly disintegrated, more openness on borders prompted an urgent need for new mechanisms to facilitate flows of persons and products across international borders,[5] but in others, such as between some of the states of the former Soviet Union, these changes have resulted in less openness.

In North America, where the process of regional integration is less advanced through movement to a free trade area as opposed to economic union

This checkpoint on the German-Netherlands border near Nijmegen is now closed, 2002. *Photograph by Paul Ganster*

The border between Enschede, the Netherlands, and Gronau, Germany, is marked only by a ditch, 1995. *Photograph by Paul Ganster*

as in Europe, it is likely to be many years before the concept of internal and external borders becomes a reality.[6] In fact, due mainly to the reluctance of the U.S. Congress to grant fast-track authority (the presidency negotiates and Congress approves or disapproves trade agreements) to President Clinton and his trade negotiators, regional integration in South America, especially among the MERCOSUR countries of Brazil, Argentina, Paraguay, and Uruguay, is advancing far more rapidly than in the NAFTA countries.

In summary, for internal EU borders the traditional economic functions are changing significantly, but for external EU borders they are still relevant. Nevertheless, economic barriers on external EU borders are also receding due to the expanding influence and coverage of the WTO and the IMF throughout the entire world economy. Still, where borders are contested, such as those between some of the republics of the former Soviet Union, or are relatively closed for national security reasons, such as between Estonia and Russia, the volume of transboundary crossings of both goods (exports, imports, and border transactions) and people is increasing.

Globalization and Border Regional Development

The decade of the 1990s can be viewed as a watershed decade in economic history, marking the end of the post-World War II period, characterized by the Cold War and the East-West division of the global economy. The new period we are now entering is distinguished by the integration of the centrally planned economies of the East—and increasingly China and India—into the increasingly globalized, market-oriented economy of the West. This New Economy is driven mainly by technological innovation and an increasingly open and competitive international economic environment. In response, firms throughout the world are now experiencing a dramatic revolution in both structure (how they are organized) and function (how they do business). Technological change has made it possible for firms producing tradeable goods that are mainly manufactured items to operate on a global level with geographic location of the various phases of their operations determined less and less on the basis of traditional cost considerations. In fact, for many firms, profits and market share now depend more on rapid product development than simple cost reduction. Thus, it is increasingly important for such firms to locate their research and development facilities in a milieu that supports innovation[7] while the production phases are located in lower cost, export processing zones (EPZs) throughout the world. The *maquiladoras* of Mexico's northern border are typical of these manufacturing operations.

These and many other factors have resulted in different spatial patterns of economic activity and traditional core-periphery distribution has become more variegated, providing new economic opportunities for regions that previously found themselves condemned to the periphery. Meanwhile, traditional macroeconomic stabilization and industrial policies at the national level have become less effective and politically less acceptable while ideological factors have led to a devolution of economic powers from federal to local governments, forcing them to accept more responsibility for their own economic development.

The economic development prospects of border regions are changing dramatically. Residents of localities adjacent to international borders that formerly were isolated and/or underpopulated and usually poor are now actively searching for development policies that often include collaboration with localities on the other side. Many of these communities benefitted from the development of trading activity at the border, and the storage of goods and earnings derived from the collection of duties (Hansen 1981, p.25). Now, however, with the virtual disappearance of barriers to goods and people among member nations the economic activities associated with the border that were often a large part of the region's economic base have also dwindled or, in some cases, disappeared. Such localities may differ greatly in geographical size, population density, economic characteristics and problems, and degree of development, as well as cultural-linguistic characteristics, and, therefore, frequently have difficulty in forming collaborative relationships (Martinos and Caspara 1990, p.3).

It is in this context that the economic development potential of many border regions can change in response to changing, externally imposed economic circumstances on their particular boundary, as in the implementation of NAFTA in the case of the U.S.–Mexican border, and/or other factors outside the control of the regions themselves, as with the extension of EU membership in the case of the Austrian-Slovenian border. Alternatively, the economic development potential of particular border regions can be changed by internally generated transboundary collaborative efforts as people and governments formerly separated by international borders attempt to improve living standards and resolve the many local transborder economic, social, political, and environmental problems that cannot be prevented from spilling over international borders.

It should be noted that international boundaries often do not coincide with natural boundaries such as bodies of water or mountains, and they often divide cultural and/or economic regions. Traditionally, boundaries served as symbols of, and instruments for, maintaining national sovereignty and carrying out national policies that frequently disrupted historical social and economic intercourse while creating additional political jurisdictions, further complicating the issue of fragmentation of governance. Thus, border regions usually suffered from a peripheral position in their respective countries. Moreover, the peripheral position was economic because of obstacles to trade, and political due to isolation from centers of political power and decision-making.

The main point here is that the emerging New Economy—characterized by increased globalization and openness—has diminished, but not eliminated, the impacts of economic borders, but political borders still remain, impeding the regionalization of decision-making. The New Economy, heavily influenced by conservative ideology stressing the benefits of market mechanisms, has also meant a diminished role for central governments in achieving full employment and economic growth. Thus, devolution of powers has meant that local/regional governments are increasingly forced to accept more responsibility for the economic development of their own jurisdictions. Consequently, international transboundary collaboration (TBC) between local governments, businesses, and nongovernmental organizations (NGOs) has expanded in many areas of the world in an attempt to regionalize decision-making across international and internal boundaries in order to reduce conflict and improve prosperity and the general quality of life.

In those areas where transborder collaboration has flourished each transborder region seems to have adopted its own unique approach to such endeavors, building on its own history, culture, resources, capacities, and position vis-à-vis its own niche in the national and international context. In the EU, transboundary programs have been institutionalized and scores of transborder regional projects have received financing under a formalized regime. However, in North America, transboundary collaboration has largely evolved utilizing informal agreements. In the final section of this essay we explore this theme in more detail.

Special Issue: The Mexican Maquiladora *Industry*

In recent years, European researchers and representatives from communities located on the EU's eastern (external) borders have demonstrated interest in the Mexican *maquiladora* (assembly plant) industry as a model for what they might do in the European context in terms of attracting capital and technology transfer from multinational corporations based in the developed (OECD) countries. Most of these communities, located in the transforming economies, have low wages, but, in many cases, their labor forces are quite educated and highly skilled. Since this industry has played a major role in transforming the economic structure—and the environmental and security issues—of the U.S.–Mexican border, a brief overview of the industry is essential.

The *maquiladora* industy, or maquila, is Mexico's version of the generalized phenomenon of export processing zones (EPZs) that in the last thirty years have become an integral part of the international economy, playing an important role in the assembly and manufacture of a growing array of goods and services. In the United States, for example, consumer goods displaying labels "Made in the U.S.A." are difficult to find these days. Instead, labels saying, "Made in China" or "Assembled in Mexico" are more common and indicate a major change in the traditional international division of labor via a new development strategy for a growing number of large and small developing nations scattered throughout the world based on export-oriented industrialization.

For the United States, the use of offshore sourcing began as a side effect of establishing manufacturing facilities in Europe behind tariff walls in order to increase sales to the giant European Economic Community. For Japan, frequently called a nation of *maquiladoras* because of its elaborate subcontracting system, the decision to use offshore EPZs was apparently part of a deliberate strategy to gain market shares in a world dominated by the United States. Mexico created the *maquiladora* industry as an EPZ because of both the demonstrated success of other EPZs in the Far East, such as Taiwan and Singapore, and Mexico's need to solve pressing social and economic problems by accelerating job creation.

The 1964 Border Industrialization Program that gave birth to the industry was designed to reduce unemployment in Mexico's northern border region, generate foreign exchange, provide higher skill levels for workers, and stimulate technology transfer to Mexico by attracting foreign manufacturing firms there to establish assembly operations. Since then, and especially as a consequence of the peso devaluations in the 1980s and again in 1994, the industry has grown rapidly.

Today *maquiladora* stands as a generic term for those firms that process (assemble and/or transform in some way) components imported into Mexico that are then re-exported. Alternatively, it can be said that *maquiladora* is an economic unit for the production of goods or services based on the temporary importation of raw materials and equipment to be transformed in Mexico and subsequently sold abroad. The term in-bond industry comes from the fact that those components that are imported into Mexico are imported under a bonded status in order to insure that they are not sold in Mexico's domestic market, but are re-exported for sale in foreign markets, mainly the United States and Canada.

The industry has evolved dramatically since its beginning in 1965. While it is still located mainly in Mexico's northern border region—almost two-thirds of the 2,823 *maquiladora* plants are located in the states next to the United States—many of the plants now utilize modern, automated technology and require high skill levels from their 948,658 workers (data as of October 1996). Products range from electronics, television sets, textile products, shoes and leather goods, wood and chemical products, furniture, toys and sporting goods, equipment and tools, and a range of automobile components and accessories. The ownership of plants has become more diversified, as many large Asian electronics manufacturers have established facilities there in order to take advantage of the tariff benefits offered to firms that produce within North America under the provisions of NAFTA.

The success of the maquila can best be illustrated by looking at its growth rate in recent years—10–20 percent by most indicators—and the fact that it now brings in more foreign exchange than any other single sector of the Mexican economy except for petroleum. The major shortfall of the industry, however, has been its inability to link up with the rest of the nation's economy—only about 2 percent of the industry's inputs are sourced from Mexican suppliers; the rest come from U.S. and Asian suppliers. Accordingly, most of the industry's expansion and linkages have been limited to the border region itself. There, the effects involve the construction industry, business services, and commerce through the expenditure of workers' wages. Another shortcoming of the *maquiladora* industry is that wages are extremely low (approximately U.S.$1 per hour) relative to living costs, which are very high in Mexico's northern border region. Thus, Mexican border economies have been growing rapidly, but real wages have stagnated and living standards have not improved.

Mexico's major challenge over the next decade will be to try to increase the industry's integration and linkages with the rest of the nation's economy. It will also need to increase real wages to a level sufficient to support a decent standard of living while maintaining a high level of investment from multinational firms that basically came to the region in search of low wages and access to the prosperous U.S. market.

The Environment and Border Regional Development

Transborder Environmental Issues

As noted in the previous section, as economic interdependency between neighboring nations has increased in recent decades, the roles of boundaries and border regions have been transformed. Economically, boundaries have become more open and the opportunities for border regional development have increased accordingly. Politically, the concerns of the residents of border regions, which traditionally were lightly populated and politically marginalized, could easily be ignored by central governments in the formulation and implementation of policies that affect border regions. Increasingly, as the barrier function of boundaries has subsided and the integrative function has emerged, the political importance of boundaries and border regions has increased. Often, they have received more attention in their respective national capitals.

While the evolution of function is a signature characteristic of boundaries and border regions in the current era, there are many economic and noneconomic factors that influence the ability of border regions to cooperate across international boundaries. These include the presence of economic asymmetries and complementarities; the relative importance of the integrative and barrier functions of the particular boundary in the national and international context; the relative importance of urban or rural populations; differential population growth rates and densities across the border; and the degree of centralization of the political-governance system.

Generally, decentralized systems facilitate local transborder cooperation while highly centralized political systems present special problems for local transborder cooperation. However, all of these features condition the processes available for dealing with environmental problems in a transborder context and highlight the complexities and difficulties in managing transborder environmental problems.

The general nature of the environmental challenge that all border regions face in this new era can be stated in relatively simple terms. As economic activity expands—either because of the increased movement of goods and services across international boundaries or because of more economic activity in the border regions themselves—the level of environmental deterioration due to higher levels of pollution and resource depletion can be expected to increase. It can be said that economic growth itself can be expected to decrease any region's quality of life. In fact, recognition of this relationship, empirically, and in hundreds of communities throughout the developed and developing world has, in fact, led to the search for sustainable development at the regional level as part of a growing global movement (Pezzoli 1997; Ganster 1998b).

This generalized environmental problem has special meaning for asymmetrical border regions. While relatively symmetrical border regions tend to have relatively uniform environmental standards and levels of enforcement along with relatively well-developed institutional structures for collaborative environmental management, asymmetrical border regions usually do not. Therefore, there is ample opportunity for exploiting these asymmetries by firms (and individuals) that find it more profitable to assign the various research, production, distribution, and consumption phases of their activities to that side of the border region that offers the lowest cost alternative. Additionally, governments that have insufficient resources are likely to ignore the external effects their actions might have, not only on their own territory, but also on the environment of the entire border region. This is particularly true for developing countries with high population growth rates and significant unemployment and, therefore, great internal pressure to create jobs no matter what the unintended effects.

There are, in general, four areas of environmental problems encountered at the regional level: water quality and supply problems; hazardous and industrial waste; air pollution; and bioresource issues. All of these problems can be initiated and/or aggravated by private and/or public entities as they carry out their respective economic functions.

For example, governments are usually assigned the responsibility of disposing of sewage and solid waste in the most expedient and low-cost manner available. These actions, however, if not done properly, can result in polluted rivers, lakes, underground aquifers, and ocean waters—on both sides of the border. Governments are also charged with providing their citizens with water that frequently comes from dwindling transboundary aquifers and surface sources, depriving future generations on both sides of the international boundary of an essential resource for supporting human life. Rapidly expanding populations frequently result in unbridled urban expansion that, in turn, can have negative impacts on the native flora and fauna and ecosystems. In rural areas destruction of native habitats through grazing activities or agriculture often occurs. Air pollution can damage forests indirectly through acid rain, negatively impacting resource industries and tourism. Tourism and recreation can also harm fragile ecosystems, again on both sides of the boundary. Similarly, the rapid growth of manufacturing on one side of an international boundary such as has occurred with the Mexican *maquiladora* industry can produce a great increase in industrial waste that can be difficult to manage under conditions of an asymmetric border. Largely because of the lack of infrastructure and regulatory and enforcement capacities in the U.S.–Mexican border region, particularly in Mexico, only a small percentage of hazardous waste from border maquilas is being disposed of in a fashion that would meet generally accepted international standards. The rest is being stored (often improperly), dumped in municipal landfills, or discharged into the wastewater collector system (Newman 1996).

While efforts on one side of the border can be initiated to alleviate these problems, most are doomed to failure without cooperation from the other side. Region-wide solutions must be found for problems that do not respect international boundaries.

Transborder Environmental Management Practices

As scientists, policymakers, and the public have become aware of the deleterious effects of environmental pollution, environmental protection has emerged as a national priority in both developed and developing countries. Transborder pollution issues have also attracted attention as nations have worked to develop mechanisms to resolve these complex issues. Although growing scientific evidence has been used to document the effects of the transport of pollutants over long distances, the most obvious transboundary impacts are visible in border areas where the negative results of raw sewage discharges, burning of coal, smelter operations, vehicular pollution, and improper hazardous waste disposal are immediately apparent.

There are many examples of efforts at regional transborder environmental management throughout the world. These include the formation of the

International Joint Commission along the U.S.–Canadian border to address ecosystem problems of the Great Lakes, various efforts in the Rhine River Valley for hazardous waste and thermal pollution control, agreements for natural areas in Central American border regions, and cooperation on air pollution in the Baltic region. Transborder environmental cooperation is part of the larger trend of cooperation at the regional and global levels on matters relating to the environment.

The traditional approach to pollution control utilized in the United States and other advanced countries is to identify the specific sources of the pollution and their respective social costs and through specific programs achieve the highest reduction of pollution at the lowest cost. The overall goal is to somehow hold pollution at some acceptable level by internalizing the social costs of pollution (i.e., the negative externalities) to those who through production and/or consumption are responsible for the pollution. Essentially there are three ways that governments can achieve this goal:

- Pollution Controls or Command and Control. This system imposes maximum pollution standards on businesses and/or consumers and then constructs an enforcement system to monitor compliance with the standards. Those not complying with the standards are fined and obligated to remedy the violation in the future.
- Taxes and Subsidies. In this situation taxes are imposed on the polluter in accordance with the amount of pollution, thereby increasing the firm's costs and eventually the price charged to end users. Higher prices will then, in most cases, reduce the quantity demanded of the polluting goods and therefore reduce pollution. Subsidies can be used where it is expected that they will result in less pollution by perhaps defraying the firm's cost of installing pollution control equipment or implementing less-polluting production techniques.
- Tradeable Permits. Here the government issues each firm a permit to emit a specified level of pollutants into the environment. Environmentally efficient firms that do not pollute the allowable level can then sell their permits to other firms, thereby providing an incentive to find the least costly form of pollution control.

Another way that pollution controls can be imposed is via negotiated agreements either between private parties or between governments and private parties.[8] In addition, new social accounting methods are being introduced at the national and regional levels in order to belter measure the environmental and social costs associated with resource depletion and pollution, the usual by-products of development.

There are several limitations to utilizing the traditional mainstream approach in developing and/or transforming economies. Most conspicuous is the lack of data on the sources of environmental damage. Without such data it is impossible to carry out a thorough analysis of the costs of pollution and appropriate mitigation strategies. Another limitation relates to the low incomes and low environmental awareness of many residents of poor countries. While some consumers and businesses have both the environmental awareness and economic resources sufficient to understand, purchase, and maintain pollution abatement equipment, the problem is how to devise a system that would be equitable with respect to all consumers and businesses and also be efficient. In other words, the system would need to produce significantly lower pollution at a reasonable cost. Low incomes also present another problem from the individual and community perspective. If low-cost pollution abatement equipment were available, an effective monitoring/enforcement system would also have to be created. However, the cost of such a system would, at this time, probably strain the resources of the state and local government.

Thus, on an asymmetrical border the richer community is left with several less-than-desirable options. These include (1) ignoring the spillover effects from the other side; (2) paying the costs of alleviating the most egregious sources of pollution on the other side; or, (3) working with representatives from the other side to slowly introduce the capacity, competencies, and financial resources necessary to implement the needed policies. In practice, a combination of all three options can result. And even under the best of circumstances, sustainable development practices in any region are difficult to achieve.

*Special Issue: The Evolution of Environmental Management
in the U.S.–Mexican Border Region*

The focus of this section is the evolution of management of transboundary environmental issues in the U.S.–Mexican border region. This border region is quite unique and some attention to its major characteristics is necessary prior to a discussion of environmental issues and approaches (Ganster 1995, 1997).

Demographic Characteristics. The U.S.–Mexican border region is one of the most demographically dynamic regions of the entire world. The post–World War II period saw significant development of the Southwest of the United States—known as Sunbelt growth—that stimulated similar trends on the Mexican side of the border. On the U.S. side, the population growth was largely driven by internal migration; on the Mexican side, the Mexican population explosion through natural increase and internal migration combined for extraordinary growth rates of populations in the border region. Some Mexican border cities are doubling in population every 10 to 20 years (Ganster 1998a).

The population of the border region—which grew from 8.3 million in 1990 to 10.3 million in 1995—is largely urbanized and the settlement pattern is one of U.S. and Mexican cities located across the boundary from each other—known as twin cities—and separated by vast empty spaces. Only in the lower Rio Grande Valley and in the Mexicali Valley are there significant rural populations in productive irrigated agricultural areas. Otherwise, the land of the border region is largely arid, suited only to grazing and mining activities, in addition to pockets of irrigated agriculture.

Economic Asymmetries. The U.S.–Mexican border region is also characterized by enormous economic asymmetries from north to south across the border. Although the Mexican border cities are among the wealthiest regions of Mexico, they are quite poor in contrast to their counterparts across the border in the United States. This can be seen not only in per capita incomes and regional economic activity, but also in the size of municipal budgets and urban services available in the U.S. and Mexican border twin cities. For example, in 1996 the combined budget of the City and County of San Diego was approximately U.S.$3.2 billion while the budget for the entire municipality of Tijuana was approximately U.S.$53 million. Additionally, the Gross Regional Product of San Diego currently exceeds U.S.$80 billion; that of Tijuana is approximately U.S.$5 billion. The minimum wage in San Diego is US$5.35 per hour; for Tijuana it is approximately U.S.$.44 per hour. The economy of Tijuana is heavily dependent upon that of San Diego and the United States. Approximately 3 percent of jobs and the regional product of San Diego are related to Tijuana and Mexico. Some 60 percent of employment in Tijuana is dependent on the connection to San Diego and the United States through *maquiladoras*, and cross-border tourism. Eight percent of the economically active population of Tijuana is actually employed in San Diego, and these individuals total some 40,000 who commute to work in the United States each day and account for 20 percent of total personal income in Tijuana (see Rey et al. 1998).

While the economic asymmetries are not as apparent between the other twin cities along the border, the contrast between a developed country and a developing country is still very obvious. A key difference everywhere remains the lack of local border Mexican government resources to cope with urban services and environmental issues.

Governance and Public Administration Asymmetries. Two very different systems of governance meet at the U.S.–Mexican border. The U.S. system is federal, with significant decentralization of powers to local authorities. Mexico's system is highly centralized, traditionally with little power or resources at the local municipal level, as seen in the above discussion of municipal financial resources. Moreover, many of the positions of Mexican municipal, state, and federal agencies are political appointments. Thus, when new administrations are elected, a significant number of key employees is

replaced, creating difficulties for the administrative continuity that is especially important for transborder cooperation.

On the Mexican side of the border, local administrative units are municipalities, government units that cover large urban and rural territorial areas
with one local government. However, many of the local government functions are carried out by delegates of state and federal agencies located in the
municipality. On the U.S. side, the structure varies somewhat from state to
state, but local government consists of county governments for the large territorial divisions and city governments for the urbanized areas within the
county boundaries. Thus, in a typical border region, there are many local
agencies on the U.S. side and one local agency in Mexico, along with many
state and federal agencies that need to work together to resolve local
transborder issues.

Environmental Issues. The U.S.–Mexican border region is, like other regions, plagued by a variety of air, water, waste, and biosphere problems; however, a general overview of the environmental context would probably be
helpful to understand the evolution of environmental management practices.

Rapid urbanization and population growth and the expanding *maquiladora* industry with insufficient regulatory controls have produced a range of
negative transborder environmental impacts that affect Mexican and U.S.
border twin cities. The most severe are concentrated in the transborder metropolitan regions where human activity has been most intense, but there are
also important problems and issues in rural and natural areas.

Mexico and the United States have different traditions regarding environmental protection and policies. Typically, Mexico was more concerned
with creation of jobs and providing people with basic services such as po-
table water rather than with preventing and cleaning up industrial pollution
or with providing sewage treatment and collection. Mexican officials often
felt that environmental protection and rigorous standards were a luxury that
developing countries could afford but were an unfair burden for Mexico.[9]
These different approaches to the environment stood out in strong contrast at
the border and were, at times, a source of conflict between twin city communities and between countries. These sorts of differences between developed
and developing nations are apparent everywhere in the world and have been
articulated at the global level at the Rio Summit and at other forums.

Furthermore, there were often significant differences in opinion as to
how environmental issues should be dealt with. U.S. policymakers have tended
to favor large and costly engineering solutions that depend on relatively sophisticated and expensive technology. Mexican decision makers have favored
less expensive, low-technology solutions. However, with NAFTA and changing economic realities for U.S. border cities, Mexican and U.S. policymakers
both have greater interest in low-technology, low-cost solutions to environ-

mental problems. And, for the first time, sustainable development has become a criterion for the evaluation of potential environmental projects.

Environmental Management Practices. Over the course of the last decade, Mexico has undergone a profound revolution in its economic development policy, changing from a highly protected domestic economy, with strict controls on imports and foreign investment, and heavy state participation in many sectors of the economy, to an open economy with liberalized import and investment laws. Mexico's decision to enter GATT (General Agreement on Tariffs and Trade) in 1986 was followed by implementation on January 1, 1994, of the North American Free Trade Agreement by Mexico, the United States, and Canada. These measures produced a significant growth in U.S.–Mexican bilateral trade with important consequences for the border region. Since most bilateral trade moved goods by land transportation, trade-related activities boomed in the border cities. For U.S.–Mexican trade, some 90 percent of bilateral trade moves across the land border. Of this, 75 percent is moved by truck. Consequently, infrastructure in the border cities, including customs facilities, ports of entry, and roads, has become saturated.

Debate over approval of NAFTA was particularly intense in the United States Congress and focused national attention on environmental conditions in the border region and potential impacts of the treaty on border communities. In response to strong criticism of existing governmental efforts on the border environment, U.S. and Mexican authorities developed the Integrated Border Environmental Plan for the U.S.–Mexico Border Area (IBEP). Other important actions included negotiation by Mexico and the United States of side agreements to NAFTA that led to the establishment of unique, binational entities, the North American Development Bank (NADBank) and the Border Environment Cooperation Commission (BECC). The BECC certifies border environmental infrastructure projects and then NADBank arranges financing for the certified projects. The BECC established rules and procedures after significant public comment and its deliberations and meetings are open and transparent. Another product of NAFTA was the creation of the U.S.–Canadian–Mexican Commission on Environmental Cooperation (CEC) to address trade impacts on the environment in the North American region.

The recent history of the border region, culminating in the NAFTA process, has seen a fundamental change in the role that the border region plays domestically in Mexico and the United States and also internationally in the bilateral relationship. Historically, the border has been politically marginalized in the polity of Mexico and the United States. The NAFTA process helped transform the border region from a passive recipient of policies from Washington, D.C., and Mexico City to an initiator of actions that became national and bilateral policy. The border region was key to the passage of NAFTA and will likely retain a strategic role in the unfolding economic integration of the two partners.

Perhaps the most important NAFTA border effect has been a significant improvement in bilateral cooperation at the federal level and especially at the local level along the border. New emphasis on cooperation to facilitate trade has spilled over into environmental cooperation. In fact there has been a significant increase in U.S. federal agency and Mexican federal agency direct contact and interaction at the technical level without the interference of the two foreign relations departments. At the local and state levels of government, the increase of cross-border cooperation has been startling. The new activity at the state and local levels has come about as the result of several factors. First, Mexico has been engaged in a process of transferring more governmental responsibility to state and local entities. This decentralization process has created more direct counterparts on the Mexican side of the border for U.S. entities to interact with. Second, the U.S. government and, to a lesser extent, the Mexican government have placed significant emphasis on the participation of local residents in federal policy-making in areas of concern to the border region. This has led the two foreign relations departments to realize that often resolution of local transborder issues can be accomplished best by the two federal governments facilitating local and regional transboundary efforts. For example, a new Border Liaison mechanism has been developed and is functioning in the Tijuana–San Diego area. Under the auspices of the Consul General of Mexico in San Diego and the Consul General of the United States in Tijuana, binational working groups have been convened to address transborder issues such as water quality and supply. An additional mechanism for local transborder environmental problems was the establishment in 1997 of the Ciudad Juarez–El Paso Air Basin Management Authority. Created by a joint agreement of the Mexican and U.S. governments, this authority will work to address serious air pollution problems in this binational airshed that has the worst air quality along the U.S.–Mexican border.

Third, the two governments are committed to the enhancement of free trade through NAFTA. This has enabled them to compartmentalize issues on the bilateral agenda so that disputes over illegal immigration or drug trafficking do not spill over into trade or environmental issues. This new maturity in the U.S.–Mexican relationship has enabled local and regional cross-border problem resolution to move forward without the negative repercussions of disputes at the federal level.

The current structure of environmental management on both sides of the U.S.–Mexican border is a process increasingly subject to international agreements and evolving patterns of binational, transborder cooperation. In modern times such treaties go back to 1944, when the International Boundary and Water Commission (IBWC) was created in its present form to deal with what its title implies, international boundary and water issues on the U.S.–Mexican border. Subsequently, the 1983 La Paz Agreement on Cooperation for the Protection and Improvement of the Environment in the Border Area provided a framework for addressing a broader range of border environmental issues. Then, in 1991, the Integrated Border Environmental Plan for the Mexican–U.S. Border Area, First Stage (1992–1994) (IBEP) was implemented. It was based on the La Paz Agreement and took joint cooperation on border environmental issues to a higher stage. Finally, Border XXI was presented in 1996 in order to broaden the scope of collaborative issues and increase coordination among all levels of government and border communities.

Border XXI is a comprehensive plan and process to address border environmental problems and to work toward sustainable development. The key activities of Border XXI take place through the ongoing efforts of the binational working groups, established by the La Paz Agreement and then expanded under Border XXI to include nine areas of work: air, water, hazardous and solid waste, natural resources, environmental health, pollution prevention, cooperation enforcement and compliance, environmental information resources, and contingency planning and emergency response. Initially constructed only with federal agency representatives, the working groups soon included the informal representatives of state and local agencies. At a March 1998 meeting of the working groups, the states pushed for formal seats in the working groups. There is also pressure to open the groups to public and academic participation.

Conclusions: Environmental Management
in the U.S.–Mexican Border Region

At this point a myriad of governmental agencies and nongovernmental organizations are involved in defining and managing U.S.–Mexican border environmental issues (Ganster 1996). Nevertheless, the general objective of this new constellation of organizations is that bringing together technical monitoring, academic analysis, and grass-roots participation with governmental processes and financial leverage can result in a politically acceptable and environmentally sound set of policies. Because the process is relatively new it is still too early to assess its overall performance. Still, the concept represents a great deal of progress over the traditional top-down processes dictated by the two nations' capitals that prevailed for so many years.

In the past, a major bottleneck has been the unwillingness of the U.S. Congress to spend funds to address problems that originate in Mexico. This stands in strong contrast to the EU, where providing funding for projects for poorer partners or for areas adjacent to the EU is well-established. This may be changing through the mechanism of the U.S. Environmental Protection Agency allocating funds to projects certified by the BECC and funded and managed by NADBank. On the Mexican side, the bottleneck has been the lack of resources, but with decentralization in public administration and governance and the emerging power of the municipalities, this may be changing.

These recent developments are positive and will hopefully open the way for more efficient transborder cooperation at the local level. However, the excessive population growth in the region has the potential to continue to overwhelm the available institutional resources. If that happens, residents of U.S. border cities may feel that Mexico is threatening their security and quality of life. That would bring a deterioration of transborder political cooperation in the region.

Perhaps the outstanding feature of the U.S.–Mexican bilateral environmental policy is its complexity and inclusiveness. A set of institutions has evolved to deal with the issues in a broad, comprehensive fashion. At the same time, a range of mechanisms is developing to cope with micro-regional transborder environmental issues. Our impression is that the U.S.–Mexican border is somewhat distinct from environmental management in border regions of Europe. There, it seems that efforts most often are multinational and focus on issues such as implementation of Agenda 21 in the Baltic Sea, regional activities such as the Lake Constance management efforts, or the Rhine River cooperative efforts.

Security and Border Regional Development

This section examines security issues in international border regions. It presents a framework for discussing and understanding various elements of security and their impact on development of border areas in the context of a changing global economic and geopolitical order.

Security and Borders: Traditional and Emerging Perspectives

As noted in previous sections, until relatively recently, the boundary region separating two countries has served to demarcate the physical limits of the nation-state. Border regions were seen as politically, economically, and socially peripheral to the main activities of the country, which generally took place far from the border zones. Border regions tended to be sparsely populated and undeveloped for the most part. Moreover, many border regions were militarized and seen as the first line of defense against would-be aggressors. Since the end of the Second World War, however, some border regions have emerged as vibrant areas of economic growth and have served as positive, integrative elements in relations between the nations that share the border region. Some examples of such border regions are those between France and Germany, Germany and Holland, the Nordic countries, and the United States and Canada.[10]

The end of the Cold War has given rise, on the one hand, to some boundaries as barriers that serve as focal points of conflict between the states separated by the boundary and, on the other hand, to integrative boundaries where the border regions are more unified and transboundary collaboration is growing between neighboring states. Examples of the former are the new boundaries of the former Yugoslavia, and those separating the former republics of the Soviet Union. Many of these new border regions are heavily militarized and in some cases are regions of violent conflict.

At the same time, however, some regions separated by an international boundary have grown closer, have become more integrated, and conflictive issues have been resolved.[11] The U.S.–Mexican border region, the internal boundaries within the European Union, the border between Venezuela and Colombia, and the Russian–Finnish border are examples that come to mind. In the case of Germany, the political border between East and West Germany has disappeared altogether, although some argue that another boundary, of an economic and psychological nature, has replaced the former physical border.

As boundaries and border regions have taken on new roles and meanings in the international system, so has the concept of security. During the Cold War era, roughly from 1948 to 1990, security generally referred to issues related to maintaining the political and physical integrity of the nation-state. This involved training and equipping large military forces, developing strategies for their use, and, most important, dealing with the almost 50,000 nuclear weapons that were in existence by the end of the Cold War.

Recently, however, the concept of security has expanded to encompass non-defense-related issues, such as how to deal with organized crime, drug trafficking, smuggling, illegal migration, and serious environmental problems that pose a threat to human health or the underlying ecology of the region. Although this broadened notion of security lends a certain ambiguity to the term, it is useful when discussing conflict and cooperation in border regions, because most security-related problems in border areas today do not deal with issues directly related to military forces or national defense.

In fact, one of the paradoxes of the current global system is that as traditional defense-related security concerns diminish in border regions, non-defense-related security issues increase in importance. This arises as a result of the relative opening of borders that were tightly controlled during the Cold War era. For example, during this period, the East-West dividing line through Central Europe was a highly militarized border region where questions of security referred to deployment of armed forces, questions having to do with nuclear weapons, and defense against armed attack. Since the militarized border region was meant to serve as a barrier against invasion, there obviously was very little interaction across the boundary or transborder collaboration. Here the boundary served the classical role as a barrier between two regions (in this case two different political systems or blocs) and delimited the limits of the states involved. In these circumstances, the possibility of invasion and war were ever-present, but the likelihood of problems arising from organized crime, illegal migration, drug trafficking, and so forth, were non-existent or very small.

Today, however, this same region in Central Europe has borders that are much more open to the movement of goods, people and capital than at any time during the last fifty years. As a result, the possibility of military invasion or conflict is at the lowest level of any time during this century, but there has been a marked increase in smuggling, illegal movement of people, arms trafficking and organized crime.

This situation is not limited to Central and Eastern Europe by any means. A similar set of circumstances is observed, in varying degrees, in the Finnish–Russian border region, the Baltic–Nordic maritime border, and the Russian–Chinese border areas, to name but a few. In each case, a former militarized border has become more open with increased transboundary interaction and border region development. At the same time, however, non-defense-related security problems have arisen.

The U.S.–Mexican case is more complex than the examples just mentioned because the border region has not been the scene of military conflict for more than 150 years.[12] However, due to rapidly expanding trade between the countries and the opening of the Mexican economy in the 1980s, cross-border interactions have dramatically increased in recent years, and with that many of the non-defense security problems noted earlier have emerged. Many of these issues have been associated with the border region for decades, but they have increased significantly in public perception and awareness during the last few years.

A central theme of this section is that security-related problems in border regions play an increasingly important role in the success or failure of efforts to develop and improve transborder cooperation. The perception of security-related issues, as well as the actual management and resolution of these issues, among the general public and local and federal elites is becoming increasingly important as border regions strive to become more integrated and compete effectively in the global economy. Failure to adequately address non-defense-related security issues in the border region could eventually undermine efforts to build trust and cooperation across the border and thus weaken efforts at developing an integrated border region.

Transborder regions can be seen as one element of the ever-increasing globalization of the international economy. Leaders in many border areas around the world are attempting to build on what they perceive as competitive advantages of being located in a binational, asymmetrical border region. These competitive advantages, relative to nonworker regions, result from combining complementary elements that exist on both sides of the border in a synergistic manner. For example, in the U.S.–Mexican case, high technology and skills, coupled with investment capital, tend to be located on the U.S. side of the border, while relatively low wages, a large labor pool, and quick access to U.S. and Canadian markets are found on the Mexican side of the boundary. Taken together, these elements can constitute a competitive advantage for the border region in the global economy, relative to interior parts of Mexico or of the United States. As noted above, considerations such as these have led to rapid growth of the *maquiladora* sector in Mexico, which now employs some 1,000,000 Mexican workers and is a major source of foreign capital in the Mexican economy (*El Financiero Internacional* 1998).

A similar set of complementary elements also exist in the German–Polish border regions and the Finnish–Russian border areas. In the Finnish–Russian example, one finds an abundance of natural resources, such as forests, on the Russian side and, on the Finnish side of the border, an efficient, modern and well-developed wood and paper processing sector. By combining these elements in a synergistic manner, the border region as a whole possesses advantages that each side by itself could not effectively exploit.

For the border regions between Germany and Poland and Germany and the Czech Republic, the complementarity is not found in natural resource distribution, but rather in the very large wage differences between Germany and its eastern neighbors. These differences can be as large as that between the United States and Mexico, which is about a factor of five. It is not surprising, therefore, to find German companies setting up production facilities in Poland and the Czech Republic, bypassing, in many cases, the eastern part of Germany.

Of course, not all border regions, or even national economies, will or can compete successfully in the global economy. It is clear, however, that the high degree of transboundary collaboration that is required for competing in the international economy cannot be achieved unless and until many of the security-related issues in border regions are adequately addressed.

Although management of security issues in border zones will be required for efficient economic development to take place, there is a natural tension between development and security. The optimum condition for economic development and cultural exchange would be completely open borders with free movement of people, capital, and goods. For management of security-related problems, however, just the opposite is the case. A balance needs to be struck, a difficult and politically sensitive task in many border regions. A recent case along the U.S.–Mexican border illustrates the point. The head of the U.S. Customs Service recently resigned under pressure because he was under mounting criticism that he allowed the focus of the agency to shift from drug interdiction to facilitating trade across the nation's borders (Alvord 1997).

The increasing security measures now commonly found at many international border crossings inevitably increase the transaction costs (see below) of doing business in the border region due to increased waiting times at the border, increased documentation required, time-consuming inspections of goods, and so forth. Thus, there is a natural tension between managing security at the boundary and within the border area, and encouraging transborder business and development of the binational region. One of the main challenges for federal and local officials, the business sector, and those charged with economic development will be to develop strategies and policies that respond to the legitimate security-related concerns of people living in the border regions while at the same time encouraging transboundary collaboration and development.

Elements of the New Security

As noted earlier, the term security is somewhat vague and not well-defined. In addition to the more traditional meaning of political and military security, phrases such as economic security, environmental security, comprehensive security, personal security, and internal and external security are commonly found in the literature today. The intent here is not to debate the relative merits or demerits of the varying notions of security. Rather, it is to highlight concrete issues and problems that exist in border regions that, for better or worse, have been lumped together under the rubric of security. A functional way to separate security problems from the myriad of activities that take place in border areas is to examine which agencies deal with particular issues. Thus, smuggling of materials related to nuclear weapons, illegal arms transfers, and large-scale shipments of drugs are dealt with by agencies such as federal police—the Federal Bureau of Investigation (FBI), Central Intelligence Agency (CIA), and the Drug Enforcement Administration (DEA) in the U.S. case—as well as customs police at the border. Clearly, these examples fall into the category of security-related issues.

    Migration. More problematic is the contentious issue of illegal migration. Whether this should be thought of as a security problem or not depends very much on how one sees the underlying factors that give rise to unsanctioned movements of large numbers of people across boundaries. If one concludes that individuals on one side of the border are responding to a need for labor on the other side of the boundary, then people are acting rationally by crossing the border in response to market forces. In this case, migrants would not be thought of in criminal terms or as a security problem. On the other hand, if one views the influx of a large number of people, especially if they are of a different color and speak a different language from the resident population, as disruptive, a source of crime, and requiring unpaid-for social services, then the whole question of migration becomes lumped together with other security-related issues in the border region.

    Since these are very different views about the nature of migration, it is not surprising that methods for dealing with cross-border flows of people vary widely. At one extreme, there are those who call for an impenetrable physical barrier at the border and a dramatic increase in the use of police and military forces to patrol the border region. At the other end of the spectrum are those who argue for a more open border, greatly increasing the legal flow of migrants and providing better social and legal services to migrants. The tension between these two opposing views of migration, and the methods for dealing with the issue, is an important characteristic of many border regions in the world today. How these issues are dealt with has important implications for the success or failure of transboundary collaboration.

In contrast to the European Community, where boundaries are disappearing, the border between Mexico and the United States is increasingly marked by the erection of fences to deter undocumented crossings. Barrier on the border between Nogales, Arizona, and Nogales, Mexico, 2003. *Photograph by Paul Ganster*

Internal and External Security. In addition to the non-defense security-related issues already noted, there are some important elements that should be pointed out regarding the lines between the internal and external security of the state. This subject has attracted attention in recent years as supranational trade blocs, such as the EU and NAFTA region, have evolved (Bigo 1997a, 1997b). Traditionally, external security dealt with issues of defense and securing national boundaries against invasion. These functions were carried out by the armed forces and militarized border patrols. Internal security usually referred to questions related to crime and maintaining order within the boundaries of the state and were dealt with by national and local police authorities. Recently, however, the distinction between internal and external security has become blurred and a convergence between the two realms appears to be emerging. Increasingly, organized crime, terrorists and the countries that support them, drug trafficking, and illegal migration have begun to be viewed as security threats to the state itself. This set of threats has, to some extent, replaced the overriding national security concern of nuclear war that existed during the Cold War period. Many of the same agencies that used to deal with the external enemy (the Soviet Union in the West's case and the United States in the Soviet case) now appear to be focusing much of their resources on the above-mentioned spectrum of threats as they seek to redefine their roles, as well as protect their budgets, in the post-Cold War era. Thus, the CIA is now concerned with drug-related intelligence and even gathering economic intelligence information; the former Soviet KGB is dealing with organized crime and the Russian Mafia as well as smuggling; and the regular armed forces of the United States are heavily involved in drug interdiction along the U.S.–Mexican border.

Related to these developments has been the appearance of internal borders located away from the internationally recognized exterior boundary of the state. These internal borders are not the familiar lines separating administrative units, such as states in the United States, provinces in Canada, or Länder in Germany. Rather, they are locations *anywhere* within a nation's boundaries and serve as checkpoints on the movement of people and goods. In the United States, these internal borders or checkpoints are usually operated by border patrol agents, even though they are far from the international border. Within the territory of the European Union, it is common for individuals to be stopped and checked for proper immigration status, functions that previously were performed at the border before entering EU territory. More often than not, people of color and ethnicity different from the majority are the ones checked, a situation that occurs in the United States as well. This becomes then a question of human rights and not just border-related security.

Taken together, the securitization of activities previously thought of as criminal in nature, the elevation of migration to a security-related issue, the appearance of internal checkpoints, and the role of central agencies heretofore engaged in national security roles have resulted in border security becoming very complex and intertwined with competing interests and competition between different sectors of society and agencies of the government.

Natural Resources and Environmental Security. Natural resource allocation and environmental issues can also be thought of as security-related when the problem threatens the underlying ecosystem of the border region or has a direct impact on the health of border communities.[13] A good example would be the construction of a dam on one side of the border along a river shared by both nations. If the dam should fail, there could be catastrophic consequences for those on the other side of the boundary. In fact, the damming of internationally shared rivers for flood control and power production is a contentious issue that has led to serious tensions in various regions of the world, such as between those states that share the Euphrates and the Danube rivers.

Another example is that of shared underground aquifers. Should the aquifer become contaminated, it would cause a grave health risk to communities on both sides of the border. Managing shared aquifers also raises important questions related to managing natural resources in border areas. Air pollution is yet another arena where transboundary cooperation is critical in dealing with border regions that share a common airshed, such as the El Paso–Ciudad Juarez region along the U.S.–Mexican border or the Baltic Sea air basin.

Energy, like water, is another resource that has important implications in border areas since it is the lifeblood of all modern societies and is vital to the security of any state. A secure and adequate supply of energy is critical to the stability, well-being, and economic development of any region, including border areas. Energy resources, in the form of oil, coal, natural gas, and electricity, are commodities traded worldwide. In many cases, these energy commodities must pass across international boundaries. The transfer of natural gas from Russia to Northern and Central Europe, and the movement of Canadian natural gas to the United States are some examples of cross-boundary energy transfers. For electricity, which can be viewed as a manufactured product, cross-boundary transfers of power take place via connected power grids throughout Europe and North America.

Because secure access to energy resources is seen as vital to national security, most states would prefer to be independent of foreign energy supplies. Unfortunately, nature has been most uncooperative, and energy resources are very unevenly distributed throughout the globe. The major industrial nations of today, such as the United States and Japan, are both heavily dependent on foreign energy supplies. Europe as a whole appears to have sufficient indigenous energy resources, owing to the offshore gas and oil fields of the North Sea. No single country, however, is energy independent, with the exception of a few, such as Norway, the United Kingdom, and Russia.

Although the energy system is global in nature, in some border regions synergies exist that make sharing of energy resources beneficial to the whole border area. This usually occurs where there is a surplus of energy resources such as natural gas, electricity production, or coal in or near the border zone on one side of the boundary and a large demand center on the other. A few examples of these circumstances are the excess generating capacity of the nuclear power complex at Ignalina in Lithuania that is used to service the demand center in St. Petersburg. Another case is the exchange of electricity between Baja California in Mexico and California to meet varying demands throughout the year on both sides of the border. In both cases, the energy resource (nuclear in the case of Lithuania and geothermal in the case of Mexico) is located on one side of the border and the demand on the other.

Until recently, energy has not generally been viewed as a shared resource in border regions. There are many reasons for this, including the relation between energy supplies and national security. Most governments would prefer not to become too dependent on critical energy supplies located in other countries. With the growing competition among regions forced to operate in a global economy, however, shared energy resources that cross national boundaries are increasingly viewed as one element of a binational region's comparative advantage relative to areas lacking in these resources. Questions and concerns about energy security are giving way to economic realities of global competition.

This means, for example, that in the U.S.–Mexican border region, increased sharing of energy resources will increase. The United States is already supplying Mexico with natural gas for use in the northern border cities that are not connected to the Mexican gas pipeline system. This occurs despite the fact that Mexico is a major producer of natural gas. For the first time, Mexican border cities can benefit from relatively clean-burning natural gas obtained from the United States. This is a good example of how a border city can benefit by proximity to a region with resources and infrastructure. U.S. border cities also benefit, as in the case of San Diego, by utilizing electricity generated from large geothermal fields located across the border in Mexico. This helps keep the price of electricity low, reduces air pollution, and keeps *the whole binational region* more competitive in the global economy.[14]

An important example of these trends is the growing integration of North American energy markets. Although energy trade was not included in the 1994 NAFTA accords between Canada, the United States, and Mexico, the energy sectors in all three countries are undergoing a dramatic restructuring. This phenomenon is being driven by inefficiencies in the state-run enterprises in Mexico and the huge amount of capital required to modernize its energy sector, the relatively high cost of electricity and lack of competition in the electric industry in the United States, and the integration of the Canadian energy industry into world markets. Taken together, private companies, local and state agencies, and even individuals will be able to purchase energy supplies from a variety of sources and service providers, not unlike choosing a telephone carrier today.

Special Issue: NATO Expansion and Border Regions

Sometimes, an issue that clearly falls in the arena of international security and appears to have no direct bearing on border questions can, in fact, impact relations in border regions. A good case in point is the planned expansion of NATO to include several countries in Central Europe. The main argument presented by those countries most often mentioned for membership in NATO— Poland, the Czech Republic, and Hungary—is that they currently exist in a kind of security vacuum and that stability cannot be achieved in Central Europe unless they are allowed to become full members of NATO. Membership in NATO is viewed, along with membership in the European Union, as the sign of full acceptance into the family of Western European states. The principal arguments presented against expanding NATO to the east are that it could result in another East–West division of Europe, unnecessarily provoke Russia, and jeopardize Russian cooperation with other important security-related issues such as control of nuclear weapons materials. Moreover, it is suggested that the resources needed to upgrade the armed forces of new NATO members could be better spent for economic development in the region.

Rarely, if ever, discussed is the impact NATO expansion could have on transborder cooperation in the region. Should the three countries mentioned above become full members of the alliance, a'NATO border would then exist between Poland and Belarus, between Kaliningrad and Lithuania, and between Hungary and Ukraine. Nothing precludes cooperative activities from taking place in these border regions, but the fact that there could be military implications for NATO would seem to discourage transborder ventures. If for no other reason, these boundaries would become the outer borders of NATO-controlled territory and thus assume a military function they would not otherwise have. Under these conditions, development in the border regions would likely suffer.

The inclusion of Poland, the Czech Republic, and Hungary into NATO will result in a rather unusual political configuration indeed in the Nordic–Baltic region. It will have NATO states (Norway, Denmark, Germany, Poland), EU states (Denmark, Germany, Sweden, Finland), and non-EU and non-NATO states (Russia, Lithuania, Latvia, Estonia). This grouping of states is somewhat reminiscent of the Cold War period and if it remains in place for a long period of time will inevitably weaken Baltic Sea-region cooperation. For this reason, the enlargement of NATO to Central Europe could have implications for northern Europe as well.

The situation in Finland is quite different from what exists in Central Europe. The understandable desire for the Central and East European states to be incorporated into Western European structures does not apply to Finland, because it already is fully incorporated into all major western institutions, most importantly the European Union. Thus, there is no compelling security reason for Finland to seek membership in NATO at this time. The Finnish government recognizes this and in its most recent statement of Finnish security policy has said that Finland is not seeking NATO membership,

228 Borders and Border Politics in a Globalizing World

but is closely following the effects of NATO enlargement on the Baltic Sea region in relations between NATO and Russia (Council of State 1997). Should the situation change and Finland decide to seek NATO membership, this would very likely have negative consequences for cooperation in the Finnish–Russian border region. Finnish membership in NATO would be certainly seen as a provocation in Russia, and even as threatening to Russian vital interests in the region. Such a state of affairs would hardly be conducive to increased border collaboration, and could even result in a militarization of the border region.

Because of the close relation between Sweden and Finland on defense and security questions, the future course of Swedish security policy is also of great importance to Finland. At the moment, declared Swedish policy is to maintain its traditional stance of nonparticipation in military alliances in peacetime leading to neutrality in war. Should Sweden decide to alter this position and seek closer ties with NATO, this could put Finland in a very awkward and delicate position. Therefore, very careful thought must be given to any decision resulting in a change in direction of Swedish security policy since it will have repercussions not only in Finland, but throughout the whole Baltic Sea region.

The reverse situation also could have implications for security and borders in the Nordic region. Should Finland, and not Sweden, become a member of NATO, then Sweden would find itself sandwiched between two NATO states, Norway and Finland. This potentially could lead to some complicating factors related to the very open borders that currently exist in the Nordic area. For example, practice military maneuvers between two NATO states, Norway and Finland, would be more complicated than, say, between France and Germany, because of the intervention of non-NATO territory (Sweden).

Conclusions: Border Regional Development and Security

The main theme running throughout this section is that traditional and nontraditional aspects of security must be taken into account and managed properly if transboundary cooperation and development is to take place. The managing of security-related problems in international border regions will become increasingly important if these regions are to develop their full potential as truly binational, transborder actors in the global economy. Until the day is reached when borders completely disappear between nation-states, an unlikely event in the foreseeable future, various types of control and regulation of borders and within border regions will remain. The task for those concerned with creating a cooperative and vibrant border region will be to develop a realistic balance between legitimate security needs and the desires of those in the region for a more prosperous, healthy, and secure existence.

A Conceptual Framework of Transborder Collaboration

In this section we synthesize the implications of the first three sections in order to develop a conceptual framework for analyzing the complex constellation of elements involved in promoting transboundary collaboration as a vehicle for achieving border regional development. Border regional development is defined as: higher levels of economic prosperity, a higher quality of life, and reduction of cross-border conflict. We first look at the main economic factors underlying the concept of transboundary collaboration (TBC) and then outline the dynamics of TBC, the objectives, the major factors influencing the TBC process in specific contexts, and, finally, the main concepts underlying the inherently complex and interdependent nature of this process.

The Economic Forces Underlying Transboundary Collaboration

From an economic perspective there are three basic concepts that support the concept of transborder cooperation:

- economies of scale
- externalities
- transaction costs

The concept of economies of scale in this context is usually associated with the creation of the physical infrastructure facilities needed to support the development process. That is, the construction of bridges, highways, and port facilities frequently is only feasible if financed by all parties deriving the benefits, or the positive externalities, they generate. And even if only one side were able to finance the construction of, say, a regional airport, some of the benefits would accrue automatically to the other side in the form of increased access and lower travel costs. The same can be said for the provision of social infrastructure such as educational and health services as well as police and fire protection. Similarly, regional marketing efforts to promote the region's exports and transborder tourism as well as extol the region's virtues as a retirement haven or a good place to invest and do business can frequently be done at a lower cost and more effectively in concert. Lobbying efforts in the two nations' capitals or before transnational governmental bodies such as the EU in Brussels can frequently be much more effective if done collaboratively.

There are also negative externalities that must be taken into account and managed in the border context. Thus, for example, communicable diseases as well as air and water pollution present on one side of the border can spill over to the other side, raising health costs and lowering the quality of life.

Transborder collaboration can result in better management of such problems, increasing [*sic*] the quality of life on both sides of the border.

Finally, transaction costs—the costs associated with buying/selling, including gathering information on market conditions, negotiating and enforcing agreements—in cross-border situations are likely to be high in comparison with expected profits, thus discouraging economic activity. That is, faced with a lack of information regarding market conditions, legal constraints, common business practices, and language and culture on the other side, entrepreneurs are reluctant to do business there, even though it would otherwise be regarded as part of the local or regional market area. High transaction costs can also inhibit the realization of economies of scale in the production of private goods by limiting the size of the market.

It should also be acknowledged that even when a strong element of transborder collaboration exists there will still be competition between the two subregions in such areas as attracting tourism and new investment. Nevertheless, it can be argued that virtually anything that increases economic activity on one side of the border can result in some increased activity on the other through a variety of cross-border flows that arise because of the many asymmetries and complementarities between the subregions.

The Dynamics of Transboundary Collaboration

As noted above, transboundary relationships on unequal borders are characterized not only by economic and non-economic *asymmetries* but also economic *complementarities* that, in turn, generate a variety of economic and non-economic transboundary *linkages* including transboundary flows based on economic transactions, environmental interdependencies, and cultural interactions through person-to-person contacts between the two, and in some cases three, sides of the border region. The significance of these transboundary linkages is that they represent *opportunities* (issues that, if properly acted upon, could contribute to higher levels of development) and *challenges* (problems that potentially could hinder development). Thus, in order to properly manage these linkages, transboundary collaboration is necessary. TBC has two principal features:

- The provision of physical infrastructure, ranging from border-crossing facilities and highways and bridges to facilities for private and public air, rail, and sea transportation.
- A management framework or capacity built on informal or formal relationships capable of providing ongoing consultation and cooperation on an ever-increasing set of border region issues ranging from economic development to environmental and security issues.

The overall challenge is to economically, administratively, and culturally integrate regions that are divided by an international boundary. Not only must
border regions do everything that every other region must do in terms of
increasing their competitiveness, but they must do so *in collaboration with*
the region(s) on the other side, which is likely to be economically and politically organized very differently. This not only increases the number of decision makers but also increases the heterogeneity of the decision-making body
and complexity of the decision-making process. The existence of such mechanisms does not imply anything *a priori* about the nature of the transborder
relationship that can range from peaceful coexistence to partners in development. Also, it must be noted that in addition to cooperation there will be a
strong element of *competition* between the two regions that must be accepted
from the outset.[15]

In a *static* sense, it is widely recognized that successful transborder collaboration is a function of a myriad of factors including demographic characteristics ranging from culture and language to population growth rates and
density; levels of economic development; national economic and political
decision-making patterns; and legal/administrative systems and competencies as well as cross-border communications and infrastructure. The historic
legacy of transborder conflict and/or cooperation at the national and/or regional level may also play an important role in conditioning current transborder
collaborative efforts. Finally, an important determinant is likely to be the
transnational institutional context that can vary from an economic and political union, as with the European Union, to a free trade area, the North American Free Trade Agreement, to simple membership in the international global
economy, as in the case of the World Trade Organization.

In a *dynamic* sense there may be observable and predictable patterns as
transborder relationships evolve over time. One such pattern may be the pro-
gression from local, informal, and non-binding transborder relationships, to
formal and non-binding relationships, and then to formal and binding relationships enforced by transborder institutions established by international
treaty.

Another key aspect of the TBC process that flows from the analysis carried out in the preceding three sections is that of trade-offs among the three
stated objectives of TBC. That is, higher levels of prosperity can dramatically
impact the quality of life on both sides of the border, provoking higher levels
of cross-border conflict as the negative externalities spill over the boundary
to the other side. Alternatively, in the terms of the analysis presented above
we can say that, under certain scenarios, higher levels of economic development can result in environmental deterioration on both sides of the border
that, in turn, can impact on the security of the region by threatening the health
and/or well-being of the residents.

There are a number of other trade-offs that should be noted in this context.

- In order to fully integrate and economically develop the subregion adjacent to an international boundary there should be open access in order to fully exploit the opportunities created by the cross-border complementarities and asymmetries. However, open access also implies that there would be little or no regulation of the entry (or exit) of materials that could be harmful to the environment and/or people who might carry out undesirable actions.
- Economic development requires stability and security as well as a high quality of life in order to attract firms and a quality labor force. However, promoting security in border regions usually requires inspections on the boundary that require time and effort to administer, increasing transaction costs and reducing incentives to exploit cross-border opportunities.
- A high-quality environment requires regions to enact regulations and enforce them in an efficient manner, without discouraging investment in the region. That, in turn, requires that both sides of the border region maintain a relatively uniform level of regulation and enforcement in order to avoid the pirating of firms and the emergence of cross-border hostilities.

Final Comments

Clearly, there will be both benefits and costs resulting from transborder collaboration, and only when the benefits are perceived as greater than the costs for a majority of residents in each subregion will there be a willingness to participate. The exact nature and division of these benefits and costs as well as the ultimate consequences of TBC will depend on the specific circumstances inherent in each region. However, there are a few observations that can be made at the conceptual level.

First, it should be noted that TBC implies a higher level of economic, political, and social integration between the two or more subregions. Such integration across an international boundary usually results in some loss of national sovereignty and ability to fully manage one's own security, the need to interact with people from the other side in spite of deeply rooted resentments and/or hostilities, and the usual risks associated with any new venture such as the risk of investing a great deal of resources in a process that could fail at any time.

Second, in order to pursue the objectives of TBC each subregion is opening itself to new social, political, and economic forces. These new forces are likely to benefit one side of the boundary more than the other. Additionally, some sectors of each subregional community are likely to benefit while others will be hurt. There are always winners and losers in such integration and the benefits and losses are never evenly distributed.

Third, the complex nature of these relationships implies that irrespective of the outcome of TBC, the process itself will result in a loss of hegemony by central governments to sub-national actors—a consequence that can be viewed from a variety of perspectives, either negatively or positively, but perhaps always with some anxiety. The omnipresent danger, of course, is that the process of TBC can, under certain circumstances, result in the fragmentation of the nation-state.

Any of these consequences could generate conflict, despite economic and/or environmental benefits.

Notes

1. The terms boundary and border can be used interchangeably; however, in order to avoid confusion we will use the former term to mean a line that fixes the limit of a nation's territory, thereby referring exclusively to its international character. The two (or more) subregions adjoining such a boundary will be referred to as border regions.

2. In the orthodox economic literature barriers to trade are generally regarded as barriers to economic development; however, economic history is replete with examples of how protectionism was used to stimulate national development. Indeed, it can be argued that import-substitution industrialization, which usually provides for high degrees of protection, has been an important phase in the development of most countries, from Japan and the U.S. to the NICs (newly industrialized countries) of the post-World War II era.

3. A recent study of border-crossers at San Diego-Tijuana ports of entry resulted in the following classification of primary purpose (listed in order of declining importance): shopping, social visits, work, tourism, and other (including attendance at cultural and sporting events). See San Diego Dialogue.

4. Some data on these flows are available to border communities in the United States and Mexico (e.g., exports, imports, border crossings and international tourism). However, one important category, local transborder shopping expenditures and purchases (border transactions), usually goes unreported. For many years Mexico's central bank regularly conducted surveys of these *transacciones fronterizas* and reported them in its national Balance of Payments statement for the border region as a whole, but not for each individual set of twin cities (e.g., San Diego-Tijuana). This survey was apparently terminated in the early 1990s.

5. Crossings on borders between Western European and Soviet-bloc countries were strictly regulated during the Cold War. With the sudden disintegration and/or liberalization of the old order came sudden and unanticipated border traffic of people as well as goods. Anecdotal evidence suggests that most local governments were not prepared for such events and a great deal of chaos and improvisation occurred.

6. A free trade area provides for the elimination (over a specified period of years) of trade barriers between member countries on a specified group of goods (or all goods), with each country determining its own level of external tariffs against non-members. The next higher level of integration, a customs union, provides for free trade and a common external tariff while a common market adds free movement of

labor and capital. Finally, an economic union includes group-determined policies (e.g., macroeconomic stabilization policies), harmonization of standards and eventually a common currency.

7. Since 1985 an international group of scholars called GREMI (Groupe de Recherche Européenne sur les Milieux Innovateurs) has been engaged in the study of technological innovation processes and policies at the regional and local level. For an example of recent GREMI publications in English see Aydalot and Keeble, 1988.

8. In general terms there are two methods of reducing pollution: pollution control, the most common strategy, which utilizes end-of-pipe technology for cleaning up the environment; and pollution prevention, which reduces emissions at the source by improving efficiency in the use of inputs and by reducing the use of environmentally harmful substances/activities.

9. This is the classic dilemma that is addressed in the Bruntland Commission Report 1987.

10. For a good description of border regions in the pre-1950 and 1950–1990 periods see Herzog 1992.

11. For a comprehensive study of borders and border regions see Ganster et al. 1997.

12. The U.S.–Mexican border initially was the northern fringe of the Spanish colony of New Spain and then, after 1821, of the newly independent republic of Mexico. Mexico lost much of its northern territory first through the revolt ofAnglo settlers in Texas in 1835 and then through a war with the United States in 1846. The Treaty of Guadalupe Hidalgo, signed in 1848 to end the war, ceded much of the north to the United States. This, along with the sale of parts of New Mexico and Arizona by the Gadsden Purchase in 1854, established the international boundary that exists today.

13. There is a vast literature on the relation between environment and security. For a good guide to the literature see Simmons 1996.

14. For a complete description of the energy sector in the U.S.–Mexico and California-Baja California border region see Sweedler 1995 and Sweedler et al. 1995.

15. Some competition can be minimized if complementarities can be identified and made operational. For example, a study is currently being carried out in the San Diego-Tijuana region on the U.S.–Mexican border to explore the feasibility of a cross-border industrial strategy. Such a strategy, based on the comparative advantages of each region, could increase economic activity on both sides of the border by attracting reverse investment and replacing imported components with components manufactured in the region.

References

Alvord, Valerie (1997), "Customs Chief Resigning as Criticism Refuses to Die," *The San Diego Union-Tribune* (April 17).

Aydalot, Philippe and David Keeble (eds.) (1988), *High Technology Industry and Innovative Environments*. Routledge, London.

Bigo, Didier (1997a), "Security(s): Internal and External, the Mobious Ribbon" (in French), *Cultures and Conflits*, vol. 16/17.

Bigo, Didier (1997b), "Security, Borders and the State," in Paul Ganster, Alan Sweedler, James Scott and Wolf-Dieter Eberwein (eds.), *Borders and Border Regions in Europe and North America*. Institute for Regional Studies of the Californias, San Diego State University, San Diego.

Bruntland Commission Report (1987), *World Commission on Environment and Development, Our Common Future*. Oxford University Press, New York.

Council of State (1997), *The European Security Development and Finnish Defence*. Report by the Council of State to Parliament on 17 March 1997, Second Revised Edition, Helsinki.

El Financiero Internacional (1998), "Maquiladoras Hit the Million Mark" (January 26–February 1, 1998).

Ganster, Paul (1995), "The United States-Mexico Border Region and Growing Transborder Interdependence," in Stephen J. Randall and Herman W. Konrad, *NAFTA in Transition*. University of Calgary Press, Calgary.

Ganster, Paul (1996), *Environmental Issues of the California–Baja California Border Region*. Border Environment Research Report # 1, June 1996, Southwest Center for Environmental Research & Policy. San Diego State University.

Ganster, Paul (1997), "On the Road to Interdependence? The United States–Mexico Border Region," in Paul Ganster, Alan Sweedler, James Scott and Wolf-Dieter Eberwein (eds.), *Borders and Border Regions in Europe and North America*. Institute for Regional Studies of the Califomias, San Diego State University, San Diego.

Ganster, Paul (1998a), "Environmental Implications of Population Growth in the San Diego-Tijuana Region," to be published by the Center for U.S.–Mexican Studies, University of California, San Diego, La Jolla, California, forthcoming.

Ganster, Paul (1998b), "Sustainable Development in San Diego andTijuana: A View from San Diego," to be published by the Center for U.S.–Mexican Studies, University of California, San Diego, La Jolla, California, forthcoming.

Ganster, Paul, Alan Sweedler, James Scott and Wolf-Dieter Eberwein (eds.) (1997), *Borders and Border Regions in Europe and North America*. Institute for Regional Studies of the Califomias, San Diego State University, San Diego.

Hansen, Niles (1981), *The Border Economy: Regional Development in the Southwest*. University of Texas Press, Austin.

Herzog, Lawrence A. (1992), "Changing Boundaries in the Americas," in Lawrence A. Herzog (ed.). *Changing Boundaries in the Americas*. La Jolla, California: Center for U.S.–Mexican Studies, University of California, San Diego.

Martinos, H. and A. Caspara (1990), *Cooperation between Border Regions for Local and Regional Development*. Commission of the European Communities, Directorate-General XVI, Brussels.

Newman, Joseph (1996), "Maquiladoras Achieve only 12 Percent Estimated Hazmat Compliance," *EnviroMéxico*, V:9 November.

Pezzoli, Keith (1997), "Sustainable Development: A Transdisciplinary Overview of the Literature," *Journal of Environmental Planning and Management*, 40(5), pp. 549–74.

Rey, Serge, Paul Ganster, Gustavo del Castillo, Juan Alvarez, Ken Shell-hammer, Alan Sweedler and Norris Clement (1998), "The San Diego–Tijuana Region," to be published in James W. Wilkie and Clint E. Smith (eds.), *Integrating Cities and Regions: NAFTA and the Caribbean Face Globalization*, forthcoming.

San Diego Dialogue (1994), *Who Crosses the Border: A View of the San Diego/Tijuana Metropolitan Region*. University of California, San Diego Extension, San Diego.

Simmons, P. J. (ed.) (1996), *Environmental Change and Security Project Report*, Woodrow Wilson Center, Issue 2 (Spring 1996).

Sweedler, Alan (1995), "Energy and Environment in the United States–Mexico Border Region," in Stephen J. Randall and Herman W. Konrad (eds.), *NAFTA in Transition*. University of Calgary Press, Calgary.

Sweedler, Alan, Paul Ganster and Patricia Bennett (eds.) (1995), *Energy and Environment in the California-Baja California Region*. Institute for Regional Studies of the Californias, San Diego State University, San Diego.

14

Disaster on the Danube

Brian Erskine

Large water infrastructure projects, such as dams to generate electricity, con-trol floods, or divert water for agriculture, frequently have significant envi-ronmental impacts that include unintended effects. These projects are particularly complex in regions that share water resources— whether river, lake, or underground aquifer—across international boundaries. This article discusses a scheme begun in 1977 by Czechoslovakia (later, Slovakia) and Hungary to construct a dam and related hydraulic works on the Danube River system. By diverting the flow of the Danube into an alternate channel and drying up part of the river, the project risked contaminating the water—which eventually feeds into an aquifer for drinking—with carcinogenic poisons. Fish stocks were also threatened. The project was called off, but when Slovakia became independent in 1993, it decided to move forward. Hungary has chal-lenged Slovakia's decision in the International Court of Justice.

Brian Erskine is a research assistant at the Harvard International Review.

Sixteen years ago, Czechoslovakia and Hungary began a massive construc-tion project to harness the waters of the Danube for hydroelectric power, navigation and flood control. Neither state envisioned that the scheme would cause an international dispute that would outlast the Warsaw Pact and create an ecological nightmare serious enough to jeopardize their planned objectives.

From Brian Erskine, "Disaster on the Danube: A Hydroelectric Plant Wreaks Havoc," *Harvard International Review* 16, no. 2 (Spring 1994): 56–60. Reprinted by permission of *Harvard International Review*.

One of the most ambitious river management designs ever conceived in Europe, the Gabcikovo-Nagymaros River Barrage System (GNRBS) stands today as a concrete monument to environmental devastation, Brezhnev-era hubris and resurgent nationalism. Newly independent Slovakia, facing an uphill battle for economic survival, ignored the strident protests of Hungary and worked frantically late last year to finish the highly controversial hydro-power project.

The original 1977 agreement between Czechoslovakia and Hungary provided for the coordinated construction of three large dams. These river barrages were complemented by a water control system designed not only to alter the course of a 20 kilometer stretch of the Danube, but also to provide locks, fill a huge reservoir and engineer an unusual water release mechanism. To understand why these drastic measures were necessary to make the entire hydroelectric project effective, a knowledge of the local geography is necessary.

The Danube broadens and slows before it enters the flat region east of Vienna. After passing Bratislava, the Slovak capital, the river flows along the Slovak-Hungarian border for about 175 km, then suddenly turns south. It then divides Budapest and the rest of Hungary before continuing toward Belgrade.

In this region, the Danube slopes gradually, falling only one meter per two kilometer stretch. On both sides of the river lies a flat, fertile flood-plain. Though it carries a great volume of water, its flow is gentle. Its branches meander into bayous, nourishing farms, wetlands and a unique inland delta. The Danube is also the chief water source for the region and is the backbone of Europe's largest aquifer. In some places as deep as 200 m, this aquifer contains 10 billion liters of fresh water. Millions of Hungarians and Slovaks either drink filtered river water or depend on the underground water resources provided by the Danube.

Because of the gradual river slope and flat terrain, dams built in the river channel create a difference in water level, known as a "head," of only a few meters. This contrasts markedly with dams in the western United States, where there is often a convenient canyon or gorge to contain the artificial lake, creating a head size that is limited only by the height of the canyon. Conversely, a reservoir behind a Danube dam would spill widely into the surrounding countryside.

Cheap Energy

Despite these difficulties, dam construction generally remains an attractive energy option for several reasons. Hydropower is the cleanest large-scale source of electricity available, as it is non-polluting and renewable. If properly engineered and managed, river dams can provide electricity for millions of people at a very low cost with minimal ecological impact. In addition, the building and maintenance of dams provides jobs, bolstering the local economy.

The joint Danube hydropower project was first formally proposed in 1951, but did not receive serious consideration until the Oil Producing and Exporting Countries [*sic*; Organization of Petroleum Exporting Countries] (OPEC) embargo in the mid-1970s. Though propagandists confidently asserted that the oil supply shock did not affect the Eastern bloc, the Soviet Union and Romania capitalized on the opportunity to sell their high-quality oil to the West at high market prices for hard currency instead of wasting it on their communist European allies. The other nations of Eastern Europe, despite Soviet occupation, were thus dealt a severe blow by the OPEC embargo. Even when they could get shipments of Soviet oil, it was contaminated with sulfur and heavy metals, rendering it potentially lethal when burned. The power grids of Czechoslovakia and Hungary were forced to resort to unsafe, poorly designed nuclear reactors and imported Soviet electricity. Their main source of power, however, was low-quality but locally available lignite coal.

Lignite has a very high content of sulfur and other impurities. When burned, it forms noisome clouds and pollutants that combine with atmospheric water to form acid rain. Strip-mining to obtain the coal also ruined huge areas of the countryside. The communist regimes were not overly concerned with ecology, but the hydroelectric project provided them with some respite from polluted air, corrosive rain and unreliable electricity. In addition, when completed, the planners hoped the GNRBS would make Czechoslovakia and Hungary more energy self-sufficient.

Power Surges

In designing a useful Danube hydroelectric project for Czechoslovakia and Hungary, two factors necessary for large-scale hydropower generation were considered: a large volume of water and a large head. In addition to variables such as the number of turbines, turbine blade size and generator design, greater water volume and increased head size provide increased power.

The Danube provides a volume of flow which is more than adequate. However, the flat floodplain and gentle slope of the Danube necessitate the flooding of land two kilometers upstream for every additional meter of head. Even a relatively small dam, comparable in size to the Bonneville Dam on the Columbia River in the northwestern United States, requires a reservoir over a dozen kilometers wide and 50 km long to generate the same amount of power.

Engineers working on the GNRBS project, however, devised a dramatic solution. The project diverts almost the entire Danube flow into an artificially constructed side channel. Sloping only half as steeply as the river, the channel extends parallel to the river for about 20 km. The river then flows through the dam back into the natural river-bed. This diversion creates an artificially large head size and significantly increases power generated at the dam. It also eliminates the need for a reservoir and the attendant problems arising from the flat terrain.

This "power canal," hundreds of meters wide, was originally planned to begin about 40 km downriver from Bratislava. The river flow is thus to be diverted north to a course wholly within Slovakia. Running parallel to the dry river bed, it reenters the Danube north of the Hungarian city of Györ. A short distance from the end of the canal the diverted river drives the eight turbines of the Gabcikovo Dam, generating hundreds of megawatts of electrical power.

Because of the artificially slight slope of the canal, a sizable head of 19 m could be obtained at the Gabcikovo dam. This solution, however, did not produce enough power to satisfy the planners. They modified the plan so the dam would not run moderately and steadily around-the-clock, but would provide maximum power in sudden bursts during morning and evening peak electrical demand hours. To make this possible, the Danube was to be held back for half a day, then released to the dam at the proper times.

In order to generate the extra power, the planners engineered a reservoir, the Dunakiliti-Hrusov Reservoir, capable of containing about two days' worth of Danube flow above the entrance to the power canal. This required a great enlargement of the diversion dam, which was designed not to produce power but to contain the reservoir at the downstream end and direct its flow into the canal. To prevent this reservoir from flooding the plain, 96 km of asphalt-covered sand and rock dikes were built. The controlling sluices of the diversion dam were planned for the Hungarian side of the river. This change was designed to increase the power potential of the Gabcikovo dam to an impressive 720 mW [megawatts].

This modification, however, created a serious problem. With the Gabcikovo dam closed most of the time, the river level below the dam dropped drastically, by as much as 12 m. It is inefficient to allow this downstream section of the river to flow away and become extremely shallow while the power station is closed, and then to unleash a torrent of water downriver when the power station operates twice a day. To control the stretch of river below the Gabcikovo dam, a third dam was planned at Nagymaros in Hungary, about 50 km north of Budapest and just before the river turns south. With the control of the Nagymaros dam and dredging of the Danube bed just below the Gabcikovo dam, the stretch of river between the dams would remain closer to the normal level. The Nagymaros dam would also add about 150 mW of power to the productive potential of the system.

Calamitous Consequences

In 1977 both countries began work on the GNRBS. Once work began, professional opposition to the mammoth project was silenced by the Hungarian and Czechoslovakian governments. Within a few years, however, it became obvious in competent government circles that the great impact of the dams on the local ecosystem had not been fully considered. The Hungarian-Czechoslovakian Economic and Technical-Scientific Cooperation Committee agreed in 1981 to suspend work on the dams and canal. Meanwhile, scientific commissions on both sides of the border evaluated the effects of the GNRBS.

Four scientists at the Laboratory of Fishery Research and Hydrobiology in Bratislava prepared a report predicting that the annual harvest of fish from the river would fall 75 percent within two years of completion as the dam and river diversion would kill millions of fish. Another Czechoslovakian investigation detailed some other likely adverse effects of the project on the aquifer, such as depression of the water table. Prague immediately suppressed the data.

Budapest did not even bother to wait for the more extensive report of the Hungarian Academy of Sciences, which predicted widespread ecological devastation, warned of irreversible damage to the aquifer and advocated immediate postponement or cancellation of the GNRBS. By the summer of 1983, the Cooperation Committee had agreed to resume work, and the heads of state added their approval in the fall.

What were the scientists so concerned about? It was not in the nature of communist regimes to show any regard for ecology when industrial development was at stake. However, the two-year delay in further construction demonstrates that the ecological consequences of the project were too severe and too practical to ignore. Anything that might damage or pollute the aquifer, from which over four million Hungarians and Slovaks draw drinking water, commanded the attention of the governments.

With 20 km of Danube River nearly dry and a concrete-lined canal sealing off water that would normally feed the aquifer, several outcomes were likely. First, the paved walls of the Dunakiliti-Hrusov Reservoir would expose the aquifer to poisons from carcinogens in the pavement tar.

Second, the stagnant reservoir would ruin the filtration process that feeds the aquifer. The banks and bottom of the Danube act as a natural filter, freshening water as it percolates into the aquifer. This action depends on the natural balance of oxygen and organic matter in the river, which naturally contains a high concentration of oxygen and a low concentration of organic matter. Without continual flow, this natural equilibrium would eventually be reversed. If this balance is disrupted, the aquifer would be damaged. The immense fish kill combined with stagnation would accelerate the reversal of equilibrium, causing the concentration of organic matter in the water to rise abruptly and the oxygen concentration to quickly drop to a level incapable of sustaining life.

Third, the water table would fall precipitously not only from the massive diversion into the concrete and plastic canal, but also because of the fall in river level below the Gabcikovo dam. This fall in the water table would cause wells to dry out, farmers to lose access to water and pumping stations to run dry.

Finally, the force of the twice-daily deluge from the Gabcikovo dam on the weak, shallow river below the dam would drive accumulated filth and pollutants downward into the aquifer.

More heavily industrialized than Hungary, Czechoslovakia needed its share of the additional power the dams would generate. Ignoring the warnings of its scientists, Prague immediately resumed work on the dam. In Hungary, however, opposition stubbornly persisted as further studies confirmed that Hungary would bear the brunt of the environmental damage. While these disputes raged in Budapest, Hungary unilaterally postponed work and, needing an excuse, pleaded poverty to the Czechoslovaks.

Foreign Entanglements

Frustrated by this new delay, the Czechoslovakian government opened negotiations with Austria for yet another dam, to be located between Bratislava and Vienna, upriver from the GNRBS. Disagreement over the exact site and allocation of power caused Austria to break off the talks and to begin planning its own dam at Hainburg, in Austria, but less than 15 km from Bratislava. Snubbed, Prague retaliated in ironic fashion. Official protests to Vienna over the disruption of the ecological balance and the danger of flooding in Bratislava posed by the Hainburg dam were timed to coincide neatly with demonstrations by the Austrian Green Party. Vienna was forced to abandon the project. This left the Austrian construction firms without work and the capitalists without an investment. The Austrians, then, proposed to solve Hungary's "problem." Offering an agreement by which Austrian firms would supply capital and Austrian workers would participate in construction on the Nagymaros dam, Austria asked in exchange for a large share, over 20 years, of the dam's electrical output.

Hungary found itself in a difficult position. Under pressure and treaty obligation from Czechoslovakia to resume work, with its bluff ruined by the Austrian offer, and with its own government in a state of indecision, Budapest was forced to return to the project in the face of increasing domestic opposition and the dire predictions of its Academy of Sciences. Failure to complete the project would have cost the heavily indebted Hungarian government 55 billion forints—30 billion to Czechoslovakia, eight to Austria for loss of investment and 17 to restore the Nagymaros site.

Even worse for the regime, the dissident Hungarian journalist Janos Vargha was arousing troublesome popular opposition to the project on ecological and nationalist grounds. Hungarians resented Czechoslovakian pressure and Austria's perceived attempt to farm out environmental damage to Hungary while Austria reaped electricity. A minority in the Hungarian parliament demanded debate on what was becoming a national crisis.

Political Transformation

While Hungarian engineers worked just enough to maintain the incomplete structure, Parliament thoroughly discredited itself by allowing the Communist Party to impose its will. A majority of the members of Parliament voted in October 1988 to resume work. It proved to be the communists' last stand in Budapest; soon afterward, the Party lost its monopoly on power. Seven months later, in the face of growing domestic opposition and popular protest, Parliament reversed the decision.

Austria and Czechoslovakia furiously demanded compensation, but a conference at Budapest in August resolved nothing. In early November 1989, the Czechoslovakian government outrageously threatened to use the nearly completed Gabcikovo dam to cause massive floods in Hungary. Seventeen days after making that threat the Prague communists were ousted. The new government of Vaclav Havel agreed to cancel the project.

The core of Havel's program, however, was the preservation of the Czechoslovakian federation. When this became impossible, Havel resigned. Under pressure from the Slovak minority, the federal government announced resumption of the project. Hungary countered by officially renouncing the 1977 treaty. With autonomy and the promise of independence provided by Havel's political weakness and fall, the Slovaks were more determined than ever to press forward and complete work on the Gabcikovo dam. The Slovakian flag will fly from the engineering office, and shipping tolls will be payable to the Slovakian treasury. To the Slovaks, the Gabcikovo dam is a symbol of sovereignty, decisiveness and will.

Technical Revision

Independent for the first time in history, Slovakia has decided to prioritize energy self-sufficiency over environmental concerns. Slovakia argued that the investment of time and capital in the dam is great and claims the ecological damage is irreversible. Assuming this, Slovakian leaders asserted, the only sensible course of action was to finish the project.

To finish on their own, Slovakian engineers modified the plan. Extending the power canal another 15 km upriver, the engineers placed the point of diversion at Cunovo along the short stretch of Danube entirely within Slovakia. Here workers built a new breakwater. The whole water management scheme thus became an internal affair.

This reinforced Slovakian determination to generate as much electricity as possible at the Gabcikovo dam. The Slovakian power grid draws part of its electricity from Ukraine, part from two antiquated and polluting brown-coal power plants, but over half from the Bohunice complex of four Soviet-designed nuclear reactors that provide 440 mW of power each. None of these sources is remarkably attractive. A 720 mW boost from the Gabcikovo dam would enable Slovakia to reduce dependence on imported energy, to eliminate the pollution from the coal plants or to close the two older, less safe reactors.

Meanwhile, Hungary has pressed its legitimate grievances at the International Court of Justice and in the European Community. Both Slovakia and Hungary are competing for Western aid and the diplomatic spotlight. Slovakia wants aid to modernize its power grid, arguing that it honored the original agreement and is trying to responsibly provide energy for itself. Hungary draws attention to its ecological concern in trying to attract aid to demolish its part of the project and bring international pressure to bear on Slovakia to stop work on the dam.

Uncertain Future

Neither approach is likely to result in complete success. Currently, Hungary and Slovakia are moving toward an agreement. An EC committee of two dam experts from Denmark and the Netherlands, as well as two river ecologists from Germany and Austria, has helped the Hungarian and Slovakian representatives arrive at a compromise by which Slovakia will operate the dam at

25 percent capacity with a continuous water flow, generating 180 mW, and permit 75 percent of the Danube to flow in its original bed. However, Slovakia has been diverting over 80 percent of the river volume into the power canal, causing a 2m drop in the local water table and drying out wells and wetlands in Hungary.

The final resolution of the thorny dispute between Hungary and Slovakia remains to be reached by the diplomats. However, only time can reveal the full ecological impact of the dam. Questions remain as to whether the citizens of Bratislava and Györ will have safe drinking water, whether the farmers of the Hungarian floodplain or Slovakia's "Wheat Island" will have water for their crops and whether the ecological damage is controllable. Any damage the dam causes will continue to fuel the international political tension.

15

Border Regions and Transborder Conservation in Central America

Pascal O. Girot

Even though the border regions of Central America are home to poor and isolated populations, they also include some of the most important natural areas. After decades of wars, massive human migration, and failed initiatives, the 1990s saw a new focus on sustainable development by Central America's leaders. Border areas will play an important role in any successful regional development effort. With scarce government resources, nongovernmental organizations (NGOs) and grassroots agencies will need to take an active role in implementing plans to protect natural areas and promote economic development in a sustainable way. The problems of protecting natural resources are common throughout the developing world but are particularly difficult in border regions, where two or more governments and nonprofit sectors must coordinate their programs.

Pascal Girot is a geographer in the Escuela de Geografía at the University of Costa Rica, San José. He received an Advanced Studies Diploma at the University of Paris III and the M.S. at the University of Wisconsin-Madison. He has worked in Central America since 1989 in areas relating to international borders and boundaries, natural resource management, community forestry, and regional planning.

From Pascal O. Girot, "Border Regions, Integration, and Transborder Conservation Initiatives in Central America," in *Borders and Border Regions in Europe and North America,* ed. Paul Ganster et al. (San Diego: Institute for Regional Studies of the Californias and San Diego State University Press, 1997), 333–54. Appendix and figures omitted. Reprinted by permission.

Introduction

After undergoing a decade of war, disintegration, and impoverishment dur-
ing the 1980s, Central America is witnessing a resurgence of innovative regional initiatives. A trend that began in 1987 with the Central American Peace
Plan, earning the Nobel Peace Prize for the then President of Costa Rica,
Oscar Arias Sánchez, produced in the early nineties an unprecedented flurry
of integration initiatives. During 1994 alone, the presidents of the Central
American region (Guatemala, El Salvador, Honduras, Nicaragua, Costa Rica,
Panama, and Belize) held no less than five summit meetings, culminating in
the signing in November of the Alliance for Sustainable Development in Cen-
tral America.

Such a process of intense regional consultations, in an area at war only a
few years before, is in itself noteworthy. However, questions remain as to
how these sweeping regional agreements will result in tangible improvements
in a zone plagued with abysmal levels of poverty, health, and economic growth
(with notable exceptions). The emphasis on sustainable development as the
new paradigm for regional integration comes as an innovative departure from
previous regional initiatives. While the Central American Common Market
experiment of the 1960s centered on fostering early industrialization through
protective trade barriers and the opening of national borders to regional commerce, the present-day integration model aspires to join the North American
Free Trade Agreement (NAFTA), and is centered on free trade and open
borders.

Questions obviously arise. How well does sustainable development fare
in a Central America open to free trade? How will the Central American
economies compete by opening their borders to far more powerful partners
to the north? What role will border regions play in such a scenario? Sustainable development as the paradigm of the nineties provides a challenging framework in which to analyze the effect of free trade on the environment, territories,
and societies of the Central American isthmus. In this article, we will address
critically some of the crucial issues facing Central America at the close of the
century. Sustainable development as a very broad concept forces us to think
ahead: What will Central America have to offer to its future generations in
the next century? How can the integrity of their cultures, landscapes, economies, and peoples be preserved while participating in the structural overhaul
underway at a hemispheric level?

A pivotal point of convergence of these regional initiatives has been, and
will be, border regions. Whether closed to foreign trade through tariffs, or
open to the free flow of goods, peoples, and services, borders will continue to
operate as the safety valve for Central American economies. However, these
regions are among the most destitute, socially marginalized and politically
peripheral. But they are also the richest in natural resources, with unique

cultural and biological diversity. Border regions have historically played a particular function in the formation of the territorial state in Central America. As refuges for marginalized populations, indigenous people, and *ladinos* (people of mixed racial heritage), border regions have traditionally been marked by contraband, political intrigue, armed conflict, and transboundary networks of all manner, including more recently drug trafficking. Border regions have functioned throughout the 1980s as the main receptors and assimilators of massive flows of refugees, mostly from El Salvador, Nicaragua, and Guatemala.

How can states undergoing processes of structural adjustment, with ever-shrinking national budgets and drastic reductions in government services, face the growing challenge of integrating, policing, developing, and protecting the margins of their national territories? Faced with a shrinking central government, local authorities, NGOs (nongovernmental organizations), and grassroots organizations are called on to play a more important role in territorial administration. Local governments in border regions are ill-prepared for assuming new tasks such as environmental protection, road building, sanitary and land use planning, and so forth. However, there have been some notable transboundary initiatives that, when combined, provide a promising alternative. The thrust of this article is to suggest that integration begins and ends with border regions. Strengthening local governments and fostering transboundary initiatives may help solve problems of isolation, insecurity, and environmental degradation. One of the main testing grounds of the Alliance for Sustainable Development will be, without a doubt, the border regions of Central America.

The Historical Role of Border Regions in Central America

The history of territorial formation in Central America provides a useful backdrop for understanding the role assigned to border regions. As in many other countries of Latin America, the process of national integration was late in coming and subject to the ebb and flow of political and economic events. In several countries, vast regions, particularly the Caribbean lowlands of the Mosquito Coast, still remain isolated from their respective national economies because of lack of access. The famous dichotomy between the Pacific heartland and the Caribbean rimland formulated three decades ago by West and Augelli (1966, 1989) still applies in much of the area. The dominant national cultures are generally based in Pacific and intermontane regions, while much of the Caribbean rim is still considered peripheral, both culturally and economically.

The contrast between densely populated highlands and sparsely inhabited Caribbean lowlands is evolving fast, and the process of agricultural colonization that began in the 1960s is reaching some of the most remote corners of national territories. While the agricultural frontier in El Salvador is estimated to have reached the political boundaries of the country in the 1930s, in Costa Rica the contraction of the agricultural frontier drew to a close in the 1980s (Augelli 1987). In Panama, Honduras, and Nicaragua, the agricultural frontier is alive and well and constitutes a key safety valve for agrarian conflicts as in many other Latin American nations.

The territories undergoing processes of agricultural colonization coincide in many cases with peripheral border regions. These regions, long neglected due to difficult access, inhospitable climate, and rough terrain, have functioned for centuries as refuges for displaced populations fleeing war, political persecution, economic indigence, and land dispossession. Their function as regions of refuge has fostered a unique combination of cultural and biological diversity. The co-existence between indigenous people and tropical forests in Central America coincides often with border regions, as illustrated by the Chapin (1992) map by *National Geographic*'s Research and Exploration. As we shall see further along, these remote regions constitute the setting for border parks and indigenous territories that are under increasing encroachment by *ladino* settlers. The refuge function of border regions was most convincingly illustrated during the war-torn decade of the 1980s. As a reception and processing platform for internally displaced and refugee populations, border regions played a crucial role in the dramatic events of the last decade. Frontier societies have by definition a greater capacity to absorb and assimilate foreign elements than do most of their respective national societies (Girot and Granados 1993). A notable exception to this rule is Belize, in which the massive influx of Salvadorean and Guatemalan refugees over the past decade has signified a dramatic demographic transformation of its entire society. One could almost argue that Belize as a whole has functioned as a border region in terms of its capacity to absorb foreign elements.

Finally, Central America's border regions have also been marked historically by a limited effective control by central governments. The presence of transboundary plantation enclaves, established as early as the 1890s, across the borders between Costa Rica, Panama, Honduras, and Guatemala illustrates the scant control by nation-states of these remote regions until the second half of the twentieth century. Despite being converted into some of the most intensive agricultural-production areas, few if any of these banana enclaves have resulted in the integrated development of border regions. Today, lax government control over these remote border regions makes them prime targets for drug traffickers and contraband operations. The impact of these activities on border societies and economies remains to be determined. However, the destabilizing effect of money-laundering through land speculation, not only in border regions but in most of Central America's urban centers today, can already be seen.

Regional and National Territorial Integration

The political history of Central America has been marked by the swing of the pendulum between unionism and nationalism, and initiatives for regional integration and the safeguarding of national sovereignties through protectionism (Pérez Brignoli 1989; Salisbury 1984). While the object of this article is not to document the history of regional integration initiatives per se, several elements are important to point out in order to understand the formation of the territorial state in Central America and its relation to larger polities.

Overall, an important distinction must be made between the political discourse regarding integration, and the territorial setting in which these policies are, or are not, put into practice. At the end of the colonial era, Central America was characterized by scattered nuclei of densely settled populations, essentially in the volcanic highlands and the Pacific seaboard. Although the colonial administration had regrouped the isthmus under the Captaincy General of Guatemala, the countries were poorly interconnected, and lived essentially in a state of local autarky. The experiment of the Central American Federation (1821–1842) foundered precisely because of the lack of any real territorial, economic, and social integration among isolated provincial polities. As a result, warring factions set the conditions for the emergence of nation-states, based on the territorial divisions of provincial boundaries (Girot and Granados 1993).

The use of colonial administrative limits as the political boundaries between emerging nation-states provided a fertile terrain for litigious and conflictual interpretations of colonial texts by jurists from neighboring countries. Until the mid-twentieth century most of the border regions were remote peripheral domains, and conflict over use and occupation emerged as in most of Latin America. A notable exception to this has been the boundary between Costa Rica and Nicaragua, which closely follows a potential route for an inter-oceanic canal, and was the object of intense rivalry and legal analysis throughout the second half of the nineteenth century. The dialectics between projected canal ventures and boundary litigation between Costa Rica and Nicaragua has been well documented (Girot 1994). In most other border regions, isolation and remoteness relegated them to a very marginal role in national affairs, even up to the present.

Following the break-up of the Central American Federation in 1842, there have been recurrent attempts at reviving the unionist spirit. Between 1842 and 1863 alone, there were no less than eight initiatives directed at reconstructing the Central American Union (Karnes 1982: 156). Discrete differences existed between the Unionists, who sought the creation of a unitary Central American state, and the Federalists, who vouched for the creation of a Federation of Autonomous Nation-States. All these integration forces have emerged and subsided throughout Central American history, without ever really going beyond the rhetoric stage of political discourse. Several factors contribute to explain the failure of unionism in Central America. In the first place, scant attention was paid to the economic and social fabric of which to weave a regionally integrated whole. In this sense, the attempts at political fusion were constructed on very weak foundations. The opening up of Central America to the export trade during the second half of the nineteenth century, under successive liberal governments, confirmed the consolidation of national economies. The construction of export-oriented trade networks, essentially geared to the coffee trade, signified the consolidation of a road infrastructure that linked the coffee-growing highlands to coastal ports, especially on the Pacific. The linkages between Central American states remained extremely weak until the second half of the twentieth century (Girot and Granados 1993: 9).

The giddy growth of export economies of Central America consecrated the model of the liberal nation-state and provided further incentives for expanding cultivated areas, predominantly for the coffee trade. By the end of the nineteenth century, the opening up of new lands for incorporation into the export economy had occupied most of the best volcanic soils of the highlands. The expansion of the agricultural frontier was bolstered at the turn of the century by the installation of banana plantation enclaves in Caribbean lowlands of Costa Rica, Panama, and Honduras (Boza 1994). These enclaves contributed to the construction of the export empire of the United Fruit Company, which dominated the region during the first half of the twentieth century. Several of these enclaves were clearly transborder operations, particularly between Costa Rica and Panama, in which Standard Fruit and United Fruit banana plantations literally straddled the boundary. To this day, these border enclaves constitute an illustrative example of how transnational corporations transcend political boundaries in practice.

By the mid-twentieth century, the process of national territorial integration was culminating in several countries of Central America. In El Salvador, for instance, the agricultural frontier has reached the political boundaries of this small country (21,000 km², as well as the limits of lands favorable to coffee production. In most other countries of the region, agricultural colonization has continued as a fundamental mechanism, not only of conversion of tropical forests into agriculture or pastures, but of integration of remote regions into the national economy. In the case of Costa Rica, the agricultural frontier reached its limits by the end of the 1970s. In Panama, Honduras, Nicaragua, and Guatemala the process continues to this day with varying intensity from one country to the next.

What was considered a century ago remote and inaccessible is today part of a peripheral but increasingly integrated region of the national territory. Perhaps one of the factors that accelerated the process of national integration was, paradoxically, the creation of the Central American Common Market during the 1960s.

The integration principle differs in many ways from the unionist doctrine of the nineteenth century. First and foremost, it takes as its starting point the existence of sovereign states and precludes any notion of political fusion or union. It places a crucial emphasis on economics as the main motor behind regional integration. The Central American Common Market (CACM) was designed during the 1950s and put into practice in the 1960s. The principal thrust of the CACM was to create a larger single market, eliminating trade and tariff barriers within the region and creating a single unified trade policy for the region. The creation of a regional market was the basis on which to build a regional industry aimed at substituting costly imports of manufactured consumer goods.

The integration experiment of the 1960s had a profound impact on intra-regional trade networks and fostered incipient industrialization processes in several Central American countries. By 1980, intra-regional trade reached a total value of one billion U.S. dollars, and represented a fifth of the total trade value of the region (Lizano 1989: 285). The growth of national industries was significant, but regionally skewed. The main beneficiaries of the experiment were El Salvador and Guatemala, bolstered by a cheaper and more abundant labor supply compared to their southern neighbors. The principal losers in the regional venture were Honduras and Nicaragua, left behind in the race to control markets and secure an industrial base. Costa Rica, favored by a more up-to-date infrastructure and qualified labor supply, managed to remain afloat.

Many works have discussed the demise of the Central American Common Market (Cáceres 1980; Lizano 1989), and this article does not aim to address them. However, it is necessary to point out that one of the most important shortcomings of the integration effort was to have placed excessive attention on economic growth and commerce, neglecting the processes that affect the territories and societies and, between them, the border regions of Central America. Perhaps the best illustration of this was the famed Soccer War of 1969, which set Honduras against El Salvador in a short but intense armed conflict. The war was first and foremost a border conflict and had roots imbedded in the history of the two countries. With a land-poor and densely populated El Salvador neighboring a larger, less densely populated Honduras, the law of communicating vessels applied and exacerbated the historic migration of land-hungry Salvadoreans into Honduras during the 1960s. This process culminated in armed conflict over control of the *bolsones,* prized alluvial strips on either side of the meandering Lempa River, which separates the two countries.

The Soccer War of 1969 dealt a lethal blow to the integration effort, and by the mid-1970s the process had ground to a halt. The oil crisis of the 1970s, and the impact of the global recession that followed set the scene for a deepening social and political crisis that culminated in the war-torn decade of the 1980s. Perhaps the greatest losers of the eighties were the border regions of the isthmus. Ignored by the process of industrialization and excluded from the benefits of commercial integration, border regions played a relatively marginal role, with few exceptions, in the economic articulation of the isthmus. There were only a few more border crossings in 1980 than there had been at the close of the 1950s. Nevertheless, border regions acted as the main recipients of the increased flow of migrants and refugees fleeing war and economic collapse. The civil war of Guatemala and the revolutionary and counterrevolutionary wars of El Salvador and Nicaragua used border regions as stages for transboundary operations and bases. The Sandinista revolution in Nicaragua of 1979 was made possible in many respects by a solid, transboundary, logistical supply system. The Nicaraguan revolution closed a decade of deepening crisis in Central America with a short-lived period of hope.

House of subsistence farmer at Barra de Colorado, Costa Rica, near the border with Nicaragua, 1981. Such farmers are a persistent problem for conservation areas in Central America. *Photograph by Paul Ganster*

The Lost Decade of the 1980s

The decade of the 1980s comes as a stark reminder of the intrinsic vulnerability of the Central American isthmus in world affairs, particularly in terms of geopolitics and macro-economic policies (Girot and Granados 1993). All of a sudden, Central America was the main focus of U.S. foreign policy under the Reagan administration. The crux of the policy was geared to the containment of the Sandinista revolution, in order to avoid the contagious effect such a movement could have on neighboring countries, especially Mexico. In practice, U.S. policy toward Central America included a trade embargo against Nicaragua, massive military aid to the Honduran and Salvadorean armies, and the use of Costa Rica as a model of democracy and development. These policies were combined with deep structural problems of the region (such as distorted patterns of land tenure, *latifundios/minifundios*, and the social division of labor that accompany them), and a particularly aggravating wider economic setting (world energy crisis, recession, political polarization between the superpowers).

Paradoxically, the two countries most affected by war, El Salvador and Nicaragua, can be placed on opposite extremes of the population-land ratio. The largest and smallest of Central American countries underwent widely differing consequences of the integration experiment of the 1960s. While land tenure, access to land, and greater distribution of economic power was at the heart of the Salvadorean civil war, land shortage has hardly been a crucial issue in Nicaragua (the largest country of the region with 130,000 km²). While El Salvador boasts a greater rate of urbanization and industrialization, and a far greater percentage of its economy is in the secondary and tertiary sectors, Nicaragua has one of the lowest population densities in the region, vast tracts of state-owned lands, autonomous indigenous regions, and the longest borders of the Central American states.

The impact of the war differed widely from one country to the next. While the most devastating in terms of human impact were the revolutionary wars of Nicaragua and El Salvador, every single country in the region was affected directly or indirectly by displaced populations, either internally or across borders. Estimates are that between 1.8 and 2.8 million persons were displaced in Central America during the 1980s (Aguayo 1989: 21). Over a quarter of El Salvador's population was displaced during that period, with over 400,000 internally displaced, and another 350,000 refugees in neighboring countries. The brunt of the movement of the refugee population passed through, and settled in, border regions.

The environmental impacts of a decade of war are more difficult to ascertain. While some authors have suggested that armed conflict was a violent form of conservation by stopping and repelling the advance of the agricultural frontier (much of the remaining forested areas of Nicaragua, for instance, are former combat zones [Nietschmann 1990]), others argue that the massive displacement of populations triggered by armed conflict concentrated environmental problems in receptor areas, such as urban centers, border posts, and transit zones (*Epoca* 1985; OAS/DRD 1993).

The 1980s truly brought about heightened tensions at a regional level. Aside from the fratricidal wars of El Salvador and Nicaragua, Panama was undergoing a geopolitical upheaval that culminated in December 1989 with the U.S. invasion of Panama to capture General Manuel Antonio Noriega. A long and protracted civil war in Guatemala, and a latent confrontation between the Guatemalan government and nascent Belize, which became independent from Britain in 1981, also had great impacts. Overall, one can summarize the geographical consequences of the war years as follows:

1. The intensification of the armed conflict between El Salvador's regular army and FMLN (Frente Farabundo Martí para la Liberación Nacional) guerrillas had several effects. The war culminated in the occupation and creation of liberated territories in the departments of Chalatenango and Morazán (Lungo 1990). At its height, this armed conflict meant the displacement and emigration of almost one out of four Salvadoreans.

2. Staged in a larger territorial context, the revolutionary wars of
Nicaragua (1977–1979 and 1981–1988) displaced far more
populations internally than they created international refugees.
Nevertheless, with the intensification in 1983–1984 of the Contra-
revolutionary warfare, border regions were the principal theater for
armed conflict. The northern front of the Segovias, Río Bocay, and
Río Coco, bordering on the Honduran border provinces
of Danlí, Río Patuca, Olancho, and the Mosquito Coast, was the
setting for the most violent armed conflicts of the 1980s in Central
America. The southern front, which encompasses the middle and
lower sections of the San Juan River drainage basin between Nicaragua and Costa Rica, was another transboundary battlefield. The 1983
campaign brought about the evacuation, as in the case of the Río
Coco Misquito Indians, of the *campesino* population on the agricultural frontier (Girot and Nietschmann 1992). Much of the evacuated
populations was then resettled in FSLN (Frente Sandinista de
Liberación Nacional)-organized communities, thereby increasing the
flow of migrants and refugees, principally into Costa Rica. By the
mid-1980s, over 300,000 illegal Nicaraguan immigrants were
reported (OAS/DRD 1993).

3. In Guatemala, a war of attrition between the army and the guerrillas
from the early 1970s escalated by 1978–1980 into total war along the
border regions with Mexico. In particular, the areas of the Río San
Pedro and Río La Pasión, all tributaries of the transboundary
Usumacinta watershed, were theaters of intense armed conflict during
the early 1980s. Hundreds of thousands of Guatemalan refugees
sought protection north of the border in Mexico and in Belize,
transforming the demographic and social composition of the neighboring regions. Chiapas was among the states most affected by
Guatemalan migrants during the 1980s. Belize's population literally
doubled during the 1980s, due in great part to the flow of Salvadorean and Guatemalan refugees.

4. Although Costa Rica did not undergo any internal warfare during
this period, it did lend its territory as a logistical support base for
the Contra-revolutionary war during the first half of the 1980s.
The increased militarization of Costa Rica's northern border was
the object of serious concern in a country that had abolished its
army in 1948 (Granados and Quesada 1986). One of President
Oscar Arias's achievements was to defuse this dangerous escalation,
and disengage Costa Rica from the Nicaraguan war (Fernández
1989).

5. In practically all countries, armed warfare was essentially waged in, or supplied through, border regions. These border regions became the focus of international attention, and projects were quickly implemented to attend to refugee populations and the dire needs of border populations. As war vanished from the border regions, and from Central America as a whole in the 1990s, it also disappeared from television screens. Unfortunately, Central America only makes the news when it is plagued by war, natural disasters, or some other calamity.

The 1990s and New Regional Initiatives

Neo-Integrationism and Its Limitations

The decade of the 1990s inaugurated a new era in Central America and was hailed by many as a period of peace, reconciliation, and reconstruction of national societies torn apart by war (Arias and Nations 1992). Several momentous political shifts occurred at the onset of the decade that have marked developments since. Two discrete processes came to a head in 1990. First was the Nicaraguan presidential elections in which Violeta Chamorro came to power leading a loose coalition of parties opposed to the Sandinista regime. The transition went smoothly. By the end of 1990, another major event occurred with the United Nations-mediated settlement of El Salvador's bloody civil war. Thus, by the end of 1990, the two deadliest wars of the past decade were settled through peaceful reconciliation between warring parties, both participating in and respecting the outcome of the electoral game. Settlements included concessions concerning the role of the armies, both the United States-backed Salvadorean and the Sandinista Popular Armies. An accent on mutually conducted, verified, and UN/OEA-supervised demilitarization of society characterized both El Salvador's reforms and Nicaragua's political direction.

The year 1990 brought newly elected governments in practically every country of Central America. In August 1990, the presidents of Central America and Panama signed the Declaration of Antigua. This constituted a clear transition from the peace-seeking efforts of the Contadora and the Arias Peace Plan of the eighties. This time, the theme of regional integration was constructed through a series of summits and ministerial missions, resulting in the creation of the Central American Integration System (SICA). While it contains the usual dose of rhetoric and defines an extremely ambitious series of objectives, the latest version of the integration model differs from the previous in many respects:

1. It centers on economic issues essentially fixing regional economic union as a goal.

2. The integration process proposed by the SICA is driven by a free regional market, framed by a single tariff policy, with a major difference in its openness to the northern partners in NAFTA.

3. During the 1960s, emphasis was put on the protection of national industries and competition limited to regional partners. The SICA initiative implies joining forces to compete within a hemispheric free-trade bloc.

4. The economic bias of the system attributes social and environmental problems to economic policy and structural adjustments.

5. The opening up of economies weakened by ten years of war, as in the case of Nicaragua, to a free-market arena pitting Mexican, American, and Canadian businesses against each other, is bound to have dire repercussions, and affect their reconstruction effort.

6. The intra-regional disparities, already apparent in the 1960s, have increased. There is, on the one hand, an ever-widening gap in living standards between Costa Rica and Panama. Costa Rica's GDP (gross domestic product) per capita is U.S.$2,180 and that of Panama is U.S.$1,930. On the other hand, there are ever-deepening social and economic crises in Nicaragua, Honduras, and Guatemala. The 1991 GDP per capita figure was, in U.S. dollars, for Nicaragua $340, for Honduras $570, and for Guatemala $930 (OAS/DRD 1993: 14). Nicaragua is still the only country experiencing negative GDP growth, some 15 percent for the period 1988–1993 (OAS/DRD 1993: 15).

7. The import-substitution model has been replaced by one centered on commerce, import-export trade, and offshore services. The Panamanian example illustrates the model, with an extremely dynamic corridor linked to site-specific advantages of the Canal Zone and a poorly articulated hinterland.

8. The model of integration proposed by the SICA favors the transisthmic, free-trade zone, and investment corridors as in the case of Panama, and increasingly Costa Rica, more than north-south regional integration through the Pan-American highway.

9. Needless to say, the proposal ignores completely the role of border regions, but the summit meeting declarations are replete with references to redoubling joint efforts in fighting poverty, corruption,

crime, drug trafficking, and terrorism. These are precisely the ills that have been plaguing border regions in Central America for decades.

Still, one must make a clear distinction between the integration process proposed by the SICA (which is still very tentative), and the initiatives derived from the regular summit meetings that have brought Central American presidents together several times a year since 1990. Despite its shortcomings, the new integration process has produced a flurry of parallel initiatives by civil groups, NGOs, local governments, and chambers of commerce. Both the private sector (FEDEPRICAP) and the local communities and *campesinos* (ASOCODE) have their regional institutional structures to participate in regional summits. However, the integration process is still very much centered on the executive powers of the presidential summits. Although the legislatures have their regional body (Comisión Interparlamentaria Centroamericana), the key parts of these regional initiatives are decided at a presidential level, after consultations with the private and public sectors.

Sustainable Development: Risks and Opportunities

The culmination of the renewed integration efforts of the early 1990s came in November 1994 with the signing of the Central American Alliance for Sustainable Development. Framed in similar language as the SICA, the alliance does, however, introduce a strong environmental dimension to regional integration initiatives, which so far had been notoriously absent.

The Alliance is organized according to seven guiding principles, which include:

1. Respect for life in all its forms
2. An improved quality of life
3. Respect for, and sustainable use of, the land
4. Peace and democracy as basic forms of coexistence
5. The ethnic and cultural diversity of the Central American region
6. A greater degree of integration within countries of the region and others around the world
7. Intergenerational responsibility, which is one of the basic tenets of the doctrine of sustainable development.

The text of the Alliance then fixes four fundamental axes around which sustainable development will be organized. These are: (a) democracy, (b) sociocultural development, (c) sustainable economic development, and (d) sustainable management of natural resources and improvement of environmental quality. Two new institutions have been created: the National Councils for Sustainable Development, which, together, form the Central American Council for Sustainable Development. The creation of a permanent council designed to monitor the carrying out of these accords adds to the already long list of international conventions (including Agenda 21 of the Rio Summit in 1992), which require regular follow-up by the region's governments.

While the Alliance constitutes a clear departure from the traditional economic integration initiatives centered on markets, industries, and commerce, it remains extremely general in its scope. It places a new emphasis on the environmental and social dimension of development and, as such, provides a sort of guiding charter creating an overarching institutional framework within which many existing initiatives can be channeled. Although the text of the Alliance makes no mention of border regions, it is sufficiently broad in scope to incorporate a vision integrating local development and the conservation of natural resources.

It is too soon to judge the effects of the Alliance for Sustainable Development in Central America. However, new actors are emerging in the region. The insistence on reinforcing the full participation of local populations in matters of sustainability has fostered a number of forums that bring together government agencies, NGOs, and civil society over issues relating to local development, conservation, and production. For instance, in recent months there has been a number of regional entities, like the Central American Council for Forests (Consejo Centroamericano de Bosques), in which government officials in charge of the forestry sector, representatives of indigenous communities, *campesino* organizations, and environmental NGOs participate. A similar initiative is under way that is integrating the national parks systems of Central America.

Project-Oriented Border Region Development

Although practically all of the official texts marking the new integration movement in Central America skirted the issue of border regions, the matter was discussed during several summit meetings held in the early 1990s. In the December 1992 meeting in Panama, the presidents decided to back an action plan involving the SIECA, the Organization of American States (OAS), and the Interamerican Institute for Cooperation in Agriculture (IICA), focusing on the development and integration of border regions in Central America. The emphasis of the initiative is captured by the phrase "integration through projects" (OAS/DRD 1993: 4). An argument in favor of project-oriented integration is that it avoids delicate issues like boundaries, sovereignty, and macro-economic policies. Moreover, this approach posits achieving tangible results in shorter periods of time. The border projects proposed during the

Forum of Central American Vice-Presidents held in Washington, D.C., in November 1993 were geared around three interrelated objectives: (1) regional development of areas that extend over international boundary lines; (2) reversal of ecological degradation and implementation of programs of environmental management; and (3) combating poverty in areas of retarded development (OAS/DRD 1993: 20).

The project-focused border region development policy designed by the OAS is one of the official initiatives that underlines regional disparities, voicing concern about the contrast between free trade and deepening poverty levels in border regions. Specifically, the OAS maintains that: "the extent and depth of poverty in Central America is incompatible with the process of peace and democratization that the governments have embraced and could eventually undermine the model of openness and modernization now being pursued" (OAS/DRD 1993: 17). Central Americans are without a doubt poorer today than they were 30 years ago. The proportion of the total population of the region living in poverty went from 60 percent in 1980 to 68 percent in 1990, and the portion in extreme poverty increased from 38 percent to 46 percent in the same period. In some countries such as Honduras and Nicaragua, the 1990 poverty figures exceed 75 percent of the population while over half the population of El Salvador, Guatemala, and Honduras live in extreme poverty (OAS/DRD 1993: 18). Border regions are among the hardest hit by rural poverty and all the symptoms of underdevelopment, abandonment, and marginalization. The events in Chiapas and the economic slump of 1995 and 1996 in Mexico should serve as a sobering reminder that border regions can trigger change at an unsuspected scale.

Of the 18 border development projects listed by the OAS, practically all have a strong environmental component targeted at the last remaining pristine ecosystems of the region. Among the two oldest initiatives, the Trifinio (the international park at the junction between the boundaries of Guatemala, Honduras, and El Salvador) and La Amistad International Park between Costa Rica and Panama centered on a protected nucleus and geared actions around the preservation of these biosphere reserves. The Talamanca mountain range between Costa Rica and Panama was declared a World Heritage Site by UNESCO in 1990.

The above list of border region development projects reflects, on the one hand, a growing concern by central governments over the last remaining frontiers of their own territory. Even though the figures are approximate, these border region projects involve about 10 percent of Central America's population and almost a third of the land surface of the isthmus. This indicates the importance of the territories at stake. On the other hand, these proposed projects are, for the most part, at an early stage of formulation and have involved scant participation by local communities and border region governments.

Mario Boza (1994) outlines a strategy for biodiversity and development in Mesoamerica, an area ranging from the Yucatán Peninsula to the Darién Gap. The major strategy coincides with the OAS development proposals in that it recommends the creation of a Mesoamerican Biological Corridor uniting 17 major biodiversity sites, all of which are located in or near border areas. This would enable preservation of some of the region's most extraordinary biological heritage.

Much of the remaining tropical forests of Central America have been under the custody and stewardship of indigenous peoples. At least 12 of the 18 projects outlined by the OAS involve regions predominantly populated by indigenous groups. Historically assigned a minor role in development planning, for generations most of these indigenous communities have fostered transboundary trade, kinship ties, and networks. They are by definition transborder cultures, as in the case of the Emberá and Kuna between Panama and Colombia, the Bribri and Ngobe between Costa Rica and Panama, and the Misquito between Honduras and Nicaragua. The degree of decentralization, true regional autonomy, and self-determination varies enormously from one context to the next. Panama boasts perhaps the most progressive indigenous legislation in Latin America, some of it dating back to the 1920s with the creation of the Kuna Yala Comarca in San Blas. In Nicaragua, the historical struggle by the Misquito people to secure regional autonomy has been marked by distrust, intrigue, and, most recently, war. Any border development project that ignores the cultural and ecological intricacies of these marginalized regions is bound to fail.

The willingness by the region's governments to sacrifice centralized control of remote border regions and to share the responsibility for the long-term management of natural resources with people who have co-existed for centuries with tropical ecosystems is still tenuous, if not unacceptable, in most countries. However, it is becoming increasingly clear that the preservation of Central America's extraordinary biological endowment will not be made possible by the work of central governments alone (Boza 1994). Many border regions encompass ecological- and cultural-heritage sites that have been preserved for centuries through the presence of thriving indigenous communities. New mechanisms for involving local communities and regional governments in joint-management ventures are being timidly developed, while serious challenges, such as claims for regional autonomy and self-rule by border populations, remain. These create serious geopolitical tensions within and between Central American states. Furthermore, increased incursions by *ladino* farmers and ranchers are common, and reckless timber and mining concessions continue to be granted in indigenous territories with little or no previous consultations in the regions affected. The 1990s will probably witness an increase in conflict between nation-states and indigenous communities along border regions.

Conclusion

Bringing Central American integration down from the realm of political discourse to the stark reality of border regions is a necessary step, but one full of
unpredictable liabilities. One can forcefully argue that integration begins and
ends with border regions. For generations, they have witnessed the praxis of
integration in their daily lives. Border residents have been the primary victims of the wars of the 1980s, as well as their main actors. Transboundary
networks through kinship systems, commercial alliances, and contraband
partnerships are activated or deactivated according to complex mechanisms.
These are yet to be carefully documented for Central America. However, it is
plausible to argue that therein lies one of the major potentials for consolidat-
ing long-lasting border development. Populations on both sides of political
borders in Central America often differ in their appreciation of fiscal policy,
migration, customs regulations, and trade restrictions. They often work around
them, against them, or with them, according to their particular interests.

The historical role of border regions as refuges for displaced populations makes them particularly adaptable to the influx of outside populations.
Their capacity for absorption was clearly demonstrated during the war-torn
decade of the 1980s. However, the prerogatives of national sovereignty and
the centralizing character of Central American states make for a difficult
dialogue between center and periphery, between the capital and border regions. The economic development produced by earlier integration experiments was circumscribed to urban areas and adjacent commercial
thoroughfares. Trade liberalization, and the creation of a Central American
appendix to NAFTA (which is foremost in the political agenda of the region's
politicians) will probably benefit most those areas involved in export/import
activities, both in urban zones and across the inter-oceanic corridors present
in most countries. One can wonder whether much of the prosperity promised
by the proponents of these liberalization schemes will ever reach border
populations.

The renewed interest in regional integration, particularly under the new
paradigm of sustainable development, is occurring in a region profoundly
impoverished by war and national disintegration. While the official language
of integration is analogous to similiar earlier experiments, the broad orienta-
tions of the present-day initiatives differ significantly from the integration
process of the 1960s. There is a clear emergence of a new set of actors, drawn
from civil society in the political arena, originating from both the private/
entrepreneurial and local/grassroots sectors of society. In a context of structural adjustment, ever-shrinking government entities face ever-increasing tasks.
The transfer of responsibilities to civil society is a process fraught with im-
ponderable outcomes in Central America. Local governments, peasant and
indigenous organizations, chambers of commerce, and other nongovernmen-

tal organizations are assuming progressively a more important role in territorial administration.While in many countries, matters of national sovereignty and national security are still the exclusive preserve of the armed forces, there is a progressive transfer of responsibilities to local governments over natural resources, land tenure issues, water supply, and other locally managed systems.

The transfer of responsibilities from central governments to civil society will inevitably affect border regions. Although most local border region governments are ill-prepared for assuming these new requirements, many interesting initiatives are taking place. The project-centered approach for border regions' development can be easily criticized. It is still in the hands of technocrats and experts, and the very nature of these projects is seldom discussed and decided at a local level. The greatest merit of the approach forged by the OAS in the region is to provide the inventory of transboundary projects and point out the very critical environmental and social conditions prevailing in border regions. Whether these conditions will be reversed or preserved through projects remains to be seen. One would argue more in favor of processes that include the conduct of transboundary initiatives geared to resolve the problems many of the border regions have in common. These are often very basic and linked to immediate tangible results such as the access to markets, schooling, and medical care across political boundaries. The few ongoing experiments, such as in La Amistad between Panama and Costa Rica, have proven quite effective. Grand transborder development schemes seldom work, especially if they have been conceived in San José or Washington, D.C.

In conclusion, Central America as a whole is undergoing momentous change in the 1990s, and border regions are not immune to these transformations. Perhaps the most significant development of recent years is the greater role assumed by civil society in matters traditionally reserved for the political class. The reform and reduction of the state creates a vacuum that is being filled by a contrasting but vigorous series of local and national initiatives. The Alliance for Sustainable Development in Central America reinforces this trend. It is too soon to judge its merits or limitations. These regional initiatives open, without a doubt, a new page in Central American history. Whether they will provide answers to such pressing needs is an open question. Surely, the border regions of Central America will provide a key testing ground.

References

Aguayo, Sergio. 1989. "Las poblaciones desplazadas y la recuperación y el desarrollo centroamericano." In *Recuperación y desarrollo en Centroamérica*, William Ascher and Ann Hubbard, eds. San José: Trejos Hnos.

Arias, Oscar, and James Nations. 1992. "A Call for Central American Peace Parks." In *Poverty, Natural Resources and Public Policy in Central America*,

Sheldon Annis et al., eds., New Brunswick: Transaction Publishers, ODC, U.S.-Third World Policy Perspectives.

Ascher, William, and Ann Hubbard, eds. 1989. *Recuperación y desarrollo en Centroamérica*. San José: Trejos Hnos.

Augelli, John 1987. "Costa Rica's Frontier Legacy." *The Geographical Review* 77 (1).

Boza, Mario. 1994. *Biodiversidad y desarrollo en Mesoamérica*. San José: CCC-WCS/COSE-FORMA GTZ.

Cáceres, René Luis. 1980. *Integración económica y subdesarrollo en Centroamérica*. México, D.F.: Fondo de Cultura Económica.

Chapin, Mac. 1992. "The Coexistence of Indigenous Peoples and the Natural Environment in Central America." *National Geographic Society Research and Exploration* (special map supplement). Spring.

Epoca. 1985. "Militarization in Central America: The Environmental Impact." San Francisco: Epoca.

Fernández, Guido. 1989. *El desafío de la paz en Centroamérica*. San José: Editorial Costa Rica.

Girot, Pascal Olivier. 1991a. "Origen y estructuración de una frontera viva: El caso de la región norte de Costa Rica." *Geoistmo* 3 (2).

Girot, Pascal Olivier. 1991b. "Perspectiva canaleras en Centroamérica." In *La política exterior de Estados Unidos hacia Centroamérica*, José Luis Barros and Mónica Verea, eds. México, D.F.: Editorial Miguel Angel Porrúa.

Girot, Pascal Olivier, and Bernard Q. Nietschmann. 1992. "Geopolitics and Ecopolitics of the Río San Juan." *National Geographic Society Research and Exploration* 1.

Girot, Pascal Olivier, and Carlos Granados. 1993. "La integración centroamericana y las regiones fronterizas ¿Competir o compartir?" *Presencia* 5 (19).

Girot, Pascal Olivier. 1994. "The Interoceanic Canal and Boundaries in Central America: The Case of the San Juan River." In *The Americas: World Boundaries*, Vol. 4, Pascal O. Girot, ed. London: Routledge.

Granados, Carlos, and Liliana Quesada. 1986. "Los intereses geopolíticos y el desarrollo de la zona nor-atlantica costarricense." *Estudios Sociales Centroamericanos* 40 (Enero-Abril).

Karnes, T. 1982. *Los fracasos de la Unión*. San José: ICAP.

Lizano, Eduardo. 1989. "Perspectivas de la integración regional." In *Recuperación y desarrollo en Centroamérica*, William Ascher and Ann Hubbard, eds. San José: Trejos Hnos.

Lungo, Mario. 1990. *El Salvador en los 80: contrainsurgencia y revolución*. San José: Facultad de Ciencias Sociales, Editorial Universitaria Centroamericana.

Menjívar, Rafael, and Juan Diego Trejos. 1992. *La pobreza en América Central*. San José: FLACSO.

Nietschmann, Bernard Q. 1990. "Conservation by Conflict." *Natural History* (November).

Organization of American States, Department of Regional Development and Environment. 1993. *The Development of Border Regions in Central America*. Washington, D.C.: OAS/DRD

Pérez Brignoli, Héctor. 1989. *Breve historia de Centroamérica*. Madrid: Alianza Editorial.

Salisbury, Richard V. 1984. *Costa Rica y el Istmo 1900–1934*. San José: Editorial Costa Rica.

Segura, Olman, ed. 1992. *Desarrollo sostenible y políticas económicas en América Latina*. San José: DEI.

West, Robert, and John Augelli. 1966, 1989. *Middle America: Its Lands and Peoples*. Englewood Cliffs: Prentice-Hall.

16

The U.S.-Mexican Border as Locator of Innovation and Vice

Kirk S. Bowman

Borders often mark very different legal, economic, and cultural systems where the availability and cost of goods and services vary considerably from one side to the other. Consequently, people travel to the other side to purchase goods and services that are either not obtainable or more costly at home. On the U.S.-Mexican border, discrepancies in laws and regulations that control industries dealing with sex, gambling, and alcohol have created what is often referred to as "border vice." This essay discusses the history and characteristics of border vice in this region. It also points out how border vice is found within the United States along many state boundaries.

Kirk S. Bowman is a political scientist in the Sam Nunn School of International Affairs at the Georgia Institute of Technology. His research includes Latin American political development, Third World militarization, political dynamics of borderlands, and democratization. Bowman is the author of a book on militarization and some fifteen articles on various Latin American topics.

The border is a powerful influence on the cultural, social, political and economic landscape. Often, the United States-Mexico "border" represents a general area where the two nations meet, blend and encroach. The growing Hispanic population in the southwestern United States and the increasing economic resources of the *fronterizos* of Mexico have combined to enlarge

From Kirk S. Bowman, "The Border as Locator and Innovator of Vice," *Journal of Borderlands Studies* 9, no. 1 (1994): 51–67. Reprinted by permission of the Texas Center for Border Economic and Enterprise Development.

that region often referred to as Mexamerica (Langley 1988). Even Las Vegas, Nevada, located in a state which is not contiguous to Mexico, relies heavily on Mexican shopping and tourist dollars, has a large Spanish-speaking population, serves many *platos típicos*, and by many definitions can be properly considered a border city.

The border can also provide for more concentrated and geographical-specific phenomena. At any border, be it city, state or international, the legal boundary is the precise line which separates often-differing codes, ordinances and laws. Even in a single city, zoning ordinances create borders where business X is forbidden on one side of the street yet welcomed and even encouraged on the other side. If laws on side A of the border prohibit a business or practice which is legal on side B, and if a sufficient number of inhabitants from side A wish to enjoy the services of such a business, then a border-specific industry will surely develop. On the *frontera* shared by Mexico and the United States, discrepancies in legal norms which regulate industries dealing with sex, gambling and alcohol have created that characteristic known as border vice. Border vice is an opportunist, a chameleon and a survivor. Changes in laws, evolution in society, and the consequences of history have often altered and battered the sin business; but like a roach reacting to pesticides, vice has repeatedly mutated and re-emerged as a significant component of the Mexican-American frontier.

The proposition of this article is that the border is not merely the place where vice exists, but an active and dynamic force both in locating vice businesses and in innovating the type of and marketing of legal vice being offered.[1] Gambling in Nevada and around Utah will be used to illustrate the hypothesis that the border is a powerful stimulus in determining the location of businesses which feature legal vice. Then the Mexican-American border will be used to demonstrate the adaptive and mercurial phenomenon of border and vice. While changes in social mores and laws in the United States have undermined traditional vice industries, entrepreneurs south of the border have adapted and repositioned themselves in order to capitalize on the legal advantages which proclaim "Welcome to Mexico." The long partnership between the border and vice in Northern Mexico will be described. Finally, the contemporary results of that partnership —prostitution, betting and gaming and teenage consumption of alcohol—will be analyzed.

The Border and the Location of Vice: Nevada and Utah

The growth of centers of legalized gambling in Nevada and the encroachment of vice centers outside the Utah border provide excellent illustrations of the spatial dimension of legal border vice. These two states confirm the hypothesis that when two contiguous territories have different laws governing businesses dealing with sex, gambling, or alcohol, vice businesses will be situated in the area with the more liberal laws and as close as possible to the population centers of the area with the more stringent laws governing vice industries.

For decades, Nevada has been renowned for adult entertainment centered around gambling: Las Vegas is known throughout the world as "Sin City." The state's two largest cities, Las Vegas and Reno, are both relatively close to the California border. Another tourist area, Lake Tahoe, sits on the Nevada-California border. Las Vegas mainly draws from southern California, and the gambling halls of Reno and Lake Tahoe are mostly frequented by residents of central and northern California. Table games such as blackjack, paigow, craps and roulette, as well as slot machines and video-poker machines, are illegal in California. In addition, wagering on team sports is sanctioned only in Nevada.

With the growth of populations throughout the West, and with the increasing mobility brought about by the widespread ownership of automobiles, the Nevada borderlands have, like a magnet, drawn new casinos to lure in gamblers as soon as they cross the state line. Stateline, Nevada, just north of the California-Nevada boundary on Interstate 15, has grown from a service station to a thriving mini-Las Vegas. Four large casino-hotels flourish in what would be the middle of nowhere, but are actually situated *somewhere* solely because they are on the gambling side of the border.

When Don Laughlin flew over South Point, Nevada, twenty-six years ago, he saw a few shabby motel rooms and four bars with slot machines. Laughlin realized that this piece of desert, where summer highs regularly reach 120 degrees, was also "within a 30-mile radius of . . . Kingman, Arizona and Needles, California, and 15,000 people who needed a place to gamble" (Goodman 1991:18). The City of Laughlin was born soonafter and today, largely because of its location on the Arizona border and near the California frontier, has grown into a gambling mecca. The town's 7,200 rooms handily outnumber the population of 5,000 and annual gaming revenues approach $400 million (Yoshihashi 1990:B4).

It is in the twin cities of Wendover that the power of a single line to determine the location of vice establishments can be best demonstrated. The white line running across Route 40 is where the contrasting laws governing vice in Nevada and Utah meet. In Wendover, Utah (population 1,300), there are a couple of motels, a Mexican restaurant, and a pair of used car lots. More than 260 families are on welfare and 150 families have moved in the past three years to that thriving metropolis—Wendover, Nevada.

In Wendover, Nevada (population 2,000) there is a new golf course, equestrian park, medical clinic, library and throngs of visitors from Utah pouring coins into slot machines (Lamb 1989:4). While the Utah establishment abhors gambling, the citizenry of Salt Lake City drives two hours across the desert and drops more than $1 million each week in the Wendover, Nevada, casinos. Fearing that their town would disappear, a group from Wendover, Utah, petitioned the legislature for a special amendment allowing them to have legalized gambling like their neighbors across the white line. "What's next?" cried the Mormon church-owned *Deseret News*, "Demands for legalized brothels in Utah just because they are permitted in some parts of Nevada" (Lamb 1989:4). According to Dr. Bill Eadington, an economist and director of the Institute for the Study of Gambling and Commercial Gaming at the University of Nevada at Reno, Utah will never permit any type of wagering: "Of all the states in the U.S., the only one that will probably never contemplate gambling is Utah, because of the Mormon influence" (quoted in *New York Times* 1993:A8).

The Wendover case also demonstrates how border vice circumvents the intentions of the laws. All forms of gambling are illegal in Utah because gaming is an evil "based on the morally wrong philosophy of getting something for nothing, of taking money without giving fair value" (Mormon doctrine quoted in *New York Times* 1993:A8). With a different law on the other side of a permeable frontier, casinos can still be erected which solely attract Utahans. While gambling in Utah is illegal, casino advertising is not, and the highways of Salt Lake County are well stocked with billboards featuring the games of Wendover, Nevada.

As one of only two states without so much as a lottery, Utah is an excellent exemplar of our hypothesis. The lack of any legal gaming in Utah has attracted a myriad of vice establishments right to its border. The Mormon "church's opposition last year helped defeat a measure that would have allowed modest, state-run betting at county fairs" (*New York Times* 1993:A8). To provide an outlet for northern Utah's horse-bettors, the Wyoming Downs Racetrack is located in the border town of Evanston, Wyoming. Mesquite, Nevada, is a booming casino town due to its proximity to St. George, Utah. Grand Junction, Colorado, sells large quantities of lottery tickets to the citizens of eastern Utah. The towns of southern Idaho provide such large quantities of lottery tickets to their Utah neighbors that Idahoans commonly joke about the "Utah Lottery of Idaho."[2] Even Fredonia, Arizona (population 1,207), has found a way to capitalize on the lack of legal vice in Utah. Arizona sanctions gambling on horse and dog racing. With modern technology permitting live feeds and instantaneous updates of the betting line, Fredonia has installed pari-mutuel betting facilities to lure over the residents of southern Utah.[3]

In addition to gaming, Utah's neighbors profit from differences in laws governing alcohol. Utah only permits 3.2 proof beer. Since Wyoming approves sales of a much stronger brew, many northern Utahans cross the border into Evanston to purchase alcoholic beverages.

As shown with the cases of Nevada and Utah, the border is a partner of vice in locating establishments featuring gaming and alcohol.[4] The analysis will now focus on the Mexican-American border to illustrate the role of the border in the evolution and innovation of vice.

The Border and Vice Innovation: Mexamerica

The history of Mexican-American border vice has been well documented. The available research will be reviewed to reveal the dynamic nature of legal border vice. Then the contemporary manifestations of border vice of the northern Mexican frontier will be discussed.

Machado (1982) provides an excellent overview of the period 1910–1930. "Throughout the 1910–1920 period increasing numbers of states began to prohibit the sale and production of liquor. Texas dried up in 1918 and thus eliminated 250 drinking establishments, 50 liquor stores and related enterprises in El Paso" (Machado 1982:2). Likewise, a dry California forced United States investors in gambling, prostitution and ponies to set up shop over the line in Baja California. Martínez (1988:115) reviews the general phenomena of border vice, the upswings in the industry during Prohibition and World War II, and the recent lull in "the thunder of the Mexican border nightlife."

At one point, Tijuana was such a single-commodity town that of the 1,091 residents, 200 were listed as prostitutes (Hedges 1991:A11). The specific model for the compound zones immortalized by the alluring tales of Weisman (1986) and Miller (1985) actually dates from the United States military occupation of Chihuahua in 1916. General Pershing's troops spent seven months at Colonia Dublán:

> . . . during which time the vice vendors congregated around the camp. The alarming number of men with venereal disease and the fear instilled in the Mexican population by American soldiers on the prowl for women led the local bishop to advise Pershing to set up a restricted district on the southern limits of the camp. A Mexican managed the district and only Mexican prostitutes were allowed. Pershing assigned a military physician as health inspector, fixed a flat fee at two dollars, and the disease rate tumbled (Curtis and Arreola 1991:342).

Excellent specific historical accounts of the boom and bust cycles of vice in Tijuana and Ciudad Juárez are available. Martínez (1986) details the rise and fall of the vice business in Juárez from 1900 to the 1980s. The border location has left Juárez highly dependent on fluctuations in the U.S. economy, foreign affairs, and social and legal changes.

Piñera and Ortiz (1989), Cárdenas (1955) and Espinosa (1990) provide an exhaustive study of vice in Tijuana. The history of Tijuana demonstrates the resourcefulness inherent in the border industry and its ability to innovate and change with the times. In response to the morality movement sweeping the nation, gambling and bars were prohibited in the Golden State in 1911 (Piñera and Ortiz 1989:93). The promoters moved south of the border and set up shop on A Avenue, known today as Avenida Revolución. When the United States invaded Veracruz in 1914, Victoriano Huerta ordered the border closed and the vice industry faced a certain demise until the problem was resolved in June of 1915 (Piñera and Ortiz 1989:94). In 1915 and 1916, San Diego hosted a large influx of visitors due to its San Diego Expo. Tijuana took advantage of the situation and invited the tourists south of the border to enjoy the many pleasures not available in San Diego. More than ten thousand attended the opening of the American-owned Tijuana racetrack in 1916 (Piñera and Ortiz 1989:98).

In 1916 the Casino Monte Carlo started a trend by taking advantage of the geographical component of border vice, opening between the existing race track and the international boundary (Piñera and Ortiz 1989:98). Even today, legal border vice establishments jockey for position by locating as close to their cross-border clientele as possible.

The success of the horse track and the large numbers of tourists partaking of the pleasures of Tijuana provoked strong attacks from the California media and religious community. While their stated goals included dry zones in both California and Baja California, their major accomplishments were temporary early closings of the border crossings (Piñera and Ortiz 1989:99). Mexico's neutrality in World War I caused the U.S. to close the border many times and to forbid Americans from entering Mexico without a valid passport, seriously damaging industry in Tijuana.

After the war, tourism flourished as never before with the enactment of the Volstead Act. Bars and other centers of vice sprouted in Tijuana, including the 170 meter-long mega-bar La Ballena (The Whale). The twenties were the golden years of Tijuana. A second race track opened along with other casinos, houses of ill repute and bars. The most famous was the grand Agua Caliente, which featured a luxurious casino frequented by Jimmy Durante, Buster Keaton, Laurel and Hardy, and many other celebrities, the Patio Andaluz restaurant where Rita Hayworth was discovered, a greyhound track, a golf course and a hotel (Espinosa 1990).

It would be incorrect to assume that Mexican authorities are a morally bankrupt homogeneous group of sin-sellers who have always encouraged the sex and liquor business on the border. The Carranza administration was ideologically aligned with the moralists in the United States. The officials could not, however, entirely give up the revenue produced by booze. As a solution, they outlawed hard liquor and permitted the sale of *cerveza* in the saloons. Governors, generals and mayors also imposed their morals on the iniquity dealers.

Chronic alcohol consumption in Mexico forced the new revolutionary regimes to move against this particular social vice. General Francisco Murguía, military commander of Chihuahua, decreed in March 1917 an unflagging prohibition on the sale and consumption of alcoholic beverages throughout the state. Murguía's decree of March 23 warned that all persons selling liquor, "no matter what nationality or makeup . . . ," would be summarily executed. Unconfirmed reports already abounded that at least four Mexicans had been killed for violation of the order (Machado 1982:5).

Billboard in Tijuana advertising cabarets to U.S. visitors, 2003. *Photograph by Paul Ganster*

The Great Depression began to be felt along the border in 1931. Prohibition was repealed in 1933, depriving the Mexican border towns of a generous comparative advantage in competing for the entertainment dollar. Just two years later, President Cárdenas outlawed all games of chance, permanently closing the doors of the glorious casinos such as Agua Caliente (Cárdenas 1955:59). The glamorous era of Tijuana was over, and, to flourish, the vice peddlers would need to discard the champagne, chandelier, and Charlie Chaplin image and discover a novel niche and new clientele.

World War II provided the new clientele and the border vice was able to transform itself to service the customers. Military bases dotted the borderlands and hundreds of thousands of soldiers and sailors were willing participants in the creation of the "black legend" (Espinosa 1990) and "Boys Towns" where the "ladies of the evening" of the 1920s were replaced with "prostitutes" and the glamorous marble of the casinos was replaced with fake velvet in seedy cabarets. In the new *zona rosa* or *zona de tolerancia*, there emerged lurid tales of aging whores with bountiful breasts who "accommodated customers with solely upper-torso fixations right at the bar . . . , (and where) you could see a woman and a man, two women and a man, two men and a woman, or a human (male or female) and a dog or a pig or a burro" (Langley 1988:32).

Swelling populations of mobile university students augmented the client base. Fraternity boys, military men, and the general population of the exploding U.S. border population frequented the adult playpens from Tijuana to Matamoros. Adding to the availability of nude shows and cheap sex was the psychological allure.

> Something falls off you when you cross the border into Mexico. You may be a faithfully married, church-going man in the United States but over here you can grope and paw and make a fool of yourself and no one says a word about it. If you want a temporary liaison, your whore takes you by the arm and parades you to the bar where you pay twenty-three dollars—twenty for the sex and three for a bed. You head out back to a courtyard lined by a promenade of rooms. A half-hour later you emerge. Indeed, the biggest attraction at the red-light district is not sexual at all. It is psychological. No man is ever rejected in Boys Town (Miller 1985:63–4).

The relative contribution of vice to the economies of the cities and towns south of the border began to decline in recent decades. Topless and bottomless bars are now common on the American side of the Rio Grande. X-rated movies and videos, sexual permissiveness at home, and a fear of AIDS have all made a sordid image of Tijuana and Ciudad Juárez unpalatable to many (Martínez 1986:146). The vice industry fought the decline by offering a more diversified menu. The more extreme experiences offered across the border include the transvestites. The transvestites work in such establishments as the Dallas Cowboys: "Most of their clientele are ostensibly robust Texas heterosexuals who are somehow titillated by the idea of a companion hooked on hormone shots and silicone" (Weisman 1986:40).

Despite their finest efforts, the decline of the vice industry continued at the same time that many border cities matured and developed. Tijuana, which celebrated its centenary in 1989, now projects itself as "A New City," "the New Hong Kong," and an industrial giant with the second largest population on the North American Pacific coast and no unemployment (Espinosa 1990). Headlines announce that "Tijuana has Lost its Ill Repute," and "Bustling Tijuana Lives Down Hooch and Honky-Tonk Past" (Rohter 1989:A1). Other Mexican border cities are also downplaying their past and emphasizing the *desarrollo* of the present *maquila* boom and the North American Free Trade

Agreement. Is the vice industry of Mexamerica doomed? The reality is that very different laws governing popular aspects of American vice still converge at the border separating Mexico and the United States. Not surprisingly, the potent partnership of border and vice found ways to innovate and capitalize on this border-specific characteristic. Contemporary border vice still includes prostitution, but now features sports gaming and underage alcohol consumption.

Prostitution

As recently as the early 1970s, prostitution added nearly two million dollars to the Ciudad Juárez coffers and "was probably the city's major industry" (Curtis and Arreola 1991:334). As stated earlier, the last two decades have witnessed a sharp decline in prostitution on the border. "There are one hundred registered prostitutes in Juárez today when twenty-five years ago there were seven thousand" (Langley 1988:37). Curtis and Arreola's field research, conducted between 1987 and 1990 in eighteen urban centers on the Mexican side of the border, revealed that a distinct *zona de tolerancia* still existed in Tijuana, Mexicali, San Luis Río Colorado, Nogales, Agua Prieta, Las Palomas, Ciudad Juárez, Ojinaga, Ciudad Acuña, Piedras Negras, Nuevo Laredo and Reynosa. Contrary to the popular everything-revolves-around-America belief, most prostitutes in these areas have long served a Mexican clientele (Curtis and Arreola 1991:337). A study from 1973 reported that 700 of the 1,000 Tijuana prostitutes catered to a Mexican clientele (Price 1973:94). The proportion of prostitutes servicing *gringos* has probably diminished, "as the number of *zona* visitors from the United States and other foreign countries has plummeted and as Mexicans have come to represent an even larger majority of *zona* patrons" (Curtis and Arreola 1991:337).

Although the *zonas* persist in twelve of the eighteen urban centers featured in their study, Curtis and Arreola conclude that some zones have been eliminated or moved to less conspicuous sites. The surviving zones are in a state of obvious decline and "represent relics of a previous era during which prostitution and adult entertainment played a far more important role in tourism than they do now" (Curtis and Arreola 1991:337).

Even in its decline, border prostitution feeds many families. The zones of tolerance offer little to contemporary connoisseurs of hedonism, just lower prices and an exotic setting. These two comparative advantages are sufficient to lure a steady stream of college boys and U.S. servicemen to patronize the prostitutes of the northern Mexico border and preserve the border component of sex.

Each weekend, Tijuana's Avenida Revolución is invaded by hundreds of off-duty marines and sailors looking for inexpensive sex. "American boys come here to do what they can't do at home. That is only a small part of what

Tijuana is. We are an industrial town. Most of us never go to Avenida Revolución. Never" (Tijuana resident quoted in Lowry 1992:23).

Gaming

While prostitution is in decline, entrepreneurs have capitalized on the popularity of sports in America and the potency of the border/vice partnership to produce a gaming bonanza. The popularity of sports betting in the United States is evident in the construction of mega-sports books in Las Vegas such as the 30,000-square-feet Las Vegas Hilton Super Book. Betting lines for all major sports and sporting events are carried in newspapers throughout the United States. Nationally syndicated radio shows feature professional oddsmakers who give their advice on picking winners. With Nevada being the only legal location in the western United States to wager on team sporting events, where do all of the people play? If one lives near the border, chances are that one wagers in Mexico.

The New Juárez Sports Book and Racetrack Company owns five border betting halls: three in Ciudad Juárez, one in Nogales, and one in San Luis Río Colorado.[5] Tijuana alone features five sports books and additional books are in Mexicali and Algodones. In addition to the offerings of football, basketball, baseball and hockey, all of these establishments feature wagering on horse and dog races. The New Juárez Sports Book and Racetrack Company has been so successful with its five border locations, they have opened in the interior of Mexico in Mazatlán, Puebla, and Veracruz and will soon be opening in five other locations.

Mexican sports books purchase the lines (point spreads) and odds directly from Las Vegas and offer the same "parlays" and "teasers" popular at Caesar's Palace or the Stardust. New Juárez Sports Book and Racetrack Company officials estimate that over ninety percent of the sports book players are from north of the border. The New Juárez Sports Book and Racetrack of Nogales is housed in the Hotel Fray Marcos de Niza, located within walking distance of the international border. A satellite feed supplies the large number of monitors with live broadcasts of horse and dog races, baseball games, weekend football matches, and other contests featured on the betting boards.

Tijuana betting is controlled by the owners of the Agua Caliente racetrack. The Mexican government first authorized racetracks to handle bets on foreign sporting events in June 1989. This change was expected to generate $60 million in Tijuana in the first year alone (Reza 1989:29). Jorge Hank Rhon, colorful proprietor of the Agua Caliente, estimates that 120,000 U.S. gamblers a week enter Baja California to wager on sports. Some of Tijuana's sports books are quite swank: the Pueblo Amigo parlor, located just 300 yards from the border, features private rooms, a 50-dollar admission fee (refundable in bets), and 42 television monitors (Crist 1991:B14). Wagers are not accepted on sporting events played in Mexico.

Gaming in Mexico has many advantages over Las Vegas and also raises some serious ethical questions. The major advantage for American borderlanders is location. Since neither Nevada nor Mexico permits inter-state telephone wagering, location is very important. Many sports bettors are casual players who like to place a bet of support on their favorite team. Others are more serious and play seasons, football season or baseball season. Both types of gamblers will be attracted to Mexican sports books if they live near the border. The sports book in Nogales advertises quite heavily both on radio and in newspapers in Tucson. Since the odds or line are similar to what is found in Las Vegas, the actual mechanism is identical and convenience or proximity becomes the major factor.

For the very serious bettor, Mexico offers a very serious advantage. Federal taxes are automatically deducted from large winnings in Las Vegas while no tax is deducted or reported from winnings in Mexico: "Whatever you do with your money is up to you" (Tijuana gaming official quoted in Reza 1989:29).

Sports wagering has a reputation for attracting mobsters and cons who attempt to fix the outcome of sporting events. Past instances of boxers and baseball players purposefully losing under pressure and temptation from bettors have been well documented. In recent years, college basketball has witnessed the disbanding of whole programs when it was discovered that players were attempting to keep their score under the established line so that gamblers could enrich themselves with "sure bets." One major college coach was forced to resign when photos of his players enjoying a whirlpool with a convicted gaming cheat appeared in the local press.[6] Due to the many temptations associated with gaming, Nevada sports books are prohibited from posting a line or accepting any wagers on team sporting events played in Nevada or on any Nevada college team even if the game is to be played outside of the state.

No such restrictions apply to sports betting in Mexico. On that stretch of Mexamerica from Ciudad Juárez to Tijuana, three large universities with major sports programs (University of Texas at El Paso, New Mexico State University and San Diego State University) are located on the border and the University of Arizona sits only an hour from Nogales. Players, coaches, alumni and fans from these universities can legally wager on their own football and basketball games just by conveniently crossing over the line. Tremendous amounts of money can be made simply by intentionally missing one free-throw. Since modern wagers are based on a point spread, one would not even need to "throw" the game to insure windfall profits. Given the past peccadilloes which surfaced when gaming and college athletics met, the new and exploding phenomenon of border sports books represents a new challenge to universities of the Southwest.

Teenage Drinking

Prohibition gave Mexican border *cantinas* a monopoly on the booze market and a reputation as a refuge for drinkers. Today with the ubiquitous pub, lounge, or sports bar dotting American cities, and with the once-seedy image of cities such as Tijuana being rehabilitated, one may assume that contemporary border vice would not include alcohol. However, the border has been most adaptive to changes in the laws governing alcohol consumption.

Border towns are schizophrenic. Tijuana by day attracts the families and the yuppies looking for a few nice souvenirs, a Gucci shirt, and a reasonably priced meal; Tijuana on Friday and Saturday night is dominated by two things—booze and American teenagers (Espinosa 1990).

Thousands of young San Diegans invade Tijuana Friday and Saturday night to party (Castañeda and Pastor 1988:299). Located so close to home and with such a convenient border crossing, Avenida Revolución is not so much a foreign country but a lenient suburb where drinks flow freely for adolescents and where the clubs stay open all night. Even for those over the legal age of twenty-one in California, the northern bars close at 2:00 A.M., thus driving thousands of twenty-something drinkers to spend their dollars at the Tijuana Red Onion and other clubs.[7]

With every "Tequila Slammer" shaken while in the mouth of a teenager, the malleability and resilience of border vice become more apparent. The border does not require antithetical legal juxtapositions such as Prohibition to thrive in vice peddling: *la frontera* can utilize niche marketing and its allure to exploit minor legal discrepancies and technicalities in order to nourish and redirect the vice industry. Today's alcohol niche market is teen drinking. From Tijuana to Nuevo Laredo, United States teenagers as young as fourteen regularly cross the border to drink (Associated Press 1993:A9).

The 1991 highway death of eighteen-year-old Brian Martínez shocked the community of Tucson, Arizona. The night of his death, Martínez had been doing what many high-schoolers and young adults did on weekends since Arizona raised the drinking age from eighteen to twenty-one: partying in Nogales, Sonora.[8]

Investigations after the Martínez accident revealed that Nogales's Calle Elías was a weekend playground for Arizona teens. Children as young as age fourteen were welcome in the nightclubs seventy miles south of Tucson. Clubs such as Harlows and La Posta, which catered principally to an Arizona teenage clientele, advertised on Tucson radio stations. Pricing policies such as that found at Harlows, where on weekends the cover charge is seven dollars but after entering all drinks are free, encouraged excessive alcohol consumption.[9]

The victim's mother, who "thought I always knew where Brian was," attempted to change the situation. The "In Memory of Brian" foundation was started in order to galvanize support for changes in the teenage drinking scene in Nogales. The Arizona-Mexico Commission and the governors of Arizona and Sonora were included in discussions. In an effort to raise awareness, Ms. Martínez spent many weekends camped out at the border crossing passing out coffee to teenagers returning from their night of drinking.

Much like the attempts by religious groups of the 1920s to combat border vice and establish dry zones, the results of the "In Memory of Brian" movement have been modest. Tucson radio stations no longer accept advertising from teen-oriented Nogales clubs. This has not greatly affected the ability of the nightclubs to reach their clientele; now they pay students to hand out fliers at school. Under pressure from the mayor, the police of Nogales, Sonora, began raiding the suspected clubs and checking for patrons under the age of eighteen. Club owners are confident that this will be a temporary nuisance but believe that the 3:00 A.M. closing enforcement will continue.

A spatial analysis of the nightclubs in Nogales illustrates the geographic component of border vice. There are many nightclubs in Nogales which in part rely on American clientele. Epidaurus is the largest club, relies on American patrons for only a small percentage of its business, and attracts the 26–40 crowd. This club is located approximately four miles from the border. Mr. Don is a spacious club and is as modern and chic as any found in New York or Las Vegas. Mr. Don attracts a twenty-something crowd and its clientele is evenly split between Mexicans and Americans. Mr. Don is located approximately fifteen blocks from the international border, the distance discouraging American teenagers who normally walk across the border. Harlows caters to the Arizona teenager and is located one block from the border crossing. As previously demonstrated with the cases of Nevada and Utah, the border is magnetic, attracting both supply and demand for border vice.

Conclusion

The proposition of this article is that the border has a major influence on vice. The border's influence is composed of two dimensions: geographical location and product innovation.

The border is a powerful determinant of the location of legal vice centers. The tremendous growth of Nevada gaming establishments located as close as legally possible to their California, Utah and Arizona clientele supports this hypothesis. The same pattern is evident in the spatial distribution of nightclubs in Nogales, Sonora. With very strict laws governing vice, Utah is surrounded by vice establishments peddling lottery tickets, casino action and stronger alcoholic beverages to Utahans.

The border is also a powerful innovator of vice. Prohibition created the robust supply-and-demand interplay where drinkers and places to drink converged on the border. The 1920s were the "golden years" of border vice. Grand casinos and plush resorts emerged in border towns such as Tijuana. The end of Prohibition, the Great Depression and the pious administration of Lazaro Cárdenas combined to bring Tijuana's glamour era to a close.

World War II brought thousands of servicemen to the military bases of the borderlands and a self-metamorphosed border-vice industry thrived. Instead of elegant casinos and four star restaurants, border towns in the World War II era featured seedy cabarets and prostitution.

In recent years, the growth of legal vice industries in the United States, sexual promiscuity and the AIDS virus have battered the sex-oriented vice industries of northern Mexico. Despite these obstacles, legal border vice has been able to survive, adapt and even flourish in niche markets.

Although important, Mexican-American border vice no longer dominates the economies of Mexamerican towns such as Tijuana, Nogales and Ciudad Juárez and scholars have virtually ignored contemporary border vice. Despite its decline in recent decades, prostitution is still an important element of the border dynamic.

Sports betting and teenage drinking are growing industries on the border. The success of sports books and teen-oriented nightclubs demonstrates the resilience of border vice and its ability to change with the times. Arturo Alemany, Agua Caliente director for American operations, understands that border vice must remain a chameleon and an opportunist to survive: "We always have to offer something more, so now we have added New York racing. If race books like ours come to California, we'll get sports betting. If California gets sports betting, we'll get casinos. If California gets casinos? Well, we'd have to throw in the girls" (Crist 1991:B14). As long as different laws governing gambling, sex and alcohol meet at permeable borders, vice will continue to be a feature of the borderlands.

Notes

1. This article focuses on legal border vice. Legal border vice includes those activities, thought to be immoral or sinful to some, which are legal or quasi-legal on only one side of the border. The border region is also affected by illegal vice, most notably narcotics. Since vices of this type are illegal on both sides of the border, they do not fit into the purpose of this research. Also, smuggling where "Legal exchange of commerce on one side of the border becomes a crime when it passes illicitly across the border to the adjoining nation-state in violation of its laws" is not a part of this research (Lupsha 1981:58).

2. From a telephone interview with Vance Witbeck, resident of the Idaho-Utah borderlands.

3. Indian gaming in Arizona also supports the hypothesis. The State of Arizona recently signed compacts with several tribes permitting casinos with slot machines. As would be expected from our model, the tribes are locating the casinos as close as possible to the tribal border and near a major population center or a busy highway.

4. The same geographical phenomenon is evident at the county level in Nevada. Prostitution is legal in Nevada but illegal in the two most populous counties, Clark and Washoe. As expected, legal houses of ill repute have been located on the Clark and Washoe county borders as close as possible to the major cities of Las Vegas and Reno.

5. All information about the New Juárez Sports Book and Racetrack Company was obtained through a telephone interview with Howard Jones, corporate president, in November 1992.

6. Photos of three University of Nevada at Las Vegas (UNLV) basketball players sitting in a Jacuzzi with Richard "The Fixer" Perry appeared in the *Las Vegas Review Journal* in March 1992. Perry had previously been convicted of paying college athletes to keep the winning score under the betting line. Rumors of an FBI investigation into the UNLV Final Four loss to Duke in 1991 surfaced soonafter. UNLV coach Jerry Tarkanian was soonafter forced to resign. All UNLV players were cleared by the FBI.

7. With changes in mayors or governors, the particulars of drinking age and operating hours can alter. With a PAN mayor in Tijuana for example, bars have been ordered to close at 2:00 A.M. and the eighteen-year-old drinking age is more strictly enforced. This type of action is not new and, given the past history, is probably temporary (Hamann 1992:B1).

8. K-Gun Arizona reporter Laura Castañeda was instrumental in this research. Castañeda provided three video tape stories which dealt with teen drinking in Nogales, Sonora, the death of Brian Martínez, and the attempts to ameliorate the situation.

9. Long-time "Harlows" disk-jockey Saul Bonilla provided the bulk of the information about Nogales nightlife and attempts to curb underage drinking activities. An interview was conducted 13 November 1992 at the club.

References

Acevedo Cárdenas, Conrado. 1955. *Tijuana*. Mexico City: Editorial Stylo.

Associated Press. 1993. "Texas, Mexico Working to Halt Drunken Driving by U.S. Teens," *Arizona Daily Star* 27 August.

Castañeda, Jorge G. and Robert A. Pastor. 1988. *Limits to Friendship: The United States and Mexico*. New York: Alfred A. Knopf.

Crist, Steven. 1991. "Aging Pioneer Discovers Fresh Plan for Survival," *Los Angeles Times* 8 February.

Curtis, James R. and Daniel D. Arreola. 1991. "Zonas de Tolerancia on the Northern Mexican Border," *Geographical Review* 81:333–46.

Espinosa, Paul. 1990. "The New Tijuana," documentary produced by KPBS, San Diego, California.

Hamann, Carlos. 1992. "Mexico Tries to Lure Tourist to Tijuana," *Wall Street Journal* 26 August:B1.

Hedges, Curtis. 1991. "Glitter and Sleaze of Tijuana Still Beckon to U.S. Servicemen," *New York Times* 23 June.

Goodman, Eric. 1991. "Don Laughlin's Desert Dream," *Los Angeles Times* 18 August.

Lamb, David. 1989. "Utah Draws the Line on the Glittering Ambitions of Wendover as the Parade Keeps Passing It By," *Los Angeles Times* 15 May.

Langley, Lester D. 1988. *MexAmerica: Two Countries, One Future*. New York: Crown Publishers.

Lowry, Beverly. 1992. "In Tijuana, Tacky Days and Velvet Nights," *New York Times* 1 March.

Lupsha, Peter A. 1981. "The Border Underworld," in *The Border Economy: Regional Development in the Southwest*. Joint Border Research Institute, New Mexico State University, Las Cruces, New Mexico.

Machado, M.A., Jr. 1982. "Booze, Broads, and the Border: Vice and U.S. Mexican Relations, 1910–1930," pp. 349–361 in C. Richard Bath, ed., *Change and Perspective on Latin American Studies*, Center for Inter-American and Border Studies, University of Texas at El Paso, Texas.

Martínez, Oscar A. 1988. *Troublesome Border*. Tucson: University of Arizona Press.

Martínez, Oscar A. 1986. "The Foreign Orientation of the Ciudad Juárez Economy," pp. 141–151 in G. Young, ed., *The Social Ecology and Economic Development of Ciudad Juárez*. Boulder: Westview Press.

Miller, Tom. 1985. *On the Border: Portraits of America's Southwestern Frontier*. Tucson: University of Arizona Press.

New York Times. 1993. "Nevada Town Booms with Proceeds from Gambling Mormons," 14 June.

Piñera Ramírez, David and Jesús Ortiz Figueroa, eds. 1989. *Historia de Tijuana: 1889–1989*. Tijuana, Baja California: Universidad Autónoma de Baja California.

Price, J. A. 1973. *Tijuana: Urbanization in the Border Culture*. Notre Dame: University of Notre Dame Press.

Reza, H. G. 1989. "Tijuana Ready to Take on Las Vegas," *Los Angeles Times* 29 July.

Rohter, Larry. 1989. "Bustling Tijuana Lives Down Hooch- and Honky-Tonk Past," *New York Times* 2 August.

Weisman, Alan. 1986. *La Frontera: The United States Border with Mexico*. San Diego: Harcourt, Brace, Jovanovich.

Yoshihashi, Pauline. 1990. "Laughlin, Nevada, Casinos Fed by Meat-and-Potatoes Diet," *Wall Street Journal* 24 September.

17

Cross-Border Shopping

Canada and the United States

Dallen J. Timothy and
Richard W. Butler

*International boundaries often reveal sharp differences in the availability
and cost of consumer goods and attract shoppers from both sides. Shopping
is no longer a simple matter of procuring daily necessities; instead, it has
become for many people a form of leisure and an important component of
tourism. Cross-border shopping and tourism are thus two aspects of the movement of people and goods across international borders. This essay examines
cross-border shopping and tourism between Canada and the United States.*

*Dallen J. Timothy is a member of the Department of Recreation Manage-
ment and Tourism at Arizona State University. His research interests include
borders and tourism, tourism planning in developing and peripheral regions,
and global tourism. Richard W. Butler is currently professor of tourism at the
School of Management, University of Surrey, Guilford, UK. He spent thirty
years in Canada at the University of Western Ontario in London, Ontario.
His major research interests are in destination development and cycles, the
impacts of tourism, and sustainability.*

Introduction

Traditional definitions of a tourist normally include the element of travel on
a temporary basis, involve crossing an international border, and frequently
involve the element of pleasure as a purpose of the trip (Burkart and Medlik

From Dallen J. Timothy and Richard W. Butler, "Cross-Border Shopping: A North
American Perspective," *Annals of Tourism Research* 22, no. 1: 16–34. Figures omitted. © 1995. Reprinted by permission of Elsevier.

1974; IUOTO 1986; Murphy 1985). The definitions do not include reference to shopping as a motivation for, or an essential purpose of, tourism. However, it appears clear in the North American context at least, and probably also in Europe, that shopping can be a powerful motivating force in the decision to undertake a cross-border trip. There are strong indications that under some conditions shopping is the primary motive, if not the only significant one, in the decision to make such a trip.

This proposition in itself is not new. Humans have made shopping trips since specialization in production took place in prehistoric times, and those living in remote locations often had to travel considerable distances, sometimes involving overnight stays and crossing international borders. What is new, however, is the fact that shopping is becoming an ever increasingly important element in trips which are primarily of a leisure or tourism nature. This trend reflects the increasing emphasis on consumption in modern society, and the importance which the acquisition of material goods has assumed in many peoples' lives (Featherstone 1991; Shields 1992). It is not the purpose of this paper to discuss this trend, although it will be referred to again in the discussion. Rather, it is the role of shopping in tourism and leisure which is of concern. (This paper regards tourism as a form of pleasure travel; business and other forms of travel that are not primarily pleasure-oriented, whether they involve shopping or not, are not considered here.)

Jansen-Verbeke notes that the role of shopping in leisure time has changed greatly, and that "a series of interconnected social, economic and cultural trends are creating new behavior patterns and new demands" (1990a:4). These trends include major changes in family and lifestyle, increased mobility, changes in urban form, and changes in the nature of shopping itself. Shopping is no longer a simple everyday activity undertaken to acquire the daily necessities.

Lesser and Hughes (1986) categorized shoppers into seven types (active, inactive, traditional, service, dedicated, price, and transitional) and described some characteristics of each. Active shoppers are those who enjoy shopping, with price being a major consideration in the purchase of goods, whereas inactive shoppers do not express much enjoyment or interest in shopping. Similarly, traditional shoppers do not show much enthusiasm for shopping; they do it merely to get by. Service shoppers demand a high level of in-store service, and price is not always a consideration in the purchase decision. Dedicated fringe shoppers are devoted to catalogue shopping as opposed to shopping in person in stores. Price shoppers are those who always compare prices and search most diligently for good deals. Transitional shoppers generally have no interest in searching for low prices; they buy whatever is available.

Many people view shopping as a way of fulfilling part of their need for leisure and tourism. It is clear that for many people, this type of activity is a form of recreation and provides enjoyment and even relaxation (Bussey 1987; Gratton and Taylor 1987). Nonessential shopping is especially viewed as a leisure activity, whereas shopping for essential goods is often considered laborious (Martin and Mason 1987). Recent research offers a great deal of insight about shopping as one of today's leading recreational activities (Chubb and Chubb 1981; Jackson 1991; Jansen-Verbeke 1987, 1991; Johnson and Mannell 1983; Prus and Dawson 1991; Roberts 1987; Ryan 1991). Many of those interviewed by Prus and Dawson in southern Ontario considered shopping one of their most enjoyable recreational activities as it helped them escape from their daily routines, a finding echoed in a study of leisure activities in England (Jansen 1989).

Shopping has become a major leisure activity in part because the setting for shopping has become much more leisure oriented, as malls and other shopping centers continue to add amenities for customers such as food outlets, fitness studios, skating rinks, cinemas, and swimming pools (Martin and Mason 1987). The widespread distribution of shopping malls, especially in North America (Kowinski 1982), has meant that many people have easy access to such facilities. The appearance of supermalls such as West Edmonton Mall has served to blur the distinction between shopping and leisure places even further, as such facilities are openly aiming at leisure visitors as well as shoppers (Hopkins 1991; Jackson 1991). Roberts (1987) also attributes much of the rapid growth of shopping as a leisure activity to the establishment of pedestrian-only streets.

If it is accepted that shopping has now become a leisure activity of considerable significance, it is not surprising that it should also be an important element in tourism. Indeed, shopping has long been an important tourist activity in many destinations. The importance of shopping as one of the oldest and most important aspects of tourism has often been addressed and several researchers have concluded that for many visitors no trip is complete without having spent time shopping (Hudman and Hawkins 1989; Keowin 1989; Prinsky 1977). Actually, Kent, Shock and Snow (1983) have shown that shopping is often the most popular tourist activity in many destinations.

Brown, in his review of tourism and symbolic consumption, talks of tourism as an essential form of consumptive behavior, but argues that "traditional models that have been used to examine and predict consumer behavior are inappropriate for the study of tourism as symbolic consumption" (1992:64). He feels that it is necessary to delve deeper into the reasoning behind tourist shopping, as the behavior is not related necessarily to rational decision making as in normal purchasing. In particular, in the context of the purchase of souvenirs, he quotes Gordon that "people feel the need to bring things home with them from sacred, extraordinary time or space" (1986:36). Such items may not necessarily be particularly sacred, except to the purchaser, although they may be extraordinary. Kurosawa notes somewhat cynically that "no-one ever went broke underestimating the taste of the trinket-buying traveller" (1992:62).

There is little doubt that when he/she is a tourist, a person's shopping and purchasing habits often vary considerably from their normal pattern at home (Stansfield 1971). The transformation of shopping into a hedonistic activity is encouraged in many tourism locations by the nature of the shops, the hours and days of opening, the range of goods available, and the general ambience of such sections of resort communities. The unique and distinctive pattern and location of specific shops and services catering to the tourist in many resorts is a distinguishing feature of such communities and is identified by the term Recreational Business District, to differentiate the area from the traditional Central Business District of most urban centers (Stansfield and Rickert 1970). The concept of establishing distinctive shopping areas for tourists has continued in more recently established destinations. Getz (1993) discusses the planning of tourist shopping villages as tourism attractions, and the creation of duty-free shopping centers at virtually all major airports and cruise ship ports is further evidence of the propensity of tourists to purchase goods during their travels.

Increasingly, however, the range of goods purchased by tourists is broadening and no longer consists just of souvenirs and necessary personal items forgotten in packing. This now includes items such as clothes and major electronic goods. Retail stores are now an important part of the infrastructure in many destinations (Hudman and Hawkins 1989; Pearce 1989), and as the use of self-catering accommodation continues to increase, the amount of grocery shopping by tourists will also increase.

Shopping as Tourism

The discussion has so far focused upon shopping as one activity undertaken as a part of tourism, rather than as the primary reason for tourism. Jansen-Verbeke (1990a, 1990b) has noted the difficulty in defining leisure shopping and how it becomes a leisure experience and resolving whether shopping areas can be defined as tourism resources. While acknowledging this problem, it is reasonable to argue that the desire and need for shopping is an appropriate motivation for tourist travel, comparable to the need and desire to sunbathe, for example. As already noted, shopping provides a form of relaxation, an escape from normal routine, and an element of challenge. Such attributes match closely the two fundamental forces Iso-Ahola suggests as the motivation for leisure and recreation, namely, seeking and escaping. Escaping refers to leaving behind one's routine environment, such as work and other responsibilities or personal problems, for the purpose of achieving some kind of satisfaction. Seeking refers to the pursuit of perceived benefits such as relaxation, pleasure, or a learning experience by engaging in leisure/

tourism activities. Iso-Ahola also suggests that it is useless to try to separate escape and seek forces because tourism can be generated by both the need to avoid something and the need to seek something (Iso-Ahola 1982).

In a similar vein, Crompton concluded that, for most people, the basic tourism motivation is a break from the normal routine or a type of escape (Crompton 1979). Dann (1981) has defined these basic forces as push and pull factors. Push factors are those things that cause people to want to escape, while pull factors are those perceived rewards that a destination can offer. In the context of shopping and tourism, the push factors can be viewed as the relative unattractiveness or over-familiarity of the home shopping environment, and the pull factors the attraction of new and perhaps unvisited shopping opportunities which may offer a range of items not available in the home area.

Tourism attractions are those events, places, or features that draw visitors from near and far. An attraction must be interesting and pleasurable enough to sufficiently motivate people to travel for the purpose of experiencing it. For example, the Louvre may satisfy the needs of art enthusiasts, while a trip to Hawaii may be fulfilling to those who enjoy beaches, warm climates, and cultural experiences. If the opportunity to shop can motivate people to travel by serving their needs and providing enjoyment, then it too may be regarded as a tourism attraction.

Lundberg presupposes the possibility that the urge to shop may be as much a human instinct as the nesting behavior in some animals (Lundberg 1990). Many people find it very pleasurable to hunt bargains, to spend, and to go somewhere different. This is especially true if going somewhere different entails traveling abroad, as this adds intrigue and fascination to a trip. Many people find it attractive to experience cultural differences, spend foreign currency, and eat exotic foods. Shopping abroad is popular, as there is often a different and more alluring selection of merchandise than can be found in the shopper's home community.

Butler (1991) outlines a six-hierarchy order of tourism attractions by their geographic sphere of influence and appeal: attractions with global appeal; global but appealing to only certain groups; places with national appeal; places that attract visitors in conjunction with other attractions; regional attractions; and local attractions. He suggests that shopping areas as tourism attractions can be ordered in a similar fashion. For example, Hong Kong and Paris feature global shopping which appeals to most tourists; Venice (for glass) and Bangkok (for gems) are global centers whose specialized items appeal to only some tourists. Attractions for shoppers at the national level include such places as Harrod's in London and West Edmonton Mall in Canada. Major shopping malls may draw visitors from abroad, but generally only in conjunction with other attractions. On the regional scale, shopping attractions may include malls which are less well known than West Edmonton Mall. For example, the malls in border communities like Port Huron (Michigan) and Niagara Falls (New York) attract visitors from neighboring regions, both in the United States and Canada. Finally, local shopping attractions consist of department stores, malls, grocery stores and other retail establishments that draw people from the local area.

One study conducted in Amsterdam examined how a major shopping area serves as an attraction to many types of visitors (Jansen 1989), and a study by Dilley, Hartviksen and Nord (1991) demonstrated how shopping centers in Duluth (Minnesota) are the most important attraction for visitors from nearby Ontario. Keowin (1989) noted the importance of shopping opportunities to Japanese tourists in Hawaii and modeled the tourist propensity to buy while on holiday. It is reasonable to argue from these examples that shopping opportunities themselves can often function as attractions and that shopping can be the primary purpose of tourism travel (Ryan 1991).

Cross-Border Shopping

It is against this background discussion of the role of shopping in tourism that attention is focused on one particular aspect of shopping and tourism, the phenomenon of cross-border shopping. This particular activity is not a new element in travel. As Jansen-Verbeke comments, "Shopping tourism in border areas is a well-known pattern all over the world and the tourist flows are changing, in intensity and in direction, according to the price fluctuations in the neighboring countries" (1990a:11). Ryan (1991) has emphasized the rapid growth of cross-border shopping in North America and Europe, and a comprehensive analysis has been written about the significance of cross-border shopping between the Republic of Ireland and Northern Ireland (Fitzgerald, Quin, Whelan and Williams 1988). Weigand (1990) notes the dimensions and characteristics of cross-border shopping tourism across the Danish-German border, and as the effects of the Maastricht Treaty further reduce the effects of customs and tariffs between members of the European Community, this activity should continue to increase in Europe.

In North America, cross-border shopping has long been a feature of both trade and tourism between Canada and the United States. Tourist traffic between these two countries is of considerable dimensions, and is dominated by automobile travel. The relative ease with which the border can be crossed, the number of crossing points and the familiarity and similarity between the two countries all facilitate the frequent movement of people between them. Over 90% of Canada's foreign visitors are from the United States. In 1970, Americans entered Canada over 37 million times, and in 1980 this had increased to over 38.5 million. However, in 1990 less than 35 million trips were made by Americans to Canada (84% of these were by car). There has, therefore, been a notable overall decrease in Americans visiting Canada since 1980, with a significant drop of over one million American visits in just one year, between 1990 and 1991 (Statistics Canada 1972–1992).

The number of trips to Canada made by residents of the United States for all types of transportation and all lengths of stay notably increased from 1980 to 1981. This has largely been attributed to the decreased value of the Canadian dollar in the late 1970s and early 1980s, which made it cheaper for Americans to travel in Canada (Chadee and Mieczkowski 1987). The rapid increase of American visitors in the mid-1980s, and its peak in 1986, appear to correspond with Expo '86 which was held in Vancouver, British Columbia. Although the 1988 Winter Olympics were held in Calgary, Alberta, no increase in American visitors can be detected. Instead, a regular decline is visible from 1986 to 1991. This is felt to have been caused in part by the economic recession, and the higher value of the Canadian dollar (approximately U.S.85–89 cents). The notable decrease in 1991 may have been somewhat accentuated by strikes which Canada experienced throughout the summer months which slowed and at times halted the services of many government agencies, including customs and immigration offices at border crossings.

The total number of 1980–1991 returns from the United States by Canadian residents for all lengths of stay and all types of transportation also decreased. The low numbers in the early 1980s have been attributed to the low value of the Canadian dollar, which made traveling in this neighboring country expensive (Chadee and Mieczkowski 1987). However, as the value of the dollar began to increase and as Canadians were attracted to the United States for economic and recreational purposes, the number of departures increased dramatically, especially at the end of the 1980s and the beginning of the 1990s (Waters 1990).

In 1991, over 12 million Canadian trips of two or more nights were made to the United States by car. Over 2 million spent one night traveling by car, and over 59 million drove to the U.S. and returned the same day. In that same year, 6.5 million Americans traveled to Canada by car and stayed more than two nights. Almost 2 million stayed one night, and almost 20 million Americans drove to Canada and returned the same day (Statistics Canada 1972–1992). This imbalance in tourist flows between the two countries has had heavy economic impacts on the Canadian economy. Between July and September 1991, American expenditures in Canada dropped 0.4% to CAN $1.1 billion related to the decline in Americans visiting Canada. During the same period, Canadian expenditures in the United States rose 3.5% to CAN $2.4 billion. The relative significance of these visitation figures can be appreciated in the context of the relative populations of the two countries, Canada having approximately one-tenth of the population of the United States.

Since no actual data exist regarding how many people cross the border between Canada and the United States strictly for shopping, cross-border shoppers are statistically defined by government agencies as those people who cross the border by car and return the same day (New Brunswick 1992; Ontario 1991). This border crossing—by far the most common type of trip made by Canadians—has been in practice for years. However, since the late 1980s, there has been a phenomenally rapid and steady increase in the number of Canadians shopping in the United States. In 1987 almost 31 million Canadians shopped in the United States; this number almost doubled to over 59 million by 1991.

Similar to the general pattern of tourist flows, there is a noticeable seasonality in cross-border shopping on same-day trips in 1991. In March the increase was due to the school holidays in many parts of the country and the onset of better weather. The continued growth in May and June, reaching its peak in July and August, reflects increased availability of family leisure time and better weather. But the flow decreased drastically in September, at the beginning of the school year, to rise again in October, November, and December. This final increase was almost certainly the result of Canadians doing much of their Christmas shopping in the United States.

Research has shown that the primary reason Canadians shop south of the border is that prices are generally lower in the United States, caused by lower profit margins, more retail competition, and lower taxes (London Free Press 1992; New Brunswick 1992; Ontario 1991). Other causes of heavy cross-border shopping relate to the relative strength of the Canadian dollar since 1986 (which improved Canadian purchasing power in the United States), a larger variety of goods, better service, active promotion (such as special sales on shopping weekends), free amenities, and businesses accepting Canadian currency at par with the U.S. dollar—a saving of from 10 to 20% depending upon exchange rates in the period examined (London Free Press 1992; New Brunswick 1992; Waters 1990). The availability of Sunday shopping is another major consideration. One research project conducted in the United Kingdom showed that although Sunday shopping trips accounted for only 3% or 4% of all shopping trips, there was a clear demand for Sunday shopping (Wrigley, Guy and Dunn 1984). An Ontario study found that 74% of that province's consumers who shopped across the border on Sunday would shop at home if stores were open that day (London Free Press 1992).

A particular attraction for many Canadians to shop in the United States has been the lack of enforcement of tax collection at the border by Canada Customs. Although rates of duty on many items have decreased since a free trade agreement was signed between Canada and the United States in 1990, Canadians are not allowed to import any taxable items tax-free if their stay out of the country has been less than 24 hours in duration. However, many Canadians discovered that they could routinely make day trips and relatively small purchases without being charged tax on them at ports-of-entry. The sheer numbers of returning Canadians, along with normal traffic at border crossing points, resulted in delays of several hours if custom officials examined even a quarter of vehicles.

Media coverage has also contributed to the growth of cross-border shopping by suggesting that all goods are cheaper in the United States than in Canada. American businesses took advantage of media promotion by conducting intensive advertising campaigns in Canadian newspapers and on Canadian television. American hotels, attempting to lure their Canadian neighbors, often offered discounted room rates that could be paid with Canadian money at par (London Free Press 1992). Malls catered to Canadian shoppers by promoting store-wide sales and accepting Canadian currency at par in many shops. One other factor that was considered to be a major influence in the increase in cross-border shopping toward the end of this period was the introduction of a value-added tax, the "Goods and Services Tax," by the federal government at the beginning of 1991. This has proved to be the most unpopular tax in Canadian history, and replaced an invisible manufacturing tax on a limited range of products with a smaller but highly visible and almost universal tax. Although some authors (Chatterjee 1991) do not feel this was a major factor in the increase of cross-border shopping, the popular perception and reaction was that it was of considerable importance.

The growth in cross-border shopping from 1986 onward greatly increased the balance of trade deficit between Canada and the United States. This traffic was also felt to be one of the major reasons for an increase in lost jobs and retail bankruptcies in Canada within the past few years (London Free Press 1992). An increase of almost 91% in such events since 1987 supported this assumption. Cross-border shopping has been blamed also for millions of dollars in lost revenue for federal and provincial governments. The financial loss to the province of Ontario alone was estimated at around CAN$600 million for 1990 and CAN$1 billion for 1991 (Ontario 1991).

Canadian border communities have been most adversely affected by this shopping phenomenon, although the effects have been felt in all parts of Canada. According to the Standing Committee on Finance and Economic Affairs for the province of Ontario (1991), cross-border shopping was assumed responsible for the loss of over 4,000 jobs in border communities of Ontario.

In contrast to Canada, American businesses thrived on Canadian patronage as they continued to offer the selection, service, and prices that attracted their northern neighbors. Retail stores and hotels were not the only businesses that benefited from cross-border shopping; petrol was the most commonly bought item, with food as the next most frequent purchase. Other components of U.S. tourism that benefited from cross-border shopping included local transport services, cinemas, museums, and banks. While these shoppers were contributing to the loss of revenue and jobs in Canada, they were clearly causing the creation of jobs and increases in receipts across the border (Kendall and Kreck 1992; Kreck 1985).

The spectacular and rapid rise in the cross-border shopping trips from 1986 onward assumed such dimensions and apparent severe effects that political and legislative action was felt necessary. Several ideas for decreasing the number of Canadians crossing the border to shop were proposed. Agreement to combine collection of the provincial sales tax with the federal goods and services tax at border crossings would in effect increase duty on goods being brought back into Canada, and thereby discourage cross-border shopping and raise revenues for provincial governments. The establishment of Sunday shopping, especially in communities near the border, would eliminate an American advantage. Attaching smaller increases to the costs of goods as they move through the distribution channels would make prices more competitive in Canada. The establishment of more brand-name outlet stores and more competition between retailers would increase the attraction of shopping in Canada (London Free Press 1992). While action has been taken in a number of directions (noted below), legislative action on the combining of tax collection has not taken place. This is in part due to philosophical and ideological differences between some of the provincial governments and the federal government, but also reflects the desires of the Canadian public, who generally did not want further restrictions (Chatterjee 1991).

In May 1992, because of the high travel deficit, and to celebrate Canada's 125th anniversary, the federal government of Canada launched a new advertising campaign to promote domestic tourism. The government encouraged Canadians to stay in their own country to experience its scenery and historical sites, and to explore its cities (London Free Press 1992). Extensive television advertising and billboards, some of them promoting shopping in Canada, were seen in many communities as part of the federal government's crusade to keep its citizens home.

Early in the summer of 1992, Sunday shopping became legal in the province of Ontario. As already mentioned, many respondents had indicated that they would stay in that province to shop on Sundays if stores were allowed to open. It remains to be seen, however, whether or not this is truly the case. This development would merit investigation to evaluate the effect of legalized Sunday shopping on cross-border shopping.

As of July 1, 1992, Canadians are required to pay a CAN$5 handling fee to Canada Post Corporation for every parcel received from the United States through the mail, aimed at orders from mail order catalogues, as well as the federal goods and service tax and duties on parcels valued at CAN$20 or more. Formerly, Canadians were allowed CAN$40 worth of American mail order merchandise tax-free (York Region Business Journal 1992).

The province of Ontario recently legalized gambling within its borders. While many people view this as a strategy for keeping Canadians at home, it is also expected to draw American tourists from neighboring states where gambling is not permitted.

Analysts have concluded that from 1992 onward, there will be a marked decrease in cross-border shopping owing to a variety of reasons: the reduced value of the Canadian dollar makes shopping in the United States more expensive; prices there have been raised significantly (even on commonly purchased goods like gasoline), whereas many Canadian retailers have reduced their prices; Canada Customs has cracked down on smuggling; the Canadian government has removed tariffs from many imported goods; and anger has diminished somewhat after more than a year of the 7% goods and services tax.

The dimensions and extremely dynamic nature of the cross-border shopping between Canada and the United States in the 1980s raise questions as to whether such activity is tourism, or is simply primarily functional shopping without a leisure or tourism dimension. This doubt is supported to some extent by the fact that the rise in participation was clearly strongly related to the relative value of the Canadian dollar compared to its U.S. counterpart. The value of the Canadian dollar began to fall in 1992, and in March 1992 the first decline in cross-border shopping was recorded since September 1986 (Kemp 1992). This decline has continued through 1993, as has the decline in the Canadian dollar, such that at the end of the summer of 1993 it had fallen to U.S. 75 cents, from 89 cents in 1989.

However, studies would appear to contradict the view that cross-border shopping is not a form of tourism. The Canadian Chamber of Commerce reported that "the available data suggests [*sic*] that Canadians are not only visiting the United States more, they are also doing so with the express purpose of shopping there, and appear to be spending increasing amounts of time and money with each trip" (1992:1). It then went on to note that "many respondents to the cross-border shopping survey say that one of their main reasons for shopping in the U.S. is because it allows them to get away from home and experience change. The trip is a family outing and, depending on the length of stay, may even be seen as vacation" (1992:6). A similar finding was reported by Dilley and Hartviksen who, as a follow-up to their earlier study (1991), examined the effect of the free trade agreement between Canada and the United States on cross-border trips between Ontario and Minnesota. They concluded that the effect of the agreement was to "increase somewhat the number of people making trips and to increase significantly the frequency with which they go" (1993:17). However, although such a finding might suggest that the primary motivation for the increase in numbers and frequency of the trips was economic (the effect of the agreement being to reduce tariffs and duty on goods), Dilley and Hartviksen concluded that the trip was "above all a *tourist* experience" (1993:17; emphasis original). These apparently contradictory conclusions imply that cross-border shopping can be both highly rational (i.e., it responds quickly and dramatically to changes in the economic systems) and primarily pleasure focused. This incongruity needs to be reconciled, and is discussed below.

Models of Cross-Border Shopping

In order to attempt to place cross-border shopping within the tourism system in theoretical terms, it is appropriate, therefore, to model the phenomenon. Two hypothetical models have been formulated to help illustrate the nature of cross-border shopping as tourism. They build on basic assumptions about the relationships between leisure and shopping described by Jansen-Verbeke. According to her, "the only valid indicator with respect to the leisure aspect of shopping lies in the information about the place of residence and the distance travelled to the shopping area . . . the further one travels, the more likely it is the visit has a leisure based nature" (1990b:130).

Canadians who shop in the United States can be classified by where they live in the country, how often they shop in the United States, and the types of goods purchased. . . . The general pattern of cross-border shopping is based on the authors' observations, as well as on those mentioned in other discussions dealing with the subject (London Free Press 1992; New Brunswick 1992; Ontario 1991). It suggests that residents of the proximal shopping zone (the area extending approximately 50 kilometers from the border) generally cross the border frequently and are willing to go for everyday, small-ticket items like gasoline, groceries, beer, tobacco products, and restaurant meals. Chamberlain (1991) found that 31% of people in Ontario border communities had shopped in the United States in the previous month, 16% of them having shopped five or more times in the same period. Levels of shopping in the United States among residents of non-border communities was less than half these levels. Consumers who live in the medial shopping zone (50 to 200 kilometers from the border) cross the border less often and tend to buy higher-value goods. Those people who live farthest from the international boundary, in the distal shopping zone (the rest of Canada), seldom cross the border on shopping trips, but when they do, they tend to purchase big-ticket items such as clothes, appliances, and electronics.

According to this model, the farther one lives from the border the less frequently one shops in the United States, but the more costly one's purchases are likely to be. However, variations from this pattern obviously exist. For example, proximal residents are probably just as likely to purchase big-ticket items on one of their more frequent trips as are people who live in the distal zone. It is likely that when consumers from either the distal or medial zone shop in the United States, they may also dine out, purchase gas, and buy groceries.

There are two other types of cross-border shoppers not associated with this model because they live in all parts of Canada: those who shop while on a specific U.S. vacation and those who shop by mail-order catalogue. Vacationers tend to buy small items, but may include high-value goods since their duty-free allowance increases with time spent abroad. Some mail-order shoppers may never have visited the United States, but shop by mail and telephone for the same cross-border reasons—low prices and wider selection. Classifying cross-border shoppers in this way may be useful in developing marketing campaigns by segmenting the population into specific target groups. This could be worthwhile for the Canadian government in its efforts to keep its citizens shopping at home, and for American businesses wishing to entice more Canadians to shop across the border.

It is also appropriate to attempt to determine the strength of the tourist or leisure component in cross-border shopping. Some researchers agree that people who travel abroad and return to their home country the same day are, and should be considered, tourists—they cross an international boundary and spend time and money while utilizing space and facilities in the destination area (Murphy 1985; Ryan 1991). Johnston, Mauro and Dilley (1991) have called cross-border shopping a form of tourism. They assert that this activity, as a type of tourism, is rapidly taking over the traditional recreation-type tourism in the vicinity of the U.S.-Canadian border.

The fact that cross-border shopping experiences seasonality seems to support the hypothesis that many people participate in this activity in the same manner as in other forms of leisure. If seasonality did not exist, it would imply that cross-border shopping was based purely on economic motivation and would likely continue at nearly the same rate throughout the year as people feel the economic need to shop in the United States. This model is based largely on the premise that many cross-border shoppers find this activity a pleasurable experience. . . .

Conclusion

Shopping today is obviously not the laborious activity it used to be. For many, it is one of their most enjoyable leisure-time activities, and more so for tourists. In many tourism destinations, shopping is the preferred activity and tourists often spend more money on shopping than on food, lodging, and other entertainment. Shopping opportunity can also function as an attraction. There are many places that draw visitors from near and far mainly for the purpose of shopping—in this case, American border communities.

Cross-border shopping is a type of tourism that has recently nearly overrun the traditional tourist flows between the United States and Canada. A multiplicity of causes of cross-border shopping have been noted, most of them economic in nature. However, it is fairly obvious that many Canadians who shop south of the border are motivated by both economics and pleasure. In fact, it is possible that some of them may be motivated purely by pleasure. If individuals willfully cross the border to shop and are motivated by pleasure, or even a combination of economics and pleasure, they ought to be considered tourists. There should be little doubt that most cross-border shopping is as much a leisure activity as it is an economic one, and that it is one tourism-generating activity that is worthy of additional attention.

References

Brown, G. 1992. Tourism and Symbolic Consumption. In Choice and Demand in Tourism, P. Johnson and B. Thomas, eds., pp. 57–71. London: Mansell.

Burkart, A. J., and S. Medlik. 1974. Tourism: Past, Present, and Future. London: Heinemann.

Bussey, K. 1987. Leisure + Shopping = ? Leisure Management 7(9):22–26.

Butler, R. W. 1991. West Edmonton Mall as a Tourist Attraction. The Canadian Geographer 35:287–295.

Canadian Chamber of Commerce. 1992. The Cross Border Shopping Issue. Ottawa: Canadian Chamber of Commerce.

Chamberlain, L. 1991. Small Business Ontario Report No. 44—Cross Border Shopping. Toronto: Ministry of Industry, Trade and Technology.

Chadee, D., and Z. Mieczkowski. 1987. An Empirical Analysis of the Effects of the Exchange Rate on Canadian Tourism. Journal of Travel Research 26(1):13–17.

Chatterjee, A. 1991. Cross-Border Shopping: Searching for a Solution. Canadian Business Review 18 (Winter):26–31.

Chubb, M., and H. R. Chubb. 1981. One Third of Our Time? An Introduction to Recreation Behavior and Resources. New York: Wiley.

Crompton, J. L. 1979. Motivations for Pleasure Vacation. Annals of Tourism Research 6:408–424.

Dann, G. 1981. Tourism Motivation and Appraisal. Annals of Tourism Research 9:187–219.

Dilley, R. S., and K. R. Hartviksen. 1993. Duluth and Thunder Bay: Tourism after the Free Trade Agreement. The Operational Geographer 11(3):15–18.

Dilley, R. S., K. R. Hartviksen, and D. C. Nord. 1991. Duluth and Thunder Bay: A Study of Mutual Tourist Attractions. The Operational Geographer 9(4):9–13.

Featherstone, M. 1991. Consumer, Culture and Postmodernism. London: Sage.

Fitzgerald, J. D., T. P. Quinn, B. J. Whelan, and J. A. Williams. 1988. An Analysis of Cross-Border Shopping. Dublin: The Economic and Social Research Institute.

Getz, D. 1993. Tourist Shopping Villages: Development and Planning Strategies. Tourism Management 14:15–26.

Gordon, B. 1986. The Souvenir: Messages of the Extraordinary. Journal of Popular Culture 20:135–146.

Gratton, C., and P. Taylor. 1987. Leisure and Shopping: The Domesday Experience. Leisure Management 7(3):29–30.

Hopkins, J. 1991. West Edmonton Mall as a Centre for Social Interaction. The Canadian Geographer 35:268–279.

Hudman, L. E., and D. E. Hawkins. 1989. Tourism in Contemporary Society. Englewood Cliffs: Prentice-Hall.

Iso-Ahola, S. E. 1982. Toward a Social Psychological Theory of Tourism Motivation: A Rejoinder. Annals of Tourism Research 9:256–261.

IUOTO. 1968. The Economic Review of World Tourism. Madrid: World Tourism Organization.

Jackson, E. L. 1991. Shopping and Leisure: Implications of West Edmonton Mall for Leisure and for Leisure Research. The Canadian Geographer 35:280–287.

Jansen, A. C. M. 1989. "Funshopping" as a Geographical Notion, or the Attraction of the Inner City of Amsterdam as a Shopping Area. Tijdschrift voor Economische en Sociale Geografie 80(3):171–183.

Jansen-Verbeke, M. C. 1987. Women, Shopping and Leisure. Leisure Studies, 6:71–86.

1990a From Leisure Shopping to Shopping Tourism. In Proceedings I.S.A. Conference, pp. 1–17. Madrid.

1990b Leisure and Shopping: Tourism Product Mix. In Marketing Tourism Places. G. Ashworth and B. Goodall, eds., pp. 128–135. London: Routledge.

1991 Leisure Shopping: A Magic Concept for the Tourism Industry? Tourism Management 12.9–14.

Johnson, R. C. A., and R. C. Mannell. 1983. The Relationship of Crowd Density and Environmental Amenities to Perceptions of Malls as Leisure Shopping Environments. Recreation Research Review 10(4):18–23.

Johnston, M., R. Mauro, and R. S. Dilley. 1991. Trans-Border Tourism in a Regional Context. Paper presented at annual meeting of Canadian Association of Geographers, Kingston, Ontario.

Kemp, K. 1992. Cross-Border Shopping—Trends and Measurement Issues. Canadian Economic Observer (December):5.1–5.13.

Kendall, K. W., and L. A. Kreck. 1992. The Effect of the Across-the-border Travel of Canadian Tourists on the City of Spokane: A Replication. Journal of Travel Research 30(4):53–58.

Kent, W. E., P. J. Shock, and R. E. Snow. 1983. Shopping: Tourism's Unsung Hero(in). Journal of Travel Research 21(4):2–4.

Keowin, C. F. 1989. A Model of Tourists' Propensity to Buy: Case of Japanese Visitors to Hawaii. Journal of Travel Research 27(3):31–34.

Kowinski, W. 1982. The Malling of America. New York: William Morrow.

Kreck, L. A. 1985. The Effect of Across-the-border Commerce of Canadian Tourists on the City of Spokane. Journal of Travel Research 24(1):27–31.

Kurosawa, S. 1992. Token Gestures. The Australian Magazine (September): 62.

Lesser, J. A., and M. A. Hughes. 1986. Towards a Typology of Shoppers. Business Horizons 29(6):56–62.

London Free Press. 1992. Various Issues (January-September).

Lundberg, D. E. 1990. The Tourist Business. New York: Van Nostrand Reinhold.

Martin, B., and S. Mason. 1987. Current Trends in Leisure. Leisure Studies, 6:93–97.

Murphy, P. E. 1985. Tourism: A Community Approach. London: Methuen.

New Brunswick, Government of. 1992. A Discussion Paper on Cross Border Shopping. Fredericton: Department of Economic Development and Tourism.

Ontario, Government of. 1991. Report on Cross-Border Shopping. Toronto: Standing Committee on Finance and Economic Affairs.

Pearce, D. G. 1989. Tourist Development. London: Longman.

Prinsky, R. 1977. Within Eastern Bloc, Tourists Go Byebye Mostly to Buy Buy. Wall Street Journal (January 14):1.

Prus, R., and L. Dawson. 1991. Shop 'til You Drop: Shopping as Recreational and Laborious Activity. Canadian Journal of Sociology 16(2):145–164.

Roberts, J. 1987. Buying Leisure. Leisure Studies 6:87–91.

Ryan, C. 1991. Recreational Tourism: A Social Science Perspective. New York: Routledge.

Shields, R. 1992. Lifestyle Shopping: The Subject of Consumption. London: Routledge.

Stansfield, C. A. 1971. The Nature of Seafront Development and Social Status of Seaside Resorts. Society and Leisure 4:117–141.

Stansfield, C. A., and J. E. Rickert. 1970. The Recreational Business District. Journal of Leisure Research 2:213–225.

Statistics Canada. 1972–1992. Touriscope: International Travel. Ottawa: Statistics Canada.

Waters, S. R. 1990. Travel Industry World Yearbook: The Big Picture. New York: Child and Waters.

Weigand, K. 1990. Drei Jahrzehnte Einkaufstourismus über die deutsch-dänische Grenze. Geographische Rundschau 42(5):286–290.

Wrigley, N., C. Guy, and R. Dunn. 1984. Sunday and Late-night Shopping in a British City: Evidence from the Cardiff Consumer Panel. Area 16(3):236–240.

York Region Business Journal. 1992. Mail Order Industry 'Delighted' with Pay-First Policy. The York Region Business Journal 6(4):2.

18

Maritime Agreements and Oil Exploration in the Gulf of Thailand

Daniel J. Dzurek

The history of borders has largely centered on land boundaries. However, as transportation has improved and as technology has advanced to the point where undersea resources, such as petroleum and gas deposits, can be exploited economically, nations have moved to stake their claims to maritime regions, particularly those near shore. The Gulf of Thailand—bordered by Malaysia, Thailand, Cambodia, and Vietnam—is currently the center of an acrimonious dispute over conflicting and overlapping offshore claims.

Daniel J. Dzurek is president of International Boundaries Consultants in Washington, DC. He was formerly chief of the boundary analysis division in the Office of the Geographer, U.S. Department of State, and a fellow at the East-West Center in Honolulu. He has published extensively on offshore boundary and island sovereignty disputes.

Introduction

Maritime claims in the Gulf of Thailand have grown in tandem with oil and gas exploration, which has fed national interest in offshore jurisdiction (Dzurek, 1985: 261). From June 1971 to May 1973 Cambodia, the former South Vietnam and Thailand made unilateral claims to continental shelf areas that overlap in the central Gulf of Thailand (Prescott & Morgan, 1983). About the same time, in 1972, gas was first discovered off Thailand.

From Daniel J. Dzurek, "Maritime Agreements and Oil Exploration in the Gulf of Thailand," in *Boundaries and Energy: Problems and Prospects,* ed. Gerald Blake et al. (London: Kluwer Law International Ltd., 1998), 117–35. Tables omitted. Reprinted/adapted with permission from Kluwer Law International.

Cambodia's offshore exploration began in 1974 but came to a halt with the Vietnamese occupation in 1978 (Valencia, 1985: 167).

The countries bordering the Gulf claim the full suite of maritime jurisdictional rights. The partial continental shelf boundary between Malaysia and Thailand is the only agreed maritime boundary in the Gulf. Since Cambodia renounced its claim to Phu Quoc Island in 1976, the Gulf of Thailand does not encompass any island sovereignty disputes, but the coastal states contest several jurisdictional zones. These include three areas in active dispute, two areas under joint development, and one area under joint control. The coastal states are negotiating resolutions in several of the contested areas. Thailand and Vietnam have reportedly reached agreement on a draft maritime boundary.

The Gulf of Thailand is traditionally defined as being bounded by a line from the terminus of the Malaysia-Thailand land boundary to the southern tip of Vietnam (Mui Ca Mau). The Gulf occupies 289,000 square kilometres (sq km), which is an area larger than the United Kingdom.[1] Because the Gulf is less than 400 nautical miles (nm) across, every portion is subject to a jurisdictional claim by one of the coastal countries: Cambodia, Malaysia, Thailand or Vietnam. Sixteen percent of the Gulf is disputed: 33,000 sq km of contested continental shelf claims; 8,600 sq km of overlapping internal waters claims in the Cambodia-Vietnam joint historic waters zone; and 5,800 sq km of the Malaysia-Thailand joint development zone.[2]

Status of National Maritime Claims

The international law of the sea provides several kinds of jurisdictional claims relating to resource rights. Claims to continental shelf or exclusive economic zone (EEZ) rights usually account for most offshore oil and gas deposits, but this region is unusual because the coastal states claim 31 percent of the Gulf as internal waters (within straight baselines).

Straight Baselines

Normally, the baseline from which maritime jurisdiction is measured is the low-water line along the coast; however:

> Where the coastline is deeply indented and cut into, or if there is a fringe of islands along the coast in its immediate vicinity the method of straight baselines joining appropriate points may be employed in drawing the baseline from which the breadth of the territorial sea is measured. (United Nations, 1982: Article 7.)

The area within straight baselines is termed internal waters, where a country has absolute sovereignty like that it exercises over its landmass.

Cambodia, Malaysia, Thailand and Vietnam claim straight baselines, portions of which violate international law because they diverge from the general direction of the coast or connect islands that are not in the immediate vicinity of the coast. Thailand claims straight baselines along most of its coast; elsewhere it uses the low-water line as its baseline. The other Gulf countries claim straight baselines along their entire coasts.

In August 1992 Thailand made two modifications to its 1970 straight baselines. The first Thai cabinet decision (11 August 1992) adjusted coordinates of the baseline along the Andaman Sea coast.[3] The second cabinet decision (17 August 1992) established a new section (Area 4) of straight baselines, which extended from the baseline around Area 2, in the western Gulf, to link Ko Kra and Ko Losin islands to the Malaysia-Thailand land boundary terminus (Thailand, 1992). The new Area 4 abuts Area 2. Although the Thai Cabinet decisions were adopted six days apart, reference to the second decision, delimiting the new area, did not appear in western sources until mid-1994.

The Thai change reinforces its claim vis-à-vis both Cambodia and Vietnam in the central Gulf. By creating Area 4, Thailand expands its claimed internal waters by 129 percent in the Gulf, to a total of 52,000 sq km. Thailand's modification may have been made in preparation for negotiations with Cambodia and Vietnam. If used as a base for delimiting a median boundary line, the new Thai baselines would shift the boundary eastward, encompassing more of the Pattani Trough area.

Most baseline claims in the Gulf have been protested by other countries as excessive or violating international law. For example, the United States protested Vietnam's straight baselines claim in 1982 and historic waters claim in the Gulf of Thailand in 1987. The United States asserted its navigation rights through Cambodia's claimed internal waters beginning in 1986, and protested Cambodia's claim to historic waters in 1987 (Roach & Smith, 1994: 23–24, 26–27, 45, 48). Also in the mid-1980s, Singapore and Thailand rejected Vietnam's historic waters and straight-baseline claims (Singapore, 1986; Thailand, 1985). In 1994, on behalf of the European Union, Germany protested Thailand's straight baseline around Area 4 (Germany, 1994). Since Malaysia has never published the coordinates of its baseline, other countries have probably not had sufficient basis to formulate diplomatic protests.

Several segments of straight baseline claims extend well into the Gulf. For example, the Vietnamese basepoint A1, at Hon Nhan in the Tho Chu group, lies 150 km from the nearest mainland point (Geographer, 1983: 6). A point on the Thai straight-baseline segment between Ko Kra and Ko Losin is 107 km from the nearest mainland point. In 1982 the People's Republic of Kampuchea (PRK) delimited a straight-baseline system from the terminus of its land boundary with Thailand to an undefined point on the southwest limit of the 1982 PRK-Vietnam historic waters area (FBIS, Daily Report: Asia and the Pacific, 9 August 1982: H1). The coordinates of Malaysia's straight baselines have not been published but have been inferred from its 1979 continental shelf claim (Malaysia, 1979; Prescott, 1985: 213).

Historic Waters

One special justification for straight baselines is a claim to historic waters. To establish such a claim,

> a state must demonstrate its open, effective, long-term, and continuous exercise of authority over the body of water, coupled with acquiescence by foreign states in the exercise of that authority. (Roach & Smith, 1994: 23.)

In 1959 Thailand claimed the inner part of the Gulf of Thailand (the Bight of Thailand) as a historic bay and closed it with a straight bay-closing line (Thailand, 1959). The enclosed area is 9,300 sq km.

In 1982 Cambodia and Vietnam claimed a joint area of historic waters, to be divided later (FBIS, Daily Report: Asia and the Pacific, 9 July 1982: K3-4). This joint area encloses 8,600 sq km. When eventually divided, their straight baselines will be linked at sea on a line connecting Cambodia's Poulo Wai island with a point in Vietnam's Tho Chu archipelago. Such a "floating" basepoint is unusual but not unknown in the international law of the sea.[4]

Territorial Sea

All of the Gulf of Thailand countries claim 12 nm (22.2 km) territorial seas, which are measured seaward from their baselines. Within its territorial sea a country exercises absolute resource rights but must allow the innocent passage of other countries' ships (United Nations, 1982, Articles 17–26). For the purposes of this paper, which focuses on oil and gas rights, territorial sea jurisdiction has been subsumed under continental shelf claims.

Continental Shelf

Continental shelf claims of the Gulf countries often preceded delimitation of straight baselines. Although most countries bordering the Gulf assert the use of a median line (equidistant from the nearest points of the respective countries) for the seaward limit of their shelf claims, they have ignored or given special effect to various islands in order to maximize national shelf jurisdiction. This explains the divergence among the claim lines in the central Gulf.

Thailand's continental shelf claim has probably been formulated to accord with the proportionality principle of maritime boundary delimitation. The fraction of Gulf area claimed by Thailand is very close to its proportion of the total coastline or baseline around the Gulf; Thailand claims 72 percent

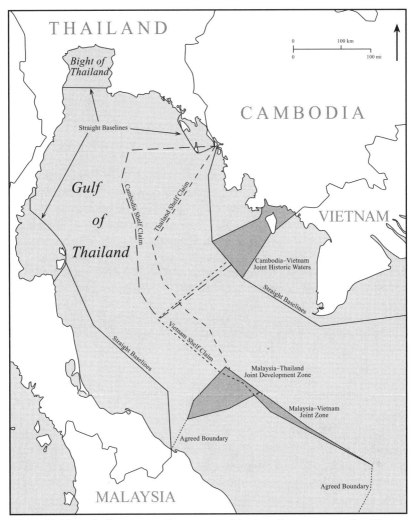

of the Gulf, excluding internal waters, and its baseline accounts for 73 percent of the coastline around the Gulf. Similarly, if one ignores straight baselines, Thailand claims 67 percent of the Gulf as either internal waters or continental shelf, and its low-water coastline accounts for 69 percent of the perimeter of the Gulf. The similarity in proportions between the coastal length and the area claimed is remarkable and probably not coincidental.

Despite civil wars in Cambodia and Vietnam, the successor regimes seem to maintain the positions promulgated by their predecessors. The Khmer Republic delimited its continental shelf claim on 1 July 1972 (République Khmère, 1972). Recent maps produced by the Cambodian Ministry of Industry continue to depict the continental shelf claim delimited in 1972 (Praing,

1992), except the portion in the southern Gulf, which radiated from Cambodia's former claim to Phu Quoc Island.[5] Cambodia claims 48,000 sq km of shelf area.

Vietnam appears to claim the same continental shelf area in the Gulf of Thailand as that delimited by the Saigon regime in 1971 (Prescott, 1985: 223). In 1992 Vietnam elaborated its continental shelf claim to extend to water depths of 1,500 metres (m) (Huynh, 1992). Because the Gulf of Thailand is shallow, this depth criterion only has effect beyond the Gulf in the South China Sea proper, where Vietnam is in conflict with the PRC [People's Republic of China]. Within the Gulf, Vietnam claims 33,000 sq km.

Exclusive Economic Zone

All four countries claim EEZs, which can extend to 200 nm from their respective baselines. Because the Gulf of Thailand is less than 400 nm wide, no country can claim a full EEZ. The precise extent of these claims is unclear. The EEZ claims may coincide with earlier continental shelf limits, but EEZs need not conform with continental shelf claims. Countries can revise claims and sometimes do so when preparing to negotiate a maritime boundary, as the United States and Canada did in the case of the Gulf of Maine. Countries bordering the Gulf of Thailand could claim more extensive EEZs on the basis of recently delimited straight baselines. There have been no EEZ agreements in the Gulf of Thailand.

Disputes

Cambodia-Thailand

The largest disputed area (approximately 27,000 sq km) in the Gulf is that overlapped by the Cambodian and Thai continental shelf claims. Cambodia has, perhaps, the most unusual shelf claim in the world, because it cuts through Thai territory and internal waters. The northern limit of the Cambodian claim intersects the highest point of Thailand's Ko Kut Island and proceeds nearly due west into the Gulf. The Cambodian claim is based on an unusual interpretation of the 1907 Franco-Siamese land boundary protocol, which specified that "the boundary between French Indo-China and Siam leaves the sea at the point opposite the highest point of Koh Kut island" (Prescott, 1985: 223; Geographer, 1966). This Cambodian segment not only cuts through Thai land territory; it also discounts the Thai coast in the northeastern Gulf.

In drawing its limit. Thailand ignored the Thai islands of Ko Kra and Ko Losin, the Cambodian islands of Poulo Wai, and the Vietnamese Tho Chu islands (Prescott, 1985: 223). However, Cambodia and Vietnam subsequently used these islands as base points in their straight-baseline systems. Vietnam apparently convinced Thailand to use Tho Chu as a basepoint in their current negotiations.

Because coastal geography restricts its potential shelf area, Cambodia has more to gain than Thailand from an equitable settlement. An estimated one-third of Cambodia's potential oil and gas deposits lies offshore (Praing, 1992: 3). Much of that is in the area disputed with Thailand. Beginning in 1991, Cambodia resumed awarding offshore contracts (FEER, 9 July 1992: 68–69; *Offshore*, August 1993: 18).

In 1992 Cambodian Ministry of Industry officials and Thai petroleum representatives reportedly agreed in principle to resolve the dispute. The government in Cambodia has pressed for a joint technical and economic agreement modelled on the Malaysia-Thailand accord (*Business Times*, 7 October 1992; *Offshore*, August 1992: 18).

Cambodia-Vietnam

Within their straight-baseline claims, Cambodia and Vietnam dispute 8,600 sq km of historic waters. This area of claimed internal waters extends some 100 km from their mainlands. Their 1982 agreement delimited the area in dispute and permitted both sides to patrol the zone. The agreement also recognized the 1939 French-colonial Brevie Line as determining the sovereignty of islands in the area,[6] thus reiterating Cambodian renunciation of a claim to Phu Quoc (FEER, 7 August 1982: 25).

If it maintains its claim up to the Brevie Line, Cambodia would claim 79 percent of the joint zone. Reportedly, the new Cambodian government wants to renegotiate boundary agreements signed by the former Hun Sen regime, including the 1982 historic waters accord. Technical committees have been established to address the issues. A Vietnamese official has suggested that agreement in the Gulf of Thailand would be more difficult than reaching resolution of land-boundary issues. Vietnam has indicated willingness to renegotiate the agreements as long as Cambodia does not raise the issue of sovereignty over the Mekong Delta, which Vietnam gained in the eighteenth century (FEER, 9 September 1992: 13; FBIS, 12 May 1993: 51).

Until the historic waters dispute is resolved, it is unlikely that the overlapping continental shelf claims beyond the baselines can be settled. The area of overlap is some 1,100 sq km. It lies between the Vietnamese claim line and the Cambodian claim, which follows the Brevie Line.

Cambodia-Thailand-Vietnam

There is a small sliver of area (150 sq km) that appears to be overlapped by continental shelf claims from Cambodia, Thailand and Vietnam. Thailand is negotiating with both Cambodia and Vietnam over the areas it contests with them but it is unclear how the parties are treating the trilaterally disputed area or the eventual delimitation of a tripoint.

Thailand-Vietnam

Thailand and Vietnam dispute an area of approximately 5,800 sq km. During meetings in 1992 and 1993 the two sides agreed to conduct a joint delimitation of their overlapping area and establish joint development arrangements (*Offshore*, October 1993: 16; FBIS, 21 May 1993: 47). Talks continued in 1994 (*Reuters*, 25 February 1994). The two sides met in January 1995, when they apparently agreed to seek a continental shelf boundary delimitation but also consider a joint development zone (FBIS, 6 January 1995: 77, and 17 January 1995: 83, 89). Some Thai reporting said that the boundary would be delimited "based on the relative lengths of the coastlines" (proportionality) (FBIS, 28 February 1995: 81).

Part of an eventual Cambodia-Vietnam shelf boundary would provide the northern limit of any Thai-Vietnamese boundary line. Thai officials have observed that an EEZ claim by the new Cambodian government could complicate a Thai-Vietnamese agreement.

Malaysia-Thailand-Vietnam

A small area (about 880 sq km) of overlap exists between Vietnam's continental shelf claim and the northeastern edge of the Malaysia-Thailand joint development area. The status of Vietnam's claim with respect to the joint area is uncertain.

Joint Development Agreements

There are many joint offshore oil and gas development agreements, which have had differing levels of success. The 1982 UN Convention specifically calls for provisional arrangements pending boundary delimitations for the continental shelf and the EEZ but gives no further guidance (United Nations, 1982, Articles 74 and 83). Joint zones have been used in the Persian Gulf since 1958. Commentators suggest that factors favouring a joint zone solution include the adaptability of the resource to joint management, the potential for a cooperative relationship between the parties, and their willingness to balance control and share technology. On the other hand, if the parties are sensitive to security in the area, have incompatible political relations or dependent economic ties, or are reluctant to share technology, then joint arrangements are less likely (Jagota, 1993: 117).

Two joint development agreements are in force in the Gulf of Thailand area; the 1979 Malaysia-Thailand agreement and the 1993 Malaysia-Vietnam accord. These differ in their institutional arrangements and in the amount of time elapsed before implementation. The Malaysia-Thailand model established a joint development inter-governmental authority and extensive legislative framework. The Malaysia-Vietnam model resembles some arrangements in the Persian Gulf, where one country negotiates the contract with an oil firm and the other country simply obtains a share of the proceeds. The Malaysia-Thailand agreement took 14 years to complete; the Malaysia-Vietnam arrangement appears to have been negotiated in two years.

Malaysia-Thailand

In 1979 Malaysia and Thailand signed a series of agreements that delimited their territorial sea boundary and the nearshore segments of their continental shelf boundary, and established a Joint Authority for the disputed 7,250 sq km continental shelf area. The memorandum of understanding on the joint development area (JDA) was ratified the same year. The boundary delimitation agreements entered into force in 1982.

It took 13 years to implement the memorandum of understanding. Major issues included reconciling Malaysia's production-sharing system with Thailand's concession system and agreeing on the legal framework for the Authority. In 1991 a supplemental agreement on the constitution of the Malaysia-Thailand Joint Authority was made, and implementing legislation was promulgated by both countries (Kurujit & Premrutai, 1992; Jagota, 1993: 122–23; *Boundary and Security Bulletin*, July 1993: 39). The Authority administers three production-sharing contract blocks. The Malaysian and Thai governments will divide a 10 percent royalty (Kurujit & Premrutai, 1992; FEER, 21 April 1994: 80). Triton Energy reported the discovery of several gas finds in the JDA during 1996 (*Offshore*, January 1996: 11; *Reuters*, 5 June 1996).

Malaysia-Vietnam

A sliver of area (about 1,000 sq km) southeast of the Malaysia-Thailand JDA is contested by Malaysia and Vietnam. In November 1991 Vietnam protested to Malaysia over operations by a Hamilton Oil-led group of foreign oil companies in the area (*Offshore*, September 1993: 81). On 4 June 1993 the two countries exchanged diplomatic notes, establishing a 40-year agreement to exploit the disputed area jointly.

Although the text of the agreement is not available, it appears to resemble a commercial arrangement. The national oil companies, Petronas and PetroVietnam, will work out a plan and share costs and profits. The foreign group is expected to continue work in the area under the Malaysian contract. Apparently Malaysia and Vietnam will split the revenue from the existing production-sharing contract. There is no joint government authority, just a joint committee of Petronas and PetroVietnam (*Straits Times*, 5 June 1993; FBIS, 8 June 1993: 31).

Recent Developments

In its negotiations with both Cambodia and Vietnam, Thailand has pressed for a formal boundary and resisted the joint development option. In early January 1995 Maersk Oil Thailand reported finding better-than-expected deposits of crude, natural gas and condensate in the Sunflower Field (FBIS, 6 January 1995: 76). In May 1996 Enterprise hit some gas off Cambodia in Block One, but the wildcat was plugged and abandoned because of the apparent small size of the deposit (*Reuters*, 30 May 1996; *Offshore*, July 1996: 20). Unocal and BHP, among others, expressed interest in the Cambodia-Thailand overlapping area (*Reuters*, 8 May 1996). Triton Energy spent $52 million to develop its prospects in the Gulf during 1996 (*Reuters*, 28 January 1997). Statoil and Unocal found a prospective gas deposit in Thailand's Block B10/32 during March 1997 (*Reuters*, 13 March 1996). Promising finds in the Gulf were counterbalanced by disappointment off Vietnam's South China Sea coast (*Reuters*, 28 June, 20 May and 14 March 1996; FBIS, 7 March 1996).

Cambodia-Thailand Negotiations

In 1992 Cambodian Ministry of Industry officials and Thai petroleum representatives reportedly agreed in principle to resolve the dispute. The Thai modification of its straight baseline in 1992 may have been a gambit to offset the Cambodian and Vietnamese baselines in anticipated negotiations. Cambodia expressed interest in a joint technical and economic agreement modelled on the Malaysia-Thailand agreement (*Business Times*, 7 October 1992).

Discoveries of oil and gas near the disputed area during 1994 appeared to accelerate interest in resolving the dispute (*Offshore*, March 1994: 13; June 1994: 14). In February Pou Sothirak, Cambodian Minister of Industry, Mines and Energy, stated that Cambodia wanted a joint development area and "was prepared to take 50 percent of the proceeds of future discoveries in the disputed [Pattani] trench" (Quiambao, 1995). This suggests a joint arrangement similar to the Malaysia-Vietnam model. Thailand invited Cambodia to begin talks at the end of April 1995. They held their first technical working group meeting in July 1995, but in October Thailand proposed a fixed boundary and indicated that negotiations for a joint development agreement would take a long time (*Reuters*, 24 March 1995; FBIS, 4 October 1995).

During 1996 Cambodia appeared to grow more desperate for a resolution. Before an April visit to Thailand, Foreign Minister Ing Huot endorsed joint development as a solution and said that "Cambodia hopes the overlapping boundaries with Thailand could be resolved rapidly, at least not take the 14 years it took Thailand and Malaysia to resolve their problem" (FBIS, 2 April 1996). In June the Cambodian media reported that the visiting Thai Prime Minister had agreed to joint development of the disputed area using the Malaysia-Thailand model (FBIS, 19 and 22 June 1996).

Reports of Thai exploration drilling in the contested area were discounted by Cambodia's Pou Sothirak during March 1997, but he called for an agreement to permit foreign companies to begin survey work (FBIS, 12 March 1997). The overlapping claims were on the agenda during Thai Prime Minister Chavalit's visit to Cambodia in June (*Bangkok Post*, 28 May 1997; *The Nation*, 17 March 1997). The coup by Jun Sen during July 1997 will delay resolution of Cambodia's maritime boundaries. Presumably Cambodia's new paramount leader would like to regularize relations with Thailand; but at what price?

Thailand-Vietnam Negotiations

Early in 1995 Vietnam apparently abandoned joint development and accepted the Thai proposal for a fixed boundary. Despite repeated clashes over fishing, the sides agreed in September 1995 to use Vietnam's Tho Chu islands as a basepoint for determining a boundary (FBIS, 6 September 1995; *Reuters*, 4 September 1995). Discussion of using a particular island and comments about it being populated suggest that the two sides are not relying on their respective straight baselines. Rather, they seem to be referring to Article 121 of the 1982 UN Convention on the Law of the Sea, which provides that inhabited islands have continental shelves and EEZs.

When the sides held a sixth round of negotiations in December 1995, there were rumours that a draft agreement combined a partial boundary with a joint development zone. Reports following the seventh round, in April, continued to suggest that Thailand and Vietnam were close to resolving their overlapping claims, but the two sides scheduled the next session for December—a seven-month pause suggesting that there might be problems. When asked about the dispute in Hanoi on 18 April, the Thai Foreign Minister gave an equivocal answer (*Reuters*, 11 January 1996; *The Nation*, 27 April 1996: A2; FBIS, 19 April 1996). During October a Vietnamese attack on Thai fishing trawlers prompted calls for joint patrols of the overlapping zone (FBIS, 11 and 17 October 1996).

The maritime dispute figured in talks during Prime Minister Chavalit's visit to Vietnam in March 1997 (FBIS, 15, 19 and 31 March 1997; *The Nation*, 26 March 1997). In late April, a Vietnamese Defense Ministry team visited Thailand to discuss joint patrols for their overlapping claims (FBIS, 26 April 1997). On 28 July a Thai Foreign Ministry official said that a draft maritime boundary agreement had been reached with Vietnam. Although he gave few specifics, the accord reportedly includes provisions dealing with transboundary deposits and dispute settlement (*The Nation*, 28 July 1997).

Cambodia-Vietnam Negotiations

The offshore dispute between Cambodia and Vietnam was overshadowed by tensions along their land frontier. On 17 January 1996 Cambodia's First Prime Minister alleged two border incursions by Vietnamese forces (UPI, 17 and 30 January 1996; *Reuters*, 18 January 1996; *Boundary and Security Bulletin*, Spring 1996: 37–38). It was not until April that the issue was defused and the two countries agreed to handle the problem at a lower level (*Reuters*, 10 April 1996; FBIS, 15 May 1996). No negotiations have been reported on the unresolved maritime boundary, but in January 1997 a Vietnamese publication complained about continuing piracy and smuggling in the joint historic waters zone (FBIS, 1 January 1997). The change in government in Phnom Penh is likely to retard resolution of Cambodia's land and maritime disputes with Vietnam.

Prognosis

> International law does not require that maritime boundaries be delimited in accordance with any particular method; rather, it requires that they be delimited in accordance with equitable principles, taking into account all of the relevant circumstances of the case so as to produce an equitable result. The equitable principles are indeterminate and the relevant circumstances are theoretically unlimited. (Charney, 1994: 230.)

The resolution of maritime boundary disputes may be couched in legal terms but it is ultimately a political process. Despite a decade of international negotiations, the 320 Articles of the 1982 UN Convention on the Law of the Sea give little guidance on resolving boundary disputes and exclude them from binding dispute-settlement provisions (United Nations, 1982, Articles 298 and 299). The Articles dealing with delimitation of the continental shelf or EEZ both call for agreement on the basis of international law and make reference to the statute of the International Court of Justice (ICJ). The ICJ statute calls for settlement on the basis of equitable principles (which are not well defined).

Other conventions, court decisions and bilateral boundary agreements provide many principles and methods: equidistance, natural prolongation, geologic structure, coastal fronts, historic usage, perpendiculars to the general direction of the coast, etc. However, "coastal geometry is preponderant in maritime boundary delimitation law" (Charney, 1994: 253). Often countries come to agreements on the basis of political and economic considerations, then justify themselves on legal grounds. Some agreements contain only vague references to international legal principles or the United Nations charter. There is no way to examine a maritime boundary dispute and predict the exact form of an eventual settlement.

The only likely avenue for settling outstanding jurisdictional disputes in the Gulf of Thailand is through negotiation. It seems unlikely that Southeast Asian countries, especially Thailand, would go to the ICJ (Englefield, 1994: 36–37). On 15 June 1962 the ICJ decided in favour of Cambodia in a case it had brought against Thailand over a territorial dispute (International Court of Justice, 1962; Whiteman, 1965, 3: 648–61); since Thailand lost so decisively, it is unlikely to submit a maritime boundary dispute to adjudication by the ICJ or another body.

If Cambodia and Thailand delimit a full maritime boundary (continental shelf and/or EEZ), it is unlikely that Thailand could maintain strict proportionality. Cambodia would likely abandon its questionable shelf claim in the north and seek to gain area in the Pattani Trough region. All of the claimants, including Vietnam, are likely to settle on some version of a median line. It is not possible to estimate all the possible modifications to such a line.

Continental shelf and EEZ claims are subject to change.[7] Until there are agreed maritime boundaries, the extent of national jurisdiction and areas of overlap will be uncertain. However, the Gulf of Thailand is an area ripe for exploitation and the countries that border it seem willing to negotiate on an equitable basis. In this regard, it holds more promise than other parts of the South China Sea.

Notes

1. In order to ensure comparability, all the coastline length and area measurements for this study were made by the author from "Southeast Asia: Gulf of Thailand," U.S. Defense Mapping Agency chart No. 93010, 5th edn. (3 July 1993), scale 1:1,000,000. Length and area measurements differ among published sources. This area (289,013 sq km) is consistent with the value of 85,521 sq nm (293,521 sq km) found in Morgan & Valencia, 1983: 4.

2. Part of the Malaysia-Thailand zone (1,380 sq km) extends outside of the Gulf.

3. The Thai 1970 claim is found in U.S. Department of State, Office of the Geographer (Geographer, 1971). The modification of the Andaman Sea baseline (Area 3) is found in "Announcement of the Office of the Prime Minister Concerning the Straight Baselines and Internal Waters of Thailand," which promulgated a Cabinet decision of 11 August 1992, *Official Gazette*, Vol. 110, chap. 18 (18 February 1993), reprinted in United Nations, 1993: 29.

4. Sweden and Finland link their baselines on a line joining two islets (Prescott, 1985: 278; Whiteman, 1965, 4: 184–85). Ecuador's baseline terminates on the Ecuador-Peru maritime boundary; Argentina and Uruguay share a closing line across the mouth of the Rio de la Plata (Roach & Smith, 1994: 73).

5. The southern section of the former claim overlapped a large portion of Vietnam's shelf claim. That previous claim line extended 190 km southeast of the current line to 7°34'N, 103°21'E.

6. In 1939 French Governor-General Brevie of Indo-China settled a sovereignty dispute between Cambodia and Cochin China over islands in the Gulf of Thailand by drawing a line with an azimuth of 126° counter-clockwise from the north meridian (i.e., a 234° bearing) from the coastal terminus of their land boundary.

7. While Canada and the U.S. were preparing their cases for the World Court over the Gulf of Maine boundary, they each revised their claims in the area.

Bibliography

Birnie, P. (1987) "Delimitation of Maritime Boundaries: Emergent Legal Principles and Problems" in Blake, G. (ed.) *Maritime Boundaries and Ocean Resources*, London: Croom Helm: 15–37.

Charney, J. I. (1989) "The Delimitation of Ocean Boundaries" in Dallmeyer, D. G. & DeVorsey, L., Jr. (eds.) *Rights to Oceanic Resources*, Dordrecht: Martinus Nijhoff: 25–49.

Charney, J. I. (1994) "Progress in International Maritime Boundary Delimitation Law," *American Journal of International Law* 88: 227–56.

Dzurek, D. J. (1985) "Boundary and Resource Disputes in the South China Sea," *Ocean Yearbook* 5: 254–84.

Englefield, G. (1994) *Boundary and Security Bulletin* 2, July: 36–38.

Geographer, Office of the, (1966) *Cambodia-Thailand Boundary, International Boundary Study*, No. 40 (revised), Washington, DC: U.S. Department of State.

Geographer, Office of the, (1971) "Straight Baselines: Thailand," *Limits in the Seas*, No. 31, Washington, DC: U.S. Department of State.

Geographer, Office of the, (1983) "Straight Baselines: Vietnam," *Limits in the Seas*, No. 99, Washington, DC: U.S. Department of State.

Germany (1994), Note verbale dated 23 December 1994 from the German Embassy in Bangkok addressed to the Ministry of Foreign Affairs of Thailand, reprinted in (1995) "Division for Ocean Affairs and the Law of the Sea," *Law of the Sea Bulletin*, No. 28, New York: United Nations: 31.

Huynh Minh Chinh (1992) "Thu Chinh Bank Is on Vietnam's Continental Shelf," *Vietnam Courier* (Hanoi), No. 34, August.

International Court of Justice (1962), Case Concerning the Temple of Preah Vihear (Cambodia v. Thailand), Judgment (Merits), 15 June 1962, International Court of Justice Reports.

Jagota, S. P. (1993) "Maritime Boundary and Joint Development Zones: Emerging Trends," *Ocean Yearbook* 10: 110–31.

Malaysia (1979), Director of National Mapping, map entitled *Sempadan Pelantar Behua Malaysia* [Continental Shelf boundaries of Malaysia], 2 sheets.

Morgan, J. R. & Valencia, M. J. (eds.) (1983) *Atlas for Marine Policy in Southeast Asian Seas*, Berkeley: University of California Press.

Nakornthap, K. & Vinaiphat, P. (1992) "Malaysia-Thailand Joint Development Area," paper presented to the National Conference on Geologic Resources of Thailand, 17–24 November 1992, Bangkok.

Praing, Ith. (1992) "Status of Oil and Gas Exploration in Cambodia," paper presented to the 19th Offshore South East Asia Conference, 1–4 December, Singapore.

Prescott, J. R. V. & Morgan, J. R. (1983) "Maritime Jurisdictions and Boundaries" in Morgan, J. R. & Valencia, M. J. (eds.) *Atlas for Marine Policy in Southeast Asian Seas*, Berkeley: University of California Press, 40–55.

Prescott, J. R. V. (1985) *The Maritime Political Boundaries of the World*, London: Methuen.

Quiambao, C. (1995) *Journal of Commerce*, 16 February.

République Khmère (1972) Ordonne No. 439–72/PRK, 1 July.

Roach, J. A. S. & Smith, R. W. (1994) "Excessive Maritime Claims," *International Law Studies*, Vol. 66, Newport, RI: U.S. Naval War College.

Singapore (1986) Permanent Mission of the Republic of Singapore to the United Nations, "Note Dated 5 December 1986" in United Nations, Office for Ocean Affairs and the Law of the Sea, "The Law of the Sea: Current Developments in State Practice," No. II, New York: 1989: 84–85.

Thailand (1959) Declaration of the Office of the Prime Minister concerning the Inner Part of the Gulf of Thailand, 22 September 1959, *Official Gazette*, Vol. 76, chap. 91, Special Supplement, 26 September B.E. 2502 (translated in Chalermpon Ake-uru, "Thailand and the Law of the Sea," Annex 2, paper presented at the International Conference on East Asia and the Law of the Sea, Kyungnam University, Seoul, Korea, 3–6 July 1984).

Thailand (1985) Statement Dated 22 November 1985 by the Ministry of Foreign Affairs of Thailand, United Nations General Assembly doc. A/40/1033, 12 December 1985: 2–3.

Thailand (1992) "Announcement of the Office of the Prime Minister Concerning Straight Baselines and Internal Waters of Thailand," 17 August 1992, *Official Gazette*, Vol. 109, chap. 89 (19 August 1992), reprinted in *Law of the Sea Bulletin*, No. 25 (June 1994): 82–83.

United Nations (1982) United Nations Convention on the Law of the Sea, UN pub. No. E.83.V.5., New York.

United Nations (1993) "Division for Ocean Affairs and the Law of the Sea," *Law of the Sea Bulletin*, No. 23, June.

UPI (1996) United Press International, 17 and 30 January.

Valencia, M. J. (1985) "Oil and Gas Potential, Overlapping Claims, and Political Relations" in Kent, G. and Valencia, M. J. (eds.) *Marine Policy in Southeast Asia*, Berkeley: University of California Press, 155–87.

Whiteman, M. (1965) *Digest of International Law*, Washington, DC: U.S. Department of State.

Other Sources

Bangkok Post, Bangkok.

Boundary and Security Bulletin, Durham, UK: International Boundaries Research Unit, University of Durham.

Business Times, Singapore.

Far Eastern Economic Review (FEER), Hong Kong.

FBIS (Foreign Broadcast Information Agency), Daily Report: East Asia (unless otherwise indicated), Washington DC: United States, National Technical Information Service.

Offshore, Houston, USA.

Reuters.

Straits Times, Singapore.

The Nation, Bangkok.

19

New Borders

The Sea and Outer Space

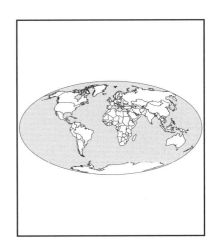

Malcolm Anderson

In this last selection, the author notes that borders—or frontiers, as he calls them—have changed dramatically over time. Innovations in modern communications have rendered many of their functions obsolete; national borders are no longer barriers to the entry of radio and television signals or the Internet. The most recent example of boundary making is in outer space. States attempt to extend their reach to uninhabited areas in order to gain benefits, establish rights, and prevent other states from staking claims there, always with the hope of some future strategic advantage.

Malcolm Anderson is professor emeritus of political science at the University of Edinburgh and former Senior Fellow in the Centre of European Policy Studies in Brussels. In recent years he has specialized in justice and home affairs in cooperation with the European Union. Among his publications in this field (with J. Apap) is Striking a Balance between Freedom, Security and Justice in an Enlarged European Union *(Brussels, 2002).*

Introduction

The general role of frontiers in contemporary political life is seldom explicitly analyzed by political scientists. This is partly because boundary effects on the behavior and values of the populations enclosed by them are almost impossible to assess, let alone measure. Indeed, attempts to measure them

From Malcolm Anderson, "The Political Science of Frontiers" in *Borders and Border Regions in Europe and North America*, ed. Paul Ganster, et al. (San Diego: Institute for Regional Studies of the Califomias and San Diego State University Press, 1997), 27–45.

seem shallow and produce obvious results which derive directly from the assumptions on which they are based.[1] More significantly, there are basic differences of view about frontiers in the historical and political science literature that are seldom made explicit.

Some historians and political scientists regard the characteristics and functions of frontiers and borders as dependent on the internal organization of societies, and the way in which political power is exercised in the core regions of states. Debates between realist, pluralist, Marxist, and interdependence theorists in international relations arise out of different views about the nature of the state; frontiers are regarded as epiphenomena whose role and function are dependent on the core characteristics of the state. For others (including most political geographers), the characteristics of the frontier are fundamental influences on the way a society develops and on the political options open to it. The vast literature specifically on frontiers—the historical classics of Turner and Prescott Webb, geographical treatises, borderland studies, and a very diverse literature on border disputes—gives little guidance for the examination of the great changes now occurring as states are easing frontier controls or finding that they cannot use frontier controls to police and control their territory.

Definition of the International Frontier

Any attempt at a general political analysis of frontiers must have a clear point of departure. The starting point here is that frontiers can be analyzed (and, in normative political theory, criticized) in the same way as other political institutions and processes. Frontiers are not simply lines on maps, the unproblematic givens of political life, where one jurisdiction ends and another begins. In the contemporary world, frontiers between states may be regarded as important institutions and processes. As institutions, they are established by political decisions and regulated by legal texts. The frontier is the *basic* political institution: no rule-bound economic, social, or political life in advanced societies could be organized without them. This primordial character of frontiers is embodied in public international law by the 1978 Vienna Convention on State Succession. When a state collapses, the agreements concerning its frontiers remain in force; frontiers are therefore regarded as prior to the reconstitution of a state and are recognized to be a prerequisite of this reconstitution. Also, frontiers and borders define, in a legal sense, the identity of individuals because the conditions for claims to nationality and exercise of rights of citizenship are delimited by them.

Within its frontiers the state is a sovereign jurisdiction, and the Weberian doctrine of the monopoly of the legitimate use of force on its territory is still almost universally recognized. The doctrine of sovereignty remains a central part of thinking about states and relations among them. The doctrine implies that states have absolute control over their territories and can impose this control at their frontiers. The claim of the modern state to be "the sole, exclusive fount of all powers and prerogatives of rule" (Poggi 1978: 92) could only be realized if its frontiers were made impermeable to unwanted external influences. But this view of the frontier of the sovereign state is not part of an immutable, natural order. Different conceptions of the frontier as an institution existed before the modern sovereign state, and other kinds will emerge after its demise. In this regard, there are now signs of seismic political change.

Frontiers are part of political processes with four defining dimensions. First, frontiers are instruments of state policy because governments attempt to change, to their own advantage, the location or the functions of frontiers. Although there is no simple relationship between frontiers and inequalities of wealth and power, government policy on frontiers is intended to protect and to promote interests. Second, the policies and practices of the state are constrained by the degree of *de facto* control that the government exercises over the state frontier. The incapacity of governments in the contemporary world to control much of the traffic of persons, goods, and information across their frontiers is changing the nature of both states and frontiers. Third, frontiers are basic markers of identity, in the twentieth century usually national identity, but political identities may be larger or smaller than the nation-state. Frontiers, in this sense, are part of political beliefs and myths about the unity of the people, and sometimes myths about the natural unity of the territory. These "imagined communities," to use Benedict Andersen's (1991) phrase concerning nations, are now a universal phenomenon and often have profound historical roots. They are linked to the most powerful form of ideological bonding in the modern world—nationalism. Imagined communities may transcend the confines of the state, and myths of regional, continental, and hemispheric unity have also marked boundaries between friend and foe (Connor 1969). But *myths* of unity can be created or transformed with remarkable rapidity during wars, revolutions, and political upheavals.

Lastly, frontier is a term of discourse. Meanings are given both to frontiers in general and to particular frontiers, and these meanings change from time to time. Frontier is a term of discourse in law, diplomacy, and politics, and its meaning varies depending on the context in which it is used. In the scholarly languages of anthropology, economics, history, political science, public international law, and sociology, it has different meanings according to the theoretical approach used. Sometimes scholarship is the servant of political power when frontiers are in dispute,[2] while at other times, it is part of the scarcely heard disquisition of the classroom. People who live in frontier regions, or those whose daily life is directly affected by frontiers as obstacles to communication and contact, have a richer form of discourse. For them, the term frontier is associated with the (often irksome) rules imposed by frontiers as institutions, and is also suffused with popular symbolism based on how the frontier is perceived, as either barrier or junction (Strassoldo 1970). The layers of discourse—political, scholarly, popular—always overlap but never coincide. Divergent mental images of frontiers are an integral part of frontiers as processes.

What frontiers are, and what they represent, is constantly reconstituted by human beings who are regulated, influenced, and limited by them. But these reconstructions are influenced by political change and the often unpredictable outcome of great conflicts, against a background of technological change. The military technology developed in the closing stages of the Second World War altered the strategic significance of control of territory; the military independence of many sovereign states was drastically reduced, and the frontiers of these states became indefensible. Now, with instantaneous communication of information, *information sovereignty* has been lost; the development of mass, rapid, and inexpensive systems of transport has resulted in all developed countries, and frontier crossings by individuals annually number more than the total population. New territorial questions have consequently emerged on the political agenda.

New Frontiers

The most interesting questions—because they put frontier disputes into a radically different perspective—concern boundary-making, and the related attempt to establish international regimes, in uninhabited spaces. The thinking about these spaces has the potential to effect major revisions in concepts and perceptions of the frontiers between states. Uninhabited spaces, and the activities that take place in them, are having effects upon the politics of territory and on thinking about frontiers in inhabited regions.

Clearly, some empty spaces are so vast and so inhospitable that no serious attempt has been made to establish sovereignty rights within them. But boundaries are drawn in some spaces that are not normally inhabited or are occupied only on a temporary basis. Consequently, conflicts arise about many uninhabited zones. The large number of international treaties, conventions, understandings, and case law concerning them indicate serious potential for conflict as states attempt to establish various kinds of positions in them. Empty spaces are an increasingly important domain of public international law. International regimes are sometimes considered necessary because spaces that belong to no one or for which no one feels responsible offer temptations to plunder, exploit, or misuse, without regard to the interests of others or to the longer-term consequences of activities.

The public international law developed for empty space departs from the traditional focus of acquisition of territory and conflicts over frontiers. New concepts have been developed. Some derive from ordinary language, such as "the common heritage of mankind"; others have analogies with the concepts of private-law notions of property rather than with territorial dominion implied by the doctrine of sovereignty. According to one influential view, private property is a complex bundle of relationships between people involving rights, duties, and obligations (Honoré 1961). This may also describe the legal regime for uninhabited spaces in that much of it (the major exception is airspace where absolute "territorial" sovereignty has generally prevailed) concerns rights, duties, and obligations established between states rather than absolute territorial dominion.

Unfortunately, this observation does not go very far in the quest for understanding boundaries in uninhabited spaces and the ways in which they may be similar or dissimilar to the frontiers between human groups. As Jeremy Waldron (1988: 28) has written about private property, "If that were all, there would be no problem about definition if [the bundle of rights] remained constant; for all or most cases that we want to describe as private property, the bundle as a whole could be defined by its contents. The problem is, of course, it does not remain constant, and that is where the difficulties begin." This is *a fortiori* true of the regime for uninhabited spaces. The regime for each category of empty space is specific to it. No regime, with the exception of aspects of maritime law, remains stable for long periods. Although concepts associated with environmental protection are forming a link between them, no rights and obligations common to all uninhabited spaces are even hypothetically suggested. However, the argument here is that states attempt, as far as they are able, to acquire property rights in order to facilitate exploitation or use of the resources of these spaces. Mutual recognition of other states' rights is often, although by no means always, necessary to achieve this end.

Categories of Empty Spaces

Boundary questions concerning uninhabited land, seas and oceans, airspace, and outer space have therefore the potential to transform perceptions and rules concerning frontiers between states. From the eighteenth to the twentieth centuries, land areas regarded as uninhabited gradually diminished in number and importance. Claims to territory based on discovery (and even effective occupation) have disappeared. The Empty Quarter of Arabia, the great deserts of Africa, Asia, Australia, and the smaller deserts of North and South America are now regarded as under the effective occupation and control of states. Even the vast, sparsely populated Arctic tundra, with its scattering of perhaps forty indigenous peoples across Europe, Asia, and North America, who are now often outnumbered locally by colonizers from the south, is under the effective sovereign control of the states (Malaurie 1992). The single great wilderness remaining is Antarctica, where no claim to state sovereignty is yet recognized by the international community. Instead, an unusual treaty regime, based on a compromise between claimants and other interested parties, has regulated the territory's use; increasingly, its stability is in question.

The Antarctic continent, like oceans, seas, and estuaries, is uninhabited in the conventional meaning of the term—all inhabitants are temporary residents. A few hundred people stay in the various scientific stations throughout the winter. In the summer months, several thousand arrive, supplemented by a few tourists. The international interest in Antarctica has been the belief that it contains mineral reserves of very considerable value;[3] it is also a focus of scientific interest as the last great wilderness and a unique natural environment, rich in research possibilities. Among the many factors that will determine whether or not Antarctica is exploited are discovery of new resources elsewhere, commodity prices, technological progress, and the political regime agreed for the continent.[4]

The remoteness and the inhospitable nature of the climate and the terrain of the continent make the traditional bases of claims to territory—discovery, occupation, historical rights, proximity, and geographical contiguity—in international law virtually inapplicable. A situation has arisen in which "Antarctica is unique—an entire continent of disputed territory" (Auburn 1982). No established rules of international law exist that allow states to successfully uphold claims to sovereignty in it.[5] Seven states have formal claims to territory (Argentina, Australia, Chile, France, New Zealand, Norway, and the United Kingdom), with about one-sixth of the continent remaining unclaimed. With the exception of Norway, no state has considered unilaterally renouncing its claim. States with an interest in Antarctica scrupulously avoid any action that might implicitly involve the recognition of the claims of others. This evasion of the issue of sovereignty was a second-best solution for claimant states. As Peterson writes, "The compromise on sovereignty, forming the basis of the Antarctic regime, was not the first choice of most participants. The claimants would have preferred acceptance of their claims" (Peterson 1988).

The 1959 Antarctic Treaty System (ATS) was signed by 12 states, including the USSR and the United States, as well as those with territorial claims.[6] The 13 original consultative parties were subsequently joined by other states as participants or observers until, by 1991, a total of 41 states were associated with the system. The signatory states all had active scientific programs in Antarctica and accepted responsibility for the continent. They reached no conclusion about the basis of territorial sovereignty in the continent, but they specifically excluded the presence of military bases and military forces. Flowing from this basic treaty, four other agreements have been negotiated—Agreed Measures for the Conservation of Antarctic Flora and Fauna (1964), Convention for the Protection of Antarctic Seals (1972), Convention for the

Conservation of Antarctic Marine Living Resources (1980), and the Protocol on Environmental Protection (1990).

Difficulties arose over the agreement for a conditional ban on exploitation of resources, reached in the 1988 Convention for the Regulation of Antarctic Mineral Resources Activities (CRAMRA). Australia and France refused to ratify it, instead jointly proposing an international natural park, preserved in perpetuity. The idea of the Antarctic as the common heritage of mankind goes back to the 1950s, and was championed by the World Conference on National Parks in 1972 and by Greenpeace (using the phrase "global commons"). The increasing national and international importance of the ecological movement was a cause of tension in the ATS. France and Australia jointly proposed the negotiation of a comprehensive environmental-protection convention. Nongovernmental organizations and vocal Third World countries at the UN alleged that the ATS was a secretive club. Signatories to environmental protection agreements have been accused of ignoring their spirit, and some of them were suspected of preparing the ground for exploitation of mineral deposits (Charney 1982).

Traditional international law does not provide any precedents that could help to design a regime for the continent. There is general agreement among its members that the ATS should be improved, but there is little prospect of a new regime until a new factor emerges (such as a rogue state engaging in mining). The continuation of the present regime remains the second-best choice of most states and the majority of all interested parties, but it can only be replaced by another international regime and not by a reversion to the principle of territorial sovereignty.

Parallel developments have been taking place over oceanic international waters and the deep-sea bed. In the last 30 years the basis for delimiting maritime boundaries has been highly controversial, but it is now agreed on in broad principle.[7] There are many current sea-boundary disputes both because large resources are at stake, because the technical problems of drawing boundaries in coastal waters can be intractable, and because sea boundaries may be part of a series of interlocking disputes between neighboring states. According to one estimate (Johnstone 1989), there are 300 bilateral delimitation issues outstanding, and other estimates put the potential figure even higher. The extension of the territorial rights of states beyond the old three-mile limit and the concept of the Exclusive Economic Zone have been sources of new disputes. These new disputes have sometimes stimulated creative solutions. An agreed delimitation is not the only possibility—joint development or management zones that cross hypothetical boundaries have, in some cases, been adopted.

Although prior to the 1960s there had been attempts to extend territorial waters to protect resources (particularly fisheries), the great impetus for renewed interest in maritime boundaries was the discovery and exploitation of offshore oil and natural gas reserves after 1945. In the United States, off-shore exploitation in the Gulf of Mexico led to the Truman Declaration that expressed a claim to the continental shelf as the natural extension of national territory for the purposes of exploiting resources. The precedent was followed in the Persian Gulf, in the North Sea, and in the Mediterranean where, sometimes with difficulty, the continental shelf was partitioned by the riverine states. The stakes in maritime boundary-drawing are high because their impact could change global balances in the next century if, as seems certain, competition for mineral resources becomes intense.

The legal issues are complex and are subject to fine legal analysis.[8] The third United Nations Conference on the Law of the Sea (UNCLOS III) successfully negotiated the 1982 Convention, which entered into force in November 1994. The Convention established three maritime zones to which states could lay claim—the territorial sea (up to 12 nautical miles), the contiguous zone (another 12 miles), and the Exclusive Economic Zone (200 nautical miles), all distances measured from the low-water mark. In addition, states may, according to the Convention, claim jurisdiction over the continental shelf, which varies in extent and often has to be partitioned between neighboring states. The implications of claims to the continental shelf and to the EEZ vary from one region of the world to another, some of which have been intensively studied.[9] On the deep-sea bed, the less developed countries at the United Nations have taken the view that the rich countries should not exploit sea-bed resources to their own exclusive advantage. The 1982 Convention embodies the principle that the high-sea and the deep-sea beds form part of the common heritage of mankind.

In terms of damage to the marine environment, a particular focus has been on dumping of nuclear waste and other noxious materials. Before the 1980s, most nations that had nuclear-power stations and nuclear weapons routinely dumped at sea. In response to pressure, a convention was signed by the nuclear powers in London in 1983 for a ten-year moratorium on dumping. The facts were, however, hard to establish. There were suspicions, but little evidence, about Russia's dumping activities until 1993. When the countries involved in the 1983 Convention reassembled in London ten years later, Russia revealed extensive and potentially dangerous dumping north of the Arctic Circle and in the Sea of Japan. The making permanent of the ban on dumping showed that the rich countries were prepared to support an international regime for the protection of the high seas, but any agreement is virtually impossible to monitor. Moreover, the problem of dumping at sea is much wider than that of radioactive materials. It also includes the dumping of munitions, dredged material—often heavily contaminated—from rivers and estuaries, and chemical wastes. Although regional attempts have been made to place curbs on these other forms of dumping, they remain a major hazard. The issue, however, has been placed firmly on the international agenda.

Airspace boundaries are normally regarded as coextensive with land boundaries, although there is some technical dispute about exactly what that means. A line drawn vertically from the outer territorial limits of the state, extending to the limits of the atmosphere, has been regarded as within the sovereign jurisdiction of the state. At what altitude airspace ceases is uncertain and has never been defined in an international treaty. The conventional limit is the so-called von Karman line where aerodynamic flight becomes impossible.[10] Sovereignty over airspace, in the twentieth century, has been important for two main reasons. The first is military; any armed intrusion into airspace is regarded with almost the same seriousness as terrestrial intrusions. During times of international tension, approaching and infringing on the airspace of opposing states has been regarded as a method of showing determination to pursue a quarrel. The principle that countries may respond forcibly to intrusions is universally recognized although overreaction, such as the 1983 shooting down of the South Korean airliner in the Soviet Far East, is the subject of considerable international outcry.[11]

The second reason for the importance of sovereignty over airspace is commercial. With the associated, but distinct, right to control landing rights, it has been used as a powerful means of protection of national airlines. The ability to restrict overflying rights and landing rights for foreign airlines has allowed national airlines to benefit from a monopoly rent and to enter into cartel agreements with other national carriers to share lucrative routes. However, three pressures are making inroads into sovereignty over airspace. The first is deregulation of the market for air travel, which has been spreading in the highly industrialized world; the logic of this deregulation is an open-skies policy. The second is concern about atmospheric pollution (part of more general issues of environmental protection discussed below). The third is the technical requirements of air-traffic control in places where airspace became congested across international frontiers.

To illustrate the last of these pressures—all states are bound by air-traffic control arrangements, negotiated through the International Civil Aviation Organization (ICAO), from which they can only withdraw at the cost of damaging their own interests. Even when they disapprove of the principles on which these arrangements are based, state protests are either verbal, or the states temporarily withdraw from the arrangements. The ICAO acts as an arbitrator and does not, in principle, infringe upon state sovereignty. But an agreement for European airspace—Eurocontrol, established in 1961—contained elements of supranationality. Although members of Eurocontrol became dissatisfied and diminished its supranational aspects by a revised convention in 1981, supranational practice is necessary in very busy airspace in order to achieve the necessary coordination of air traffic (Weber 1983). Although the principle of sovereignty over airspace is not denied,[12] the large number of aircraft on international routes has effectively removed, in all but the most unusual circumstances, the options of closing airspace or modifying international air-traffic agreements.

In outer space, five significant agreements have been reached.[13] Issues relating to outer space, with the exceptions of satellite broadcasting and observation satellites, have been pushed down the international political agenda. The real fear in the 1980s, of the progressive militarization of space, was prompted by the development of antisatellite and antimissile technology.[14] According to the 1967 Treaty, although defensive action was permissible,[15] nuclear and other offensive weapons were banned. The Strategic Arms Limitation Agreements (SALT) of 1972 and 1979 and the Anti-Ballistic Missile Treaty of 1972 banned interference by the Soviet Union and the United States with each other's satellites engaged in the monitoring of these agreements. In 1983, the Strategic Defense Initiative (SDI) was launched by President Reagan, who defended this Star Wars initiative as defensive—incoming Soviet missiles would be destroyed by lasers in space. Whether the laser-beam weapons stationed in space function effectively remains an unanswered question, but the United States partially abandoned the program as a result of arms-limitation agreements with the Russians and the virtual disappearance of a direct Russian military threat.

Very difficult problems of outer space, with military implications, remain. The most obvious is development of high-resolution observation satellites for commercial purposes by a French-Belgian-Swedish consortium. In 1986 SPOT 1 (Satellite Pour l'Observation de la Terre) and in 1990 SPOT 2 broke the super-power monopoly on this technology that, although developed for ostensibly civil surveying, became available for military purposes (Krepon et al. 1990). Whether the spread of this technology will affect the stability of the international system is a matter of speculation, but it is certain that more states will be able to see more clearly what is occurring in other states' territory, further eroding the sanctuary provided by territorial sovereignty. Another potentially important issue is the pollution of outer space by the debris of space vehicles, which can endanger the safety of satellites (Reijnen and de Graff, 1989). The responsibility for clean-up costs of debris from satellites that damage private property on reentry to the atmosphere or to another state's territory is a practical legal issue (regulated in principle by the 1972 Convention on International Liability for Damage Caused by Space Objects) and will increase in importance if schemes for hundreds of low-level satellites for multimedia communications come to fruition.

A basic problem of extra-atmospheric space is similar to the problem in Antarctica, although in a very different physical context—how to establish a regime where states exercise rights to conduct non-harmful activities, where territorial sovereignty and boundary making are inappropriate. The 1967 Treaty governing the activities of states in exploration and utilization of extra-atmospheric space, including the moon and other celestial bodies (which by 1990 had been ratified by 92 states), recognized that territorial rivalries could not be transferred from the earth to outer space. Article I, subsection 1 established a new principle, that the exploration and utilization of space was the "province of all mankind," and thus it was made equivalent to the principle adopted by the United Nations Conference on the Law of the Sea, which accepted that the seas were "the common heritage of all mankind," a notion that sharply contrasts with sovereignty.[16] The Bogotá Declaration, contesting this, has been ignored by all states with satellite-launching capabilities.[17]

The 1967 Treaty also affirmed the principle that states bear international responsibility for their activities in outer space. The absence of a doctrine of sovereignty raises interesting legal issues of jurisdiction, civil responsibility, intellectual property rights for technical and scientific discoveries, and copyright.[18] It is difficult to envisage how these problems can be solved to the satisfaction of all without the establishment of a genuine international jurisdiction. Without this, the states that have technological superiority will have an overwhelming practical advantage in any disputes that arise.

Empty Spaces and the Frontiers of States

There are now intrusions across frontiers that have the potential to cause radical change in the way large numbers of people, particularly in the rich countries, perceive the territory of their states and the significance of their frontiers. One has already been discussed—the availability to a significant minority of states (and private corporations) of high-resolution observation satellites makes it impossible for states to hide any major activity, even in remote and inaccessible locations. A second kind of intrusion is transfrontier pollution and the harmful, potentially disastrous effects of some forms of economic activity. A third is the cultural and political impact of international telecommunications, an impact that commenced in a minor way during the First World War and reached its culmination with the introduction of direct satellite broadcasting of television in the late 1980s. Frontiers and sovereign control of territory provide, at best, very limited defenses against the impact of these phenomena.

The protection of the environment has become a major political issue, although scientific knowledge of the environment is still limited and there is no definitive answer yet to the basic question of why the biosphere should be protected. There is, however, agreement that much of the effort of environmental protection must be based on international cooperation. A core difficulty is that any measure of environmental protection inevitably promotes some interests and harms others.[19] The first recognition of a common interest in environmental protection dates from the beginning of the twentieth century

(Lyster 1985). After the Second World War, the United Nations and its specialized agencies took a leading role.[20] The UN was flanked by others—the World Meteorological Organization, the International Maritime Organization, the International Civil Aviation Organization,[21] and the International Atomic Energy Agency. Regional organizations—the Organization for Economic Cooperation and Development,[22] the European Community/Union,[23] the Council of Europe[24]—have given an increasing place to environmental issues in their deliberations and decisions. Nongovernmental organizations, such as the International Union for the Conservation of Nature and Its Resources (established in 1948) and its better known progeny, the International Wildlife Fund (1961), have mobilized nonofficial groups and interests. The Worldwatch Institute, with its widely noticed reports and studies, and, above all, Greenpeace, with its spectacular direct action, have helped to effect changes in international environmental matters. Nongovernmental organizations with international membership and outlook have been influential actors in establishing international environmental regimes.

There are certain key dates and events in the development of international environmental regulation that include a mixture of environmental catastrophes that have popularized certain ideas or concepts. The 1967 wreck of the oil tanker *Torrey Canyon* on the Scilly Isles had great impact because it affected two countries, Britain and France, simultaneously, and because the areas of spillage were tourist destinations and sites of great natural beauty. More than thirty major spills have taken place since the *Torrey Canyon*, but perhaps only the 1989 *Exxon Valdez* spill in the ecologically fragile Alaskan fjords has made a comparably great impact, because of massive U.S. and international media coverage. Another catastrophe, the 1984 explosion of the Union Carbide plant at Bhopal in India, stimulated debate on two major issues—the export of toxic-waste materials and the relocation of dangerous manufacturing processes in countries with minimal environmental regulation.[25] [Another] landmark catastrophe was the explosion in April 1986 of one of the four Soviet (now Ukrainian) nuclear reactors at Chernobyl, 120 kilometers north of Kiev. The catastrophic consequences illustrated dramatically that state frontiers afford no protection against a major incident and that international cooperation of a systematic kind is necessary to control and remedy the consequences. The environmental, financial, and international regulatory consequences of Chernobyl have not yet been fully resolved.

Among influential developments that introduced or popularized concepts are the 1970 UNESCO report *Man and the Biosphere*, the 1972 UN Convention on the Protection of the Global Cultural and Natural Patrimony, and the UN Program for the Environment. These UN initiatives made the idea of the interdependence of environmental issues familiar, which in turn promoted the ideas of the common heritage of mankind and global stewardship.[26] The term "common heritage of mankind" entered common usage in international proposals and legal texts by UNESCO. The new discourse on the environment modified the traditional discourse about frontiers.

Despite all the problems of defining the general objective of environmental protection and of designing internationally enforceable regimes, some progress has been made. International organizations (such as the International Atomic Energy Authority) have assumed responsibilities for research, exchange of information, regulation, control of the application of rules, and even management of natural resources. Institutions and arrangements have been set up at global, regional, subregional, multilateral, and bilateral levels, depending on the nature of the problem. Some problems are truly global, such as the protection of whales and the ozone layer. Others are local, such as the purity of water, which is a matter for cooperation between neighboring states. For example, some relatively old bilateral agreements infringed on the territorial principle, such as the 1944 International Boundary and Water Commission between Mexico and the United States, which gives diplomatic immunity and freedom of movement to officials of both nationalities to inspect water shortage and pollution problems.[27] But when disputes about the trade-off between economic development and environmental protection occur across international frontiers, the disagreements tend to remain unresolved.

The regional level of international organization has assumed a major role in environmental protection, especially in Europe. Between 1967 and 1991, the EC adopted no fewer than eighty directives containing measures of environmental protection directly applicable in the member states. The EU member states of the EC take the collective view that common environmental rules are essential in the construction of a unified market.[28] Regional environmental problems, such as pollution of the Mediterranean,[29] sometimes have to be tackled without the help of a pre-existing regional organization that groups all the interested states. However, the general system of international arrangements for environmental protection is emerging as a real constraint on the exercise of state sovereignty. Influential international nongovernmental organizations and transfrontier political coalitions have been established, which apply pressure on both governments and international organizations. Perceptions of territorial sovereignty are changing because, in environmental matters, states no longer appear to have the right to sanction activities within their frontiers.

International broadcasting is a different kind of intrusion into state territory, but its potential impact on mentalities and cultural identities may be greater than issues of environmental protection. International radio broadcasting has been a powerful instrument for pursuing military, political, and economic objectives during most of the twentieth century (Wasburn 1992). But the Cold War use of radio and the dominance of Western, mainly American, media were in due course subject to vigorous criticism from left-wing critics and from Third World governments. Noam Chomsky (1982) was a late but distinguished critic of the Cold War broadcast propaganda. The influence of the Western media in the poor countries has been variously described as electronic colonialism, cultural domination, and media imperialism.[30] These phrases were invented by left-wing scholars, advancing one form or another of dependency theory. They represented the poorer countries as pawns in the hands of advanced capitalist countries, often held in thrall by their own belief systems that had been deliberately manipulated by Western capitalist interests. Demands were formulated for a new world-information order. Proposals were put forward in the UNESCO Report (1979) of the International Commission for the Study of Communication, which suggested a number of radical ways of reducing Western media dominance. These were almost entirely disregarded.

The appearance of direct television broadcasting by satellite provided potentially an even more powerful instrument of transfrontier influence than radio, particularly in the case of broadcasting services devoted to news and information (CNN is currently the only truly global satellite news service). A specific image of global relations can be projected along with selective factual, linguistic, political, and social propaganda, which, though unlikely to affect decisively the outcome of particular crises, can, through cumulative long-term effects, powerfully influence perceptions of the issues at stake in global competition. The ending of the Cold War does not presage the termination of international conflict over such matters as the environment, access to scarce and valuable resources, economic competition, and movement of people. In the future, control of information and powerful means of communication are likely to be more, rather than less, important.

There have been few attempts to create an international regime for regulating direct television broadcasting. A UN General Assembly resolution of 1982 on principles governing utilization by states of artificial satellites was hostile toward direct television broadcasting, because Third World governments were concerned about the political implications of unrestricted reception of these broadcasts in their territories. This resolution attracted a large majority but was not supported by the industrialized countries that had access or could easily acquire access to the necessary technology. There is little that Third World countries can do to control the effects of direct satellite broadcasting, except for the extreme of banning the discs and aerials necessary for reception of the broadcasts (a step that Iran took in April 1994). Other moves have been limited to Europe and, far from being restrictive, have been concerned about guaranteeing free communication of information, unless it conflicts with views of public morality.[31] The European Community was also concerned about arriving at a common European approach to satellite broadcasting so that it could negotiate as a bloc with the United States and Japan.

Conclusion

International negotiations about uninhabited spaces have become more intensive in the last twenty years; the trend is likely to continue. States attempt to extend their "reach" into empty spaces to gain benefits, to establish rights, and to prevent other states from establishing positions that, at some time in the future, may be to their strategic advantage. Activities in these spaces, made possible by new technologies, have raised fundamental questions about frontiers and sovereignty. However, arrangements have been established that encourage states to cooperate within recognized forums rather than engage in unrestrained competition, even though the medium-term stability of these arrangements is uncertain. Uninhabited spaces have already been the focus of attempts to create global, comprehensive, and enforceable regimes. International regimes, which may be defined as "collective action by states, based on shared principles, norms, rules, and decision-making procedures which constrain the behavior of individual states" (List and Rittberger 1992: 86), are essential to the management of the problems raised. The degree to which decisions are enforced depends on the assimilation of international agreements into the domestic law of states. This varies because of the uneven ratification procedures of states. Progress on creating global regimes is, and will continue to be, one measure of the extent to which sovereign states, in principle having complete dominion over their territories, are constrained by cooperative and regulatory arrangements. Global regimes will make the concept of sovereignty obsolescent and will alter the nature of the international frontier as a political institution. Frontiers will take on some of the character of boundaries between states in a federal system.

In general, the technologies of telecommunications, transportation, surveillance from space, and mineral extraction have altered the significance of the control of territory and of the frontiers between state territories. The ease of crossing frontiers, of communication across frontiers, of establishing transfrontier economic and social relationships, and of utilizing empty spaces in pursuit of interests has altered perceptions of frontiers as effective barriers to human activity. These altered perceptions influence all the political processes that occur at or across frontiers. Developed states are no longer greatly concerned about changing the location of frontiers to their advantage, but they are intensely concerned with the functions of frontiers and the purposes they serve. Since states are now unable to control most transfrontier transactions, a much more complex search for comparative advantage over competitor states has become apparent. Moreover, states are now operating in a changing cultural environment. In cultural terms, frontiers have lost some of their sharp-edged quality. Participation in transfrontier and sometimes global cultures affects political identities and political institutions within states.

An allusion to these themes is sufficient indication of the complexity of frontier processes and that much work remains to be done in the political science of frontiers.

Notes

1. For example, J. R. MacKay (1969). But when statistical analyses of boundary effects are firmly embedded in historical accounts of the development of boundary relations, a much enriched account may result. See Z. Rykiel (1985).
2. The relationship between the Nazi regime and an academic discipline (*Ostforschung*—research on the East) is a chilling example. See M. Burleigh (1988).
3. There have been a number of estimates of doubtful reliability. See J. F. Splettstoesser and G. M. Dreschhoff (1990).
4. See discussions in J. F. Lovering and J. R. V Prescott (1979) and G. D. Triggs (1987); there are also three useful contributions in C. H. Schofield (1994).
5. *Antarctic Treaty System Handbook*, 6th edition, 1989: viii.
6. For the text of the Treaty and all other relevant legal instruments relating to the Antarctic see W. M. Bush (1982–1988).
7. For an excellent up-to-date survey of this complex field see W. C. Gilmore (1994).
8. See especially P. Weil (1989).
9. See, for example, J. P. Craven, J. Schneider, and C. Stimson (1989); more generally see G. H. Blake (1987), F. Earney (1990), and B. Kwiatkowska (1989).
10. J. R. V Prescott (1987); V. Enscalada (1979); P. J. Martin et al. (1977).
11. It was also subject to radically different interpretations. See M. Parenti (1986).
12. The right of overflight of international straits lying within territorial waters, even for military flights, is, however, included in the 1982 Law of the Sea Convention and according to some authorities already was part of customary international law.
13. For the texts of these, see T. L. Zwann (1988); for a review of all the treaties and agreements on outer space or having implications for space travel and exploration see G. H. Reynolds amd R. P. Merges (1989), especially chapters 3–8.
14. There was no treaty ban on antisatellite technology, and it was relatively easy to develop. See J. S. Nye and J. A. Schear (1987).
15. Some, however, argue that the effects of Articles I and IV of the Treaty are to ban all military activity.
16. A. Cocca (1986); N. M. Matte (1987).
17. The 1976 Bogotá Declaration of eight equatorial states (Brazil, Colombia, Congo, Ecuador, Indonesia, Kenya, Uganda, and Zaire) claimed sovereign rights over that part of the geostationary orbit above their territory—the rest, they admitted, was "the common heritage of mankind." They based their claim on two propositions: first, that the 1967 Treaty did not define outer space; second, that they were not provided with the relevant technical knowledge when the 1967 Treaty was being negotiated. A basic weakness of this claim was the difficulty, in practice, of asserting sovereign rights at the altitude of the geostationary orbit (35,800 kilometers). Also the 1969 and 1979 conventions on outer space ban the appropriation of outer space, the moon, and other celestial bodies.

18. For a review of these, see P. M. Martin (1992).

19. However, Ambassador R. E. Benedict argues strongly the case for some states proceeding more quickly than others in environmental standards in order to raise the standards of global stewardship; Benedick (1991).

20. See P. S. Thacher (1991). This collection is a basic source on the philosophical, legal, political, and institutional issues of international environmental protection.

21. Ships and aircraft have been regarded as major international polluters and, as a consequence, the IMO has adopted rules (exceptionally difficult to enforce) against cleaning out of bilges, and the ICAO has made rules against noise and gas emissions.

22. In 1970, the OECD established a committee for the environment that produced a series of studies, declarations of principle, and recommendations, particularly *Problems of Transfrontier Pollution* (1974), *Legal Aspects of Transfrontier Pollution* (1976), and *OECD and the Environment* (1978).

23. The EC has played the most important role in terms of enforceable directives that apply to its member states. Its first major project was the First Action Program on the Environment (1974–1976).

24. Notably, the 1968 European Convention for Water, the 1972 European Convention for Soils, and the 1970 Declaration on the Environment.

25. For examples of both on the U.S.-Mexican border see C. R. Bath (1992).

26. These ideas were an essential intellectual basis for the banning of CFC [chlorofluorocarbon] gases by the 1985 Vienna Convention for the Protection of the Ozone Layer, the 1987 Montreal Protocol, and the 1990 London Revisions of the Montreal Protocol.

27. S. Weintraub (1990). In February 1992, after much criticism of the often U.S.-generated pollution of the Mexican frontier region, the two countries adopted an action plan for the environment of the Mexican-U.S. border region. This plan, although lacking adequate financial support, is a model of flexible cooperation.

28. The interconnection of environmental and economic matters goes back to the origins of the ecologist movement from the protagonists of zero growth in the early 1970s (Dennis Meadows and his associates at MIT), the Club of Rome, and the Greenpeace movement. The phasing out of the use of CFC was explicit in international agreements such as the 1987 Montreal Protocol, and in influential reports such as the 1987 Bruntland Report. However, it is only in the context of the EC that there is a direct link between environmental and economic regulation.

29. See P. M. Haas (1990).

30. See, for example, T. L. McPhail (1981).

31. Where stations are broadcasting pornography for profit by selling decoders, it is possible to ban the marketing of these devices. The station Red Hot Dutch had its revenues withheld in this way by a British government decision in 1993.

References

Anderson, B. 1991. *Imagined Communities: An Enquiry into the Origins and Spread of Nationalism* (revised edition). New York: Verso.

Antarctic Treaty System Handbook. 6th edition. 1989. Cambridge, UK: Polar Publication.

Auburn, F. M. 1982. *Antarctic Law and Politics.* London: Hurst.

Bath, C. R. 1992. "The Emerging Environmental Crisis along the United States-Mexico Boundary." In *The Changing Boundaries in the Americas: New*

Perspectives on the U.S.-Mexican, Central American, and South American Borders, Lawrence A. Herzog, ed. San Diego: Center for U.S.-Mexican Studies, University of California at San Diego.

Benedick, R. E. 1991. *Ozone Diplomacy: New Directions in Safeguarding the Planet.* Cambridge: Harvard University Press.

Blake, G. H., ed. 1987. *Maritime Boundaries and Ocean Resources.* London: Croom Helm.

Burleigh, M. 1988. *Germany Turns Eastwards: A Study of Ostforschung in the Third Reich.* Cambridge: Cambridge University Press.

Bush, W. M. 1982–1988. *Antarctica and International Law: A Collection of Inter-State and National Documents.* 4 vols. Dobbs Ferry, NY: Oceana Publications.

Charney, J. I., ed. 1982. *The New Nationalism and the Use of Common Space: Issues in Marine Pollution and the Exploitation of Antarctica.* Totowa, NJ: Allanheld, Osmun.

Chomsky, N. 1982. *Towards a New Cold War.* New York: Pantheon.

Cocca, A. 1986. "The Common Heritage of Mankind: Doctrine and Principle of Space Law." *Proceedings of the International Institute of Space Law*, 17–24.

Connor, W. 1969. "Myths of Hemispheric, Continental, Regional, and State Unity." *Political Science Quarterly* 84 (4).

Craven, J. P., J. Schneider, and C. Stimson, eds. 1989. *The International Implications of Intended Maritime Jurisdiction in the Pacific.* Honolulu: University of Hawaii, Law of the Sea Institute.

Earney, F. 1990. *Marine Mineral Resources.* London: Routledge.

Enscalada, V. 1979. *Air Law.* Alphen aan den Rijn: Sijthoff and Nordhoff.

Gilmore, W. C. 1994. "Sea and Continental Shelf." *Stair Encyclopedia of Scots Law.* Vol. 21. London: Butterworths.

Haas, P. M. 1990. *Saving the Mediterranean: The Politics of International Environmental Co-operation.* New York: Columbia University Press.

Honoré, A. M. 1961. "Ownership." In *Oxford Essays in Jurisprudence*, A. G. Guest, ed. Oxford: Oxford University Press.

Johnstone, D. M. 1989. *The Theory and History of Ocean Boundary Making.* Kingston: McGill-Queens University Press.

Krepon, M., et al. 1990. *Commercial Observation Satellites and International Security.* New York: MacMillan and the Carnegie Foundation for International Peace.

Kwiatkowska, B. 1989. *The 200 Mile Exclusive Economic Zone in the New Law of the Sea.* Dordrecht: Nijhoff.

List, M., and V. Rittberger. 1992. "Regime Theory and International Environmental Management." In *The International Politics of the Environment*, A. Hurrell and B. Kingsbury, eds. Oxford: Clarendon Press.

Lovering, J. F., and J. R. V Prescott. 1979. *Last of Lands: Antarctica.* Melbourne: Melbourne University Press.

Lyster, S. 1985. *International Wildlife Law.* Cambridge: Grotius.

MacKay, J. R. 1969. "The Interactive Hypothesis and Boundaries in Canada: A Preliminary Study." In *Spatial Analysis: A Reader in Statistical Geography*, B. J. L. Berry and D. F. Marble, eds. Englewood Cliffs: Prentice-Hall.

Malaurie, J. 1989. *Les Derniers Rois de Thúle, Avec les Esquimaux polaires face à leur destin*. Paris: Pion.

Malaurie, J. 1992. "L'Arctique soviétique, face aux miroirs brisés de l'occident." *Hérodote* 64 (January–March).

Martin P. J., et al. 1977. *Shawcross and Beaumont on Air Law*. London: Butterworths.

Martin, P. M. 1992. *Droit des activités spatiales*. Paris: Masson.

Matte, N. M. 1987. "The Common Heritage of Mankind Principle in Outer Space." *Annals of Air and Space Law*.

McPhail, T. L. 1981. *Electronic Colonialism: The Future of International Broadcasting*. London: Sage.

Nye, J. S., and J. A. Schear, eds. 1987. *Seeking Stability in Space: Anti-Satellite Weapons and the Evolving Space Race*. New York: University Press of America.

OECD. 1974. *Problems of Transfrontier Pollution*. Paris: OECD.

OECD. 1976. *Legal Aspects of Transfrontier Pollution*. Paris: OECD.

OECD. 1978. *OECD and the Environment*. Paris: OECD.

Parenti, M. 1986. *Inventing Reality: The Politics of the Mass Media*. New York: St. Martin's Press.

Peterson, M. J. 1988. *Managing the Frozen South*. Berkeley: University of California Press.

Poggi, G. 1978. *The Development of the Modern State*. London: Hutchinson.

Prescott, J. R. V. 1987. *Political Frontiers and Boundaries*. London: Allen and Unwin.

Reijnen, G. C. M., and W. de Graff. 1989. *The Pollution of Outer Space, in Particular of the Geostationary Orbit: Scientific, Policy and Legal Aspects*. Dordrecht: Nijhoff.

Reynolds, G. H., and R. H. Merges. 1989. *Outer Space: Problems of Law and Policy*. Boulder: Westview Press.

Rykiel, Z. 1985. "Regional Integration and Boundary Effects in the Katowice Region." In *Proceedings of the 7th British-Polish Geographical Seminar, 23–30 May 1983*, J. B. Goddard and Z. Taylor, eds. Warsaw: Polish Scientific Publishers.

Schofield, C. H., ed. 1994. *Global Boundaries*. London: Routledge.

Splettstoesser, J. F., and G. M. Dreschhoff, eds. 1990. *Mineral Resources Potential of Antarctica*. Washington, DC: American Geophysical Union.

Strassoldo, R. 1970. *From Barrier to Junction: Towards a Sociological Theory of Borders*. Gorizia: ISIG.

Thacher, Peter S. 1992. *Background to Institutional Options for Management of the Global Environment and Commons*. N.p.

Triggs, G. D., ed. 1987. *The Atlantic Treaty Regime: Law, Environment, and Resources*. Cambridge: Cambridge University Press.

Waldron, J. 1988. *The Right to Private Property*. Oxford: Clarendon Press.

Wasburn, P. C. 1992. *Broadcasting Propaganda: International Radio Broadcasting and the Construction of Political Reality*. London: Praeger.

Weber, L. 1983. "European Organization for the Safety of Air Navigation (Eurocontrol)." *Encyclopedia of Public International Law*, Vol. 6. Amsterdam: North Holland.

Weil, P. 1989. *The Law of Maritime Delimitation—Reflections*. Cambridge: Grotius.

Weintraub, S. 1990. *A Marriage of Convenience: Relations between Mexico and the United States*. New York: Oxford University Press.

Zwann, T. L., ed. 1988. *Space Law: Views of the Future*. London: Kluwer.

Suggested Readings

The *Journal of Borderlands Studies* is the leading interdisciplinary scholarly journal devoted to studies of border regions. Although it has a heavy emphasis on the U.S.-Mexican border, it does include articles on other border regions around the world.

U.S.-Mexican Border

Andreas, Peter. *Border Games: Policing the U.S.-Mexico Divide.* Ithaca: Cornell University Press, 2000.

Arreola, Daniel D., and James R. Curtis. *The Mexican Border Cities.* Tucson: University of Arizona Press, 1993.

Clement, Norris C., ed. *The U.S.-Mexican Border Environment: U.S.-Mexican Border Communities in the NAFTA Era.* San Diego: San Diego State University Press, 2002.

Clement, Norris C., and Eduardo Zepeda Miramontes, eds. *San Diego-Tijuana in Transition: A Regional Analysis.* San Diego: Institute for Regional Studies of the Californias, San Diego State University, 1993.

Deutsch, Sarah. *No Separate Refuge: Culture, Class, and Gender on an Anglo-Hispanic Frontier, 1880–1940.* New York: Oxford University Press, 1987.

Ganster, Paul, ed. *The U.S.-Mexican Border Environment: A Road Map to a Sustainable 2020 (Southwest Center for Environmental Research and Policy Monograph Series, No. 1).* San Diego: San Diego State University Press, 2000.

Ganster, Paul, Felipe Cuamea Velázquez, José Luis Castro Ruiz, and Angélica Villegas, eds. *Tecate, Baja California: Realities and Challenges in a Mexican Border Community.* San Diego: San Diego State University Press, 2002.

García, Mario T. *Desert Immigrants: The Mexicans of El Paso, 1880–1920.* New Haven: Yale University Press, 1981.

Hinojosa, Gilberto Miguel. *A Borderlands Town in Transition: Laredo, 1755–1870.* College Station: Texas A&M University Press, 1983.

Kearney, Milo, and Anthony Knopp. *Boom and Bust: The Historical Cycles of Matamoros and Brownsville.* Austin: Eakin Press, 1991.

Klein, Alan M. *Baseball at the Border: A Tale of Two Laredos.* Princeton: Princeton University Press, 1997.

Lorey, David E. *The U.S.-Mexican Border in the Twentieth Century: A History of Social and Economic Transformation.* Wilmington: Scholarly Resources, 1999.

_____, ed. *United States-Mexico Border Statistics since 1900.* Los Angeles: UCLA Latin American Center Publications, 1990.

_____, ed. *United States-Mexico Border Statistics since 1900: 1990 Update.* Los Angeles: UCLA Latin American Center Publications, 1993.

Lowenthal, Abraham F., and Katrina Burgess, eds. *The California-Mexico Connection.* Stanford: Stanford University Press, 1993.

Martínez, Oscar J. *Border Boom Town: Ciudad Juárez since 1848.* Austin: University of Texas Press, 1978.

_____. *Border People: Life and Society in the U.S.-Mexico Borderlands.* Tucson: University of Arizona Press, 1994.

_____. *Troublesome Border.* Tucson: University of Arizona Press, 1988.

_____, ed. *U.S.-Mexico Borderlands: Historical and Contemporary Perspectives.* Wilmington: Scholarly Resources, 1996.

Nevins, Joseph. *Operation Gatekeeper: The Rise of the "Illegal Alien" and the Remaking of the U.S.-Mexico Boundary.* New York: Routledge, 2002.

Proffitt, T. D., III. *Tijuana: The History of a Mexican Metropolis.* San Diego: San Diego State University Press, 1994.

Raat, Dirk W. *Revoltosos: Mexico's Rebels in the United States, 1903–1923.* College Station: Texas A&M University Press, 1981.

Ross, Stanley R., ed. *Views across the Border: The United States and Mexico.* Albuquerque: University of New Mexico Press, 1978.

Rotella, Sebastian. *Twilight on the Line: Underworlds and Politics at the U.S.-Mexico Border.* New York: W. W. Norton & Company, 1998.

Ruíz, Vicki L., and Susan Tiano, eds. *Women on the U.S.-Mexico Border: Responses to Change.* Boston: Allen & Unwin, 1987.

Spalding, Mark J. *Sustainable Development in San Diego-Tijuana: Environmental, Social, and Economic Implications of Interdependence.* La Jolla: Center for U.S.-Mexican Studies, University of California at San Diego, 1999.

Timmons, Wilbert H. *El Paso: A Borderlands History.* El Paso: University of Texas Press, 1990.

Vila, Pablo. *Crossing Borders, Reinforcing Borders: Social Categories, Metaphors, and Narrative Identities on the U.S.-Mexico Frontier.* Austin: University of Texas Press, 2000.

Westerhoff, Paul, ed. *The U.S.-Mexican Border Environment: Water Issues along the U.S. Mexican Border (Southwest Center for Environmental Research and Policy Monograph Series, No. 2).* San Diego: San Diego State University Press, 2000.

Williams, Edward J., and John T. Passé-Smith. *The Unionization of the Maquiladora Industry: The Tamaulipan Case in National Context.* San Diego: Institute for Regional Studies of the Californias, San Diego State University, 1992.

Wilson, Patricia A. *Exports and Local Development: Mexico's New Maquiladoras.* Austin: University of Texas Press, 1992.

Young, Gay, ed. *The Social Ecology and Economic Development of Ciudad Juárez.* Boulder: Westview Press, 1986.

European Borders

Blatter, Joachim, and Norris Clement, eds. *Journal of Borderlands Studies Special Number: European Perspectives on Borderlands* 15:1: Spring 2000.

Dahlström, Margareta, Heikki Eskelinen, and Ulf Wiberg, eds. *The East-West Interface in the European North.* Uppsala, Sweden: Nordisk Samhällsgeografisk Tidskrift, 1995.

Joenniemi, Pertti, ed. *Cooperation in the Baltic Sea Region.* Washington: Taylor & Francis, 1993.

Kirkinen, Heikki, and Leena Westman, eds. *On the Border of the European Union: From the Gulf of Finland to the Arctic Ocean.* Joensuu, Finland: Joensuu University Press, 1996.

Lezzi, Maria. *Transboundary Co-operation in Switzerland: A Training for Europe.* Basel, Switzerland: Regio Basiliensis, 2000.

Sahlins, Peter. *Boundaries: The Making of France and Spain in the Pyrenees.* Berkeley: University of California Press, 1989.

Comparative Borders and International Borders

Anderson, Malcolm, and Eberhard Bort, eds. *The Irish Border: History, Politics, Culture.* Liverpool: Liverpool University Press,

Banuazizi, Ali, and Myron Weiner, eds. *The New Geopolitics of Central Asia and Its Borderlands.* Bloomington: Indiana University Press, 1995.

Blake, Gerald, Chia Lin Sien, Carl Grundy-Warr, Martin Pratt, and Clive Schofield, eds. *International Boundaries and Environmental Security: Frameworks for Regional Cooperation.* London: Kluwer Law International, 1997.

Blake, Gerald, Martin Pratt, Clive Schofield, and Janet Allison Brown, eds. *Boundaries and Energy: Problems and Prospects.* London: Kluwer Law International, 1998.

Butalia, Urvashi. *The Other Side of Silence: Voices from the Partition of India.* Durham: Duke University Press, 2000.

Dworsky, Leonard B., Julie A. Mauer, and Albert E. Utton, eds. *Managing North American Transboundary Water Resources, Part 1 (Natural Resources Journal 33:1).* Albuquerque: University of New Mexico School of Law, 1993.

_____, eds. *Managing North American Transboundary Water Resources, Part 2 (Natural Resources Journal 33:2).* Albuquerque: University of New Mexico School of Law, 1993.

Eskelinen, Heikki, Ilkka Liikanen, and Jukka Oksa, eds. *Curtains of Iron and Gold: Reconstructing Borders and Scales of Interaction.* Aldershot, Eng.: Ashgate, 1999.

Finnie, David H. *Shifting Lines in the Sand: Kuwait's Elusive Frontier with Iraq.* Cambridge: Harvard University Press, 1992.

Ganster, Paul, ed. *Cooperation, Environment, and Sustainability in Border Regions.* San Diego: San Diego State University Press and Institute for Regional Studies of the Californias, 2001.

Ganster, Paul, Alan Sweedler, James Scott, and Wolf-Dieter Eberwein, eds. *Borders and Border Regions of Europe and North America*. San Diego: San Diego State University Press and Institute for Regional Studies of the Californias, 1997.

Gibert, Stephen P., ed. *Security In Northeast Asia: Approaching the Pacific Century*. Boulder: Westview Press, 1988.

Herbst, Jeffrey. *States and Power in Africa: Comparative Lessons in Authority and Control*. Princeton: Princeton University Press, 2000

Herzog, Lawrence A., ed. *Changing Boundaries in the Americas*. San Diego: Center for U.S.-Mexican Studies, University of California at San Diego, 1992.

Kiy, Richard, and John D. Wirth, eds. *Environmental Management on North America's Borders*. College Station: Texas A&M University Press, 1998.

Little, Paul E. *Amazonia: Territorial Struggles on Perennial Frontiers*. Baltimore: Johns Hopkins University Press, 2001.

Newman, David, ed. *Boundaries, Territories, and Postmodernity*. London: Frank Cass, 1999.

Perkmann, Markus, and Ngai-Ling Sum, eds. *Globalization, Regionalization, and Cross-Border Regions*. New York: Palgrave Macmillan, 2002.

Robins, Melinda B., and Robert L. Hilliard, eds. *Beyond Boundaries: Cyberspace in Africa*. Portsmouth: Heinemann, 2002.

Rumley, Dennis, and Julian V. Minghi. *The Geography of Border Landscapes*. London: Routledge, 1991.

Shapland, Greg. *Rivers of Discord: International Water Disputes in the Middle East*. New York: St. Martin's Press, 1997.

Swietochowski, Tadeusz. *Russia and Azerbaijan: A Borderland in Transition*. New York: Columbia University Press, 1995.

Tsui, Tien-hua. *The Sino-Soviet Border Dispute in the 1970s*. Oakville, Ont.: Mosaic Press, 1984.

Wilson, Thomas M., and Hastings Donnan, eds. *Border Identities: Nation and State at International Frontiers*. Cambridge: Cambridge University Press, 1998.

Xuechengliu. *The Sino-Indian Border Dispute and Sino-Indian Relations*. New York: University Press of America, 1994.

Index

accidental theory, 97
Achuar people, 108, 109; border politics influence on, 110–15
Adams, Forbes, 56
a fortiori, xxiii, 321
Africa, 23; boundary-making in West, 97–104
Agenda 21, xxiii
Agrarian Reform, 53
Agreed Measures for the Conservation of Antarctic Flora and Fauna, 322
Agricola, Julius, 2, 6
Aguaruna-Huambisa Council, 110
Aguaruna people, 108
Ahtisaari (Finnish president), 124
AIDS, 44, 85, 276, 282
air-lift, 24
airspace, 325–26
Akwesasne reserve, 160
alae, xxiii
Alaska, 152, 163
Alberta, border between Montana and, 160, 163, 291
alcohol: border vice and, 126, 166n18, 269, 270, 272–73, 274–75; youths and, 280–82
Alemany, Arturo, 282
Al Haj 'Umar, 98
Aliens Control Act, 74
Alimami Sattan Lahai, 102
Alliance for Sustainable Development, xxiii, 248, 250, 261, 265
Amazon Indians, 108
Amsterdam, 290
Anaheim, CA, 58
Andersen, Benedict, 319
Anderson, Malcolm, 317
Anglo-Irish Agreement of 1985, 172
antagonism, xxiii
Antarctica, 322
Antarctic Treaty System (ATS), 322, 323
Anti-Ballistic Missile Treaty, 326
antipode, xxiii
antithetical, xxiii
Antonine Wall, 6, 7
Antoninus, Pius, 6
apartheid, xxiii; ethnic, 170
aquifer, xxiii
Arabs, 184; Israeli Jews and Palestinian, 177–97; resistance tactics and, 185, 195. *See also* Muslims

Arafat, Yasir, 186, 187
Arctic border, 154, 165n7
Argentina, 57, 171, 204
Arias, Oscar, 257
Arizona, 280
Armstrong, Neil, 56
Arreola, Daniel D., 277
Arutam (symbolic message), 112
asbestos, xxiii
Asia, xii, 19, 74; Central, 20; South, 20
ASOCODE (Association of Central American Rural Organizations for Cooperation and Development), xxiii, 260
Assi, Johar, 189
asymmetrical, xxiii
Atlantic Ocean, 152
Atwood, Margaret, 154
aufheben, xxiii
Augustus Caesar, 2
Austria, border between Slovakia, 205, 242
Austrian Green Party, 243
Austrian-Slovenian border, 205
autarky, xxiii
Ayahuasca, 114

Babylon, 12
Badaling Mountain, 20
Baja California, 225, 273, 278
Baker, Frederick, 21
balaclava, xxiii
Baltic-Nordic maritime border, 220
Baltic Sea, 22, 124, 218, 228
Baotou, 19
barriers, borders as, 1–10, 11–20, 21–45
the Bastille, Berlin Wall and, 30, 36–39
Battle of the Boyne, 175
battlement, xxiii
Baud, Michiel, xv, xvi
Bausinger, Hermann, 38
bayou, xxiii
Bede, 10
Beijing, 18, 19
Beirut, 178, 184
Belfast, 170
Belgium, xviii, 9, 172
Belgrade, 238
Belorussia, 127, 131
Benvenisti, Meron, 182, 193, 194

Berlin, 6, 21, 30; air-lift and, 24; Customs wall around, 23; East, 26, *27,* 28; West, 24, 25, 26, *27,* 28
Berlin Crisis, 24
the Berlin Wall, xvii, *21,* 44–45; Americans and, 26; Bastille and, 30, 36–39; Bernauer Straße and, 22, 26, 39, 40–42; Checkpoint Charlie and, 42; Cold War and construction of, 23–25; consuming, 31–32; deaths and, 26, 28–29; fall of, 29–31; first wall (1961–1964), 23, 25–26; graffiti art and, 32, *33,* 34–36; Invaliden Friedhof and, 39, 42; Kapelle Ufer and, 43; Niederkirchner Straße and, 39–40; nostalgia for, 44; Oberer Freiarchenbrücke and, 43; Pankow and, 43; Potsdamer Platz and, 23, 25, 30, 34, 35, 38, 43; preserving, 39–43; Schiffbauerdamm and, 43; second wall (1964–1976), 23, 26, *27;* third wall (1976–1989), 23, 28–29; truth about, 22–23; violence against, 26
Bernauer Straße, Berlin Wall and, 22, 26, 39, 40–42
Bethlehem, 179, 180, 189, 193
Bewcastle, 6
Bhopal, 328
BHP, 310
Binger (captain), 102
Bir Zeit, 194
Bir Zeit University, 179, 183, 186, 188
Birley, Eric, 8
Birley, Robin, 8
Birrens, 6
Black Sea, 22
Blass, Jonathan (husband), 182
Blass, Shifra (wife), 182
Blass, Shlomo (son), 182
Blyden, E. W., 101
Bogotá Declaration, 327, 332n17
bolsones, 254
bonanza, xxiii
Bonn, 35
Bonneville Dam, 240
book, xxiii
border crossings, 233n3; illegal, 82
Border Industrialization Program, 207
Border People (Martínez), xvi
border politics, indigenous people affected by, 110–15
border regions, *203, 223;* Canada-U.S., 156–61, 285–98; categories of empty spaces and, 321–27; Central America's transborder conservation and, 247–82; changing economic functions of international boundaries and, 201–4; Danube River environment and, 237–45; economic development of, 201–8; economic forces underlying transborder collaboration and,

229–30; elements of new security and, 222–26; emerging perspectives on security and, 218–22; empty spaces and frontiers of state and, 327–30; environment, development, and security in, 199–200; environment and development of, 208–18; evolution of environmental management in U.S-Mexican, 212–18; globalization and development in, 204–6; international frontier's definition and, 318–20; Mexican *Maquiladora* industry and, 206–8; NATO expansion and, 226–28; new frontiers of, 320–21; sea and outerspace, 317–32; security and development of, 218–28; transborder collaboration's dynamics and, 230–32; transborder collaboration's framework and, 229–33; transborder environmental issues and, 208–10; transborder environmental management practices and, 210–12; transnational regional integration and, 161–64; vice in, 269–82; violence in, 108
Borderland Project, 165n10
borders, 233n1; Alberta-Montana, 160; Antonine Wall, 6, 7; Arctic, 154, 165n7; Austrian-Slovenian, 205; Baltic-Nordic maritime, 220; barriers as, 1–10, 11–20, 21–45; Berlin Wall, 21–45; Canadian-U.S., xviii, 151–65, 165n2, 285–98; Chinese-Hong Kong, xi; Customs wall, 23; Danish-German, 290; Dutch-Belgian, xvii; Finnish-Swedish, xviii, 137–50; German-Netherlands, *203;* Great Wall of China, xvii, 11–20; Hadrian's Wall, xvii, 1–10, 11, 21; Han Wall, 16; Irish Catholics, Protestants and informal internal, 169–76; Israeli-Palestinian, xviii, xix, 177–97, *181;* Lebanon, 177, 178, 184, 187, 193; Lesotho, Mozambique and Zimbabwe's, 73–93; Maine-New Brunswick, 160; migrants, refugees and, 24–25; Northern Ireland, 169–76; paradox of, xi–xii; Peru-Ecuador, xviii, 107–15; Qin Wall, 16; Russian-Chinese, 220; South Africa-Mozambique, *75;* Soviet/Russian-Finnish, xiii, xviii, 97, 117–34, 137–50, 165n4, 219; U.S.-Mexican, xi, xii, xiii, xiv–xv, xvi, xviii, xix, 51–69, 127, 151, 153, 156, 158, 161–62, 165, 165n1, 200, 205, 212–26, 269–82; West Africa's, 97–104
Bosnia, 170
Boston, MA, 39
Botswana, 76
Boucher (artist), 34
boundaries. *See* borders
Bowman, Kirk S., 269
Boza, Mario, 263
braceros, xxiv, 54
Brandt, Willy, 26, 28

Bratislava, 238, 240, 241, 242, 245
Brazil, 204
Brezhnev, Leonid, *33,* 238
Brezhnev-era hubris, xxiv
Britannia, *5*
British Airways, 31
British Columbia, 152, 157, 162, 291
Britons, 8
Brocchus, Aelius, 9
Brown, G., 287
Brownsville, TX, xiii, 158
Brunschwig, Henri, 99
Budapest, 238, 241, 242
Burma, xvii
Butler, Richard W., 285, 289
Butor, Michel, 32
by-products, xxiv

CACM (Central American Common Market),
    xxiv, 248, 253, 254
Caerleon, 4
Caledonia, *5*
Caledonii, 2
California, 51, 54, 57, 62, 63; Southern, 52,
    280
Cambodia, 301, 302; continental shelf and,
    304–6; historic waters and, 304; maritime
    disputes between Thailand and, 306–7;
    maritime disputes between Vietnam and,
    307; maritime disputes between Vietnam,
    Thailand and, 307–8; negotiations between
    Thailand and, 310–11; negotiations
    between Vietnam and, 312; straight base-
    lines and, 303
campesino, xxiv, 257, 261
Canada, xix, 172, 174, 200; border between
    U.S. and, xviii, 151–65, 165n2; cross-bor-
    der shopping between U.S. and, 285–98
Canadian-U.S. border, xviii, 151, *155,* 165n2;
    comparative perspective of, 164–65; erosion
    of, 154–56; history of, 152–53; regions of,
    156–61; shopping and, 285–98; shopping as
    tourism and, 288–97; transnational regional
    integration and regions of, 161–64
cantinas, xxiv, 280
Caracalla (emperor), 8
Cárdenas, Cuauhtémoc, 54
Cárdenas, Dámaso, 53
Cárdenas, Lázaro, 53, 275
cardenismo, xxiv
Cardew (colonel), 103
Carlisle, 4, 8, 10
Carranza, Venustiano, 58, 274
Carson, Edward, 176
Carter, Jimmy, 35
Carthage, 2
Carvetii, 8
casa de cambio (exchange house), 52

Cascade Mountains, 157
Cascadia, 164
Cassivellaunus, 2
Catholics, 37; Northern Ireland, Protestants,
    informal internal borders and, 169–76;
    priests, 51, 58–60; rebels, 53; Sahuayo and,
    58–60
Cenepa River, 109
Central America, 247–48, *249, 255;* historical
    role of border regions in, 250–51; lost
    decade of 1980s, 255–58; neo-
    integrationism and limitations in, 258–60;
    1990s and new regional initiatives in,
    258–65; project-oriented border region
    development in, 261–63; protected areas
    in, *249;* regional and national territorial
    integration in, 251–54; sustainable devel-
    opment in, 260–61
Central American Peace Plan, 248
Central Asia, 20
Central Committee of the Communist Party,
    24
Central Intelligence Agency (CIA), 222, 224
Cerialis, Flavius, 9
cerveza, xxiv, 274
Chamberlain, L., 296
Chamorro, Violeta, 258
Chapala Lake, 51–52
Chapin, Mac, 250
chaquiras (beads), 110
Charles I (king), 175
Checkpoint Charlie: Berlin Wall and, 42; mu-
    seum, 37, 42
Cheng, Dalin, 11
Chenghua (emperor), 13
Chernobyl, 328
Chester, 4
Chicago, xv, 52, 54, 56, 65
Chihuahua, 273, 275
China, xi, 204; border between Russia and,
    220; Great Wall of, xvii, *11,* 12–20, 22
Chinese-Hong Kong border, xi
Chippindale, C., 39
cholo, xxiv
Chomsky, Noam, 329
Christians, 37, 178; Catholics, Protestants
    and Northern Ireland's informal internal
    borders, 169–76; Palestinian, 184; priests,
    51, 58–60; rebels, 53; Sahuayo and, 58–60
Chu state, 14
cigarettes, 166n16
CIS (Commonwealth of Independent States),
    xxiv
Cisneros, Ramón, 68
Ciudad Juárez, xiii, 158, 273, 276, 278, 282
Claudius (emperor), 2
Clement, Norris, 199
Clinton, Bill, 204

coffers, xxiv
cohesive, xxiv
the Cold War, xvii, 22, 39, 42, 45, 122, 174, 202, 204, 219, 329, 330; construction of Berlin Wall during, 23–25; East and West sectors of Berlin during, *27*
Colonial Sahuayense, migrant network of, 60–69
Colorado, xv
Colorado River, xii
Columbia River, 240
compañero, 113
Compton, CA, 52
conspiratorial theory, 97
Continuation War of 1941, 121
Convention for the Conservation of Antarctic Marine Living Resources, 323
Convention for the Protection of Antarctic Seals, 322
Convention for the Regulation of Antarctic Mineral Resources Activities (CRAMRA), 323
Corbridge, 8
core-periphery, xxiv
Corfu, Chaim, 195
Corstopitum, 8
Costa Rica, *255, 262, 263;* GDP, 259; historical role of border regions and, 250–51; regional and national territorial integration and, 251–54
Council of Europe, 134, 328
Coutts, Alberta, 162
Cristero War, 53
Croatia, 170
Crompton, J. L., 289
cross-border migration, 74–78; frequency of visits to South Africa and, 80; methods of entry into South Africa and, 81–83; profile of visitors to South Africa and, 79–80; reasons for going to South Africa and, 80–81
Cuba, 23; missile crisis and, 24
Curtis, James R., 277
Customs walls, borders and, 23
Czechoslovakia, xix; GNRBS (Gabcikovo-Nagymaros River Barrage System) and, 237–45

Dacians, 2
Danish-German border, 290
Dann, G., 289
Danube River, xix, 6, 225, *238;* calamitous consequences and, 241–42; cheap energy and, 239; disaster on, 237–45; foreign entanglements and, 242–43; political transformation and, 243–44; power surges and, 240–41; technical revision and, 244; uncertain future for, 244–45
Darmstadt University, 29

Darnton, R., 31
Datong, 18
Dawson, L., 287
deaths: Berlin Wall and, 26, 28–29; Northern Ireland's ethnic apartheid and, 170, 171
de facto, xxiv
delta, xxiv
Denmark, border between Germany and, 290
Department of Home Affairs, 75
desarrollo, xxiv, 276
Desbuissons, 101
Deseret News, 272
determinist theory, 97
Detroit, 158
development: border regions and, 230–33; border regions and economic, 201–8, *203;* environment and border region, 208–18; security and border region, 218–22, *223,* 224–29
dietary restrictions, religion and, 178
dikes, xxiv
Dilley, R. S., 290, 295, 297
DM (Deutsche Mark), xxiv, 32, 35
Donghu people, 17
dredging, xxiv
Dromi, Dalia, 192
Drug Enforcement Agency (DEA), 222
Dublin, 172
Dunakiliti-Hrusov Reservoir, 240, 242
Dunhuang, 20
Durango, xv
Durante, Jimmy, 274
Dutch-Belgian border, xvii
Dzungar, 16
Dzurek, Daniel J., 301

Eadington, Bill, 272
East Berlin, West and, 25, 26, 28
East German Communist Party, 24
East Germany, 21, 23, 24, 25, 29, 30
East Jerusalem, 178, 186, 196
EC (European Community), 120, 244, 328, 329, 330
Ecuador, border between Peru and, xviii, 107–15
Edelmann, M., 25
Eden River, 8
Edinburgh, 7
Edmonton, 157, 287, 289
EEZ (Exclusive Economic Zone), xxiv, 302, 306, 308, 324
egregious, xxiv
Egypt, 12, 104, 186, 191
elephants, fighting, 98, 104n1
Elfert, Eberhard, 39
El Paso, TX, xiii, 158, 273

El Salvador, 249, 253, 262; lost decade of 1980s and, 255–58; regional and national territorial integration and, 253–54
Elton, Catherine, 107
empty spaces, frontiers of state, border regions and, 327–30
EMU (European Monetary Union), xxiv, 123
enclaves, xxv
energy, Danube River and cheap, 239
England, 97, 287
environment: border regions and Danube River, 237–45; border regions and development of, 208–18; border regions' development, security and influence on, 199–233; data on damage to, 212; national resources and security for, 224–26; pollution control and, 211, 234n8; transborder issues on, 208–10; transborder management practices and, 210–12; U.S.-Mexican border and issues concerning, 214–15; U.S.-Mexican border management practices for, 212–14, 215–17, 218
EPA (Environmental Protection Agency), 217
EPZ (Export Processing Zone), xxv, 206, 207
Erskine, Brian, 237
Espinosa, Paul, 273
Estonia, 204
EU (European Union), xxv, 122, 123, 124, 134, 139, 200, 204, 205, 206, 217, 303, 328
EU Interreg Programme, xxv, 126
Euphrates River, 225
Eurocontrol, 325
Europe, 1, 22, 238, 290
EU Tacis Programme, xxv, 126, 128
Evanston, WY, 272
Exclusive Economic Zone, 323, 324
Exxon Valdez, 328

Faidherbe, 98
family: history of Wampui, Tukup's, 107–8; reunions, 112–15
Fasheh, Munir, 186
FEDEPRICAP (Federation of Private Businesses of Central America and Panama), xxv, 260
Federal Bureau of Investigation (FBI), 222
federalist, xxv
fief, xxv
Finland, xix, *141*; border between Russia and, xiii, xviii, 97, 117–34, 137–50, 165n4, 219; border between Sweden and, xviii; youths' perspectives on border between Russia and, 143–48, 149–50; youths' perspectives on border between Sweden and, 137–43, 148–49
Finnish Border Patrol Establishment, 123
Finnish-Russian border, 97, 165n4, 219; crossing points of, *119, 125*; de-territorial-

ization, flows and cross-border activities on, 124–29; establishment of, 121; Karelia and, 143–48; local perspective on, 130–33; post-Soviet geopolitical order and contested border discourses on, 122–24; as social practice and discourse, 117–20; youths' perspectives on, 143–48, 149–50
Finnish-Swedish border, xviii, *141,* 150; Tornio River Valley and, 138–40, 142–43; youths' perspectives on, 137–43, 148–49
Finnish Tornio, 139
First Nation, reserves, 160. *See also* Native American Indians
first wall (1961–1964), Berlin and, 23, 25–26
Fischer, Manfred, 40–41
Fisher, H. A. L., 98
Fitzgerald, David, 51
FMLN (Farabundo Martí National Liberation Front), xxv, 256
Fox, Vicente, 57
France, 2, 23, 28, 37, 97, 174
fratricide, xxv
Fredericton, 153
Fredonia, AZ, 272
"free-trade imperialism," 98
French Revolution, 36
Friedman, Thomas L., 177
frontera, xxv, 270, 280
fronterizos, xxv, 269
frontiers: definition of international, 318–20; empty spaces, border regions, and state, 327–30; new, 320–21
FSLN (Sandinista National Liberation Front), xxv
FTA (Free Trade Agreement), 154, 155, 161, 164
Fu Su (prince), 15

Gabcikovo dam, 240–41, 241, 242, 244
Galdan (Khan), 16
Galveston, TX, 54
Gambia, 98, 100
gambling, 269; border regions and, 270–73, 274, 278–80; Ontario and, 166n14, 294. *See also* gaming
gaming, U.S.-Mexican border and, 278–80
gangs, 64
Ganster, Paul, 159, 161, 162, 163, 199
Gansu province, 12, 15, 18, 19
garrison, xxv
gastarbeiter, xxv
GATT (General Agreement on Tariffs and Trade), 202
Gauls, 8
Gay, John, 73
Gaza Strip, Israel, Palestine and, 177–97
GDP (Gross Domestic Product), xxv; Costa Rica's, 259

GDR (German Democratic Republic), xxv, 24, 25, 28, 29, 30, 33
German-Netherlands border, *203*
Germans, 8, 22, 29
Germany: border between Denmark and, 290; East, 21, 23, 24, 25, 29, 30; Nazi, 25; West, 23, 25, 174
Gestapo, 39, 40
Getz, D., 288
Ghana, 74
Gibbins, Roger, 151
Girot, Pascal O., 247
Glasgow, 7
Glienicker bridge, 22
globalization, xi, xxv, 118; border regional development and, 204–6
GNP (Gross National Product), xxv
GNRBS (Gabcikovo-Nagymaros River Barrage System), xxvi; Danube River and, 237–45
Goering, Hermann, 40
Gold Coast, 99, 100, 102
Goods and Services Tax (GST), 158
Gorbachev, Mikhail, 30, 38
Gordon, B., 287
Goren, Shiomo, 196
graffiti art, Berlin Wall and, 32
Grand Junction, CO, 272
Great Britain, xix, 1, 23, 26, 28, 171, 175
Great Lakes, 153, 156, 157, 211
Great Plains, 156
the Great Depression, 202, 275
the Great Wall of China, xvii; benefits from, 19–20; first line of defense and, 12, *13,* 14; Hadrian's Wall and, 11; investment in human lives and, 18–19; many nationalities involved and, 16–18; work of many dynasties and, 14–16
Green Party, Austrian, 243
Green Party of Mexico (PVEM), 54
Greenpeace, 323, 328
Gregory of Tours, 29
GREMI (Groupe de Recherche Européenne sur les Milieux Innovateurs), 234n7
gremio (guild), 60
gringo, xxvi
Guadalajara, 52, 54, 68
Guaracha, 53
Guatemala, 249, 259, 262; historical role of border regions and, 250–51; lost decade of 1980s and, 256–58; regional and national territorial integration and, 253–54
Guizot, 98
Gulf of Maine, 306
Gulf of Thailand, *305*; continental shelf and, 304–6; disputes in, 306–8; historic waters and, 304; joint development agreements and, 308–10; maritime agreements and oil

exploration in, 301–13; prognosis for, 312–13; recent developments in, 310–12; status of national maritime claims in, 302–6; straight baselines and, 302–4; territorial sea and, 304
Gutiérrez, Carlos González, 61
Györ, 240, 245

Haapalampi, 145–46
Hadrian (emperor): reign of, 3–4; wall of, 1–10
Hadrian's Wall, xvii, 21; archeological findings and, 8–10; civil settlements and, 7–8; dimensions and scale of, 4–5; Great Wall of China and, 11; origins of, 1–2; purpose of, 6–7; Roman Empire's conquests and, 2–3
Haifa, 179
Hainburg dam, 243
Hamad, Jameel, 189, 190
Han: dynasty, 16, 18, 19, 20; state, 14, 17
Hanafi, Musa, 194, 195, 196
Handke, Peter, 29
Hanging Gardens, 12
Hansen, Niles, 157, 163
Han Wall, 16
Haparanda, 139, 140
Harare, 77
Hardy, Oliver, 274
Harel, Israel, 190
Hargreaves, John D., 97
Haring, Keith, 34
Harrod's, 289
Hartung, Klaus, 30
Hartviksen, K. R., 290, 295
Havel, Vaclav, 243
Havichek, Dieter, 41
Hawaiian Gardens, CA, 58
Hayward, CA, 54
Hayworth, Rita, 274
Hebron, 179, 189, 190
Heckel, Christa, 41
hedonism, xxvi
Helsinki, 132
Hemming, Augustus, 100
Henan, 19
Henry VIII (king), 175
herald, xxvi
Heydrich, Reinhard, 40, 42
Hidalgo, Miguel, 52
Hildebrandt, Rainer, 34
Himmler, Heinrich, 40
Hispanics, 158–59
History of Northumberland (Hodgson), 5
Hitler, Adolf, 40
Hodgson, John (Rev.), 5
Hohl-Stein, Mattias, 34
Holland, 9

Hollywood, xix
"home": Israeli-Palestinian border and Jews'
sense of, 190–93; Israeli-Palestinian border
and Muslims' sense of, 188–90
Honduras, 259, 262, 263; historical role of
border regions and, 250–51; regional and
national territorial integration and, 253–54
Honecker, Erich, 24, 25, 28, 29, 30, *33*
Hong Kong, 289; border between China and, xi
Housesteads, 8
HTAs (Hometown Associations), 62, 64, 65
Huaihe Valley, 14, 19
Huambisa people, 107–8; border politics in-
fluence on, 110–15; population of, 109
Hughes, M. A., 286
human rights, South Africa, immigration and,
90–91
Hungarian Academy of Sciences, 241
Hungarian-Czechoslovakian Economic and
Technical-Scientific Cooperation Commit-
tee, 241
Hungary, xix, 30, 43; GNRBS (Gabcikovo-
Nagymaros River Barrage System) and,
237–45
Hussein (king), 186
Hussein, Mohammed, 178
hydroelectric, xxvi
hydropower, xxvi, 239

ICJ (International Court of Justice), xxvi
iconographies, xxvi
Idaho, 158, 163
Igbo people, 104n1
Ignatieff, Michael, 169
IICA (Interamerican Institute for Cooperation
in Agriculture), xxvi, 261
Illinois, 52
Illyrians, 8
IMF (International Monetary Fund), xxvi,
204
immigration: migration *vs.,* 92; South
Africa's human rights and, 90–91; South
Africa's management of, 90
India, 12, 171, 172, 204
Indiana, 54
Indo-China, 23
information sovereignty, 320
Inglewood, CA, 58
Inkster, Norman, 166n17
Institute for the Study of Gambling and Com-
mercial Gaming, 272
Interethnic Association for the Development
of the Peruvian Amazon, 110
International Atomic Energy Agency, 328
International Boundary and Water Commis-
sion, 329
International Civil Aviation Organization
(ICAO), 325, 328

International Commission for the Study of
Communication, 330
International Court of Justice, 244
International Maritime Organization, 328
International Union for the Conservation of
Nature and Its Resources, 328
International Wildlife Fund, 328
Internet, xi, 57–58
Interreg Programme, 139
Invaliden Friedhof, Berlin Wall and, 39, 42
IRA (Irish Republican Army), xxvi, 171
Iran, 2
Iron Curtain, xxvi, 22, 43, 44, 118, 138, 202
Irthing Valley, 4
Ishteyyeh, Mohammed, 188, 189, 195
Iso-Ahola, S. E., 288, 289
Israel, 171; fault line between Palestine and,
xviii, xix, 177–97, *181*; occupation tactics,
183–85; Palestinian resistance tactics
against, 185, 195
Israeli Nature Preservation Society, 192
Israeli-Palestinian border, xviii, xix, 177,
178, 181, *181*; economics and, 180,
182–83; history of, 179, 186–87;
Jewish/Arab relations and, 193–97; Jews'
sense of "home" and, 190–93; Muslims'
sense of "home" and, 188–90; occupation
tactics and, 183–85; resistance tactics and,
185, 195; violence and, 194–96
isthmus, xxvi
Italy, 7
itip (traditional skirts), 110

Jackson, Michael, 38
Jalisco, xv, 53
James II (king), 175, 176
Jansen-Verbeke, M. C., 286, 288, 290, 296
Japan, 31, 35, 57, 207, 225, 330
Jay's Treaty, 166n17
JDA (Joint Development Area), xxvi
Jericho, 180, 190
Jerusalem, 179, 180, 190, 191; East, 178,
186, 196; West, 196
Jerusalem Post, 178, 192
Jews: occupation tactics and, 183–85; Pales-
tinian Arabs and Israeli, 177–93; relations
between Muslims and, 193–97; sense of
"home" and, 190–93; settlements and, 182
Jiayuguan Pass, 11, 16, 20
Jin: dynasty, 16, 17; state, 14
Jiquilpan, 58
Jívaro people: disputed boundary area and,
109; Peru-Ecuador border's influence on,
107–15
Johannesburg, 76
Johnston, M., 297
Jordan, 179, 180, 186, 187, 189
Jukarainen, Pirjo, 137

Julius Caesar, 2
Jussila, H., 127
Juyongguan, 16, 18

kaffiyeh, xxvi
Kang Xi (emperor), 16
Kapelle Ufer, Berlin Wall and, 43
Karelia, 97, 121, 137, 150n1; youths'
    attitudes in Finnish-Russian, 143–48
Karlis Ltd., 132
Karsch, (lieut. col.), 34
kashrut, xxvi
Keaton, Buster, 274
Kennan, George F., 23
Kennedy, John F., 24, 25
Kenny (capt.), 102
Kent, W. E., 287
Keowin, C. F., 290
Kernd'l, Alfred, 39, 40
Khmer Republic, 305
Khrushchev, Nikita Sergeyevich, 24, 30
kibbutz, xxvi
Kingman, AZ, 271
Kinnunen, P., 129
Koch, Hagen, 37, 41
Kohl, Helmut, 41
Kola Peninsula, 127
Konrad, Victor, 153, 159, 165n10
Koran, xxvi
Korff, Gottfried, 31
kosher, xxvi
the Kremlin, 30
Krenz, Egon, 30
Kumoxi, 17
Kurosawa, S., 287

ladinos, xxvi, 249, 251, 263
Lagos, 99, 102
Lake Ontario, 156
Lake Superior, 156
Lake Tahoe, 271
Lang (capt.), 102
Lange, Silvia, 40
Langshan Mountain, 15
Laos, xvii
Lapp, P. J., 28
Las Vegas, 270, 281; gambling in, 278–80
latifundio, xxvi, 255
Laughlin, Don, 271
Laurel, Stan, 274
Lebanon, 178, 184, 187, 193; border, 177
Lepidina, Sulpicia, 9
Lesotho: attitudes toward migration to South
    Africa from, 83–88; cross-border
    migration and, 79–83; future of migration
    from, 88–90; migration to South Africa
    from, 73–79; policy implications for
    migrants from, 90–93

Lesser, J. A., 286
Liao dynasty, 17
Liaoling people, 17
Liaoning province, 16
Liefeoghe, Frank, 33
lignite, xxvi
Lima, 111
Lintao, 15
Lopers, 64
López, Guido (son), 112–13
López, Santiago (father), 113
Los Angeles, xiii, 52, 54, 58, 61, 64, 158
Louis XIV (king), 175
Luguvalium, 8
Lundberg, D. E., 289
Luobupo region, 16
Lushan Mountain, 15

Maastricht Treaty, 290
Macas, Ecuador, 108
Machado, M. A., 273
macroeconomics, xxvi
Magao Grottoes, 20
Maiji Mountain, 20
Maine, 158; border between New Brunswick
    and, 160
Mainz, 6
Malaysia, 301, 302; joint development
    agreements between Thailand and, 308–9;
    joint development agreements between
    Vietnam and, 308–10; maritime disputes
    between Thailand, Vietnam and, 308;
    straight baselines and, 303
Man and the Biosphere (UNESCO), 328
Man people (Manchu), 17
Manuel, Luis, 52
maquiladora, xviii, xxvii, 204, 221, 276;
    Mexico's industry of, 206–8, 210
Marañón River, 109
maritime agreements, Gulf of Thailand, oil
    exploration and, 301–13
Martínez, Brian, 280–81
Martínez, Oscar, xiv, xvi, 273
martyrdom, 194
masato, xxvii, 108, 114
Matamoros, xiii, 158
Mattes, Robert, 73, 74
matzo, xxvii
mauer (wall), 22, 23, 32, 45
Mauro, R., 297
Mavila, H. E. Guilherme, 91
McCallum, Brian "Herbie," 170, 171
McDonald, David A., 73, 77
McKinsey, Lauren, 153, 159, 165n10
meän kieli (our language), 149
Mediterranean Sea, 19
megawatt, xxvii
Meir, Yehuda (Lieut. Col.), 194

men: Mozambican migrant, 90–93, 94n4; South African migrant, 87–88
Menashe, Alfei, 194
Meng dynasty, 16
Meng Tian (general), 15
menorah, xxvii
Merced, CA, 54, 60
MERCOSUR, xxvii, 204
Mesquite, NV, 272
Mexamerica, U.S.-Mexican border and, 270, 273–77, 282
Mexico, xx, 154, 204, 329; border between U.S. and, xi, xii, xiii–xv, xvi, xviii, xix, 51–69, 127, 151, 153, 156, 158, 161–62, 165, 165n1, 200, 205, 212–26, 269–82; *maquiladora* industry in, 206–8, 210; migrants from Sahuayo, 51–69. *See also* Tijuana
Mexico City, 52, 54, 56, 162
mezzotint, xxvii
Miami, FL, 158
Michoacán, 53, 55, 60, 63, 68
Middle East, 1
migrants: borders, refugees and, 24–25; Colonial Sahuayense, 60–69; Mozambican men and women, 90–93, 94n4; policy implications for Zimbabwe's, 90–93; priests and, 51, 58–60; Sahuayo's, 51–56; South Africa's, 73–93; transnational media and, 56–58; undocumented, 74
migration: immigration *vs.*, 92; security and, 222–23; South Africa and future of, 88–90; South Africa and perceived impact of, 85; South Africa's attitude toward, 83–88; South Africa's cross-border, 79–83
milecastles, xxvii
Miller, Daniel, 32
Miller, Tom, 273
minaret, xxvii
Ming dynasty, 16, 17, 18, 19
minifundios, xxvii, 255
Mohawks, 160
Mongol people, 17
Montana, 158, 163; border between Alberta and, 160
Monteil, P. L., 101
Montreal, 153, 156
Moors, 3
Morelia, 52, 55
Mormons, xxvii, 272
Morona River, 109
Moscow, 24
Moses, Ofra, 194, 195
mosque, xxvii
Mozambique: attitudes toward migration to South Africa from, 83–88; border between South Africa and, 75; cross-border migration and, 79–83; future of migration from,

88–90; migration to South Africa from, 73–79; policy implications for migrants from, 90–93, 94n4
muezzin, xxvii
Múgica Manzo, Salvador, 54
Murguía, Francisco, 275
Museum for German History, 41, 42
Museum of Modern Art, 35
Muslims, 178; Palestinian, 177, 179–83, 184–87, 191–93; relations between Jews and, 193–97; sense of "home" and, 188–90

Nablus, 179, 190
NAFTA (North American Free Trade Agreement), xiii, 154, 161, 164, 165n8, 202, 204, 205, 207, 214, 226, 248, 259, 264, 276
Nagymaros, Hungary, 241
Namibia, 76
National Hockey League, 165n5
national maritime claims, *305*; continental shelf, 304–6; exclusive economic zone, 306; historic waters, 304; straight baselines, 302–4; territorial sea, 304
Native American Indians, 97, 160
NATO (North Atlantic Treaty Organization), xxvii, 25, 122; border regions and expansion of, 226–28
Nawech, Fernando (son), 114–15
Nawech, Juan Flores (father), 109–10, 111, 112, 114
Nazis, 25, 39, 40
Needles, CA, 271
Nei Monggol (Inner Mongolia), 15, 18, 19
neo-colonization, xxvii
Nepos, Aulus Platorius, 6
Netherby, 6
Netherlands, border between Germany and, *203*
Nevada, 270; vice, U.S.-Mexican border, Utah and, 270–73, 278–80
New Brunswick, 296; border between Maine and, 160
Newcastle, 8
"new economy," 200, 204, 206
New England, 156
New York, xv
New York City, 62, 190, 281
New York Times, 192
NGOs (nongovernmental organizations), 206, 247, 249, 260, 261
Niagara Falls, 290
Nicaragua, 249, 259, 262, 263; lost decade of 1980s and, 255–58; regional and national territorial integration and, 251–54
Niederkirchner Straße, Berlin Wall and, 39–40
Nigeria, 171
Ningxia province, 18, 19

Nogales, 278, 280
Noir (artist), 34
Nomingo, Shapiom, 110, 113
Nord, D. C., 290
norteño, xxvii
North Africa, 1
Northern Ireland, xvii, xviii, xix, 177, 290;
    Catholics, Protestants and informal inter-
    nal borders in, 169–76
North Korea, xvii
Northumberland, 22
Norway, *141,* 322
nuclear waste, 324
Nussberg, Lew, 34
Nusseibeh, Anwar (father), 179
Nusseibeh, Sari (son), 179–80, 183, 196, 197
Nuzhen people, 17

OAS (Organization for Economic Coopera-
    tion and Development), xxvii, 261, 262,
    263, 265
Oberer Freiarchenbrücke, Berlin Wall and, 43
Ocatlán, 68
Offa's Dyke, 28
oil exploration, Gulf of Thailand, maritime
    agreements and, 301–13
Ontario, 160, 287, 296; gambling and,
    166n14, 294
OPEC (Organization of Petroleum Exporting
    Countries), xxvii, 239
Orange County, CA, 54, 55, 57, 58, 59, 68, 69
Orangeism, xxviii
Oregon, xv, 163
Organization for Economic Cooperation and
    Development, 328
Ostpolitik, 28
Ottawa, 164
outerspace, 326–27

Paasi, Anssi, 117
Pacific Northwest Economic Region
    (PNWER), 163, 164, 166n20
Pacific Ocean, 152
Palestine: Christians in, 184; fault line
    between Israel and, xviii, xix, 177–97, *181;*
    Israeli occupation tactics against, 183–85;
    Muslims in, 184, 187; resistance tactics
    and, 185
Palloy, Pierre-François, 36, 37, 38
Palm Springs, CA, 158
PAN (National Action Party), xxviii;
    Sahuayo, Mexico and, 53–54, 57
Panama, 259, 261, 262, 263; historical role of
    border regions and, 250–51; lost decade of
    1980s and, 256; regional and national terri-
    torial integration and, 253
panista, xxviii
Pankow, Berlin Wall and, 43

Paraguay, 204
parapet, xxviii
Paris, 100, 289
Parthians, 2, 3
Pastaza River, 109
PBS, 166n15
Peace of Tartu, 121, 123
Peace Treaties of Moscow, 121
peccadilloes, xxviii, 280
Pecos, TX, 52
Pello, Finnish and Swedish, 143
People's Republic of Kampuchea (PK), 303
Pérez, Clovis, 111
Pérez, Wrays, 110
peripheries, xxviii
Pershing, John Joseph, 273
Persian Gulf, 308
Peru, xviii
Peru-Ecuador border, xviii, 107–15
Peterson, M. J., 322
Petronas, 309–10
Petro Vietnam, 309–10
Phoenix, AZ, 158
Phu Quoc Island, 302
Pico Rivera, CA, 61
Picts Wall, 2. *See also* Hadrian's Wall
Piñera, Ramírez, 273
Pink Floyd, 38
platos típicos, xxviii, 270
PLO (Palestine Liberation Organization),
    xxviii, 184, 189, 191
pollution controls, 211, 234n8
Pool (Sgt.), 42
Port Huron, 290
Porto Novo, 99
Potsdamer Platz, Berlin Wall and, 23, 25, 30,
    34, 35, 38, 43
Prague, 241
praxis, xxviii
PRD (Party of the Democratic Revolution),
    xxviii, 54
PRI (Institutional Revolutionary Party),
    xxviii, 54, 57
priests, 68; migrants and, 51, 58–60
priísta, xxviii
Prince Edward Island, 160
prostitution, U.S.-Mexican border and, 276,
    277–78, 282
Protectorate, xxviii, 99
Protestants, Northern Ireland, Catholics, in-
    formal internal borders and, 169–76
Protocol on Environmental Protection, 323
Prus, R., 287

Qawasmeh, Zuhair, 193, 194
Qi: dynasty, 17, 18; state, 14, 15
Qidan people, 17
Qin: dynasty, 19; state, 14, 15

Qing dynasty, 16
Qingdao, 15
Qin Hong (commander), 17
Qin Shi Huang (emperor), 15, 16, 18
Qin Wall, 16
Québec, 153, 155, 160
Quintus Lollius Urbicus, 6
quisling, xxviii

rabbi, xxviii
Radio Shuar, 108, 111
"Rajalla/På Gränsen/At the Border," 138
Ramallah, 182, 188, 189, 195
Reagan, Ronald, 32, 326
Red Hot Dutch, 333n31
refugees, borders, migrants and, 24–25
Regensburg, 6
Regina, 153
regionalization, xxviii
Reichstag, 23, 32, 37, 38, 43
The Reichstag Graffiti (Baker and Foster), 21
religion, dietary restrictions and, 178
remittances, xxviii
Reno, 271
Republic of Ireland, 290
reunions, family, 112–15
Rhineland, 4
Rhine River, 6, 211, 218
Rhon, Jorge Hank, 278
Rio Grande River, xii, xiii, 52, 98, 276
Rio Protocol, 110, 111
Ripon (secretary), 103
Roberts, J., 287
rock concerts, 37–38
Rocky Mountains, 157
Roman Empire, 38; conquests, 2–3;
  Hadrian's Wall and, 1–10
Romania, 239
Roman Wall, 2. *See also* Hadrian's Wall
Rouran people, 17
Rouse, Roger, 63
Royal Canadian Mounted Police (RCMP),
  166n17
Rukou, 17
Russian-Chinese border, 220
Russians, 138, 204; youths' perspectives on
  border between Finland and, 143–48,
  149–50
Ryan, C., 290

Sabbath, xxviii
SADC (Southern African Development Community), xxviii, 85, 86, 92
Sahuayo, Mexico: Catholics and, 58–60; Colonial Sahuayense in, 60–69; migrants from,
  51–56; PAN (National Action Party) and,
  53–54, 57; transnational collection plate
  and, 58–60; transnational media and, 56–58

Salisbury (lord), 100
SALT (Strategic Arms Limitation
  Agreements), 326
Salt Lake City, 271
SAMP (Southern African Migration Project),
  xxviii, 92, 94n2
Samson, R., 28, 29
Sánchez, Oscar Arias, 248
San Diego, CA, xiii, xviii, xx, 158; teenage
  drinking and, 280
San Francisco, CA, 157
Santa Ana, CA, 51, 52, 54, 55, 59, 60, 61, 64,
  66, 67
Santiago River, 108, 109, 114
Sarabia, Francisco, 67
Sarajevo, 170
Sarmatians, 3
Saskatoon, 157
Schabowski, Günter, 30
schadenfreude, xxviii, 31
Scharnhorst, Gerhard Johann David von, 42
Schiffbauerdamm, Berlin Wall and, 43
Schinkel, Karl-Friedrich, 42
Schneider, Peter, 27
Scotland, 2, 6
SDI (Strategic Defense Initiative), 326
Seattle, WA, 163
second wall (1964–1976), Berlin and, 23,
  26, *27*
security: border regional development and,
  218–28; elements of new, 222–24; internal
  and external, 223–24; migration and,
  222–23; national resources and
  environmental, 224–26; NATO expansion,
  border regions and, 226–28;
  traditional/emerging perspectives on bor-
  ders and, 218–22
Selkirk Mountains, 157
Senegal, 98, 99
Senegal River, 98
Senegambia, 102
sentry, xxviii
Septimius Severus, 5
Serbia, 170
Seton-Watson, Hugh, 173
Severa, Claudia, 9
Severus (emperor), 7, 8
sex, border vice and, 269, 270, *275*
Shaanxi province, 18, 19
Shandong, 15
Shanhaiguan, 16, 20
shekels, xxix
Shils, E., 130
Shin Bet, xxix, 180; agents, 183; domestic
  intelligence service, 184
Shock, P. J., 287
shopping: tourism and, 288–97; U.S., Canada
  and cross-border, 285–98

Shuar Indians, 107–8; border politic's influ-
ence on, 110–15; population of, 109;
Shukun, Moshe, 188
SICA (Central American Integration System),
xxix, 258, 259, 260
SIECA (Central American Secretariat for
Economic Integration), xxix, 261
Sierra Leone, 99
"Sierra Leone-Guinea system," 99, 102
Silk Road, 19
Simpson, Frank G., 5
simulacra, xxix, 32
Sinaloa, xv
Singapore, 207, 303
Slovakia, 238, 240; border between Austria
and, 205
sluices, xxix
Smith, Ken, 35, 37
Snow, R. E., 287
Solway Firth, 1, 4
Somalia, 74
South Africa: attitudes toward migration to,
83–88; comparing home countries to,
83–84; cross-border migration and, 79–83;
frequency of visits to, 80; future for migration to, 88–90; immigration and human
rights in, 90–91; immigration management
and, 90; immigration policy references and,
86–87; methods of entry into, 81–83;
migration *vs.* immigration, 92; perceived
impact of migration on, 85; policy implications of immigration and, 90–93; profile of
visitors to, 79–80; reasons for going to,
80–81; regional integration and, 91–92; special status for Lesotho, 92–93; women's attitudes toward, 88; South Africa-Mozambique
border, 75
South America, xii, 204
South Asia, 20
Southern African Migration Project (SAMP),
76
Southern California, 52
South Korea, xvii, 325
South Point, NV, 271
Soviet/Russian-Finnish border, xiii, xviii, 97,
165n4, 219; social practice and discourse
on, 117–34, 137–50
Soviets, 23, 24, 26
Soviet Union, xiii, 21, 23, 29, 117, 120, 202,
204, 239
Spain, 57, 110
Spaniards, 8
SPOT 1 (Satellite Pour l'Observation de la
Terre), 326
SPOT 2 (Satellite Pour l'Observation de la
Terre), 326
Sri Lanka, 171
Stalin, Joseph, 24

Standard Fruit, 253
Star Wars initiative, 326
Stasi, 40, 43
St. George, UT, 272
St. Lawrence River, 156, 157
Strabo, 2
Strait of Juan de Fuca, 157
subsidies, taxes and, 211
Sui dynasty, 18
Suide, 15
Sweden, 121, *141*; border between Finland
and, xviii, 137–50; youths' perspectives on
border between Finland and, 137–43,
148–49
Sweedler, Alan, 159, 161, 162, 163, 199
Sweetgrass, MO, 162
synagogue, xxix
Syria, 187, 191

tahini, xxix
Taishan Mountain, 15
Taiwan Strait, xiii
Taj Mahal, 12
Taqtouq, Awad, 195
taxes, subsidies and, 211
Tay River, 7
Taylor, P. J., 122
Tayos, 110
teenage drinking, U.S.-Mexican border and,
280–82
teetotaler, xxix
Tel Aviv, 179, 190, 192, 194, 196
Temne people, 102
terrorist, label of, 189
Texas, 52, 54, 273
Thailand, xvii, *305*; joint development
agreements between Malaysia and, 308–9;
maritime disputes between Cambodia and,
306–7; maritime disputes between
Malaysia, Vietnam and, 308; maritime
disputes between Vietnam and, 308;
maritime disputes between Vietnam,
Cambodia and, 307–8; negotiations
between Cambodia and, 310–11; negotiations between Vietnam and, 311–12; oil
exploration and Gulf of, 301–13. *See also*
Gulf of Thailand
theocratic, xxix
third wall (1976–1989), Berlin and, 23,
28–29
Thracians, 8
Tijuana, xiii, xviii, xx, 158; alcohol and,
280–82; gambling in, 273, 274; prostitution in, 276, 277–78
Timothy, Dallen J., 285
Tofa (king), 99
Tohmajärvi, 145–46
Tong county, 19

Tornio-Haparanda, 138; youths' perspectives in, 139–40, 142
Tornio River Valley, 137, 143, 149
Toronto, 153
Torrey Canyon, 328
Touman City, 15
tourism, shopping as, 288–97
tradeable permits, 211
Trajan, 3
Transborder Collaboration (TBC): conceptual framework of, 229–33; dynamics of, 230–32; economic framework underlying, 229–30
Transboundary Collaboration (TBC), 206. *See also* Transborder Collaboration
transnational media, migrants and, 56–58
trawler, xxix
Treaty of Paris, 121
Triton Energy, 309
Tucson, AZ, 280
Tujue people, 17
turret, xxix
Twain, Mark, 193
20 Years of Civil Administration (Civil Administration of Israel), 196
Tyne River, 1, 8
Tyne Valley, 4

Ukraine, 127, 131, 170
Ulbricht, Walter, 24
Ulster, Northern Ireland, 171, 172, 173, 175
Ulster Volunteer Force, 169–70
UN (United Nations), xxix, 328, 330
UNESCO (United Nations Educational, Scientific, and Cultural Organization), xxix, 28, 262, 328, 329, 330
Union Carbide, 328
United Fruit Company, 253
United Kingdom, 302
United Nations, 191
United Nations Conference on the Law of the Sea (UNCLOS), 324, 327
United Nations Convention on the Protection of the Global Cultural and Natural Patrimony, 328
United Nations Program for the Environment, 328
United States (U.S.), xx, 21, 23, 174, 189–90, 329; border between Canada and, 151–65; border between Mexico and, xi, xii, xiii–xv, xvi, xviii, xix, 127, 151, 153, 156, 158, 161–62, 165, 165n1, 200, 205, 212–26, 269–82; cross-border shopping between Canada and, 285–98; dams in, 239, 240; maritime claims and, 303; Sahuayo, Mexico and colonies in, 51–69
University College, 1
University of Nevada at Reno, 272

Unocal, 310
UN/OEA, xxix
unpalatable, xxix
Uruguay, 204
U.S.-Mexican border, xi, xii, xiii, xiv–xv, xvi, xviii, xix, 51–69, 127, 151, 153, 156, 158, 165, 165n1, 200, 205, *275*; demographic characteristics of, 212–13; economic asymmetries, 213; environmental issues and, 214–15; environmental management practices and, 212–14, 215–17, 218–26; gaming and, 278–80; governance, public administration asymmetries and, 213–15; locator of innovation and vice, 269–82; Mexamerica and, 270, 273–77; Nevada, Utah and, 270–73; prostitution and, 277–78, 282; teenage drinking and, 280–82; transnational regional integration and, 161–62
Utah, vice, U.S.-Mexican border, Nevada and, 270–73
Uvijindia, Pedro, 111, 113

Vancouver, B.C., 153, 157, 291
Vancouver Island, 157
van Schendel, Willem, xv, xvi
vatican, 35
vice, 282n1; border regions and, 166n18, 269–82, *275*
Victoria, 153
Vienna, 238
Vietnam, 301, 302; continental shelf and, 304–6; historic waters and, 304; joint development agreements between Malaysia and, 308–10; maritime disputes between Cambodia and, 307; maritime disputes between Malaysia, Thailand and, 308; maritime disputes between Thailand and, 308; maritime disputes between Thailand, Cambodia and, 307–8; negotiations between Cambodia and, 312; negotiations between Thailand and, 311–12; straight baselines and, 303
Vindolanda, 8–9
violence: Berlin Wall and, 26; border regions and, 108; Israeli-Palestinian border, 193–97
vis-à-vis, xxix
de Vletter, Fion, 73
Volksblatt, 30
Volstead Act, xxix
von Karman line, 325

Waldron, Jeremy, 321
Wales, 2
The Wall, 38
Walser, Martin, 29, 32
Wampui, Tukup, family history of, 107–8
wand (wall), 22, 23, 32, 45
Warsaw Pact, 24, 237

Washington, D.C., 162, 164, 262, 265
Washington state, xv, 163
Webb, Prescott, 318
Webb, Turner, 318
Wei: dynasty, 17; state, 14, 15
Weigand, K., 290
Weisman, Alan, 273
Weissler, Sabine, 39, 41
Wenders, Wim, 29
Wendover, NV, 271, 272
Wendover, UT, 271, 272
West Africa, xviii; boundary-making in, 97–104
West Bank, Israel, Palestine and, 177–97
West Bank Data Project, 182
West Berlin, 24, 29; East and, 25, 26, 28
West Germany, 23, 25, 174
West Jerusalem, 196
Whin Sill, 4, 5
"White Paper on International Migration," 74, 92
Wilhelm Straße, 33
Wilkes, John J., 1
William of Orange, 175
Wings of Desire, 29
Winnipeg, 153
Winter War of 1939–40, 121
women: Mozambican migrant, 90–93, 94n4; South Africa and attitude of migrant, 87–88; South Africa and migrant, 79
World Meteorological Organization, 328
World Trade Organization (WTO), 202, 204, 231
World War I, 274, 327
World War II, 23, 121, 127, 130, 131, 150n2, 204, 273, 282, 328
Worldwatch Institute, 328
Wu (emperor), 16, 18, 19
Wuhuan people, 17
Wusun people, 17
Wyoming, 272

xenophobic, xxix
Xianbei people, 17

Xianyang, 19
Xinjiang, 16, 19
Xiongnu people, 15, 17, 18, 19
Xu Da, 16

Yagkur, Tito, 110
Yalu River, 12, 16
Yang (emperor), 18
Yang Bo, 18
Yangtze Valley, 14, 19
Yan state, 15
yarmulke, xxix
Yaupi River, 109
Yellow River, 15
Yeltsin, Boris, 123, 124
Yimeng Mountain, 15
York, 5
youths: alcohol and, 280–82; Finnish-Russian border and perspectives of, 143–48, 149–50; Finnish-Swedish border and perspectives of, 137–43, 148–49; West Bank Palestinian, 185
Yuan dynasty, 16, 17
Yucatán, xv
Yueshi people, 17
Yukon Territories, 152
yuppies, xxix

Zamora River, 109
Zanzibar, 104
zeitgeist, xxix
Zhao state, 14, 15
Zhongshan state, 15
Zhou dynasty, 14
Zhu Di, 16
Zhu Yuanzhang (emperor), 16
Zimbabwe: attitudes toward migration to South Africa from, 83–88; cross-border migration and, 79–83; future of migration from, 88–90; migration to South Africa from, 73–79; policy implications for migrants from, 90–93
Zinyama, Lovemore, 73
zona rosa, 276, 277